S0-AGW-101

THE NEW BOOK OF KNOWLEDGE ANNUAL

1982

HIGHLIGHTING EVENTS OF 1981

THE NEW BOOK OF KNOWLEDGE ANNUAL

THE YOUNG PEOPLE'S BOOK OF THE YEAR

GROLIER
INCORPORATED
DANBURY, CONN.

ISBN 0-7172-0613-0
ISSN 0196-0148
The Library of Congress Catalog Card Number: 79-26807

COPYRIGHT © 1982 BY GROLIER INCORPORATED

Copyright © in Canada 1982 BY GROLIER LIMITED

*No part of this book may be reproduced without
special permission in writing from the publishers*

PRINTED IN THE UNITED STATES OF AMERICA

EXECUTIVE EDITOR FERN L. MAMBERG

ART DIRECTOR MICHÈLE A. McLEAN

ASSISTANT EDITOR PAMELA CARLEY PETERSEN

EDITORIAL DEPARTMENT

EDITORS ELAINE P. SEDITO
DANIEL DOMOFF
PATRICIA M. GODFREY
WAYNE JONES
LEO SCHNEIDER
PATRICIA ELLSWORTH WILSON

INDEXERS JILL SCHULER
SUSAN DEROMEDI

PRODUCTION EDITOR MARILYN BULLOCK

PICTURE RESEARCHER DIANE T. GRACE

PROOFREADER ALEXIS KASDEN

EDITORIAL ASSISTANT SHIRLEY HOLLISTER

. . . . .

MANUFACTURING AND PRODUCTION DEPARTMENT

MANUFACTURING WESLEY J. WARREN, Senior Manager
TERESA KLUK, Manager

PRODUCTION JOSEPH J. CORLETT, Senior Manager
ALAN PHELPS, Manager

. . . . .

YOUNG PEOPLE'S PUBLICATIONS DEPARTMENT

EDITOR IN CHIEF WILLIAM E. SHAPIRO

ART AND PRODUCTION DIRECTOR FRANKLIN N. SAYLES

. . . . .

GROLIER INCORPORATED

SENIOR VICE-PRESIDENT, PUBLISHING HOWARD B. GRAHAM

VICE-PRESIDENT AND EDITORIAL DIRECTOR BERNARD S. CAYNE

VICE-PRESIDENT AND DIRECTOR OF MANUFACTURING HARRIET RIPINSKY

CONTENTS

6

CONTRIBUTORS

BLANCHARD, Wendie R.
Managing Editor, *Creative Crafts* magazine
POPULAR CRAFTS

CAPEN, Peter D.
Author and photographer, Terra Mar Productions; Fellow, the Explorers Club
WILD FLOWERS OF THE SAN JUANS

CRONKITE, Walter
CBS News Correspondent
THE YEAR IN REVIEW

FIRESTEIN, Cecily Barth
Artist in residence, Museum of Bronx History; author, *Rubbing Craft*
RUBBINGS

FREEDMAN, Russell
Author, *Tooth and Claw; How Animals Defend Their Young; Animal Architects; How Animals Learn; The Brains of Animals and Man; How Birds Fly; Growing Up Wild; Getting Born*
ANIMAL WEAPONS

GERASSI, John
Professor of Political Science, City University of New York, Queens College; author, *Fidel Castro: A Biography; The Great Fear in Latin America; The Boys of Boise*
FIDEL CASTRO

GETLEIN, Frank
Arts critic, Public Radio and Television (Maryland Center for Public Broadcasting); author, *Mary Cassatt; The French Impressionists*
MARY CASSATT

GOLDBERG, Hy
Co-ordinator of sports information, NBC Sports
SPORTS, 1981

GOLDSMITH, Harry
Former patent counsel
THE MECHANICAL MUSIC MAKER

HAHN, Charless
Stamp Editor, *Chicago Sun-Times*
STAMP COLLECTING

KULL, David J.
Senior Editor, *Medical Laboratory Observer* magazine
ANIMAL TALK

KURTZ, Henry I.
Author, *Captain John Smith; John and Sebastian Cabot*
THE VIKINGS ARE COMING
THE FRENCH FOREIGN LEGION
RIDERS IN THE NIGHT

LARRICK, Nancy
Author, *A Parent's Guide to Children's Reading; A Parent's Guide to Children's Education; A Teacher's Guide to Children's Books*
DR. SEUSS

LEERBURGER, Benedict A.
Editor in Chief, *Gateways to Science* (3rd edition)
THE SPACE SHUTTLE COLUMBIA
FACE TO FACE

LEMKE, Robert F.
Assistant to the Publisher, Krause Publications (*Numismatics News*); author, *Standard Catalog of United States Paper Money, 1981*
COIN COLLECTING

MILLER, E. Willard
Associate Dean and Professor of Geography, Department of Geography, Pennsylvania State University
ORGANIZATION OF PETROLEUM EXPORTING COUNTRIES (OPEC)

MITCHELL, Denise
Girl Scouts of the U.S.A.
SCOUTING

PASQUIER, Roger F.
Executive Assistant to the President, International Council for Bird Preservation; author, *Watching Birds: An Introduction to Ornithology*
OSTRICHES AND OTHER FLIGHTLESS BIRDS

PRICE, Harvey
Chief Scout Executive, Boy Scouts of America
SCOUTING

SACHAR, Abram L.
Chancellor, Brandeis University; author, *A History of the Jews*
QUEEN VICTORIA

SCHAFFNER, Nicholas
Author, *The Boys from Liverpool*
THE BEATLES

SHAW, Arnold
Author, *Honkers and Shouters; 52nd St: The Street of Jazz; The Rockin' 50's; The World of Soul; The Rock Revolution; Sinatra: 20th Century Romantic*
THE MUSIC SCENE

SIMS, Stella Hackel
Former Director, United States Mint
MINT

SKODNICK, Ruth
Statistician
INDEPENDENT NATIONS OF THE WORLD

SMITH, Derek G.
Associate Professor of Anthropology and Sociology, Carleton University (Ottawa); author, *Canadian Indians and the Law; Natives and Outsiders*
ESKIMOS (INUIT)

STEWART, John H.
Media consultant, martial arts subjects; Editor, *Inside Kung Fu* magazine; former Editor, *Black Belt* magazine
KARATE

TAYLOR, John H.
Professor of History, Carleton University (Ottawa); Associate Editor, *Urban History Review*
OTTAWA

TEDFORD, John
Contributing Editor, *The New Book of Popular Science*
SAVING AFRICA'S WILDLIFE

TESAR, Jenny
Author, *Introduction to Animals* (Wonders of Wildlife series); Series Consultant, *Wonders of Wildlife;* Sponsoring Editor, *Gateways to Science*
VISUAL POLLUTION
THOSE FABULOUS VIDEO MACHINES

THE WORLD IN 1981

Anwar el-Sadat, president of Egypt and Nobel peace prize winner, was assassinated on October 6, 1981. His death clouded the prospects for peace throughout the troubled Middle East.

THE YEAR IN REVIEW

by Walter Cronkite

Striking events, ranging from the tragedy of assassination to new achievements in space travel, marked the year 1981. And while long-standing disputes and economic problems continued to trouble the world, 1981 was also a year of new directions. In the United States and several other countries, new leaders took office and began to put new policies into effect.

The year began dramatically in the United States. In January, the Carter administration succeeded in negotiating with Iran for the release of 52 American hostages. The hostages had been held since November, 1979, when militant Iranian students seized the U.S. embassy in Teheran. Their release—on January 20, moments after Ronald Reagan was sworn in as president—touched off a wave of celebration.

But violence, in the form of a series of assassination attempts, seemed to haunt the world in 1981. In March, President Reagan was wounded by a would-be assassin in Washington, D.C. In May, Pope John Paul II was shot in St. Peter's Square in Rome. Both men recovered, and their assailants were captured. Then, in October, assassins succeeded in killing Egyptian President Anwar el-Sadat. Because of Sadat's role in working for peace in the troubled Middle East, his death was felt as a great loss by people in many countries.

Sadat's successor, Hosni Mubarak, pledged to uphold the peace treaty Egypt had signed with Israel in 1979. But talks between the two countries on the creation of a homeland for Palestinian Arabs continued to make little progress during the year. Meanwhile, Israel was embroiled in conflict with other Arab countries. Its planes destroyed a nuclear reactor that was under construction in Iraq and also made strikes in Lebanon, hoping to destroy bases of the Palestine Liberation Organization (PLO). The PLO struck back with attacks on Israeli towns. U.S. negotiators helped work out a cease fire in July, but the situation in the Middle East remained tense. And it was further complicated when, in December, Israel formally annexed the Golan Heights, which it had occupied since 1967.

Central America, too, was troubled by fighting in 1981. In El Salvador, leftist guerrillas opposed right-wing landowners and the military in a civil war. A land redistribution program begun by the government in 1979 failed to stop the fighting, and by mid-1981 thousands of people had been killed and thousands more made homeless. There was concern that unrest might spread to other countries in Central America, many of which seemed to share El Salvador's social and economic problems.

The Reagan administration appeared especially concerned about the part played by Communist countries, particularly Cuba and the Soviet Union, in the conflicts in the Middle East and in Central America. In an apparent attempt to counter such influence, the United States tried to strengthen ties to moderate Arab countries and increased military and economic aid to Central American countries.

Concern about the Soviet Union was also reflected in U.S. defense spending. Late in the year, the Senate approved the largest military spending bill in U.S. history. The military budget provoked much debate. Supporters of the increases said that they were necessary to make U.S. forces equal to Soviet forces. Opponents were concerned that increased spending, particularly for nuclear weapons, might prompt the Soviets to add to their own forces, leading to a full-scale arms race. The Reagan administration did not support the U.S.-Soviet arms treaty that had been worked out under President Jimmy Carter (the SALT II treaty). But late in 1981, a new round of arms talks, called the Strategic Arms Reduction Talks (START), began.

The change of administration in the United States led to other changes in policy as well. Congress approved many of President Reagan's proposals to cut government spending in areas other than defense and to reduce taxes. The administration appeared hopeful that these measures would reduce inflation and stimulate the economy. At year's end it was unclear whether or not they would do so. The economy remained sluggish, and unemployment reached its highest level since 1975.

Economic difficulties troubled many other countries in 1981. Poland faced severe problems. Despite strict rationing, food shortages were widespread. And there were disagreements between the Communist government and Solidarity, the independent labor union federation. These problems led to a change in Communist Party leadership in October. Then, in December, Solidarity said it wanted to hold a referendum on the questions of confidence in the new leaders and the establishment of a non-Communist government. The government promptly imposed martial law, banned strikes and other union activity, and arrested union leaders. The gains in personal freedom won by the unions seemed almost certain to be lost. And there was great concern that the Soviet Union might use force to aid the government, sending in the troops it had kept near its Polish border throughout the year.

In Western Europe, campaign promises of sweeping changes in economic policy helped bring socialist parties to power in two countries that had long been governed by conservatives, France and Greece. In Britain, high unemployment and inflation provoked riots in a number of cities in July. But in that same month, the British—and many people elsewhere—were cheered by the pageantry of the marriage of Prince Charles, heir to the British throne, and Lady Diana Spencer.

The year was highlighted, too, by the launching of the space shuttle *Columbia*. There was disagreement on how costly and how useful the shuttle would ultimately prove to be. But for many Americans, *Columbia*'s first two flights, in April and November, recalled the excitement of the 1960's, when U.S. astronauts became the first men to set foot on the moon. At the same time, the re-usable shuttle seemed to open a new era in space travel.

JANUARY

1 Greece became the tenth member of the European Economic Community (EEC). The organization, usually called the Common Market, was established in 1958. Its goal is to eliminate trade barriers among member nations. These members are Belgium, Britain, Denmark, France, Ireland, Italy, Luxembourg, the Netherlands, and West Germany.

1 Abdou Diouf became president of Senegal. He replaced Léopold Senghor, who had led the country since its independence in 1960.

20 Ronald W. Reagan was sworn in as the 40th president of the United States, and George H. Bush was sworn in as the 43rd vice-president. In his inaugural address, Reagan called upon Americans to begin "an era of national renewal." He stressed the need to deal with the country's economic problems and "to curb the size and influence of the federal establishment."

20 Iran freed the 52 Americans who had been held hostage for 444 days. They were released following the signing of an agreement between the United States and Iran. The hostages had been captured on November 4, 1979, when Iranians seized the U.S. embassy in Teheran. Following their release, the Americans were flown to West Germany and, several days later, to the United States.

Ronald W. Reagan is sworn in as the 40th president of the United States.

THE REAGAN CABINET

Before his inauguration, Ronald Reagan chose the people he wanted to serve as members of his Cabinet and as U.S. representative to the United Nations. By early February, all his nominations had been approved by the Senate.

Secretary of Agriculture: John R. Block, a farmer and a former director of the Illinois Department of Agriculture.

Attorney General: William French Smith, a California lawyer.

Secretary of Commerce: Malcolm Baldrige, chairman of Scovill, Incorporated, a Connecticut manufacturing firm.

Secretary of Defense: Caspar W. Weinberger, vice-president of the Bechtel Power Corporation and secretary of Health, Education and Welfare under President Richard Nixon.

Secretary of Education: Terrel H. Bell, commissioner of higher education in Utah and a former U.S. commissioner of education.

Secretary of Energy: James B. Edwards, a former governor of South Carolina.

Secretary of Health and Human Services: Richard S. Schweiker, a former senator from Pennsylvania.

Secretary of Housing and Urban Development: Samuel R. Pierce, Jr., a lawyer from New York.

Secretary of the Interior: James G. Watt, a lawyer from Colorado.

Secretary of Labor: Raymond J. Donovan, a construction company executive from New Jersey.

Secretary of State: Alexander M. Haig, Jr., a retired U.S. Army general.

Secretary of Transportation: Andrew L. Lewis, Jr., deputy chairman of the Republican National Committee.

Secretary of the Treasury: Donald T. Regan, chairman of Merrill Lynch & Company.

Representative to the United Nations: Jeane J. Kirkpatrick, a political science professor at Georgetown University.

FEBRUARY

4   Gro Harlem Brundtland became prime minister of Norway. She was the country's first woman prime minister and, at 41, the youngest person to hold the office. She succeeded Odvar Nordli, who had resigned after five years in office.

9   Wojciech Jaruzelski was named premier of Poland. He succeeded Jozef Pinkowski, who had held the position since August, 1980.

10   Cynthia Dwyer, a writer from Amherst, New York, was released by Iran after having spent more than nine months in a Teheran jail. Dwyer had gone to Iran in April, 1980, to write about the Iranian revolution. She was arrested in May on espionage charges. (Also released by Iran in February was Mohi Sobhani, an Iranian-born U.S. citizen. He had been arrested in September, 1980, and accused of spying.)

18   In a nationally televised address to Congress, President Ronald Reagan presented an economic plan aimed at curbing inflation and unemployment. He proposed sharply reducing government spending in many areas, including health, education, energy, and environmental programs; welfare and unemployment benefits; aid to the arts and humanities; and dairy price supports. Only the military budget would be increased. Reagan's proposals would

Cynthia Dwyer is reunited with her family, after having spent more than nine months in an Iranian jail.

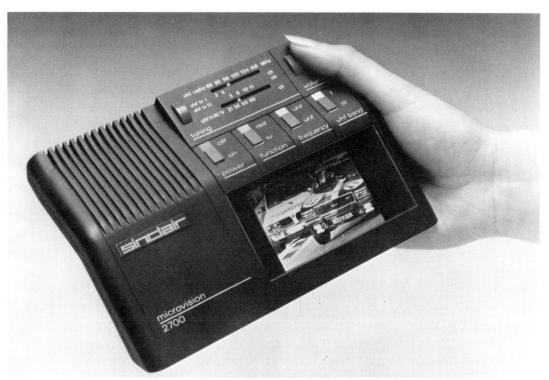
This tiny, battery-operated television is to become available in 1982.

change many social programs that had been developed over the preceding twenty years. The President also urged a reduction in taxes paid by individuals and businesses. The proposals faced a sharp debate in Congress, which controls the federal budget.

19 A British company unveiled a pocket-sized television that will sell for about $125 when it becomes available in 1982. The battery-operated TV, about the size of a paperback book, will be able to receive transmissions from almost anywhere in the world.

24 It was announced that Prince Charles, the 32-year-old heir to the British throne, would marry 19-year-old Lady Diana Spencer in July, 1981.

25 Leopoldo Calvo Sotelo become premier of Spain. He succeeded Adolfo Suárez González, who had been premier since 1976. Parliament's approval of Calvo Sotelo's appointment had been interrupted on February 23, when a group of civil guards seized control of the lower house of parliament and held about 350 members hostage. The move was part of a right-wing military uprising. King Juan Carlos was given major credit for stopping the revolt. His televised speech in support of democracy ended the possibility of any nationwide support for the uprising.

11 U.S. President Ronald Reagan and Canadian Prime Minister Pierre Elliott Trudeau ended a two-day meeting in Ottawa. It was Reagan's first trip abroad since taking office. The two leaders discussed fishing rights, pollution (particularly acid rain), the completion of the Alaska pipeline, and U.S. military aid to El Salvador.

14 Three Pakistani hijackers surrendered in Syria, ending the longest airplane hijacking in history. On March 2, the hijackers had seized a Pakistani airliner, demanding the release of political prisoners. More than 130 passengers aboard the domestic flight were taken hostage, and the plane was diverted to Afghanistan. There, the hijackers released 33 hostages but killed one, a Pakistani diplomat. On March 9, the plane was flown from Afghanistan to Syria. The hijackers threatened to blow up the plane unless their demands were met. Five days later, Pakistan agreed to free 54 political prisoners, and the remaining hostages were released.

U.S. President Ronald Reagan and Canadian Prime Minister Pierre Elliott Trudeau held a two-day meeting in Ottawa. It was Reagan's first trip abroad since taking office.

Moments after an assassination attempt against President Ronald Reagan, security officers rush to the aid of wounded presidential press secretary, James Brady, and D.C. policeman Thomas Delahanty. The assailant, John Hinckley, Jr., is being held in the background.

29 General Roberto Eduardo Viola became president of Argentina. He succeeded Jorge Rafael Videla, who had held the position since 1976.

29 Eric Williams, prime minister of Trinidad and Tobago, died at the age of 69. Williams had led the nation since it became independent in 1962. George Chambers was chosen to succeed him.

30 President Ronald Reagan was shot by a lone gunman outside the Washington Hilton Hotel. The President was rushed to a nearby hospital, where a bullet was removed from his left lung. Also wounded were James Brady, the President's press secretary; Timothy J. McCarthy, a Secret Service agent; and Thomas Delahanty, a District of Columbia policeman. John W. Hinckley, Jr., 25, of Evergreen, Colorado, was arrested at the scene of the attack and was charged with attempted assassination. (Reagan was hospitalized until April 11, when he returned to the White House. His recovery was termed excellent by his doctors, and he soon resumed his regular duties.)

6 Mark Eyskens became premier of Belgium. He succeeded Wilfried Martens, who had held the position since 1979.

8 Ferdinand E. Marcos, president of the Philippines, named Cesar Virta as the country's first premier. The appointment came after voters had approved a parliamentary system of government.

8 Omar Nelson Bradley, U.S. General of the Army, died at the age of 88. The popular World War II field commander, who had led more than a million American troops, was known as the "G.I.'s General" because of his concern for the ordinary soldier.

10 Based on the 1980 U.S. census, it was announced that the center of population in the United States is De Soto, Missouri, a small town southwest of St. Louis. The center of population is the point at which the United States would balance if it were a flat surface and every person on it weighed exactly the same. In the country's first census, taken in 1790, the center was just east of Baltimore, Maryland. It has gradually moved westward. Now, for the first time, the center is west of the Mississippi River. It is also farther south than ever before, reflecting the large population growth experienced by the South and Southwest during the 1970's.

The shifting center of population: Based on the 1980 U.S. census, De Soto, Missouri, has become the center of population in the United States. Since 1790, the center has gradually moved westward, and by 1980 it had moved farther south than ever before.

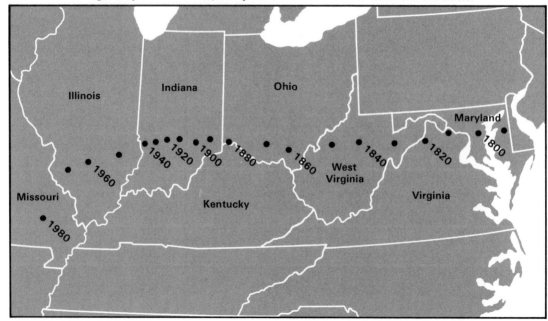

Joe Louis, the American heavyweight boxer, died at the age of 66.

12 The U.S. space shuttle *Columbia* was launched from Cape Canaveral, Florida. It was the world's first re-usable spacecraft. With two astronauts aboard, *Columbia* made 36 orbits around the Earth and, on April 14, landed in California's Mojave Desert. (A space shuttle is designed to be launched like a rocket and then to return and land like an airplane. It can be used again and again to carry astronauts and instruments into orbit around the Earth.)

12 Joe Louis, the American heavyweight boxer, died at the age of 66. Louis was the heavyweight boxing champion of the world for almost 12 years, from 1937 until 1949. His heavyweight reign was the longest of any champion in that weight class.

MAY

5 In Northern Ireland, Robert Sands died in prison on the 66th day of a hunger strike. Sands was a member of the Irish Republican Army (IRA). This organization wants Northern Ireland to become independent of Britain and to unite politically with the rest of Ireland. Sands had been jailed since 1976 for illegal possession of firearms. On March 1, 1981, he began a fast. His goal was to pressure the British Government to treat jailed IRA members as political prisoners rather than as criminals. Demonstrations and rioting followed his death. But the British Government remained firm in not granting the prisoners political status. (By the end of August, a total of ten hunger strikers had died in prisons in Northern Ireland.)

10 François Mitterrand, head of the Socialist Party, was elected president of France. He defeated Valéry Giscard d'Estaing, the conservative candidate, who had been president since 1974. (Mitterrand, the first leftist president in 23 years, took office on May 21. He appointed Pierre Mauroy as premier.)

12 Benjamin H. Sheares, president of Singapore since 1971, died at the age of 73. (In October, C. V. Devan Nair became president.)

Thousands of sympathizers gather in Belfast, Northern Ireland, for the burial of Robert Sands. Sands, a member of the IRA, died in prison as the result of a hunger strike.

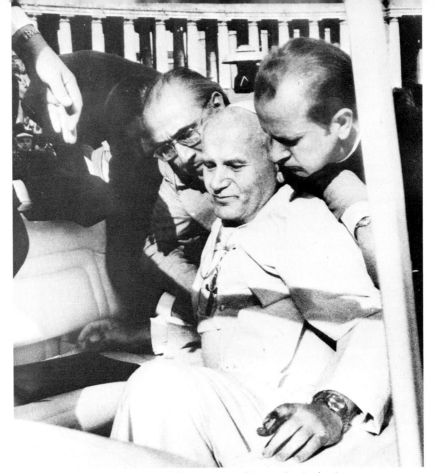

Pope John Paul II is aided by assistants after having been shot and seriously wounded in an assassination attempt.

13 Pope John Paul II, head of the Roman Catholic Church, was shot and seriously wounded. The assassination attempt took place in St. Peter's Square in Rome, Italy, as the Pope stood in an open car moving through a large crowd of worshipers. An escaped Turkish murderer, 23-year-old Mehmet Ali Agca, was arrested for the crime. (The Pope was hospitalized until June 3, when he returned to his residence in the Vatican. On July 22, Agca was found guilty and was sentenced to life imprisonment.)

18 William Saroyan, the American author and playwright, died at the age of 72. His best-known works include the novel *The Human Comedy* and the play *The Time of Your Life*.

24 Jaime Roldós Aguilera, president of Ecuador since April, 1979, died in an airplane crash. He was succeeded by Vice-President Osvaldo Hurtado Larrea.

30 Ziaur Rahman, president of Bangladesh, was assassinated during an unsuccessful attempt to overthrow the government. Ziaur Rahman had headed the government since 1977. (In November, Vice-President Abdus Sattar was elected president.)

JUNE

7 In a surprise attack, Israeli warplanes bombed and destroyed a nuclear reactor near Baghdad, Iraq. Because the reactor was not yet in operation, no radioactivity was released. Israel's prime minister, Menahem Begin, said that the Iraqis had planned to use the reactor to make atomic bombs for use against Israel. The Iraqi Government denied the charge, saying the reactor was intended for peaceful purposes only. The raid was condemned by many nations.

11 An earthquake struck southeastern Iran, killing about 3,000 people. (Six weeks later, on July 28, a second quake hit the region, killing 1,500 people.)

16 Grisha Filipov was named premier of Bulgaria. He replaced Stanko Todorov, who had held the position since 1971.

22 Ayatollah Ruhollah Khomeini dismissed Abolhassan Bani-Sadr as president of Iran. Bani-Sadr had held the position for 17 months. (Bani-Sadr went into hiding and on July 29 escaped to France, where he was given political asylum.)

25 The U.S. Supreme Court ruled that it is constitutional for Congress to limit draft registration to men. The ruling did not say that women *must* be excluded from the registration or from an actual draft. It only said that Congress *may* exclude women. Women who wish to join the Armed Forces may volunteer.

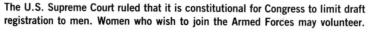

The U.S. Supreme Court ruled that it is constitutional for Congress to limit draft registration to men. Women who wish to join the Armed Forces may volunteer.

Terry Fox, whose marathon run had raised millions of dollars for the Canadian Cancer Society, died at the age of 22.

28 Terry Fox, a college student from British Columbia, died of cancer at the age of 22. In 1980, Fox had become a Canadian hero by running halfway across the country on an artificial leg to raise money for cancer. (He had lost a leg to bone cancer in 1977.) His marathon raised millions of dollars for the Canadian Cancer Society. He was later awarded the Order of Canada for his courage and perseverance. This is the highest medal a Canadian civilian can receive.

28 Giovanni Spadolini became premier of Italy. He succeeded Arnaldo Forlani, who had resigned in May after seven months in office. Spadolini, a Republican, was the first premier since 1945 not to belong to the Christian Democratic Party.

29 Hu Yaobang became chairman of the Chinese Communist Party. He succeeded Hua Guofeng, chairman since 1976.

30 Following parliamentary elections in Ireland, Garret FitzGerald was chosen prime minister of the country. He succeeded Charles J. Haughey, who had held the position since December, 1979.

JULY

1   Marcel Breuer, the Hungarian-born furniture designer and architect, died at the age of 79. Breuer designed the Whitney Museum in New York and the UNESCO headquarters in Paris.

7   President Ronald Reagan announced that he would nominate 51-year-old Sandra Day O'Connor as the first woman Supreme Court justice. O'Connor, a member of the Arizona Court of Appeals, was chosen to fill the seat of Potter Stewart, who had retired July 3.

7   The *Solar Challenger* became the first solar-powered airplane to cross the English Channel. The flight from France to England was 165 miles (266 kilometers) and took nearly 5½ hours. Energy to fly the plane was gathered by 16,000 solar cells on the wings and tail. These cells changed the sun's energy to electricity, which ran the plane's motor.

16   Britain's Parliament began a major debate on riots that had broken out throughout the country, injuring hundreds of people. The riots had begun in London and Liverpool in early July and spread to more than 30 cities and towns. Most of the rioters were black and white youths. There was disagreement on the causes of the disturbances, but many observers believed that unemployment was an important factor.

Ending a flight from France to England, the *Solar Challenger* . . .

17 Israeli jets bombed Beirut, killing 300 people. The attack marked the first time Israeli planes had deliberately hit a target in a densely populated civilian area. The target of the attack was the Palestine Liberation Organization (PLO) headquarters. The PLO retaliated with rocket attacks on Israeli towns. (On July 24, Israel and the PLO agreed to a cease-fire.)

17 Two walkways suspended above the lobby of the Hyatt Regency Hotel in Kansas City, Missouri, collapsed. The walkways crashed into the crowded lobby, and 113 people died.

21 The leaders of the seven major industrial nations ended a three-day meeting near Ottawa, Canada. The countries represented were Britain, Canada, France, Germany, Italy, Japan, and the United States. The talks focused on economic issues.

24 Mohammed Ali Rajai was elected president of Iran. He succeeded Abolhassan Bani-Sadr, who had been dismissed from office in June.

29 Prince Charles, heir to the British throne, married Lady Diana Spencer. Some 700,000,000 television viewers around the world watched the ceremony, which took place in London.

31 Panamanian General Omar Torrijos Herrera died in an airplane crash at the age of 52. Torrijos had resigned as president of Panama in 1978 but continued to be considered the main power in the country.

. . . becomes the first airplane powered by the energy of the sun to cross the English Channel.

AUGUST

1 Paddy Chayefsky, the American playwright, died at the age of 58. He won Academy Awards for three movie screenplays: *Marty* (1955), *Hospital* (1971), and *Network* (1977).

3 Egypt and Israel signed an agreement establishing an international peacekeeping force in the Sinai. The agreement would enforce the peace treaty signed by the two countries in 1979. The 1979 treaty called for Israel to withdraw from the Sinai peninsula, which it had occupied in 1967 during a war between Israel and the Arab nations. The withdrawal was to be completed in stages over a three-year period. (The peacekeeping force would be in place by April, 1982, when Israel was to complete its withdrawal from the Sinai.)

3 More than 11,000 members of the U.S. air traffic controllers union went on strike. The strike was in violation of federal law. President Ronald Reagan told the controllers to return to work or be fired. (Striking controllers ignored the back-to-work order, and dismissals began on August 5. The government kept the air traffic control system operating with nonstriking controllers and military personnel while new permanent employees were being hired. Air traffic was temporarily disrupted by the strike. But within two weeks it was functioning more smoothly.)

4 Melvyn Douglas, the American actor, died at the age of 80. He won Academy Awards for his performances in *Hud* (1963) and *Being There* (1980).

Air traffic was temporarily disrupted when more than 11,000 members of the U.S. air traffic controllers union went on strike.

"Now to see if it works"

This political cartoon asks the question: Will Reagan's tax and budget bills improve the economy and balance the budget?

4 Mohammed Javad Bahonar was named premier of Iran. He replaced Mohammed Ali Rajai, who had become president in July. (On August 30, both men were killed in a bomb explosion.)

10 U.S. Secretary of Defense Caspar Weinberger announced that the United States would produce neutron weapons. These weapons produce more radiation but less heat and blast than other nuclear weapons. They can kill people without causing extensive damage to buildings.

13 President Reagan signed into law two major economic bills, aimed at curbing inflation and unemployment. His budget bill cut spending for more than 200 domestic programs. His tax bill lowered taxes for both individuals and businesses.

19 In a brief clash about 60 miles (100 kilometers) from the coast of Libya, two U.S. jet fighter planes shot down two Libyan jet fighters. According to the U.S. Government, the Libyans had fired first. The incident took place over waters that Libya claims as part of its territory but that the United States says are international waters.

29 Lowell Thomas, the American author and news commentator, died at the age of 89. He wrote more than 50 books; his best-known book was *Lawrence of Arabia*. For 46 years, from 1930 to 1976, Thomas had a nightly news program on radio.

SEPTEMBER

1 General Gregorio Alvarez became president of Uruguay. He replaced Aparicio Méndez, who had held that position since 1976.

1 In the Central African Republic, President David Dacko was overthrown in an army-led coup. General André Kolingba became head of state.

1 Albert Speer, the German architect who was Adolf Hitler's Minister of Armaments and War Production during World War II, died at the age of 76. Speer wrote three books about his experiences as a Nazi. His best-known book was *Inside the Third Reich*.

4 General Celso Torrelio Villa became president of Bolivia. He replaced General Luis García Meza, who was forced to resign in August after a year in office.

8 Roy Wilkins, the American civil rights leader, died at the age of 80. Wilkins was a top official of the National Association for the Advancement of Colored People (NAACP) from 1931 until 1977.

14 In parliamentary elections in Norway, the Conservative Party and its allies took a majority of the seats. (On October 14, Kaare Willoch, head of the Conservatives, became prime minister. He succeeded Gro Harlem Brundtland of the Labor Party, who had held the position since February.)

15 The 36th regular session of the United Nations General Assembly opened at U.N. headquarters in New York City. Ismat Kittani of Iraq was elected to serve as assembly president for one year. (By the end of September, two newly independent nations, Vanuatu and Belize, had been admitted to the U.N. They became the 155th and 156th members of the world body.)

17 It was announced that a fossil jawbone of a small, previously unknown mammal had been discovered in Arizona. The mammal was about the size of a mouse and probably ate insects. Earlier, four teeth of a known prehistoric mammal had been found at the same site. Together, the fossils provided evidence that mammals had lived in North America 180,000,000 years ago. Other fossils of early mammals found in North America dated to only 135,000,000 years ago.

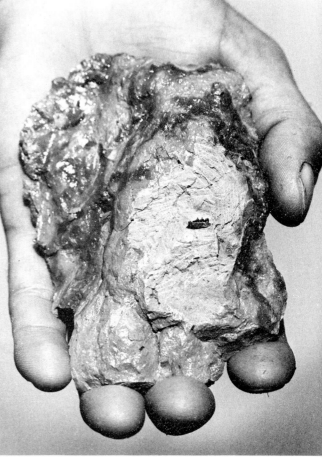

A fossil jawbone (at right and, enlarged, below) of a small, previously unknown mammal was found in Arizona. The mammal was about the size of a mouse.

21 Belize, formerly known as British Honduras, became an independent nation. The Central American country had been ruled by Britain for more than 300 years. George Price continued as prime minister.

21 The U.S. Senate voted to confirm Judge Sandra Day O'Connor as the 102nd justice of the Supreme Court. (On September 25, O'Connor took the oath of office, becoming the first woman to serve on the Supreme Court.)

27 Robert Montgomery, the American stage and screen actor, died at the age of 77. Among his best-known movies were *Night Must Fall* and *Here Comes Mr. Jordan*.

27 The world's fastest trains began commuter operations between Paris and Lyons, France. The sleek, electrically powered trains have two locomotives, one at each end, and eight passenger cars. On special tracks, the trains cruise at up to 160 miles (257 kilometers) per hour. They are capable of traveling at much higher speeds—more than 225 miles (362 kilometers) per hour.

OCTOBER

2 Hojatolislam Ali Khamenei was elected president of Iran. He succeeded Mohammed Ali Rajai, who had been assassinated in August. (On October 31, Mir Hussein Moussavi became Iran's premier.)

6 Anwar el-Sadat, president of Egypt since 1970, was assassinated as he watched a military parade in Cairo. The attackers, who were arrested, were said to be Muslim fanatics. Sadat was best known for establishing peace between Egypt and Israel, for which he and Israeli Prime Minister Menahem Begin shared a Nobel peace prize. (In an October 13 referendum, Vice-President Muhammad Hosni Mubarak was elected to succeed Sadat.)

16 Moshe Dayan, the Israeli soldier and statesman, died at the age of 66. Dayan was an architect of Israel's victories in the 1967 and 1973 wars against the Arabs. In the late 1970's, as foreign minister, he played an important role in Israeli-Egyptian peace negotiations.

18 In parliamentary elections in Greece, the Panhellenic Socialist Movement won a majority of the seats. The party's victory ended 35 years of conservative rule. (On October 21, Andreas Papandreou, head of the Socialists, became premier. He succeeded George Rallis, who had held the position since May, 1980.)

Egyptian President Anwar el-Sadat was assassinated on October 6.

PEACEMAKER

18 Prime Minister Wojciech Jaruzelski became head of Poland's Communist Party. He replaced Stanislaw Kania, who was forced to resign by the party's Central Committee. The committee wanted a tougher stand against Solidarity, the independent trade union federation formed in 1980. It also wanted effective action against the country's worsening economic crisis. Food, gasoline, and other essentials had become increasingly scarce, and Solidarity had staged strikes and demonstrations demanding greater political freedom. Meanwhile, Poland continued to face the threat that the Soviet Union would use military force or economic pressure to keep the Communist Party firmly in control.

27 Urho K. Kekkonen, president of Finland, resigned. Kekkonen, 81, had held the position since 1956. Mauno Koivisto became acting president, and elections were scheduled for January, 1982.

THE 1981 NOBEL PRIZES

Chemistry: Kenichi Fukui of Japan (the first Japanese to win the award) and Roald Hoffmann of the United States, for their independent research describing the importance of electron motion on chemical reactions. Their work helps chemists understand why some chemicals react with one another while others do not.

Economics: James Tobin of the United States, for his study of financial markets and their effect on how people and companies save, invest, and spend money. Tobin's theory provides ''a basis for understanding how subjects actually behave when they acquire different assets and incur debts.'' His theory also explains how investors balance their risks by not ''putting all their eggs in one basket.''

Literature: Elias Canetti, a Bulgarian-born writer living in Britain, for his ''writings marked by a broad outlook.'' His works, all in German, include plays, memoirs, and works of fiction.

Peace: The Office of the United Nations High Commissioner for Refugees, for aiding the ''tremendous and increasing number of refugees'' in the world. (The Organization also received the peace prize in 1954.)

Physics: Dutch-born Nicolaas Bloembergen and Arthur Schawlow of the United States and, independently, Kai M. Siegbahn of Sweden, for developing ways to study the internal structure of matter. Bloembergen and Schawlow were cited for ''their contribution to the development of laser spectroscopy.'' Siegbahn was cited for ''his contribution to the development of high-resolution electron spectroscopy.''

Physiology or Medicine: Roger W. Sperry and David H. Hubel of the United States and Torsten N. Wiesel, a Swedish citizen living in the United States, for research on the human brain. Sperry was honored for identifying the different functions of the right and left hemispheres of the brain. Hubel and Wiesel were honored for their joint studies showing how the brain processes information received through the eyes.

NOVEMBER

1 Antigua and Barbuda became an independent nation. The islands, which are located in the Caribbean, had been ruled by Britain for nearly 350 years. Vere Bird became prime minister. (On November 11, Antigua and Barbuda became the 157th member of the United Nations.)

7 Will Durant, the historian and philosopher, died at the age of 96. He and his wife, Ariel, who had died on October 25, were best known for their eleven-volume *Story of Civilization*.

9 U San Yu became president of Burma. He succeeded U Ne Win, who had been president since 1962.

12 Four men completed the first balloon voyage across the Pacific Ocean. The balloon, *Double Eagle V*, left from Japan and traveled nearly 6,000 miles (9,650 kilometers) to California. The flight took three and one half days.

14 Scientists reported that fire was used by prehistoric people called *Homo erectus* 1,400,000 years ago—almost 1,000,000 years earlier than had previously been believed. The scientists found pieces of baked clay at a site in Kenya. Tests indicated that the clay had been baked in small, controlled fires rather than in uncontrolled natural fires.

Four men on *Double Eagle V* completed the first balloon trip across the Pacific.

Natalie Wood, shown here in *West Side Story*, died at the age of 43.

14 Astronauts Joe H. Engle and Richard H. Truly ended a 54-hour mission aboard the space shuttle *Columbia*. This was the second mission of the re-usable shuttle. Although the mission was shortened because of technical problems, the astronauts completed their major objectives. They conducted various scientific observations and tested a robot arm that will be used to remove items from the cargo bay and place satellites in orbit.

16 William Holden, the American actor, was found dead. He was 63 years old. Among his best-known movies were *Sunset Boulevard, Stalag 17* (for which he won an Academy Award in 1953), and *The Bridge on the River Kwai.*

28 Roberto Suazo Córdova was elected president of Honduras. Upon his inauguration in January, 1982, he will succeed Policarpo Paz García, head of state since 1978. Suazo Córdova would become the first elected president to lead the country since an army coup in 1972.

29 Natalie Wood, the American actress, died at the age of 43. Her best-known movies included *Miracle on 34th Street, Rebel Without a Cause,* and *West Side Story.*

2 After months of controversy, the Canadian House of Commons passed the government's constitutional resolution by a vote of 246 to 24. The resolution asked the British Parliament to pass a law giving Canada control of its Constitution and the power to amend it. (The British North America [BNA] Act has formed the basis of Canada's Constitution since 1867. Until the law requested by Canada is passed, the BNA Act can in most respects be amended only by the British Parliament.) The resolution to patriate, or gain control of, the Constitution included a charter of rights and a formula for amending the Constitution. It had undergone several changes. It was first submitted to the Canadian Parliament in 1980. At that time, only two provinces, New Brunswick and Ontario, agreed to its terms. The federal government announced it would seek patriation without the consent of the other provinces, and the provinces appealed to the Supreme Court of Canada. In September, the Court ruled that although the federal government's action was legal, Canadian custom was that there be a "substantial measure of provincial consent" for any constitutional change. Prime Minister Pierre Elliott Trudeau and the ten provincial premiers then met once more, and on November 5, a compromise plan was announced. It had the approval of all the provinces except Quebec. (After passage in the House of Commons, the resolution went to the Senate, where it was passed on December 8. It was then taken immediately to London, where the British Parliament was expected to vote on it early in 1982.)

This small, white, unknown species of fish was discovered in the Pacific Ocean.

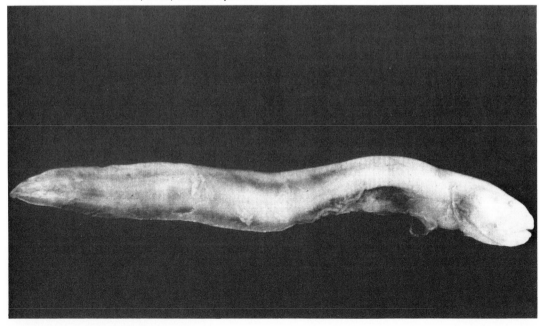

5 It was announced that what may be a previously unknown species of fish had been discovered in the Pacific Ocean. The fish lives near hot springs some 8,500 feet (2,600 meters) beneath the ocean's surface. It is white and about 10 inches (25 centimeters) long.

5 Heng Samrin, president of Cambodia, was appointed secretary-general of the People's Revolutionary Party. This is the most powerful position in the Cambodian Government.

11 General Leopoldo Galtieri was named president of Argentina. He succeeded General Roberto Eduardo Viola, who had held the position since March.

13 Martial law was declared in Poland. The military government suspended the operations of Solidarity, the independent labor union. It arrested or took into custody many union members, including Solidarity leader Lech Walesa. It also arrested some former government leaders, blaming them for the country's economic crisis. All strikes, demonstrations, and public gatherings were banned. Curfews were imposed, and travel was limited. News dispatches, except for offical government statements, were blacked out. Soldiers and police patrolled highways and city streets and were stationed in factories and other buildings. A military council was set up to rule the country. The declaration of martial law canceled the gains in personal freedom that had been won by Solidarity since 1980, when it was founded as the first independent labor union in a Communist country. The government's action followed a call by Solidarity leaders for a referendum on two questions—confidence in Poland's leaders and the establishment of a non-Communist government. (In the days following the declaration, there were reports of resistance to the government's action. Strikes and demonstrations were said to have been broken up, and a number of protesters were killed. While the Soviet Union clearly supported the government, there was no immediate evidence that Soviet troops had been sent to help. The imposition of martial law was condemned by the Polish Roman Catholic Church and by the leaders of Western countries. On December 20, the Polish ambassador to Washington, Romuald Spasowski, defected to the United States. He said that with martial law, a "cruel night of darkness and silence" had spread over Poland.)

15 Javier Pérez de Cuéllar, a Peruvian diplomat, was sworn in as the next secretary-general of the United Nations. Pérez de Cuéllar will serve a 5-year term beginning January 1, 1982. He was chosen to succeed Kurt Waldheim of Austria, who had served two terms.

THE ROYAL WEDDING

"Here is the stuff of which fairy tales are made: the Prince and Princess on their wedding day. But fairy tales usually end at this point with the simple phrase, 'They lived happily ever after.' This may be because fairy stories regard marriage as an anticlimax after the romance of courtship.

"This is not the Christian view. Our faith sees the wedding day not as the place of arrival but the place where the adventure really begins."

These words were spoken by the Most Reverend Robert Runcie, the Archbishop of Canterbury, at the year's most magnificent wedding. It was the wedding of 32-year-old Prince Charles, heir to the British throne, and 20-year-old Lady Diana Spencer.

The wedding took place in London on July 29, 1981—a day that blazed with glamour and pageantry and was filled with cheers and laughter. It was the climax of six months of excitement that had begun in February, when Charles gave Diana a brilliant sapphire and diamond ring and the couple announced their engagement.

More than 2,500 guests filled high-domed St. Paul's Cathedral, the beautiful, 300-year-old church where the wedding took place. There were kings and queens from other countries, heads of state, and other international figures. Other guests included Charles's former schoolteachers, Diana's former roommates, members of the household staffs at the royal palaces, and sailors from the naval ship that Charles had once commanded.

Outside, under sunny skies, hundreds of thousands of flag-waving spectators lined the streets between St. Paul's and Buckingham Palace, the home of the royal family. Some had waited all night to catch a glimpse of the Prince and his bride. And around the world, 700,000,000 people watched the ceremony on television.

About 10 A.M., the first of the eleven antique horse-drawn carriages that formed the wedding procession clattered through the gates of Buckingham Palace. The carriages were escorted by the royal household cavalry, in gleaming breastplates and plumed helmets. The Welsh guards, in scarlet coats and tall fur hats, lined the route. One coach carried Queen Elizabeth II and Prince Philip, the parents of Prince Charles. Later, Prince Charles, looking dignified and handsome in his Royal Navy uniform, passed through the cheering crowd. Finally, in a glass coach, came Lady Diana and her father.

The crowd oohed and aahed as Lady Diana stepped from the carriage and walked up the steps of the church. Her pale ivory taffeta gown was made of silk from the only silk farm in England, hand-embroidered with pearls, sequins, and lace. It had a full skirt, a fitted bodice, and a romantic curving neckline. On her head, Lady Diana wore a diamond tiara. And a 25-foot (7.5-meter) train swept behind her as her father led her up the aisle. Five bridesmaids and two pages accompanied them.

At the altar were the groom and his two "supporters"—his brothers Prince Andrew and Prince Edward. Throughout the ceremony, which lasted more than an hour, music filled the cathedral. And when the Archbishop pronounced the couple man and wife, Prince Charles placed a ring of Welsh gold on the third finger of the bride's left hand, and she became Diana, Princess of Wales.

After the ceremony, the royal family returned to Buckingham Palace. Charles and Diana appeared on the palace balcony, together with their parents and members of the wedding party. As the crowd below chanted, "Kiss her, kiss her," Charles turned to his bride and gave her a gentle kiss. The happy cheers of the watching crowd mingled with the sounds of trumpets and hundreds of ringing church bells.

After a wedding breakfast that included lobster, lamb, champagne, and wedding fruitcake, the Prince and Princess left on their honeymoon. The carriage that carried them away from the palace surprised and delighted everyone—the Prince's brothers had decorated it with a big bunch of heart-shaped balloons and a hand-lettered sign that read, "Just Married."

The honeymooners spent two days at a secluded country estate in southern England. Then they flew to Gibraltar, where they boarded the royal yacht, *Britannia,* for a two-week cruise of the Mediterranean.

After their return to England, they gradually took up their duties as Prince and Prin-

Diana's engagement ring and Charles's crest ring.

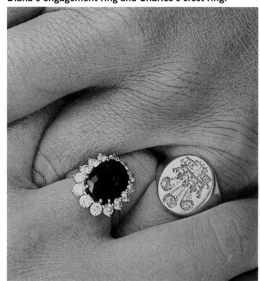

Eleven antique horse-drawn carriages formed the wedding procession to St. Paul's Cathedral. One coach carried Queen Elizabeth II and Prince Philip.

cess. Many of these are ceremonial—opening parks, planting commemorative trees, and touring factories. They will also travel to other countries as goodwill ambassadors. Wherever they are, whatever they do, Charles and Diana are expected to set an example for the British. This puts limits on what they can do and say. As Charles's sister, Princess Anne, once said: "You are always a bit on your guard. You know that because you're royal, anything you say might be given extra significance."

Like most royals, Charles and Diana will divide their time between a number of places. They have apartments in at least seven royal residences. When in London, they will live in Kensington Palace. But their own home is Highgrove, an estate in the rolling Cotswold Hills, west of London. Highgrove is rather small by royal standards. It has nine bedrooms, six bathrooms, and four large reception rooms. One wing holds a children's nursery. This wing may have a tenant soon—in November, Charles and Diana announced that their first child was expected in June, 1982.

Charles and Diana received thousands of wedding gifts—silver and crystal bowls, candlesticks, beds, kitchen utensils, cushions, and a bedspread hand-knitted by Queen Mata'aho of Tonga. The couple even received a ton of peat, a nickel-silvered mousetrap, and an herb garden for Highgrove. But the most precious gift was the love and best wishes of people everywhere.

Reverend Runcie expressed it this way: "However long they live may they always know that when they pledged themselves to each other before the altar of God they were surrounded and supported not by mere spectators, but by the sincere affection and active prayer of millions of friends."

Just Married! Diana, Princess of Wales, and Charles, future King of England, embark upon their new life as man and wife.

PRINCE CHARLES

Charles Philip Arthur George has many titles: Prince of Wales and Earl of Chester, Duke of Cornwall, Duke of Rothesay, Earl of Carrick and Baron of Renfrew, Lord of the Isles and Great Steward of Scotland. Someday he will have one of the grandest titles of all—King of England.

Charles was born on November 14, 1948. He is the oldest of the four children of Queen Elizabeth II and Prince Philip. He is the first Prince of Wales in history to be educated at a regular school, rather than by private tutors, and the first to graduate from a university. He served as an officer in both the Royal Air Force and the Royal Navy. He is a pilot who has flown helicopters, propeller planes, and jets. He has also trained as a commando, parachute jumper, and frogman. Charles's love of outdoor activities is well known. His favorite sports include polo, riding, skiing, and salmon fishing. He also loves classical music and plays the cello.

The motto of the Prince of Wales is "I serve." Charles takes this seriously. He assists with the duties of the royal family, keeps informed about politics, and meets with government leaders, in addition to managing his own vast property holdings. As one historian said, "He's the right sort of person for a modern monarch—hard working, buoyant and cheerful, with a deep sense of purpose."

DIANA, PRINCESS OF WALES

Diana Frances Spencer became the first English woman to marry an heir to the throne in more than 300 years. She was born on July 1, 1961, the daughter of the eighth Earl Spencer and his first wife, Frances. Although she is not of royal birth, she is related to royalty—the Spencers trace their lineage to the Stuart kings of England. It could be said that Charles married the girl next door. Diana spent her childhood at Park House in Sandringham, on the royal family's estate. Her playmates included Charles's brothers, Prince Andrew and Prince Edward, who are about her age. She knew the Queen well enough to call her "Aunt Lilibet."

When she was young, Diana had a private tutor. Later, she attended a boarding school and a finishing school in Switzerland. Like Charles, Diana loves music, the outdoors, and animals. She also loves children. After completing school, she worked for an American couple, caring for their young child. Later, she worked in a kindergarten in London.

Life as the wife of the future King of England will be very different from life as a commoner. Diana must address her husband as "Sir" in public. She must walk one step behind him. She cannot go anywhere unannounced—not even to see friends or to go shopping. But she will enjoy a life of great wealth and luxury with the man she loves.

THE MIDDLE EAST

Tension between Israel and the Arab countries of the Middle East remained the region's biggest problem during 1981. There was also conflict around the Persian Gulf area and in North Africa. And the assassination of Egyptian President Anwar el-Sadat in October created new uncertainty about Egypt's future and the prospects for peace throughout the Middle East.

EGYPT

Sadat, who became president in 1970, had brought Egypt into a closer relationship with the West. He had also made the first moves toward peace with Israel, which had been at war with the Arab countries since its creation in 1948 as a Jewish homeland. In 1978, Sadat and Israeli Prime Minister Menahem Begin had met at Camp David, Maryland, and agreed on terms for a peace treaty and a framework for peace throughout the region.

But Sadat's policies had separated Egypt from the other Arab countries, who rejected the Camp David accords. And Sadat also faced opposition at home. Egypt was troubled by groups of Muslim extremists. (Similar groups had overthrown the Shah of Iran in 1979.) The extremists opposed the treaty with Israel and called for a government run according to Islamic law. In June, 1981, there were riots between Muslims and Coptic Christians, who make up a small part of the population. And in September, Sadat arrested more than 1,500 of his critics.

Sadat was shot on October 6 while reviewing a military parade in Cairo. Four men dressed as soldiers broke away from the parade and fired into the reviewing stand. They were said to be connected with a Muslim extremist group. Vice-president Hosni Mubarak was confirmed as president within days of the assassination, and hundreds of people connected with terrorist groups were arrested.

Sadat's death raised questions about the future of the Camp David accords. Under

Egyptian President Mubarak embraces Israeli Prime Minister Begin after the death of Anwar el-Sadat.

the treaty, Israel was to give up the Sinai Peninsula, which it had seized from Egypt during the 1967 war. The last third of the Sinai was to be turned over in April, 1982, after which Egypt would allow the peninsula to be patrolled by an international peace-keeping force. In 1981 the United States agreed to set up the force.

Mubarak said that he would honor the peace treaty. He also indicated that he wanted to improve relations with Arab countries and that Egypt would not be aligned with any major power. But it seemed likely that U.S. aid would continue.

Mubarak also pledged to continue talks with Israel on the creation of a Palestinian Arab homeland in the West Bank, an area Israel had seized from Jordan in 1967. These talks had been called for in the Camp David framework for peace. But in two and a half years of on-and-off negotiations, Israel and Egypt had been unable to agree on any major points. And the other Arab countries and the leading Palestinian Arab group, the Palestine Liberation Organization (PLO), continued to reject the idea of a solution worked out under the Camp David accords.

ISRAEL

Conflicts with Arab countries and the PLO brought Israel to the brink of war in 1981. The greatest tension concerned Israel's involvement in Lebanon.

Since 1975, Lebanon's two main groups —Muslims and Maronite Christians—have been fighting a civil war. The war has been complicated by outside groups. In 1976, Syria sent in a peacekeeping force and in practice took control of the Lebanese Government. PLO guerrillas based in Lebanon have made raids and rocket attacks on Israel. And Israel has allied itself with the Maronites and has attacked PLO bases in Lebanon, chiefly with air strikes.

In April, 1981, Syria placed anti-aircraft missiles in central Lebanon. Israel threatened to destroy the missiles, and it was feared that war would break out between Israel and Syria. An agreement was worked out with the help of the United States. But in July, acting on reports that the PLO bases were receiving large shipments of arms, Israel staged a number of air strikes. They in-

cluded a bombing raid on Beirut, Lebanon's capital. And the PLO launched artillery attacks on Israeli towns. Finally, on July 24, Israel and the PLO agreed to a cease fire.

Israeli bombers also staged a raid on Iraq. On June 7, they destroyed a nuclear reactor that was being built near Baghdad. Israel said that the reactor would have been used to produce material for nuclear bombs. Iraq said the reactor was being built for peaceful purposes. The raid was condemned by many countries, including the United States, the Soviet Union, and France, which was building the reactor for Iraq.

The raid on Iraq and the Syrian missile crisis figured in Israel's parliamentary elections on June 30. The leading opposition party accused Begin of taking too warlike a stand. But Begin's party won by a narrow margin, and he was able to get support from minor parties and remain prime minister.

In December, Israel formally annexed the Golan Heights, an area it had taken from Syria in 1967 and had occupied ever since. The surprise move was sharply criticized by Arabs and also by Israel's allies.

THE PERSIAN GULF

In January, Iran released the 52 Americans it had held hostage since late 1979. But Iran continued its strong anti-U.S. stand. Ayatollah Ruhollah Khomeini, the Muslim cleric who had led the 1979 revolution, remained the country's most powerful leader. But the government was torn by struggles between leftists, moderates, and Muslim fundamentalists who wanted to rule strictly by Islamic religious law. During the year, leftist terrorists killed more than 100 fundamentalist leaders, and the government executed more than 1,350 leftists. In June, President Abolhassan Bani-Sadr, a moderate, was impeached. He left the country for exile in France. A fundamentalist was chosen in his place. But he and his prime minister were assassinated in August. A Muslim cleric, Hojatolislam Ali Khamenei, then took office as president in October.

The war between Iran and Iraq, which had begun in September, 1980, continued through 1981. Iraq's main objective was control of the Shatt al Arab waterway, a major shipping route that lies between the two countries and leads into the Persian Gulf. Iraqi forces held a thin strip of Iranian territory along most of the countries' common border. But Iran continued to hold the key city of Abadan, and shipping on the Shatt al Arab was blocked.

NORTH AFRICA

The stability of the Middle East was also threatened by Libya in 1981. Libya's leader, Muammar el-Qaddafi, hoped to eventually establish an Islamic state that would stretch across North Africa. He had built up the Libyan Army with aid from the Soviet Union. In 1981, Libyan troops were involved in a civil war in Chad, in skirmishes with Sudan along the Sudan-Chad border, and in a military incident with the United States.

Relations between the United States and Libya had cooled after Qaddafi seized power in 1969. In 1979, the United States had closed its embassy in Libya after it was attacked by a mob. In May, 1981, Libya's representatives in Washington were expelled on charges that they had helped kill Libyan exiles living in the United States. Later in the year, the United States charged that Libya had plotted to kill President Ronald Reagan and other top U.S. officials.

The military incident stemmed from Libya's claims to the waters off its coast. Libya had declared sovereignty over waters up to 12 miles from shore, except at the Gulf of Sidra, where its claim extended to over 100 miles. The United States recognized a territorial limit of 3 miles only. In August, two U.S. Navy planes on maneuvers over the Gulf of Sidra were fired on by two Libyan planes, 60 miles (100 kilometers) off the coast. The U.S. planes returned fire and downed both Libyan planes.

U.S. POLICY

The Middle East is especially important to Western countries because it is the source of much of the oil they use. In recent years, the United States has felt that there were growing threats to the region from the Soviet Union and extremist groups.

In 1981, the U.S. Government said that it hoped to develop a "strategic consensus" of Middle East nations, with each co-operating to ward off such threats. It reaffirmed its support of Egypt. And in November, the United States and Israel signed an agreement to work together against threats from "the Soviet Union or Soviet-controlled forces." But the United States suspended the agreement in December, after Israel annexed the Golan Heights without consulting with its allies.

The United States also tried to develop closer ties with moderate Arab countries such as Jordan and Saudi Arabia. In October, after much debate, Congress approved a sale of arms to Saudi Arabia. The debate had focused on the sale of five planes equipped with a special electronic system called AWACS (Airborne Warning and Control System). The AWACS planes were to be used for defense. But because they would give the Saudis an advantage in air battles, supporters of Israel opposed the sale.

The United States continued to press for a solution to the Palestinian Arab problem under the Camp David accords. There was also interest in a plan proposed by Saudi Arabia. The plan seemed to recognize Israel's right to exist—something no Arab country save Egypt had ever done. But the plan failed to win the support of other Arab leaders, and the Middle East's most pressing problem remained unsolved.

An AWACS plane. In 1981 the United States agreed to sell five such planes to Saudi Arabia.

CENTRAL AMERICA—TROUBLED TIMES

Political unrest and the birth of a new country kept Central America in the news in 1981. The six countries of the region—Guatemala, Honduras, El Salvador, Nicaragua, Costa Rica, and Panama—were joined by a seventh in September, when Belize gained independence from Britain. But throughout the year, a civil war raged in El Salvador. And there were tensions and troubles all along the narrow bridge of land that links North and South America.

In El Salvador, Nicaragua, and Guatemala, some 50,000 people have been killed in political violence since 1978. The disputes have pitted strong, right-wing leaders against rebels with leftist and Communist ties. Many people, especially in the United States, blame outside influence from Cuba and other Communist countries. The United States itself has long been important in the economy and the politics of Central America. But in recent years U.S. influence has lessened, and the idea of U.S. interference is strongly resented in these countries.

Central America's troubles also involve social and economic problems that go back to Spanish colonial days. In most of its colonies, Spain had set up huge plantations. One result of this was the development of two classes—a small group of wealthy landowners and a large group of impoverished workers. This unequal division of land and wealth has continued into modern times.

Also because of the plantation system, the countries of Central America came to depend on a few export crops, such as coffee and bananas. Income from these crops is used to offset the cost of goods that must be imported. In recent years, the cost of imports, especially oil, has gone up—while prices for some exports have dropped. As a result, many countries are deeply in debt. These serious economic problems have made life even harder for Central America's poor—and have helped feed political unrest.

EL SALVADOR

El Salvador is the smallest and most densely populated of the Central American countries. Most of the people are poor.

From 1932 through 1979, the country was ruled by military leaders who represented a small group of landowners called the fourteen families. In the 1970's there were attempts to bring reform through popular elections, but election frauds kept the military in power. As a result, support increased for leftist groups who wanted to overthrow the government. There were clashes between the military and leftist guerrillas.

In late 1979, a coup brought a military-civilian junta to power. The new government presented its position as a middle way between the right and the left. A land redistribution program was begun, and many large estates were broken up. But both rebels and landowners opposed the government with violence, and the reforms bogged down. Fighting increased. And there were reports of brutality on both sides. Guerrillas kidnapped and murdered business leaders and others. Government troops were charged with widespread civilian killings, including the deaths of three American nuns in 1980.

The rebels, who were being supplied with arms from Cuba, launched what they called a "final offensive" in January, 1981. But the result was a victory for neither side. The

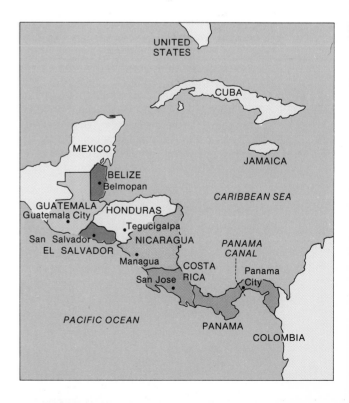

Soldiers search for rebels in a village in El Salvador. The country's civil war was the most serious of the conflicts that troubled Central America in 1981.

government promised to hold elections in March, 1982, and it asked for increased military aid. The United States sent aid and about 50 military advisers. The United States and other countries, among them France and Mexico, also urged the Salvadoran Government to negotiate with the rebels. But the government said it would not talk with the rebels or allow them to take part in the elections unless they gave up their arms. Meanwhile, the fighting continued. By mid-1981, more than 15,000 people had been killed.

NICARAGUA

In Nicaragua, moderates had banded together with leftist rebels, the Sandinistas, to overthrow the government of General Anastasio Somoza Debayle in 1979. The rebels set up a ruling junta that included both leftists and moderates. The new government aligned itself with Cuba, but it did not adopt all the policies of that country. It allowed some political opposition, and it permitted a good deal of private business.

The new government's most serious problem was the economy. The civil war had done great damage, and Nicaragua owed huge sums of money. At first the new government received economic aid from the United States. But in 1981, the United States said that because Nicaragua was channeling arms from Cuba to the rebels in El Salvador, aid would be cut off. By the fall, consumer goods and some food items were in short supply. Unemployment and prices were rising. As popular support for the Sandinistas dropped off, the government passed emergency laws to deal with the economic crisis and to tighten its political control.

GUATEMALA

Guatemala, the largest Central American country, edged closer to civil war in 1981. Poverty and illiteracy are widespread in Guatemala—especially among the Indians, who make up more than half the population. The military government has been charged with brutal repression. One human rights group estimated that the government was responsible for killing 3,000 people in 1980.

Guatemala has a history of unrest. In the early 1970's, a leftist rebellion was crushed with U.S. aid. But the rebels regrouped in Guatemala's highlands. There they hoped to win the support of the Indians, who in the past had kept out of political disputes. By 1981, the rebels were regularly ambushing government and military personnel. Government forces struck back, sometimes killing people who were not involved with the rebels. And "hit squads" assassinated government opponents.

Military aid from the United States had stopped in 1977, after the United States had criticized the government for repression. In 1981 there was talk of resuming aid—if the government could control its forces. There was hope that elections scheduled for March, 1982, would help the situation.

HONDURAS, COSTA RICA, AND PANAMA

These countries saw far less political violence than their neighbors in 1981. In Honduras, the military had been in power for nearly 20 years. But it had allowed a degree of political and press freedom and had backed land reform and trade unions. As a result, the government faced less opposition from extremist groups. But Honduras remained one of the poorest countries in Central America, and there was concern that unrest might spread from its neighbors. Hoping to prevent this, the United States increased its aid to Honduras and urged the military leaders to agree to elections restoring civilian government. Elections were held in November, and a civilian president was chosen to take office in January, 1982.

Costa Rica has a long tradition of democracy. Since 1948, it has had no army, and the major political parties are committed to human rights. Its land is divided into small farms, rather than large plantations. But even Costa Rica was touched by trouble in 1981. Sharp increases in the price of imported oil, decreases in the price of coffee (Costa Rica's main export), and expensive social programs created an economic crisis. And scattered terrorist bombings raised fears of political violence. The government, long friendly to the United States, asked for increased economic aid.

Panama was troubled by the death of General Omar Torrijos Herrera, the country's leader for thirteen years. He was killed in a plane crash on July 31, 1981. During his years in power, Torrijos had kept the country stable and had negotiated treaties that would gain control of the Panama Canal from the United States by the year 2000. He had resigned as head of government in 1978, appointing a civilian president. But he had remained head of the National Guard and the most important figure in the country. After his death, no single person came forward to take his place, although the top leaders of the National Guard seemed to be the most powerful. And like the other countries of Central America, Panama faced problems with poverty and an economic slump.

BELIZE

On September 21, 1981, Belize—Britain's last colony on the American mainland—became independent. The event was celebrated with fireworks, champagne, and dancing in the streets.

But the festivities were dampened by a dispute with Guatemala that had delayed independence for a number of years. Guatemala claimed a right to the entire territory of Belize (which was called British Honduras until 1973). Britain had been unwilling to grant Belize independence as long as Guatemala would not give up its claim. In 1981, Guatemala agreed to do so, and independence was scheduled. In July, however, negotiations with Guatemala broke down. But it was too late to cancel independence, and Britain agreed to station troops in Belize to protect its former colony. George Price, who had been prime minister since Belize was granted self-government in 1964, continued as the country's leader.

At independence, Belize had good education and health-care systems, as well as a tradition of democratic government. The people, mostly English-speaking blacks, did not seem to share the revolutionary fever that troubled some other Central American countries. But many of the people were poor. Only a small part of the country's farmland was being tilled, and there was little industry. People were hopeful that the country would soon solve these problems.

Belize, Britain's last colony on the American mainland, became independent on September 21, 1981.

444 DAYS

On the night of January 20, 1981, a group of Americans—50 men and two women—pushed through a jeering crowd to board a plane at Mehrabad Airport in Teheran, Iran. For 444 days, they had been held hostage. And they had been subjected to what were later described as "acts of barbarism." Now people around the world waited in suspense for word that the hostages' plane had taken off for freedom.

Thousands of miles away, in Washington, D.C., a drama of a different sort was unfolding. There, under a brilliant noonday sun, Ronald Reagan was being inaugurated president of the United States, succeeding Jimmy Carter.

Just minutes after Reagan took the oath of office, the hostages' plane took off. A short time later came the official U.S. announcement: The hostages were free. It was the end not only of their ordeal but also of months of worry for Americans everywhere.

HELD HOSTAGE

The events that led up to this drama began in 1979. Early in that year, a revolution had deposed Iran's ruler, Shah Mohammed Reza Pahlavi. Ayatollah Ruhollah Khomeini, a Muslim religious leader, was brought to power. In October, the exiled Shah entered a U.S. hospital for medical treatment. And on November 4, militant Iranian students seized the U.S. embassy in Teheran. They said they would hold the Americans there hostage until the Shah was returned to Iran to stand trial. Iran's new rulers backed their demand.

Some of the Americans were later released. But Iran continued to hold 52 hostages throughout 1980. Countries around the world condemned Iran's action as a violation of international law. The United States stopped trade and diplomatic relations with Iran and froze Iranian assets held in U.S. banks. It also attempted a military rescue mission. But the mission was called off when equipment broke down in the Iranian desert. Eight U.S. soldiers died during the withdrawal from the desert.

By the fall of 1980, the hostages seemed to have become less important to the Iranians. Moderate Iranian politicians were struggling for power with radical religious groups. The Shah, who had left the United States before the start of 1980, had died in Egypt in July. Iran had become involved in a war with

The U.S. hostages, free at last, wave to the jubilant crowd that greeted them when they landed in Frankfurt, West Germany.

After their return to the United States, the former hostages were honored at a White House reception.

neighboring Iraq. And because of the U.S. economic pressures, Iran was short of money and equipment to fight the war.

In November, 1980, the Iranian parliament set conditions for the release of the hostages. The conditions were that the United States would turn over the Shah's vast personal fortune, release Iran's frozen assets, promise not to interfere in Iran's affairs, and drop financial claims filed by U.S. companies whose property had been taken over by Iran's new government.

Negotiations began. Algeria was chosen as an intermediary, and proposals and counterproposals flew back and forth. The issues were complicated. The United States said that it did not have the right to cancel the claims of U.S. companies or to turn over the Shah's fortune to Iran. And no one seemed to know the exact amount of the Shah's fortune or of Iran's frozen assets. American hopes were raised—and dashed—several times.

Early in 1981, Carter stepped up the pace of the negotiations, hoping to end the crisis before he left office. And the Iranians at last seemed ready to make a deal. Deputy Secretary of State Warren M. Christopher flew to Algiers, and details of an agreement were hammered out in round-the-clock negotiating sessions. Iran's chief negotiator, Behzad Nabavi, told the Iranian parliament: "The

hostages are like a fruit from which all the juice has been squeezed out. Let us let them all go."

The agreement was signed on January 19, with the following terms:

• The United States pledged not to interfere in Iran's affairs.

• The U.S. Government would end its ban on trade and drop its own claims against Iran.

• The claims of individuals and private companies would be settled by an international tribunal.

• The Shah's personal fortune would be frozen until courts could rule on Iran's claims to it.

• And as soon as the hostages were released, the United States would begin to return Iran's frozen assets. It would immediately release $8,000,000,000 (billion) to accounts controlled by Algeria. Some of this money would go directly to Iran. Some would go to repay loans that the Shah had taken out from European and American banks. And some of the money would be held to settle the claims brought before the international tribunal.

FREEDOM

On January 20, the hostages were bused to the airport. There—pushed and shoved by a crowd of militants who shouted "Death to

Throughout the 444-day ordeal, yellow ribbons were the symbol of people's vow to remember the hostages.

America''—they boarded a waiting Algerian plane. Officials from the Swiss embassy in Teheran counted heads, and the plane took off for Algiers. The 52 Americans, together and free to speak for the first time in more than fourteen months, jumped up from their seats to exchange tales of their experiences.

At Algiers, the United States took custody of the 52. Soon they were airborne again, this time headed for West Germany. At Frankfurt, they were greeted by shouts of ''U.S.A!'' from a jubilant crowd. The former hostages, grinning and waving, were whisked onto buses and taken to a U.S. military hospital at Wiesbaden. ''There aren't words in the American language to express how happy and thankful we are,'' said one.

Just after dawn on January 21, the former hostages were at last able to phone their families, who waited anxiously in the United States. Later that day, former president Carter arrived at the hospital to formally greet them.

The 52 stayed at Wiesbaden for several days. They were tested to see what mental and physical damage they might have suffered. They rested, talked to their families on the phone, and got much-wanted haircuts, showers, and new clothes.

Meanwhile, Americans everywhere celebrated their release. Sirens blew and church bells rang. The national Christmas tree at the White House, kept dark during their captivity, was lit. Buildings and bridges were hung with flags and yellow ribbons—a symbol of people's vow to remember the hostages. And there were ceremonies of thanksgiving in cities around the country.

HOME AT LAST

On January 25, the 52 were flown to the U.S. Military Academy at West Point, New York. There they were finally reunited with their families. Two days later, they held their first news conference and then flew to Washington, D.C., for a reception at the White House. Some then went on to celebrations in various parts of the country—including a ticker-tape parade in New York City—before returning to their homes.

The hostages' experience caused some worries that did not end with their release. People wondered if the same thing might happen at other embassies and, if so, what could be done to protect diplomats. There was also concern about the long-term effects of the hostages' captivity. The doctors who had examined the 52 reported that most were in good shape. But sometimes people who have been held captive have a hard time adjusting to freedom. They may be afraid of people or of situations that remind them of their captivity. They may feel guilty that they did not manage to escape. They may be depressed and irritable, and they may have nightmares. Sometimes, after months of depending on their captors for everything, they actually feel sympathetic toward them. Homecoming can be difficult for a hostage's family, too. Family relationships sometimes change when one member is away for a long time.

But after a few months, the former hostages seemed to show few, if any, of these symptoms. Many had gone back to work. Some were on leaves of absence, and some had started new careers. A few were writing books about their experiences. The former hostages had no sympathy for their captors, and most reported only minor difficulties in picking up their lives where they had left off. As one of the 52 put it: ''It takes about five minutes to adjust to being able to sleep on clean sheets and being able to eat Chinese food whenever you want to.''

THEIR LONG CAPTIVITY

In their first phone calls home and, later, in conversations with reporters, the former hostages told about their long captivity.

Several of the hostages told their families that they had been kept in solitary confinement. Malcolm Kalp, an economics officer, said he had spent months in solitary after he tried to escape. Michael Metrinko, an embassy political officer, said that he had been in solitary more than half the time and that he never knew where he was.

Living conditions were described as dirty and uncomfortable. Bert C. Moore, the embassy's administrative counsel, told of six months in a prison cell furnished only with thin foam mattresses and a single plastic chair. Sergeant James Lopez, one of the marines at the embassy, said that it was so cold that the hostages' drinking water would freeze overnight. He also said that centipedes often walked across his face as he slept. Richard Queen, who had been released in 1980 when he became ill, told CBS News that he had been kept in a windowless basement storeroom that he called the "mushroom inn."

"It was like living in a tomb. You didn't hear the outside world. You didn't know what was going on at all," Queen said. He added that he and his cellmate were forbidden to speak and were allowed to go outside, to a courtyard, for only 20 minutes a week.

Food was unappetizing and often stale, spoiled, or infested with worms. Some hostages were kept on a bread-and-water diet for two weeks or more, and many lost weight. Robert Blucker, an economics officer, said that for part of the time he had eaten coffee grounds, tea leaves, and orange peels to supplement the food that was given to him. Later, he was fed what he called "stew number one" (vegetables) and "stew number two" (a mixture of fish, meatballs, and spaghetti).

There were many reports of beatings and of mental torture. Queen was one of several hostages who described mock firing squads. He said that one night a band of masked gunmen woke a number of the hostages and herded them into a basement room. They were lined up with their backs to the gunmen, and they heard the clicking of rifles being readied to fire. "I was sure that we had just breathed our last," he said—but no one was shot.

Other hostages said that their captors had burned piles of Christmas packages sent from the United States and had ripped up letters from home before their eyes. Marine Sergeant John McKeel, Jr., told his family that his captors had lied and said his mother was dead. They told him he could go to her funeral if he gave them information, and he was beaten when he refused.

Iranian officials said that the hostages' statements were false. But the U.S. Government said that there was "evidence of serious mistreatment in a number of cases." In their January 27 news conference, the former hostages stressed that most of them had returned in good shape. But it is certain that all 52 suffered through their ordeal. Perhaps worst of all was the fact that, for 444 days, they had lived with the fear that they might be killed at a moment's notice.

This photo of the hostages was taken on November 4, 1979, the day the U.S. embassy was seized.

MADE IN AMERICA

In the early 1900's, a U.S. manufacturer named Henry Ford found a way to produce cars cheaply in great numbers. Ford set up an assembly line, in which each worker did one small job over and over again. His company became an industrial giant. And as other companies adopted mass-production techniques, U.S. industry became known around the world for its efficiency.

But U.S. automobile manufacturers began 1981 in trouble. The big three—General Motors, Ford, and Chrysler—had together lost about $4,000,000,000 (billion) in 1980. They had closed some plants and laid off about 200,000 workers. Chrysler was saved from bankruptcy only by a billion-dollar package of government-guaranteed loans.

One reason for the problem was competition from foreign car makers. U.S. manufacturers traditionally produced big, powerful cars. But in the late 1970's, chiefly because of rising gasoline costs, many people began to want smaller cars that used less gas. Most of these people bought cars that had been made in Europe or Japan. The foreign car makers' share of the U.S. market rose from 15 percent in 1970 to more than 25 percent by 1981. At the same time, the cost of producing a car in the United States rose. This cut into the U.S. manufacturers' profits.

Rising costs and competition from abroad also hurt other industries in 1981—steelmaking, for one. But many people were worried about the automobile industry's troubles because that industry is so important to the U.S. economy. It employs about one out of every seven wage earners and buys up vast amounts of raw materials, including steel.

U.S. car makers were not so easily beaten, however. They fought back, with new products and new production methods.

MEETING THE COMPETITION

In late 1980 and 1981 a whole new class of cars began to roll off U.S. assembly lines—General Motors' J-cars, Chrysler's K-cars, Ford's Escort and EXP. They were designed to win back the buyers who had gone over to imported cars. Among their features were these:

• The cars were expected to go 25 to 30 miles per gallon (11 to 13 kilometers per liter) of gas, compared to 14 miles per gallon (6 kilometers per liter) for the average car of 1975. They got better mileage because they were lighter. They were small, and they were made of materials that were lighter than conventional steel—aluminum, plastic, and special high-strength steel.

• Many of the new cars featured front-wheel drive, which had proved popular on imported cars. In rear drive, the power produced by the engine is transferred to the rear wheels by a long, heavy drive shaft. In front wheel drive, power goes to the front wheels, and the drive shaft is eliminated. This makes the car lighter and, many people think, easier to handle.

• The U.S. manufacturers also concentrated on improving the "fit and finish"—the overall appearance and quality—of their cars. Many import buyers had felt that the foreign cars were built with more attention to detail and concern for quality than the U.S. cars.

To produce the new cars, assembly lines had to be redesigned and outfitted with new machines. This took time. To help the car makers while they made the switch, the U.S. Government urged Japan to limit the number of cars it exported to the United States. Japan agreed to do so for 1981 and 1982.

IMPROVING PRODUCTION

Simply producing and marketing new models was not enough to turn things around for the car makers. They faced another problem: high production costs. The design changes and the new materials were expensive. And labor costs were higher for U.S. car makers than for the Japanese. Wages and benefits for a worker in a U.S. plant averaged $19 an hour, compared to $11 in Japan.

The U.S. manufacturers did several things to cut their costs and improve production:

• To hold down labor costs, the car makers negotiated with labor unions to reduce workers' benefits. Workers at Chrysler agreed to give up some pay increases in exchange for a share of future profits.

Financial information is posted on the shop floor at this Detroit gear and axle plant. U.S. car makers hope that such worker-participation programs will improve productivity.

• Rather than hiring new workers, the car makers increased the amount of automation in their plants. In 1981, General Motors had about 1,200 robots on its assembly lines, and 4,000 more were on order. It was hoped that automation would improve quality as well as cut labor costs.

• The federal government helped the car makers save money by easing standards for safety devices and pollution control. Car makers estimated that this would trim about $150 from the cost of producing an average car.

• Japanese plants were turning out cars in less time than U.S. plants, and doing it with fewer workers. So the U.S. manufacturers tried to find ways to improve the productivity—the output per worker—of their plants. They took a long, hard look at the way their assembly lines had been run ever since the days of Henry Ford.

Traditionally, managers had made the decisions on what to do and how to do it, and workers had performed their single jobs. But the Japanese ran their plants differently. Workers there were considered part of the decision-making group. It was assumed that they would be just as interested in improving quality and productivity as the managers were—because their jobs depended on the company's success.

U.S. car makers began to adopt some Japanese management methods. These ranged from "quality circles," in which employees met regularly to solve production problems, to much broader programs in which workers helped design their own jobs. General Motors especially was interested in employee participation. It began "quality of worklife" programs in several plants.

These new management methods were being tried in other industries, too. Many people were enthusiastic about them. But it was too soon to tell if the new methods would help U.S. industry turn the tide against foreign competition.

The B-1 bomber is being developed to replace the aging B-52. President Reagan hopes to have the B-1 ready by 1987.

THE U.S. DEFENSE BUILDUP

In 1981, U.S. President Ronald Reagan called for one of the largest military buildups in the nation's history. But the United States was not at war.

Why did President Reagan call for the buildup? Because, since 1970, the Soviet Union had been building up its own military. Many people believed that the Soviet Union's defenses had become at least as strong as those of the United States, and in many ways stronger.

THE ARMS RACE

World War II ended in 1945, shortly after the United States dropped atomic bombs on the Japanese cities of Hiroshima and Nagasaki. The Nuclear Age had dawned. For several years after World War II, the United States was the only country that had nuclear weapons. But in the 1950's, the Soviet Union developed its own nuclear weapons. The United States and the Soviet Union then became great rivals as world powers.

The two countries never went to war with each other, but there was always the fear that they might. In the 1960's, each continued to build up its supply of nuclear bombs and warheads, and each developed sophisticated missiles and planes to carry the weapons. This was called the arms race. As each side became stronger, the United States developed a nuclear strategy called "mutual assured destruction." Under this strategy, if the Soviets launched a nuclear attack, the United States would retaliate with a nuclear attack on the Soviet Union. The belief was that neither side would want to start a war because both countries would be destroyed.

In the 1960's and 1970's, the United States fought a long and costly war in Vietnam. Because of the cost of the war, it cut back on developing new and more sophisticated weapons. But the Soviets went right on building better weapons, both nuclear and non-nuclear. In time, the Soviets began to catch up with and even to surpass the United States.

Some people say that the Soviets have become so strong that nuclear war is now possible. They say that the Soviets are strong enough to think they can win a nuclear war —and if they think they can win such a war, they just might start one. The Soviets say they would never start a nuclear war. But U.S. defense specialists make their plans as if the Soviets would.

THE U.S. AND SOVIET FORCES

The United States has developed a three-part nuclear defense, called a triad. In the event of an attack, the United States would launch its nuclear warheads from land, sea, and air.

• **On Land.** The United States has Minuteman intercontinental ballistic missiles (ICBM's). But it now appears that the Soviet Union has missiles accurate enough to destroy U.S. ICBM's as they sit in their silos (protective shelters.)

• **At Sea.** The United States has missile-carrying submarines. But the submarines would be difficult to communicate with during a nuclear war. And the missiles now in most U.S. nuclear subs are not very accurate. If sent against Soviet missile bases, many might miss their targets.

• **In the Air.** The United States has B-52 bombers carrying nuclear bombs. But the B-52's date back to the 1950's. They are old planes, and they would be very vulnerable to improved Soviet air defenses.

According to some defense analysts, the U.S. nuclear triad no longer seems able to defend the country. The Soviet's nuclear forces are too strong. The Soviets have also built up their conventional (non-nuclear) forces. Their land forces (as well as their missiles) could threaten U.S. allies in Western Europe. Their navy could threaten the Indian Ocean and the oil-rich Persian Gulf. Soviet forces now fighting in Afghanistan could also threaten the Persian Gulf. The United States has accused the Soviet Union of aggression in Africa, the Middle East, and Latin America.

In September, 1981, the U.S. Department of Defense published a booklet titled "Soviet Military Power." The booklet detailed the strength of the massive Soviet military system—nearly 5,000,000 men-at-arms, 50,000 tanks, 7,000 nuclear warheads, 5,200 helicopters, and so on. U.S. Secretary of Defense Caspar Weinberger said that much of this Soviet buildup had come within the preceding five years.

PRESIDENT REAGAN'S PROPOSALS

Under President Jimmy Carter, the United States had begun to rebuild its defenses in response to Soviet military moves. During his 1980 election campaign, Reagan promised that as president, he would build up U.S. defenses even more. This promise was part of the Republican platform.

After he took office, President Reagan called for spending cuts in most federal programs. At the same time, he asked that $1,-500,000,000,000 (trillion) be spent on defense between 1981 and 1986. He offered a number of proposals. Many of the ideas for strength-

Citizens of Moscow watch Soviet missiles on display at a parade.

ening U.S. defenses also contained some problems, however.

• **Land-based Missiles.** The Minuteman missiles would be replaced with larger, more powerful, more accurate MX missiles. It was not certain how the MX missiles would be based. The land-based MX, like the Minuteman, would be vulnerable to Soviet attack. President Reagan discussed making MX missile silos "super hard" to withstand a nuclear assault, but there was no guarantee that an MX could survive a direct hit.

An alternative would be to place the missiles in airplanes or submarines. But development of airplanes that could carry them would take several years, at least. And giving up land-based missiles would mean giving up one leg of the three-legged defense triad. Many U.S. defense planners did not want to do this.

• **Sea-based Missiles.** The United States is building six new Trident nuclear submarines to replace older nuclear subs. Each Trident would carry 24 highly accurate long-range missiles. Each missile would have 7 to 14 warheads. These numbers mean that one submarine alone could hit at least 168 and perhaps as many as 336 targets. The United States also plans to place nuclear cruise missiles in some existing subs.

An important advantage of any submarine is that it is difficult for the enemy to detect. But the Tridents are much larger than previous nuclear subs. Because of this, they might be somewhat easier for the Soviets to spot.

• **Air-based Nuclear Weapons.** To replace the aging B-52 bombers, there were proposals to build B-1 bombers, which would be ready by 1987, and to build Stealth bombers, which would be ready in the 1990's. The B-1, according to President Reagan, would be able to penetrate Soviet defenses for several years. By the time the Soviets improved their defenses again, the United States would have the Stealth bomber, which would be able to evade Soviet radar and enter Soviet air space undetected. Some critics say that the B-1 is too costly and unnecessary. The B-52, they say, would be able to perform its mission until the Stealth bomber is built.

• **Communications.** President Reagan also proposed that the United States upgrade the radar and satellite systems that would provide warning of a nuclear attack, as well as the communications systems that would keep the three parts of the defense triad in contact in the event of an attack.

CONVENTIONAL WEAPONRY

President Reagan proposed spending a far greater amount of money on weapons for conventional combat—such as tanks, fighter planes, and aircraft carriers—than on nuclear weapons. Many people agree that the United States must build up its conventional forces to match those of the Soviets.

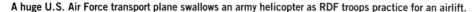

A huge U.S. Air Force transport plane swallows an army helicopter as RDF troops practice for an airlift.

In particular, the Reagan administration has called for expanding the U.S. Navy from 450 to 600 ships (especially for use in the Indian Ocean); developing the Rapid Deployment Force (RDF), which can quickly reach any "hot spot" in the world; and building more sophisticated and more powerful tanks, jeeps, fighter planes, and laser weapons. Perhaps the most important factor is manpower. Much of the money going for the defense buildup is intended for military salaries. The administration hopes that with higher salaries, trained soldiers will want to stay in the military.

There are also problems with the non-nuclear buildup:

• The new M-1 tank is by most accounts a superb fighting vehicle. It can shoot accurately on the run. It can survive direct hits by antitank missiles. But it is also so heavy (60 tons) that the largest U.S. transport plane can carry only one at a time. This means that the tank cannot be airlifted quickly in large numbers to a battle zone.

• The huge Nimitz-class aircraft carriers are formidable ships of war. Each can carry 90 fighter-bombers and can stay at sea for long periods of time. But the carriers require long stays at port for maintenance. And some defense analysts suggest that the United States needs a larger number of smaller aircraft carriers. They say that fifteen huge carriers, which the Navy will have by 1992, are not suitable for the naval wars that the United States might have to fight.

The basic question that the critics are asking is this: Is the United States spending its money on the correct weapons? Or will this huge defense buildup leave the country no better protected than before?

OTHER PROBLEMS

Even if all the problems with the various weapons systems were solved, the United States would still be faced with other, larger defense problems:

• **U.S. Allies.** Soviet nuclear missiles are aimed not only at the United States but also at the NATO allies in Western Europe (NATO stands for North Atlantic Treaty Organization) and at Japan. The United States wants its NATO allies, as well as Japan, to shoulder more of the burden of the common defense. Not all the people in these countries agree with the U.S. perception of the Soviet threat, however. Some NATO countries have agreed to allow new nuclear missiles on their soil. But there have been large antinuclear demonstrations in several NATO countries, and many Europeans have insisted that the United States begin arms reduction talks with the Soviet Union. Such talks did in fact begin in Geneva, Switzerland, at the end of November.

In Japan, antinuclear sentiment has been high ever since Hiroshima and Nagasaki. Some U.S. allies fear that the Reagan administration's tough stance may actually bring the world closer to war.

• **The Soviet Response.** How effective the U.S. defense buildup will be largely depends on how the Soviets respond. Even at this early stage of the buildup, it appears that the Soviet Union knows that the United States means business. The Soviets have come out in favor of arms reduction talks. But the U.S. arms buildup may also prompt the Soviets to increase their own arms once again. A new stage of the arms race would begin.

• **The Draft.** President Reagan has said that he is against the draft and that he still favors a volunteer army. But some experts say that the defense buildup will require so much new manpower that a return to the draft would be necessary. There would no doubt be some resistance to a return to the draft during peacetime.

• **The Economy.** One of the biggest questions concerning the defense buildup is this: Will massive defense spending lead to greater inflation? Will the United States be weakening itself economically while strengthening itself militarily?

The final and most important question is: Will the defense buildup prevent war? Will U.S. military strength deter the Soviets, or anyone, from committing acts of aggression? Defense Secretary Weinberger has said that he is optimistic that war with the Soviet Union can be avoided. Speaking in support of the buildup, he said, "I hope the history books in 50 years read that the statesmen of the 1980's and 1990's concluded that the proper course was to achieve deterrence through strength, and it worked." Only the future will tell if he is right.

FRANCE AND GREECE—A SWING TO THE LEFT

On a night in May, 1981, the streets of Paris suddenly filled with crowds of cheering people waving bright red flags. In October, similar rejoicing burst out on the streets of Athens. Both celebrations followed stunning election victories by socialist parties that had long been out of power. In France, François Mitterrand, the Socialist Party leader, was elected president on May 10. In Greece, the Panhellenic Socialist Movement won the most seats in a parliamentary election on October 18. Its leader, Andreas Papandreou, became premier.

Socialist and other left-wing parties generally favor public ownership of industry and broad programs to improve the quality of life. Right-wing, conservative parties generally favor private ownership. As France and Greece turned left, people watched to see the effects of the change—on the countries themselves, and on their relations with countries around the world.

François Mitterrand

FRANCE

Mitterrand defeated President Valéry Giscard d'Estaing, a conservative who was seeking a second 7-year term. In his campaign, Giscard d'Estaing stressed the standing that France had achieved—as a military power, in the production of nuclear energy, and in industry and agriculture. He claimed that if Mitterrand were elected, Communists as well as Socialists would come to power. The result would be vast changes in France, he warned.

Mitterrand was unclear on the role Communists would play in his administration. He accused his opponent of ignoring France's growing economic problems, and he proposed some sweeping changes to stimulate the economy and reduce unemployment.

Mitterrand won the election with 51.8 percent of the vote, ending 23 years of conservative government. He came to power at the age of 64, after almost 40 years in French politics. His slogan—"quiet strength"—fitted his reputation as a patient, intelligent politician with roots in the middle class. During World War II he had worked with the Resistance, and he entered politics after the war. When Charles de Gaulle founded the Fifth Republic in France in 1958, Mitterrand opposed him. He became leader of the Socialist Party in 1971. The 1981 election was his third attempt to win the presidency. After he took office on May 21, Mitterrand appointed a moderate, Pierre Mauroy, as premier.

Most of Mitterrand's proposed changes required the approval of the National Assembly. In June, the Socialists won a clear majority in elections for the assembly. The Communist Party then agreed to support some Socialist positions it had previously opposed, and Mitterrand appointed four Communist ministers to his 44-member cabinet. This alarmed some of France's Western allies, including the United States, because in the past the French Communist Party had supported the Soviet Union. But Mitterrand stressed his support of the West.

By August, the government had announced plans to turn over control of

France's departments, or regions, to locally elected councils. Construction of nuclear power plants had been stopped while the nuclear energy program was evaluated. And minimum wages and social security payments had been raised. Mitterrand's full economic plan called for nationalizing a number of large industrial companies and banks, shortening the workweek, and imposing new taxes on wealth. These changes had been promised in his campaign, and they seemed certain to be passed by the assembly.

But there was opposition from conservatives and others. Businesses were leery of investing in equipment or hiring new employees, and many people feared that Mitterrand's programs would raise the cost of living. Conservatives in the assembly delayed passage of laws putting the programs into effect. At the same time, some Socialists became unhappy with Mitterrand and called on him to change the country more quickly.

GREECE

Allaghi—"change"—was the one-word slogan that brought 62-year-old Andreas Papandreou to power. In his campaign, he called for major shifts both in foreign policy and at home. He opposed Greece's membership in the European Economic Community (Common Market) and in the North Atlantic Treaty Organization (NATO). He also opposed the presence of U.S. military bases in Greece. And he promised to end patronage and corruption in government and improve social services.

Conservatives had ruled Greece for 35 years. But in the October election, the Socialists won 174 seats in the 300-member Greek Parliament. Papandreou replaced George Rallis, leader of the conservative New Democracy Party, as premier.

Papandreou was not a newcomer to Greek politics. His father, George Papandreou, had served as premier several times. Andreas was educated in Greece and in the United States. He became a U.S. citizen in 1944 and, later, taught at universities in the United States, Sweden, and Canada. In 1959, he returned to Greece. He gave up his U.S. citizenship and entered politics. In 1967 the military seized power, and he was sent

Andreas Papandreou

into exile. When the military dictatorship fell in 1974, he returned and formed the Panhellenic Socialist Movement.

After the election, Papandreou announced that he would first concentrate on domestic affairs. With the cost of living rising nearly 25 percent a year, the economy was a major concern. The Socialists were expected to nationalize some industries and subsidize others, raise wages, and place controls on prices. The new government also planned to give more power to local administrations.

In his first major speech on foreign policy, in November, Papandreou said he was ready to bargain with the United States and the NATO and Common Market nations. He said he wanted to ban U.S. nuclear weapons from Greece, set a timetable for the closing of U.S. bases, and call a referendum on membership in the Common Market. In December, he announced that Greece would withdraw from some of its NATO commitments. His objection to NATO stemmed mainly from the fact that Turkey, Greece's traditional rival, was also a NATO member. The alliance thus gave Greece no protection from a country it saw as its enemy.

ASSASSINATION

On March 30, 1981, at about 2:30 P.M., U.S. President Ronald Reagan left the Hilton Hotel in Washington, D.C., where he had just delivered a speech. As he walked toward his limousine, he smiled and waved to a group of reporters and passersby who had waited on the sidewalk to catch a glimpse of him.

Suddenly, shots rang out. The President, wounded in the chest, was shoved into the car by Secret Service agents and rushed to a nearby hospital. Three men in the President's party were also wounded. And within seconds, security officers had tackled John W. Hinckley, Jr., a 25-year-old drifter who had been standing in the crowd. He was arrested and charged with the attempted assassination of the President and with the other shootings.

Just six weeks later, Pope John Paul II was shot in St. Peter's Square in Rome. The Pope had been standing in an open car, moving slowly through a crowd of worshipers, when he was wounded in the abdomen. Police immediately arrested the gunman—Mehmet Ali Agca, 23, an escaped Turkish murderer. Like the attempt on President Reagan's life, this attempt failed. Reagan recovered after emergency surgery and twelve days in the hospital; the Pope's recovery took somewhat longer.

But on May 30, President Ziaur Rahman of Bangladesh was killed by army officers who wanted to seize control of the government. And this was not the only assassination in 1981. In Iran, where Muslim clerics were struggling for power with moderate and leftist groups, a bomb explosion killed President Mohammed Ali Rajai and Premier Mohammed Javad Bahonar on August 30. Then, on October 6, Egyptian President Anwar el-Sadat was assassinated.

Sadat had been watching a military parade in Cairo. Suddenly a group of men dressed as soldiers, who seemed at first to be in the parade, opened fire on the reviewing stand. Several other people in the stand were also killed, and many were wounded. Four men were arrested; all were said to be members of an extremist Muslim group.

The assassinations and attempted assassinations of 1981 underscored the fact that for

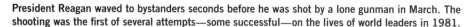

President Reagan waved to bystanders seconds before he was shot by a lone gunman in March. The shooting was the first of several attempts—some successful—on the lives of world leaders in 1981.

modern leaders, danger is ever present. But the danger of assassination is not new—it has existed since the earliest times.

ASSASSINATION IN THE PAST

The word "assassin" comes from the Arabic *hashashin,* which means "hashish eater." (Hashish is a drug derived from the hemp plant.) The *hashashin* were a group of Muslim fanatics in the Middle East in the 1100's. They were said to have murdered the leaders of their enemies (including Crusaders) after becoming intoxicated with hashish. Since that time, the word "assassin" has come to apply to anyone who kills an important public figure.

Assassins have altered the course of history more than once. Alexander the Great came to the throne of Macedonia after his father, King Philip II, was killed in 336 B.C. Many people believe that Alexander's mother, Olympias, was behind Philip's death or at least knew of the plan. Julius Caesar, who laid the foundations of the Roman Empire, was assassinated in 44 B.C. Caesar had been made dictator for life, and some Romans felt he had too much power. A group of his opponents, led by Brutus and Cassius, stabbed him as he entered the senate in Rome. And during the Middle Ages and the Renaissance, assassinations plagued the royal houses of Europe.

Assassinations have also affected modern history. In 1914, Archduke Francis Ferdinand, heir to the throne of Austria-Hungary, was shot by a Bosnian nationalist. (Bosnia was a small state ruled by Austria-Hungary.) The shooting was the spark that touched off World War I. And in the 1930's, a series of assassinations in Japan helped place the Japanese Army in control of the government. The army's policy of conquest led to Japan's involvement in World War II.

WHO ARE THE ASSASSINS?

An assassination may be the act of one person or the result of a conspiracy—a plan developed by two or more people. The motives behind this crime are complex. Many lone assassins act from personal motives—to avenge a slight or to strike out against society in general. Groups who hold extreme political beliefs sometimes resort to assassi-

In 44 B.C., Julius Caesar was assassinated in the Roman senate by a group of his opponents.

nation to call attention to their cause or simply to terrify people. Sometimes the goal is more direct—to replace a leader or eliminate an opponent. And often, more than one of these motives may be involved.

The Lone Assassin. Assassins (and would-be assassins) who act alone often seem to fit a general pattern. Many of these people have been mentally unstable types who didn't fit in with society. Many have come from unhappy homes and have had difficulty making friends. Many have joined extremist groups, only to find that they didn't fit there, either. They have held low opinions of themselves and have resented authority.

A study of people who have killed or tried to kill U.S. presidents found that most fit this pattern. John Wilkes Booth, who shot Abraham Lincoln in 1865, was the younger brother of a highly successful actor but was only mildly successful as an actor himself. According to the study, he was a failure in his own eyes. Charles Guiteau, who killed James Garfield in 1881, was a misfit who felt he had earned a job as an ambassador. When he didn't get it, he shot the President. Leon Czolgosz, who killed William McKinley in 1901, was a recluse who claimed to have acted to promote anarchism (the theory that all government is evil and should be destroyed). But the anarchists of his day disowned him. And Lee Harvey Oswald, who was arrested for shooting John F. Kennedy in 1963, had been involved with Communism but had also remained a loner.

Reagan's would-be assassin seemed to fit the pattern in several ways. After high school, Hinckley became withdrawn and gradually lost contact with his few friends. In 1978 he enlisted in the extreme right-wing American Nazi Party. Officials of that group later said he had been expelled because he seemed prone to violence.

In the months before the assassination attempt, Hinckley left the Texas college he had been attending to make trips to various parts of the country. He also began to write to an actress he had never met, Jodie Foster. His letters showed that he thought he could win her love by killing the President.

After his arrest, Hinckley was found mentally able to stand trial. The trial was scheduled to begin in 1982.

Conspiracy. The *hashashin* of the Middle Ages are an example of a group that used assassination to terrorize its opponents.

Such groups are a serious problem in many countries today. Among the more notorious groups are the Red Brigades of Italy and the Red Army faction, or Baader-Meinhoff gang, of West Germany.

Mehmet Ali Agca, who shot the Pope, appeared at first to be a lone assassin. But after investigation, an Italian court concluded that his act was part of a terrorist conspiracy.

In Turkey, Agca had belonged to the Gray Wolves, a right-wing terrorist group. He had been jailed in 1979 for the murder of a newspaper editor, but he had escaped and fled the country, apparently with outside help. He then traveled to various parts of Europe, and he seemed to have had financial help.

Agca freely admitted shooting the Pope and was sentenced to life imprisonment. He claimed to have acted alone, but the Italian court felt that the people who had helped him would not have allowed this. The court could not find enough evidence to name the others involved in the conspiracy, however.

According to the Egyptian Government, Sadat's assassins were connected with an extremist Muslim group called Takfir Wahi-

Pope John Paul II was shot while moving through a crowd of worshipers in St. Peter's Square in Rome. (The gunman's hand is circled.) Mixing with crowds exposes leaders to danger, but many choose to take the risk.

gra ("Repentance and Atonement"). The leader of the assassins was an army lieutenant, Khaled Ahmed el-Istambouly. In the parade, he replaced three of his regular crew with Muslim fanatics dressed as soldiers. The government said that these four were part of a web of revolutionaries. Several hundred soldiers and civilians who were said to have ties to extremist Muslim groups were also arrested.

There was said to be evidence that the assassins had wanted to seize power in Egypt. This was also the case in Bangladesh. There, the army officers who shot President Ziaur Rahman called on the rest of the country to rise up and overthrow the government. But the rebellion was put down within days. Its leader, Major General Manzur Ahmed, was reportedly killed by the guards who arrested him.

SECURITY

Several factors have increased the risk of assassination for modern leaders. One is the availability of guns. Another is the great publicity surrounding leaders. Their activi-

ties are widely reported in newspapers and on television. It is easy for an assassin to find a time and place to make the attempt.

But most leaders don't want less publicity. Politicians need to attend rallies, give public speeches, and mix with crowds. The Pope is committed to mingling with his followers. So efforts to prevent assassination concentrate on security measures such as bulletproof vests, bulletproof glass in car windows, police protection, and sharp detective work to identify potential assassins and keep tabs on their whereabouts.

These measures are not always successful. Sadat, for example, refused to wear a bulletproof vest. His advisers were said to have despaired over his easy-going attitude about safety. And after his death, there were questions about the efficiency of his security guards.

After the 1981 shootings, security was tightened around the Pope and President Reagan—and around other world leaders. But details of the arrangements weren't made public. To do so would provide useful information for a would-be assassin.

President Anwar el-Sadat of Egypt was assassinated while reviewing a military parade. The assassins were said to be involved in a conspiracy to overthrow the government.

63

NEWSMAKERS

Sandra Day O'Connor, an Arizona judge with a reputation for excellence, became the first woman justice of the U.S. Supreme Court in September, 1981. She is shown here with Chief Justice Warren Burger. Born March 26, 1930, O'Connor grew up on her parents' sprawling ranch in Duncan, Arizona. After graduating third in her class from Stanford Law School, she went on to an impressive career as a lawyer, legislator, and judge. She is married to a former Stanford classmate and has three sons. Of the role of women in society, O'Connor has said, "I feel strongly that qualified women should involve themselves more than they do now."

Muhammad Hosni Mubarak became president of Egypt after Anwar el-Sadat was assassinated on October 6, 1981. As vice-president, he had been Sadat's closest adviser, and as president he said, "I shall always continue his principles." Mubarak was born May 4, 1928, in the same Nile Delta province as Sadat. He was trained as a pilot in Egypt and received further military training in the Soviet Union. As commander of the Air Force, he planned and led Egypt's surprise air strike against Israel in the October, 1973, war. Mubarak, who is married and has two sons, became vice-president in 1975 and has a reputation as an efficient administrator and a shrewd politician.

Lowell Bruce Laingen was the top-ranking diplomat among the 52 American hostages freed by Iran on January 20, 1981. He had been chargé d'affaires at the U.S. embassy in Teheran. When the embassy was seized by militants, he was at the Iranian foreign ministry, and he was held there for most of the 444-day captivity. Laingen was born on August 6, 1922, in Odin Township, Minnesota. He is married and has three sons. During his more than 30 years with the U.S. Foreign Service, he has held a number of posts abroad and has become known as a dedicated and idealistic diplomat. After his return to the United States, he called the hostages' families the "real heroes" of the crisis, and he spoke on patriotism to audiences across the nation.

Jeane J. Kirkpatrick became the U.S. ambassador to the United Nations in February, 1981. She was born Jeane Jordan on November 19, 1926, in Duncan, Oklahoma. Before her appointment to the U.N., she was a professor of political science at Georgetown University and was active in the Democratic Party. She is married and has three sons. Kirkpatrick is known for her strong stand against Communism. At the U.N., she won praise as a negotiator, and she took controversial positions on U.S. relations with South Africa and Central America.

ANIMALS

Many of Africa's animal species are becoming rare or endangered. Among them is Grévy's zebra, a magnificent horse-sized animal distinguished by its large, rounded ears.

Teeth are one of the most common weapons that animals use for hunting and fighting.

ANIMAL WEAPONS

Any animal that hunts needs weapons to capture its food. Teeth and claws are the most common hunting weapons, but there are many others. Some animals catch their prey by poisoning them, electrocuting them, or even by shooting at them.

Animals also need weapons to fight off enemies. When a wild animal is threatened, it usually tries to escape. But if it is cornered or protecting its young, it will fight back. It may bite, scratch, stab, sting, or shock. It may bombard its enemy with hot gas, burning acid, or a smelly spray.

TEETH

Hunting animals usually have strong jaws and sharp teeth. If you look at the jaws of a dog or a cat, you will see four long pointed teeth—two in the upper jaw and two in the lower. These are called canine teeth, or fangs. Canines are the chief weapons of many hunting animals. Like daggers, they are used for stabbing and slashing.

Monkeys and apes also have long canine teeth, but they use them mainly for self-defense. A monkey threatens an enemy by opening its mouth and flashing its dangerous canines.

Animals such as elephants, walruses, and wild pigs are armed with tusks—extra-long teeth that grow out of an animal's mouth. An African elephant will defend her helpless calf from lions and leopards by charging and stabbing with her tusks. She can kill any enemy instantly with one powerful thrust. Tusks are used for digging up food as well as for fighting.

Fish have a greater variety of teeth than any other group of animals. Since they have no limbs to help them grasp their prey, they must rely on their teeth to seize and hold whatever they catch. Some fish have teeth not only in their jaws but also on their tongues or even far back in their throats.

A shark's teeth have jagged edges and pointed tips, like steak knives. Most sharks have several rows of teeth, lined up one behind another. New teeth are growing in all the time. When the teeth in the front row are old and worn, they drop out. Then the teeth in the row behind move in to take their place. During a ten-year period, a tiger shark will grow, use, and shed as many as 24,000 teeth.

CLAWS, TALONS, AND HOOVES

A cat's claws can be as dangerous as its teeth. Lions, tigers, and all other cats use their claws to hook their prey and pull it down. Because of the way a cat's claws are curved, they make very effective weapons. Once they dig into the flesh, the victim's struggling only serves to draw them in deeper.

Except for the cheetah, all cats can pull their claws back into their toes. When a cat walks or runs, it keeps its claws pulled in so they will not be blunted by the hard ground. When it climbs or fights, it pushes its claws out.

Other animals with claws—such as dogs, bears, and raccoons—cannot pull them in. They use their claws mainly for digging or climbing rather than hunting or fighting. Even so, their claws can still cause plenty of damage. A bear fights by striking an enemy with its front paws. When it hits its target, its heavy claws can rip and tear.

Birds of prey hunt with the pointed talons on their feet. An eagle will swoop down from the sky, snatch up a rabbit with its talons, and carry it away. Some birds, such as the flightless ostrich, defend themselves with their feet. An ostrich has long muscular legs with two toes on each foot. The big toe is armed with a thick sharp nail. The ostrich fights by kicking. Its kick can be more dangerous than that of a horse.

Hoofed animals also fight by kicking. A zebra can smash an enemy's teeth with a well-aimed kick.

HORNS AND ANTLERS

Horns are used for self-defense by grazing animals like goats, sheep, cattle, and antelope. The horns of a Rocky Mountain goat are short and curved. A mother goat protecting her kid has been known to kill a bear by stabbing it in the heart. A male bighorn sheep has thick, heavy, tightly curled horns, which it uses as battering rams.

This warthog may look harmless coming out of a mudbath, but don't get too close—its tusks are deadly.

A bear attacks by striking out with its front paws. When it hits its victim, its heavy claws can rip and tear.

Male bighorns use their heavy horns as battering rams.

When a gemsbok attacks, it lowers its head so its swordlike horns are pointing at the enemy.

In Africa, an antelope called the gemsbok has horns like swords that may be four feet long. When a gemsbok attacks, it lowers its head between its legs, so the sharp tips of its horns are pointing at the enemy. A charging gemsbok can scoop up a lion with its horns and throw the lion over its back.

Antlers are found among most members of the deer family. Unlike horns, which keep on growing throughout an animal's life, antlers last only for a few months each year. They start growing in the spring, reach their full size during the winter, then drop off. The following spring, the animal grows a new set of antlers.

The pointed tips of fully grown antlers are as sharp as pitchforks. Antlers serve as weapons only during the winter mating season, when rival males fight over females. They are also used to fight off enemies such

When a porcupine is threatened, the quills beneath its fur stand on end, like thousands of sharp needles.

as wolves. But once they have dropped off, the animal must rely for protection on speed and its sharp hooves.

QUILLS AND SPINES

A porcupine seems to know that it is well protected as it waddles slowly through the forest with its nose to the ground. Buried beneath its long fur are 30,000 dangerous quills that keep most enemies at a distance.

Quills are stiff hairs growing out of the porcupine's skin. They are as sharp as needles and may be five inches (12.5 centimeters) long. The pointed tip of each quill has tiny barbs, or hooks, that curve backward, like the barbs on harpoons.

Usually the quills lie flat against the porcupine's body. But when a porcupine is frightened, its quills stand on end. Twisting about on its short legs, the porcupine keeps its rear toward the enemy and whips its bristling tail back and forth. As a warning, it hisses and gnashes its teeth.

A porcupine can't shoot its quills, but it can swat an enemy with its tail. When the tail hits its target, it drives hundreds of quills into the enemy. As the victim backs away, the quills are pulled out of the porcupine and stay buried in the victim's body. Once a quill has stabbed an enemy, the barbed tip works its way into the flesh. A badly wounded animal can die of its injuries.

Some fish have spines similar to a porcupine's quills. The spines of a porcupine fish

The alarmed porcupine fish sticks out its spines in all directions, ready to stab its enemy.

resemble the prickly thorns of a rose bush. Usually, a porcupine fish swims about with its spines lying flat against its body. But when it is alarmed, it gulps water and swells up like a prickly balloon. Its spines stick out in all directions, ready to stab any enemy.

POISON

Poison is used as a weapon for hunting or self defense by many kinds of fish, snakes, and insects, as well as other animals. The poison, or venom, is produced by special glands in the animal's body. The animal injects its venom by biting or stinging.

Many fish are armed with venomous spines, which they use only for self-defense. A catfish has a sharp spine in the fin on its back and two more spines in the fins on its sides. All three spines are barbed, like a porcupine's quills. They are connected to glands that pump poison into an enemy's wounds. When a catfish is alarmed, it lifts its spines and locks them in place. It fights by twisting about in the water, jabbing at the enemy with its spines. Fishermen must handle catfish with great care to avoid being stung.

The deadliest of all venomous fish is the ugly little stonefish, found off the coast of Australia. A stonefish lies hidden among stones and debris in shallow water, waiting to leap forward and snap up its prey. Its body is covered with warts and coated with algae and slime, making it almost invisible.

Eighteen jagged spines jut out from its body. These fish are considered as deadly as cobras. Swimmers in Australia have died within an hour after stepping on a stonefish.

Venomous snakes use their poison to capture food, as well as in self-defense. They can strike and kill with lightning speed. A rattlesnake has two hollow fangs in its upper jaw. Each fang is connected to a poison gland in the rattler's cheek. When the snake sinks its fangs into a victim, its cheeks squeeze against the poison glands. Poison squirts into the wound through tiny holes in the tips of the fangs. A rattlesnake bite can kill a rabbit in a few minutes. It can also kill a person unless the victim receives quick medical aid.

The biggest venomous snakes are cobras, which live in Africa and Asia. A king cobra may be 18 feet (5.5 meters) long. A cobra

A rattlesnake has two hollow fangs connected to poison glands. Its deadly bite can kill a small animal in minutes.

warns an enemy by rearing up, hissing loudly, and spreading the skin of its neck into a wide hood. Some cobras can spit their poison through small holes in the front of their fangs. They are said to aim at the eyes of their enemies.

Spiders capture food just as some snakes do—with a poisonous bite. Like a rattle-snake, a spider has two sharp fangs connected to poison glands in its head. All spiders are poisonous, but only a few, like the black widow, are dangerous to humans. Most spiders are so small that their fangs cannot pierce human skin.

Hornets, wasps, and bees have poisonous stingers at the tips of their tails. A bee's venom is similar to a snake's, but it is not as dangerous because it is released in much smaller amounts. Some ants also have poisonous stingers in their tails, which they use to kill enemies and capture the creatures they eat. Ants can also bite with their powerful ice-tong jaws. An ant will often bite an enemy, then turn around and squirt poison into the wound.

CHEMICAL WARFARE

A skunk cannot really injure an enemy. Yet it is armed with one of nature's most effective weapons—a bad-smelling chemical spray. Most animals quickly get out of the way when they see a skunk coming.

A skunk always gives warning before it fires. It lowers its head and drums on the ground with its front paws. It may click its teeth and growl or hiss. If the enemy doesn't retreat, the skunk lifts its bushy tail. That's the last warning. Suddenly the skunk twists around into a U-shaped position. It aims its tail at the enemy and lets go with its stinking spray.

Skunk spray comes from two stink glands beneath the skunk's tail. Each gland is connected to a small tube that lies hidden under the skin. When the skunk fires, the tubes pop out like a pair of nozzles. They squirt two streams of thick, oily fluid that join together in a misty spray.

A skunk can aim straight ahead, to either side, or up into the air. It can shoot its spray about 12 feet (3.5 meters), even more if the spray is carried by the wind. The strong smell of skunk spray can make a person or animal sick. If the spray hits the eyes, they will sting and burn until tears wash the spray out.

Skunks aren't the only animals that use odor as a weapon. Snakes, weasels, minks, wolverines, and several other animals have scent glands similar to a skunk's but not as powerful.

Some insects are also equipped for chemical warfare. When they are threatened, they release a fluid or gas that stinks, burns, or stings. A stink bug drives off enemies by giving off a repulsive smell. Some ants can spray a burning acid. The bombardier beetle attacks enemies by blasting them with hot gas that shoots out from the tail end of its body.

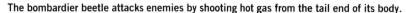

The bombardier beetle attacks enemies by shooting hot gas from the tail end of its body.

When a hungry chameleon spots an insect, it uncoils its long, sticky-tipped tongue and hauls the victim into its mouth.

UNUSUAL WEAPONS

Fish are the only animals that have the power to shock their enemies. About 250 kinds of fish can send an electrical charge into the water. The most powerful of these is the electric eel, which lives in South American rivers.

In the eel's tail are bundles of special cells that produce electricity in much the same way as an electric battery. As the eel swims along, it gives off a weak current that helps it find its way in muddy river waters. When it finds food or is alarmed, it can deliver an electric shock of up to 650 volts. That's enough power to stun the fish and frogs it feeds on and to jolt enemies like alligators.

Frogs and toads use their long sticky tongues as hunting weapons. They catch insects by flicking out their tongues. The champion tongue-flicker, however, is a reptile, the African chameleon. Usually, a chameleon's tongue is folded up inside its mouth. When it spots an insect, it creeps forward, takes aim, opens its mouth, and fires. Its tongue, longer than its body, shoots out like a spring uncoiling. The swollen tip of the tongue is coated with a sticky fluid that can trap big insects as well as small reptiles and birds. After hitting its target, the chameleon hauls its meal back into its mouth.

Of all the animals that use weapons, the archerfish is in a class by itself. It shoots water bullets at its prey. These little fish live in Australia and Southeast Asia. They hunt by waiting below the surface of a pond, with the tips of their mouths sticking out of the water. When an archerfish sees an insect or spider on a leaf or plant stem, it closes its gills and forces water into its mouth. Then it presses its tongue against the roof of its mouth and fires droplets of water in a rapid stream.

An archerfish can score a bull's-eye from several feet away. The fast jet of water knocks the insect or spider off its perch. It falls into the pond, where it is seized and swallowed by the sharpshooting archerfish.

Few animals have a weapon as unusual as that of the archerfish. But every animal uses the weapons it was born with—to hunt and to protect itself—so it can stay alive for another day.

RUSSELL FREEDMAN
Author, *Tooth and Claw*

The armadillo gets its name from its armorlike covering. Some armadillos have hairs that are so long that the armor is nearly hidden.

A PIG IN TURTLE'S CLOTHING

Feel sorry for the poor armadillo. People laugh at it and make jokes about it. They poke fun at the way it looks. Some people liken it to an army tank. Others say it has the face of a mouse and the ears of a donkey. The famous naturalist John James Audubon said it looked like "a small pig with the shell of a turtle."

THE LITTLE ARMORED ONE

There are about 20 species, or kinds, of armadillos. They are found throughout South and Central America. One species, the nine-banded armadillo, has extended its range into the southern part of the United States.

The smallest armadillo, the pichiciago, is only 6 inches (15 centimeters) long. The largest species, the giant armadillo, is up to 40 inches (100 centimeters) long—not counting its tail, which may be 20 inches (50 centimeters) long. The nine-banded armadillo is about 2 feet (60 centimeters) long, including its tail, and weighs about 14 pounds (6.5 kilograms)—it's a little larger than a house cat. It is brown speckled, with a shell over its back and its long tail.

Armadillos are usually classified in a group of mammals called edentates, or "toothless ones." Actually, armadillos have lots of teeth. One kind, the giant armadillo, has more than 90 teeth. But armadillo teeth are small, without true roots, and are more or less useless. The animal's main eating tool is its long sticky tongue.

The armadillo received its name from early Spanish explorers of the New World. The name, which translates into English as "little armored one," refers to the armorlike covering that protects the animal.

This armor consists of a series of strong, bony plates within the skin. The plates cover the back and in some cases the head and the tail of the animal. The plates are connected by flexible skin, which enables the armadillo to bend its body. Between the plates grow hard, brushlike hairs. Some kinds of armadillos have hairs that are so long and thick that they nearly hide the armor.

The undersides of the armadillo are not protected by armor. Most kinds of armadillos can roll up into a ball when they are attacked. This protects their tender undersides. Only the armor is exposed, and many of the armadillos' enemies cannot bite through it.

An armadillo has four short legs, ending in clawed feet. The middle toes on its front feet are long and heavy. These are toes used for digging.

Armadillos are surprisingly fast runners. They can run faster than people and faster than most dogs. As soon as it thinks it has outdistanced its pursuer, an armadillo quickly digs into the ground. In two minutes it can disappear from view—even in soil so hard that a person would need a pickaxe to crack it. Once underground, the armadillo uses its feet and armor to anchor itself. This makes it almost impossible to pull an armadillo out of the ground.

An armadillo can hold its breath for up to ten minutes. Thus a stream or river presents no barrier to this animal. If the stream is narrow, the animal holds its breath and walks along the bottom, under water. If the stream is wide, the armadillo inflates itself. It takes a big gulp of air before entering the water. This helps keep it afloat as it swims along the surface, with only its snout showing above the water.

Armadillos feed mainly on insects, particularly ants, termites, grasshoppers, and other destructive pests. They also eat scorpions, tarantulas, and, occasionally, snakes, mice, berries, and dead animals. In their search for food they may uproot young plants, an activity not appreciated by farmers and gardeners.

When not out looking for food, the armadillo lives in its burrow, which it may share with other armadillos or even with rabbits or a rattlesnake. The burrow usually has a long corridor that opens into a large chamber that the armadillo lines with leaves or grass.

The burrow is where a female gives birth to her young. An armadillo mother gives birth to four babies at a time—and they are all exactly alike. The mother may have four identical girls or four identical boys. Or perhaps she has "twins"—eight identical babies all of the same sex. The babies are pink and have soft shell plates. Within two weeks the armor hardens, and the babies leave their mother to live on their own.

In the 1970's, scientists discovered an unusual fact about armadillos: They catch human leprosy. This disease, which is caused by a bacterium, affects the skin and nerve tissues of humans. Armadillos are one of only two types of mammals known to contract human leprosy. Scientists are conducting research on armadillos in an effort to learn more about the disease.

Armadillos are surprisingly fast runners. This can be seen at the Armadillo Alympics, held every year in New Braunfels, Texas.

Put on a pair of foxy earphones and hear sounds the way a fennec does.

A ZOO JUST FOR YOU

How does it feel to burrow like a prairie dog? To hear like a fox? To crawl like a snail? To move like a spider on a web?

You can learn the answers to these and many other questions about animals if you visit the new Children's Zoo at the Bronx Zoo, in New York City. And you can learn not just by looking at the animals but by sharing some of their activities. You can go through an underground burrow, pop your head up through a hole in the earth, and perhaps find yourself face to face with a prairie dog who's doing the same thing. You can put on a pair of foxy earphones and hear the sounds around you the way a fennec does. You can get inside a special snail shell and crawl at a snail's pace. And you can climb a huge spiderweb made of rope.

The new Children's Zoo is divided into five areas. Each of the first four is an example of a different kind of wild place: the woodland edge, the marsh, the forest, and the desert. Each shows some of the typical animals and plants that you would find in such a place in the wild. In addition, each area gives examples of the ways animals do different things.

• In the woodland edge, you'll learn about animal homes. That's where you'll find the prairie-dog burrows and the spiderweb. You can also look for some raccoons in a hollow log—and there's another hollow log for *you* to crawl through, just to see what it's like.

• In the marsh, you'll learn how animals move—by swimming, flying, crawling, jumping. That's where the special snail shell is. There's also a glass-walled pond that lets you see ducks swimming and diving, with their feet at your eye level. You can even test your jumping ability against a bullfrog's.

Get inside a special snail shell and crawl at a snail's pace.

Climb a huge spiderweb made of rope.

• The forest area shows how animals defend themselves—with spines (a porcupine), with nasty smells (a skunk), with stings (a hornet), by being hard to see (an insect called a walking stick, which looks just like a stick that walks), by simply running away (a lizard).

• The desert area tells about animal senses —smell, taste, touch, hearing, and sight. There you'll find Freddie the Fennec, the official mascot of the Children's Zoo. Freddie is a small, sand-colored desert fox with very big, sharp ears. You'll also find the earphones shaped just like his ears.

• The fifth area has familiar domestic animals that you can pet and feed—goats, sheep, pigs, rabbits, ducks, geese, a pony, and a donkey. In the nursery, you'll see animals that have just been born.

The Children's Zoo has been created especially for you. It's a great place to have fun while learning about the creatures that share our planet with us.

The rhinoceros bears a striking resemblance to a dinosaur called . . .

Grévy's zebra

SAVING AFRICA'S WILDLIFE

With its menacing horn, massive body, and armorlike hide, the rhinoceros looks like a survivor from the prehistoric past. In fact, the rhino bears a striking resemblance to a dinosaur called *Triceratops*. *Triceratops* is extinct, of course—the last of these giant reptiles died more than 70,000,000 years ago. And today, the rhino may face the same fate.

Since ancient times, people in China and other parts of Asia have believed that powdered rhino horn has great value as a medicine. Demand for the horn caused the slaughter and finally the near extinction of Asian rhinos. Then those in Africa were hunted. Once there were many species of rhino. Now only five species remain, and all of them are rare.

The rhino is only one of many African animals whose numbers are dwindling. The leopard, Grévy's zebra, the elephant, the serval, the lechwe (an antelope), the gorilla, the aye-aye (a lemur), the Walia ibex, and the ostrich are just a few of the others. Drought and disease are partly responsible. But far more blame must go to the changes people have brought to the vast continent.

Animals in Danger. Africa is home to a matchless variety of wildlife. Dense tropical rain forests clothe the central part of the continent. Hundreds of species of forest birds chatter and call through the thick canopy formed by the treetops. Below, on the forest floor, live forest antelopes, dwarf buffalo, wild boars, leop-

... *Triceratops*. And the rhino, like other African animals, may face the same fate as the dinosaur—extinction.

Ostrich

ards, catlike genets, and elephants. The rain forest is also the home of chimpanzees, gorillas, and many species of monkeys.

North and south of the rain forest are vast grasslands, in some places dotted with trees. This is the savanna, Africa's richest wildlife domain. Herds of grazing animals—zebras, elephants, giraffes, and many kinds of antelope—feed on the grass and leaves. Meat eaters—lions, leopards, hyenas, and cheetahs—stalk the herds. Other animals of the savanna include wart hogs, baboons, jackals, and rhinos. There are big birds, such as ostriches and eagles, and countless smaller birds. Here and there are the streams and lakes preferred by hippopotamuses, buffalo, crocodiles, and such water birds as cranes, ibises, and flamingos.

For thousands of years, little happened to upset the balance of nature south of the Sahara. But things changed after Europeans began to colonize Africa in the 1800's. As the human population grew, towns and cities were built, and wilderness areas diminished. Forests were cut down for lumber. Mines were excavated, and plantations were laid out to grow crops. Roads and railroad lines penetrated the jungles. Many animals could not adapt to the changed environment, and they began to die out.

But perhaps more frightful was the tremendous slaughter of animals that began. No longer were the animals being killed mainly to fill the basic needs for food and clothing. After colonization, birds, reptiles, and mammals were being killed in vast numbers for sport or to obtain products for foreign markets. Zebras were killed for their striped coats, leopards for their spotted

Elephants

Gorilla

fur. Elephants were hunted for their ivory tusks. Crocodiles and snakes were killed for their skins. Ostriches, flamingos, and other birds were sought for their plumage. And rhinos were killed for their horns.

A Cry for Conservation. Some of the colonial powers became concerned about Africa's threatened wildlife. In 1897, Britain developed an African conservation policy. Wildlife reserves were proposed as a solution to the changing environment. And three years later, six of the colonial powers signed an agreement that banned the hunting of certain animals, protected the young of many other species, and sought to regulate trade in ivory. Over the years, the policy of conservation spread. By the end of World War II, several wildlife reserves had been established.

By the 1960's, most African nations had gained independence. The independent nations joined in to support conservation. Some countries tightened hunting regulations, and others banned hunting completely. And during the next twenty years, dozens of new wildlife reserves were established. Today, Africa has some of the largest and most impressive reserves in the world. More than 50 reserves are in East Africa. There are others in central and south-

Aye-aye

Leopards

Lechwe

ern Africa. In these reserves, the animals live undisturbed, much as they have for thousands of years.

What Does the Future Hold? Despite the wildlife reserves and other conservation efforts, there are still serious threats to Africa's wildlife. They include drought, disease, and a shortage of funds for the reserves. But the greatest threat is poaching—the illegal killing of animals. Many countries have agreed to restrict trade in products made from endangered species. The hope is that if there is less demand for the products, fewer animals will be killed. But poachers still kill huge numbers of animals.

There have also been victories in the struggle to save Africa's wildlife. By the 1940's, the white rhino population had dwindled to a few dozen. Conservationists decided to protect them in two special wildlife reserves in South Africa. The project was so successful that more than 2,000 white rhinos were shipped to reserves throughout Africa and to zoos around the world. The white rhino's success story raises the hope that other endangered species may be saved from the fate of the dinosaurs.

JOHN TEDFORD
Contributing Editor, *New Book of Popular Science*

ANIMAL TALK

Roar, hiss, chatter, twitter—these are sounds made by animals. Lions roar, snakes hiss, monkeys chatter, and birds twitter. Are these sounds just a lot of noise? Or do they mean something?

Scientists have been asking these questions for a long time, and recently one scientist came up with an exciting new theory. The scientist, Dr. Eugene Morton, believes he has discovered a language that is shared by all animals.

Morton studied the sounds made by many kinds of birds and mammals. His subjects ranged from the parakeet to the spiny rat to the rhinoceros. He recorded the sounds that each animal made when it was angry or submissive. And he found that regardless of the size and voice of each animal, they all had a common vocal pattern. Angry animals made low, harsh sounds or growls. Friendly or fearful animals made high, whining sounds.

How did Morton compare the voice of a bird to the voice of a rhino? He monitored the animal sounds with special electronic equipment that translated the animal sounds into shapes or lines on a screen. Lines that represented angry sounds looked the same for the smallest bird and the largest mammal. Lines that represented whining sounds—indicating fear or friendliness—were also the same, no matter what animal made them. But the most common animal sounds indicated interest in a situation, not fear or anger. Morton found that these sounds—chirps, barks, and grunts—all looked alike on the screen, too.

Why do birds and mammals make low sounds when they are angry and high sounds when they are frightened or friendly? Morton believes that they developed the ability to raise and lower the pitch of their voices because this ability helps them survive. Large animals normally make lower sounds than small animals. So when an animal lowers the pitch of its voice, it sounds larger than it really is. In this way, it can scare its enemies. And when an animal raises its pitch, it seems smaller and less threatening. Animals that are able to use these vocal tricks increase their chances of survival. They can deal with dangerous situations without having to resort to the possibly deadly use of force.

In Morton's theory of a universal animal language, animals express general feelings but not exact meanings. Other scientists believe that they have found a species of monkey whose language does express more precise information.

The monkeys are vervets, and they live in the jungles of eastern and southern Africa. Vervets use special sounds to warn each other whenever enemies approach. This is not unusual—many animals have danger signals. But the scientists believe that the vervets are able to tell each other what *kind* of danger to watch out for.

Vervets have three main enemies—leopards, eagles, and pythons. The monkeys seem to have a specific warning sound for each one. Their leopard warning is a series of short noises that sound like barks combined with snores. Other vervets respond to this by looking around and then heading for the nearest tree. A series of low grunts signals the monkeys to search the sky for eagles and to hide in thick foliage. A high-pitched hissing sound warns them to be wary of pythons on the ground.

The monkeys seem to learn their language by trial and error. Infant vervets sometimes make mistakes. They may give the eagle call when they see a harmless bird or a falling leaf. Or they may give the snake alert when they spot something long and thin, like a stick. Their ability to spot real dangers improves with age. Adult vervets almost always use the warnings correctly.

The scientists think that the vervets may have even more warning signals—one for baboons and one for unfamiliar people. The warning sound for people is thought to be similar to the warning sound for pythons.

DAVID J. KULL
Senior Editor
Medical Laboratory Observer magazine

Some scientists believe that the language of a vervet expresses precise meaning, rather than just general feelings.

ANIMALS IN THE NEWS

The U.S. National Zoo's giant panda Ling-Ling takes a close look at the London Zoo's Chia-Chia, who traveled to Washington, D.C., to meet her in April, 1981. Zoo officials hoped that the pandas would mate and produce a cub. Pandas are threatened with extinction in their native China, and they rarely breed in captivity. But love at first sight it was not. Ling-Ling and Chia-Chia didn't hit it off. In fact, they came to blows. Panda fans had something to be happy about later in the year, however—cubs were born in two other zoos. Ying-Ying, a panda at Mexico's Chapultepec Zoo, gave birth to a cub in July. It was her second, and also the second to be born outside China. (Ying-Ying unfortunately sat on the first cub shortly after it was born in 1980.) And in September, panda twins were born at the Peking Zoo. Only one of the twins survived.

Champion Dhandy's Favorite Woodchuck, a pug, won top honors at the 1981 Westminster Kennel Club show, in New York City. Chucky, as he is called, hails from Philadelphia, Pennsylvania. But his ancestors came from a more exotic place. The pug breed originated in China. In the 1800's traders brought the dogs to Europe, where they soon became popular pets.

This shaggy brown calf doesn't look anything like its mother. That's because the calf is a gaur—a rare type of wild ox from South Asia—and the mother is a black-and-white Holstein cow named Flossie. Scientists at the Bronx Zoo in New York City transferred a gaur embryo to Flossie in October, 1980. Ten months later, the calf was born. It was named Manhar, a Hindi name that means "he who wins everyone's heart." Manhar certainly won Flossie's heart—and the scientists were happy, too. A gaur normally gives birth to one calf a year. But by transferring gaur embryos to other animals, six to eight times that number could be born in a year. And the scientists hope to use the same technique to increase the numbers of other rare species.

Unicorns exist only in legend—or so most people think. That makes Lancelot, the Angora goat at the right, a living legend. Most Angoras have two horns, one at each side of the head. But two California biologists found a way to ensure that Lancelot would grow just one horn, smack in the middle. Lancelot lives at Marine World/Africa USA, in Redwood City, California. Apart from his horn, he resembles the mythical unicorns of the Middle Ages in other ways. He's larger than most Angoras, and he has a flowing mane. But while the medieval unicorn is said to have looked much like a horse, Lancelot is pure goat.

Incredible Creatures

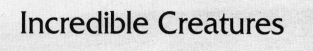

Once upon a time, people believed that the earth was populated by incredible creatures. Some of them were fascinating, but many others were truly horrible beasts.

These animals have never been seen in zoos. And no one has ever taken pictures of them. These creatures never really existed at all—they lived only in people's imaginations. But to the people who believed in them at the time, they were very much alive. They were as real as cats and dogs are to you and me.

DRAGONS

Dragons are probably the best-known imaginary creatures. Stories about dragons are found in many parts of the world.

A typical dragon had a scaly, snakelike body and four legs with huge claws. The head and front legs were like those of a crocodile, a lion, or an eagle. And many dragons had wings.

In China, Dragon Kings ruled the lakes, rivers, and seas. If people treated them well, the Dragon Kings would see to it that rain watered the farmlands. But if the Dragon Kings believed that they were being treated badly, they would cause droughts or fierce storms.

One Chinese dragon, Ch'ien T'ang, had a terrible temper. When he was angry, he would swing his enormous tail through the sea. This would cause a huge wave of water to sweep over the land. The water would drown villages and cause many deaths.

Chinese dragons were said to change themselves into other living things. Sometimes there were ways to see through their disguises. People thought that a dragon disguised as a fish would speak in a human voice while it was being cooked. But it would be more difficult to detect a dragon that had turned itself into a beautiful young woman.

In Europe during the Dark Ages, dragons were thought to be evil animals. They breathed fire and puffed smoke through their nostrils. Often, groups of three or four would entwine their tails and fly together through the air in search of food. Dragons ate cows, sheep, and people. And they had huge appetites. It was said that one dragon, kept as a pet by a man in Rome, had eaten 6,000 people a day.

MANTICORES

Manticores were fearsome creatures that were said to have originated in India. A manticore had a human face, with blue or gray eyes and a bright red complexion. Reaching from ear to ear was a wide mouth containing three rows of teeth.

A manticore had the body of a lion and a

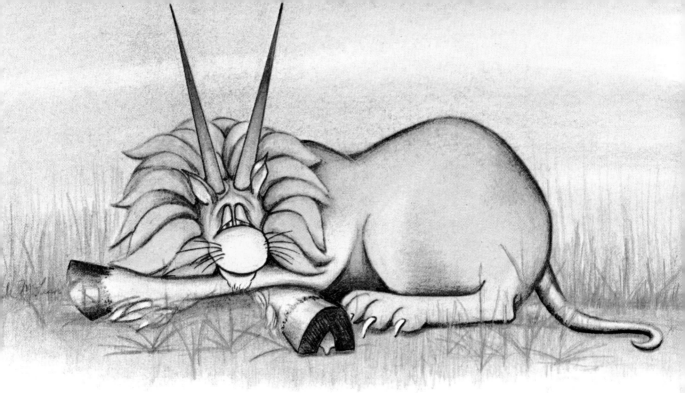

scorpionlike tail. The tail was covered with poisonous spines. If angry or frightened, a manticore would shoot these spines at its enemies.

Manticores could run very fast. They were powerful, fearsome creatures that could easily catch, knock down, and kill people.

BASILISKS

Basilisks were small poisonous reptiles, each one having a crownlike crest on top of its head. They were thought to be so poisonous that just looking at or smelling one was enough to kill a person or animal.

It was said that if a hunter speared a basilisk, the creature's poison would rise up through the spear and instantly kill him.

CENTICHORAS

The centichora was another mythical native of India. The body of a centichora was part lion and part horse. It ended in an elephantlike tail. The monster had a large round snout, eyes that were very close together, and a human voice. On top of its head were two very long, sharp horns. A centichora could move its horns, which was a great advantage during a fight.

A centichora's worst enemy was the basilisk. The venomous basilisk would bite the centichora while it was sleeping. The basilisk's poison would cause the centichora to swell up like a balloon and die.

THE CHIMERA

The Chimera was another fire-breathing creature. It was found in the mythology of the ancient Greeks. Homer, the famous poet of ancient Greece, described the Chimera as having the head of a lion, the body of a goat, and the tail of a serpent.

One story says that the Chimera was born from a mountain. The mountain had a volcano at the top, goat pastures on its side, and a colony of snakes living at its base.

The fire-breathing Chimera would creep into villages at night and kill all the inhabitants. Finally, a young Greek named Bellerophon set out to destroy the terrible beast. Bellerophon was helped by a powerful winged horse, Pegasus, that could soar like a bird through the sky. Astride Pegasus, Bellerophon flew high above the hiding place of the Chimera and slew it with arrows.

UNICORNS

Most people agreed that unicorns were beautiful animals. A unicorn was built like a horse, with a white body, purple head, and blue eyes. In the center of its forehead was a long, powerful horn. Some writers said the horn was twisted. Others said it was smooth.

One description said that the horn was white at the base, black in the middle, and red at the tip.

People believed that the powder made by crushing a unicorn horn would improve their health. During the 16th and 17th centuries, unicorn powder was sold in most European pharmacies. The powder was used as a cure for epilepsy and as an antidote to poison.

Kings, queens, and other royalty, who often worried that their enemies might try to poison them, used whole unicorn horns as drinking cups. They believed that the magical power of the horn protected them against being poisoned. Unicorn horns were thus very valuable and could only be bought for huge sums of money.

Where did people get the horns of this imaginary animal? Some horns were probably rhinoceros horns. Twisted horns probably came from the narwhal, a type of whale that has a long tusk. And unicorn powder could have been made by crushing the bones of any animal.

Unicorns were said to run so fast that they were very difficult to catch. There are many medieval tapestries and other works of art that show the hunt for the unicorn.

Unicorns were usually described as fierce animals. Yet a unicorn would be very gentle with a maiden. It would allow itself to be petted and even lie down and put its head on a maiden's lap. As a result, the unicorn became a symbol of purity. This is why it is often included in religious paintings.

The Chinese also had a unicorn. It was called Chin-Lin and was different from the European unicorn. Chin-Lin had the body of a deer, the feet of a horse, and the tail of an ox. Its horn was short and made of flesh.

Chin-Lin was a very gentle animal. It always walked carefully in order not to trample small animals on the ground.

CENTAURS

A centaur was half man and half horse. It had the head, arms, and chest of a man. The rest of its body was like the body of a horse.

Centaurs were said to have lived in ancient Greece. Most of them were nasty creatures who broke laws and fought with the Greeks. But one of them, Chiron, was famous for his goodness and intelligence. Chiron taught some of the most important heroes of ancient Greece, including Hercules and Achilles.

Unlike the other centaurs, Chiron was immortal—he could live forever. But in a battle between Hercules and the centaurs, Chiron was accidentally wounded. The wound didn't heal, and it caused Chiron great pain. The supreme god, Zeus, finally allowed Chiron to die. But Chiron is still with us. Zeus placed him among the stars as the constellation Sagittarius.

GUYASCUTUS

This critter was an American invention. It was first described in 1846 as "a monster of gigantic proportions." Specific details of the guyascutus varied greatly. Some people said it was the size of a deer, with rabbit ears and teeth like a mountain lion's. But everyone agreed on one thing: The legs of the animal were longer on one side than on the other. This made it easy for the animal to climb mountains and graze on steep hillsides.

A group of men said they had captured the guyascutus—or gyanousa, as it was sometimes called. The men traveled around the countryside to show it in a tent. At each place they stopped, a crowd of curious people would pay to see the animal. But as soon as the audience had gathered in the tent, the men would rush in and shout, "The gyanousa am loose!" The terrified customers would run for their lives—leaving behind all the money they had paid and, of course, never seeing the fabulous beast.

GRIFFINS

A griffin had a lion's body and the head and wings of an eagle. Most griffins had four lionlike legs. Others had front legs like an eagle's and hind legs like a lion's.

The griffins of the Middle Ages had an appetite for people. If a griffin caught someone, people thought, it could quickly tear the victim apart with its claws. A griffin's claws were so large and powerful that the creature could fly through the air carrying a horse or even an elephant.

The griffin was a popular symbol of strength. Many European noble families included griffins in their coats of arms.

If you've read Lewis Carroll's *Alice's Adventures in Wonderland,* you've met a griffin. This was the creature that took Alice to meet the Mock Turtle. Alice "did not quite like the look" of the griffin. But they got along well together—much better than did the people and griffins of the Middle Ages.

ANT-LIONS

Have you ever read something and misunderstood its meaning? This is how the ant-lion came to be. Some people misunderstood a Greek translation of the Hebrew Bible. They thought that a word that was used to mean "lion" actually meant "ant-lion." The people had never seen an ant-lion. But they were sure that God had a reason for creating such animals.

As you may have guessed, the front half of an ant-lion was like a lion. The back half was like an ant. These animals were destined to die soon after birth. The lion is a meat eater, and so was the ant-lion. But the ant-lion had the stomach of an ant. The stomach couldn't digest meat, and so the strange creature soon starved to death.

There were many other strange and fabulous creatures that once existed on earth—yet never really existed at all. Have you ever read about any? Have you ever imagined one of your own?

SCIENCE

On April 12, 1981, the U.S. space shuttle Columbia was launched for the first time. It returned to Earth two days later—the first space vehicle in the world that could be used again.

THE SPACE SHUTTLE COLUMBIA

FUEL TANK

BOOSTER ROCKETS

ORBITER

The space shuttle *Columbia* was launched for the first time on April 12, 1981.

On April 12, 1981, the United States launched the first space shuttle—a vehicle unlike any ever sent aloft. The shuttle *Columbia* did something no spacecraft had ever done. It returned safely to Earth, ready to be refitted and flown again.

Before *Columbia,* all spacecraft were boosted into orbit by powerful, expensive rocket assemblies. Each spacecraft and rocket assembly was used only once. Scientists at the National Aeronautics and Space Administration (NASA) reasoned that vehicles that could be used for more than one flight might save millions of dollars in future space ventures.

The result was the space shuttle, which is launched like a rocket, orbits like a spacecraft, and glides to a landing like an airplane.

THE FIRST LAUNCH

April 12 was a clear, sunny day in Cape Canaveral, Florida. At the Kennedy Space Center, the shuttle stood ready on its launching pad, its four parts visible to observers half a mile away. Looming tallest was the huge external fuel tank, filled with liquid hydrogen and liquid oxygen. It was flanked by two 15-story-high solid-fuel booster rockets. And astride the tank was the shuttle orbiter *Columbia,* a delta-winged craft about the size of a DC-9 jet.

The cabin at the front of the orbiter had been designed to hold up to seven people. But for the first flight, only two were aboard. In command of *Columbia* was John W. Young. He had made four previous space flights, including two trips to the moon. With him was Robert L. Crippen, who had been an astronaut for years but had never been in space.

At 7:00 A.M., right on schedule, *Columbia*'s three internal, liquid-fueled engines fired. They were followed two seconds later by the external booster rockets. The shuttle slowly lifted off the ground on a column of smoke and fire. The heat and blast from the engines were so great that parts of the launch pad were badly damaged.

The shuttle streaked skyward, gaining speed and rolling over so that the orbiter rode belly-up under the fuel tank. Two minutes after launch, *Columbia* reached an altitude of about 28 miles (45 kilometers), and both booster rockets were detached. Parachutes lowered them gently into the Atlantic Ocean, where recovery ships waited. The rockets were towed to shore to be used again.

Eight minutes after launch, *Columbia* had reached a speed of 16,800 miles (27,000 kilometers) an hour. It had drained the external fuel tank. The main engines were shut down, and the tank was released. (Most of the tank—the only part of the shuttle designed not to be used again—burned up in the atmosphere.) Then *Columbia*'s smaller maneuvering engines guided the craft into orbit—nearly 170 miles (275 kilometers) above Earth.

Astronauts John Young and Robert Crippen, shown during a preflight test, flew *Columbia* on its first mission.

ON BOARD COLUMBIA

Once in orbit, Young and Crippen could move weightlessly about the pressurized, air-filled front cabin. *Columbia* had been designed so that scientists and others could travel into space with a minimum of training. The facilities aboard were far more comfortable than those on the earlier Apollo and Gemini craft. *Columbia* was equipped with an oven, hot and cold water, a zero-gravity toilet, and special sleeping compartments. On this trip, however, bulky flight instruments were stored in the sleeping area. The two astronauts had to sleep in their seats.

The main purpose of *Columbia*'s first flight was to make sure the craft could go up and come back safely. One of the most important steps in the mission was to test the doors to the huge cargo bay. It was feared that heat from the sun or stress during lift-off might distort the doors, so that they would jam open or shut. Fortunately, the doors worked perfectly.

One problem involved the heat-resistant tiles that covered the orbiter. The tiles were intended to protect *Columbia* from the intense heat caused by friction with the atmosphere when the craft returned to Earth. Designing and attaching the tiles had proved quite a problem when *Columbia* was built. Now, with the craft safely in orbit, a television camera mounted in the tail showed that some tiles were missing. It was feared that if too many tiles had been loosened by launch vibrations, the orbiter could become dangerously hot on re-entry. But luckily, only a few tiles had been lost, and the heat-resistant pads beneath them were intact.

In all, *Columbia* circled the Earth 36 times, each orbit taking about 90 minutes. At about noon on April 14, Young and Crippen began the trip home.

With the craft traveling tail first over the Indian Ocean, the maneuvering engines fired again. This burst of power slowed the shuttle, and it began to descend. When *Columbia* re-entered the atmosphere, friction turned its skin a glowing red with heat.

As *Columbia* approached the coast of California, Young took over the controls from the computer that had been guiding the craft. This was a critical part of the flight. Unlike an airplane, the shuttle cannot circle the landing strip and try again if the pilot makes a bad approach. Young sent the craft into a series of curves that further slowed it. Then, at 1:21 P.M., he brought *Columbia* to a perfect landing on a dry lake bed at Edwards Air Force Base in California. The shuttle touched down at twice the speed of a landing jet airliner.

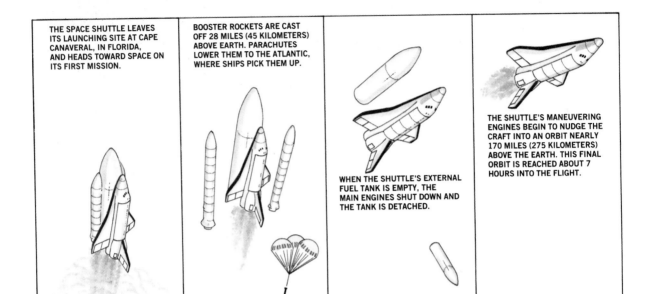

THE SPACE SHUTTLE LEAVES ITS LAUNCHING SITE AT CAPE CANAVERAL, IN FLORIDA, AND HEADS TOWARD SPACE ON ITS FIRST MISSION.

BOOSTER ROCKETS ARE CAST OFF 28 MILES (45 KILOMETERS) ABOVE EARTH. PARACHUTES LOWER THEM TO THE ATLANTIC, WHERE SHIPS PICK THEM UP.

WHEN THE SHUTTLE'S EXTERNAL FUEL TANK IS EMPTY, THE MAIN ENGINES SHUT DOWN AND THE TANK IS DETACHED.

THE SHUTTLE'S MANEUVERING ENGINES BEGIN TO NUDGE THE CRAFT INTO AN ORBIT NEARLY 170 MILES (275 KILOMETERS) ABOVE THE EARTH. THIS FINAL ORBIT IS REACHED ABOUT 7 HOURS INTO THE FLIGHT.

THE SECOND FLIGHT

After a thorough inspection, *Columbia* was carried piggy-back on a 747 aircraft to Cape Canaveral. There it was made ready for its second flight, on November 12, 1981. This mission was much like the first. But astronauts Joe H. Engle and Richard H. Truly were asked to perform more experiments.

Columbia's cargo bay carried equipment to map geological features with radar. The ship also scanned the Earth with an infrared device that can detect mineral deposits, and it observed the distribution of plant life in the oceans. Testing *Columbia*'s manipulator arm was another important part of the second flight. This remote-control mechanical arm can pluck items from the cargo bay and place satellites in orbit.

The second mission was supposed to last five days. But it was cut short when one of the craft's three fuel cells, which provide electrical power, failed. *Columbia* touched down at Edwards on November 14, after 54 hours and 36 revolutions of the Earth.

In the future, the shuttle might be used to construct a craft that would ferry people and materials to the moon.

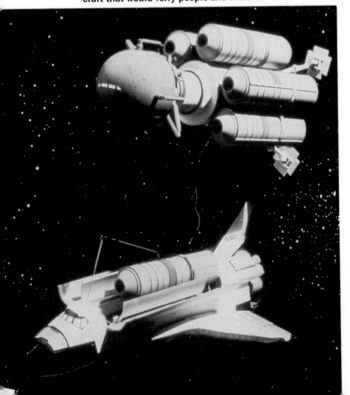

FUTURE USES OF THE SHUTTLE

With a cargo bay the size of a railroad box-car, the shuttle has been called a "space truck." Its main job will be to carry people and equipment into space and bring them safely back to Earth. Here are some of the uses scientists foresee for the shuttle:

• Communications and military satellites can be carried up in the cargo bay and placed in orbit by the manipulator arm. Technicians on the shuttle can service satellites in space, or the satellites can be brought back to Earth for repair. The shuttle could also carry up pieces of large satellites—huge antennas or solar power stations, perhaps—to be assembled in space.

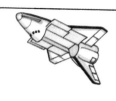

ABOUT HALF AN HOUR LATER, THE SHUTTLE RE-ENTERS THE EARTH'S ATMOSPHERE. ITS SKIN GLOWS RED-HOT FROM THE FRICTION OF RE-ENTRY.

THE SHUTTLE MAKES A PERFECT LANDING ON A DRY LAKE BED AT EDWARDS AIR FORCE BASE IN THE CALIFORNIA DESERT. GROUND CREWS CHECK THE CRAFT BEFORE THE ASTRONAUTS LEAVE IT.

IN ORBIT, THE ASTRONAUTS TEST THE CARGO BAY DOORS, FLIGHT CONTROL SYSTEMS, AND DATA PROCESSING SYSTEMS. THEY ALSO CONDUCT MANEUVERING TESTS. FLIGHT PROGRESS REPORTS ARE TELEVISED, AND THE ASTRONAUTS HAVE TWO SLEEP PERIODS.

THE CARGO BAY DOORS ARE CLOSED. WITH THE SHUTTLE TRAVELING TAIL FIRST, THE MANEUVERING ENGINES ARE FIRED TO SLOW THE CRAFT, AND IT BEGINS TO DESCEND.

• Deep-space probes can be carried into a low orbit by the shuttle. From there, the probes can fire their rockets to begin the trip to the edge of the solar system.

• Space is an ideal place to study many things—the sun, solar wind, comets, radiation, and the effects of weightlessness, to name just a few. So an orbiting laboratory, Spacelab, has been designed to fit neatly in the shuttle's cargo bay. The first Spacelab is being built by the European Space Agency. It will be made up of pressurized compartments (where scientists can work in their shirtsleeves) and instrument-carrying pallets that will be exposed to space. Spacelab will ride up and back with the shuttle, but future laboratories may be designed to stay in space.

• The shuttle is also scheduled to carry a 12-ton space telescope into orbit. Because it will be beyond the Earth's atmosphere, this telescope will be able to see much farther into space than telescopes on Earth. It will use solar energy to beam information back to Earth.

• Shuttle flights will test the possibility of manufacturing in space. The weightless and near-vacuum conditions of space seem to be ideal for making certain products. Among them are very pure silicon crystals, glass products for use in lasers and fiber optics, and certain biological materials.

Columbia is designed to fly about 100 missions, each a week to a month long. There is still uncertainty over how reliable, costly, and useful the shuttle will be. But by 1985, NASA hopes to have three more orbiters—*Challenger, Discovery,* and *Atlantis.*

BENEDICT A. LEERBURGER
Editor in Chief
Gateways to Science (3rd edition)

One day, the shuttle may even build space stations, putting the parts in place with its manipulator arm.

GET AWAY SPECIALS

Every time the space shuttle *Columbia* travels into space, it will carry experiments. These experiments will add to our understanding of space. They may also add to our understanding of life on Earth.

Imagine that you could send up your own experiment on *Columbia*. What would it be?

Hundreds of people who answered this question are getting the chance to do more than dream. They are preparing experiments that will actually travel into space aboard *Columbia*. Their experiments are called *Get Away Specials* (GAS).

ANYONE MAY APPLY

The National Aeronautics and Space Administration (NASA) has set up the GAS program for several reasons. It wants to stimulate interest in science and engineering. It wants to encourage everyone to use space. And it wants to increase people's knowledge of space.

Anyone—businesses, universities, and private individuals—with an idea for an experiment may apply to NASA. They must describe their project and show that they have the ability to carry it out and finance it.

A GAS project, or payload, may weigh up to 200 pounds (90 kilograms). It must fit into a standard container supplied by NASA. And the payload must be self-contained. That is, it must contain its own electrical power, heating, data-handling equipment, and so on.

GAS payloads will be booked on a space-available basis. Each flight of *Columbia* will carry its usual payloads. On some flights, these will not fill the total payload space available in the shuttle. The remaining space will be used for Get Away Specials.

ANTSTRONAUTS

Hundreds of Get Away Specials have already been accepted by NASA and are scheduled for future shuttle flights. One such project is being prepared by high school students in Camden, New Jersey. Their experiment will study the effects of weightlessness on a colony of ants. The colony will be the first community of animals to be sent into space.

The students found that more than just science skills are needed to carry out a space project. Students majoring in business control the finances. Art students have made posters to promote the project. Other students maintain a reference library.

Three teams of science students are working on the payload. One team is in charge of the ant colony to be sent into space.

A second team has developed and programmed a special computer. The computer will be part of the payload. It will control cameras and heating and lighting equipment.

The third team has developed the cannister that will hold the ants during their voyage into space. The cannister will provide the ants with a closed environment, containing food, water, air, and building materials. A window in the cannister will allow the ants to be observed by TV and movie cameras.

The ants will be sent into space for seven days. Following the shuttle's return to Earth, the entire payload will be returned to the students for study.

High School students have prepared a Get Away Special experiment that would study the effects of weightlessness on a colony of ants.

HEAVENLY THOUGHTS: A SPACE FANTASY

If a thing is physically possible, and it's cost-effective at some stage, then no matter how lunatic it seems, it often comes to pass.

Frank Drake, Director, Cornell University Research Institute, National Aeronautics and Ionosphere Center

The year is 2031. At Cape Canaveral, the Watson family climbs aboard the space shuttle Futura. They are starting out on an eight-hour flight to Spira I, Earth's permanently orbiting space colony. Only a decade old, Spira I is already home to some 50,000 earthlings—Americans and Soviets among them—and growing faster than the U.S. Sun Belt did in the last quarter of the 20th century.

The Watsons are a family well suited to life in space. Elliot is a solar engineer. He is employed by an interplanetary energy company that distributes solar fuel. Lauren, his wife, is an agricultural researcher. Her job will be to develop new food crops for the self-sufficient cities of Spira I.

The trip is largely uneventful. Of course, the once-empty expanse of space is now dotted with vast solar mirrors. They were erected during the early decades of the shuttle's history and are controlled by orbiting satellites. The solar mirrors beam sunlight to various regions of Earth, lengthening the growing season in the Northern Hemisphere.

At their consoles, the Watsons flip the channels on their television monitors. A wide range of programming is available, including live performances from Lincoln Center; space documentaries by Jean Cousteau (great-grandson of the 20th-century ocean explorer Jacques-Yves); up-to-the-second quotations from the world's financial capitals, Hong Kong and Calgary; and the first simulcast of the space musical *Cosmos,* featuring the Vienna Boys Choir and the Spira Symphony Orchestra. One critic called *Cosmos* "literally, the music of the heavens."

The flight plan of Futura has been designed to avoid various areas of space where satellite wars are in progress. In what most observers regard as the worst of these, laser-beam satellites belonging to Iran and Iraq are continuing the 51-year-old war between those two nations for control of islands in the Persian Gulf. The gulf region has long been depleted of oil. But the war goes on, closely watched by the Planetary Alliance—successor to the United Nations—and by the world's two superpowers, China and Brazil.

Wanting to assure the folks back home that all is well, Elliot Watson punches a set of figures on his video wristwatch, instantly reaching his parents in a suburb of Omaha, Nebraska. The tiny device allows two-way video communication with anyone on Earth who carries the portable solar antenna, which clips onto a shirt pocket like a fountain pen.

On Spira I, the Watsons will live in a two-bedroom space condominium overlooking a year-round summer of simulated parkland. Engineers have been able to devise an Earth-like gravitational pull for Spira I by having its cities gently revolve around its spaceship nucleus. But they have not so far been able to re-create Earth's change of seasons.

Still, Spira I offers some distinct advantages over its mother planet. It is a pollution-free, self-contained community, with a morale-boosting pioneer spirit. The Watsons' assignments are temporary. But if everything goes well, they plan to live out their lives in space—except for their annual two-week holiday in Florida.

VISUAL POLLUTION

- Garbage piled high on city sidewalks.
- Huge billboards lining country roads.
- Abandoned buildings, their windows gone, their doorways filled with broken furniture.
- Scattered bottles and other litter beside a quiet lake.
- "Michelle loves Tom" and other scribblings on a famous statue.

All of these are ugly. They are forms of visual pollution. Pollution is the presence of something that damages the environment. Visual pollution can be defined as something that damages the environment because it is ugly. It isn't nice to look at.

Visual pollution can be found almost everywhere—in cities and farmlands, along beaches and roads, in national parks and forests. How long has it been since you were in a place that had no visual pollution?

KINDS OF VISUAL POLLUTION

There are many kinds of visual pollution. These are some of the most common kinds.

Litter. Bits of paper, aluminum cans, bottles, and cigarette butts can be found from coast to coast, from the highest mountain to the most deserted lake, from the slums to the wealthiest communities. The total amount of litter is staggering. In Louisiana, a group of students picked up litter along a 16-mile (26-kilometer) stretch of road. They collected 11,711 pieces of paper, 9,978 bottles and cans, 3,043 cigarette butts, and assorted other trash. Why did they find so much litter? Because people were too lazy to use a trash can.

Some people even litter roadsides with their old cars. When the car has a final breakdown, it may be cheaper to abandon it than to have it towed to a junkyard. The driver removes the license plates and any other identification. The car sits on the road until the community has it towed away.

Dumps. Every day, we produce thousands of tons of garbage and rubbish. This has to be put somewhere. Some becomes litter. Some is burned or recycled or used to make landfill. But much of it ends up in open dumps. These dumps may be along roads, at the edges of rivers and lakes, even in the backyards of buildings.

Auto graveyards are another kind of dump. They are places where cars are taken when they no longer work. The cars sit in the dump, slowly rusting, waiting for people to come and strip them of usable parts. Eventually, to make room for more cars, the worst wrecks are crushed. The crushed cars are shipped off, so that the metal in them can be melted down and re-used.

Open dumps could be moved to sites that are not seen from the road. They could be screened, so they are less visible. But efforts to end this form of visual pollution have been largely unsuccessful.

Graffiti. Scribbles such as ''Michelle loves Tom'' are called graffiti. Most people would be angry if someone put graffiti on their homes or furniture or books. But many of these same people think nothing of marking up other people's property. They carve their initials into trees and restaurant tables. They write their names on public buildings and statues. Graffiti can even be found in deserts —painted on rocks or carved into cactus plants.

In New York City, it's rare to find a subway car that isn't covered with graffiti. Often, teenagers and young children ride in empty cars, scribbling when no one is watching. The more daring work at night, while the trains are sitting in underground yards. Using spray paint, they cover the entire outside of a car with huge designs. The designs often incorporate the names or initials of the designers.

Litter, one kind of visual pollution, can be found even along a lovely lake area, such as this one in Quebec, Canada.

101

Billboards. Billboards are a form of advertising—they sell things. They tell people about foods, motels, gas stations, politicians, and other things.

It's not uncommon for a billboard to be bigger than a house. At night, many are lit up brighter than Christmas trees. They tell us which motels have color TV. They tell us how many hamburgers have been sold by a fast-food chain. They tell us to smoke certain cigarettes or to buy a certain car. And while they do this, they often hide beautiful scenery. Is it true that we would rather look at billboards than scenery?

Haphazard Building. Too often, people build houses and other structures without proper planning and without thought to the damage to nature they may cause. A beautiful lake loses much of its beauty when the trees around it are cut down to make room for housing developments and motels. A majestic mountain becomes less attractive when its sides are gouged out to make room for ski lodges.

Poorly planned building can be found almost everywhere. Many parts of cities and suburbs that once were quiet, attractive places have turned into commercial jungles. Some of the ugliest building is found along highways at the edges of towns and cities. A mixture of roadsigns, billboards, run-down diners, brightly lit gas stations, fast-food restaurants, junkyards, and used-car lots lines the roads.

Most communities don't have long-range development plans. They have no guidelines that say, "This is how we want our community to grow; this is how we want it to look in the future."

THE EFFECTS OF VISUAL POLLUTION

Visual pollution affects the quality of life. It makes life unpleasant, even difficult. For example, New York City's subway trains are filthy. The floors are covered with newspaper and other litter. The subway maps that are posted on the walls of the trains are covered with graffiti. So are the windows and seats. Thus people can't read the maps to find out directions, and they can't see out of the windows to locate their subway stations.

People become angry when they see an attractive building covered with graffiti or when they have to walk through litter. But some forms of visual pollution are not only ugly, they harm the environment in other ways. This is true of strip mining, the method used to remove coal deposits that lie close to the earth's surface. Before the coal is removed, the overlying rock and soil are stripped off and piled in huge hills. This debris contains acids that are carried off in rainwater. When the water reaches lakes and rivers, plants and animals are killed by the acids.

Open dumps and piles of garbage are also more than ugly. They are health hazards. They are breeding places for germs, and they attract rats, flies, and other disease-bearing

Graffiti and auto graveyards are also visual pollution.

animals. Sometimes the dumps catch fire. The fires may burn for days, polluting the air with smoke and nasty smells.

WHAT CAN BE DONE?

Visual pollution is caused by people—all kinds of people. People who drop soda cans and candy wrappers on the street are polluters. People who put up billboards and ugly buildings are polluters. People who write on statues and subway cars are polluters. Strip miners who leave ugly scars on the land are polluters.

Here are some ways to stop the ugliness:

Stop Littering. Visual pollution would decrease greatly if people cleaned up after themselves. Litter and garbage should be put in trash cans. Many kinds of litter can be recycled. Newspapers, glass bottles, tin and aluminum cans, and tires can be recycled. Recycling cuts down on litter. It saves landfill space. It saves energy.

Anti-litter drives are a good way to clean up litter. Scouts and other student groups often have clean-up projects. These people aren't just *talking* about the problem of visual pollution. They are out there working to solve it.

Make and Use Laws. There are laws against some kinds of visual pollution. For example, there are littering laws. People who litter can be fined or even sent to jail. The same is true for people who put graffiti on public property. In 1980, New York City police arrested more than 400 young people for putting graffiti on subway cars. In many of these cases, the youngsters or their parents had to pay part of the cost of repainting the subway cars.

Sometimes there are no laws against visual pollution. But people can help pass such laws. Students at a school in Connecticut did that. They had been using a marsh near their school as a place to study wildlife. One spring, they discovered that builders had started to use the marsh as a dumping ground. Areas where fish laid their eggs were being destroyed. Mussels, clams, and oysters were being killed. The students organized. They bombarded the state legislators with letters, and they talked to people in the community. They sold buttons and bumper stickers. Their efforts helped to pass a bill

Many kinds of litter can be recycled. In Zurich, Switzerland, glass bottles are deposited according to color in these bins. This makes recycling easier.

that prohibits dumping wastes in Connecticut marshlands.

Make Your Opinions Known. People who want to change things can learn an important lesson from the Connecticut students. To change things you must discuss your goals with others. You must tell your friends and neighbors. You must tell elected officials, such as mayors, governors, senators, and representatives. You must tell polluters.

Sharing opinions can be done in person or by writing letters. Libraries have books on how to write effective letters. They can also provide the addresses of elected officials and other people to whom you should write.

Visual pollution can be stopped. It can be removed. But we must make the effort to fight it.

JENNY TESAR
Series Consultant
Wonders of Wildlife

DON'T THROW IT AWAY!

Every year, Americans buy more than 75,000,000,000 (billion) cans and bottles filled with soft drinks and beer. They drink the contents, then throw away the containers. Most containers are thrown into garbage cans. Many are thrown onto streets, beaches, parklands, and other places where they don't belong.

Metal and glass beverage containers make up about 18 percent of people's garbage, and about 20 percent of the litter found on streets and along roads. Garbage must be disposed of, usually in landfill space, which is becoming scarce. And litter is ugly.

To reduce garbage and litter, some states have passed bottle bills. These are laws that require a deposit on soft-drink and beer containers. When customers take the empty bottles and cans back to the store, their deposit is returned. And the empty containers will be re-used; they will be either refilled or recycled to make new containers.

By 1981, six states had bottle laws in effect: Connecticut, Iowa, Maine, Michigan, Oregon, and Vermont. Delaware had passed a bottle bill that would take effect in 1982. Almost every other state had considered or was considering such legislation. And a na-

tional deposit law was introduced in Congress. Many people feel that if more states pass bottle bills, action on a national law is likely. This is because each state law is slightly different, creating problems for the companies that make containers.

But passage of state bottle bills is not a simple matter. Although there is strong pressure to pass such legislation, there is equally strong pressure to prevent passage. Supporting the bills are energy-conservation and environmental groups. Opposing the bills are bottle and can manufacturers, soft-drink and beer makers, food stores, and some unions.

Here are some of the arguments:

Litter. Supporters of bottle bills say that the bills will significantly reduce street and roadside litter.

Opponents say that bottle bills will do little to clean up the environment because containers make up only a small percentage of all the litter.

Jobs. Opponents say that many people have lost their jobs in states with bottle laws. The industries that have been most affected are those that make bottles and cans.

Supporters say that the number of jobs lost is smaller than the total number of new jobs created by the bottle laws. More workers are needed to handle, transport, and recycle the returnable containers.

Water Resources. Refillable bottles must be washed before they can be used again. Bill opponents claim that this wastes water.

Supporters say that it takes less water to wash refillable bottles than to make new throwaway bottles.

Energy Resources. Opponents say that because drivers must make room on their trucks for empty containers, they must make more trips. This uses more fuel.

Supporters say that the energy savings in recycling glass and metal are very large. It takes 25 times more energy to make a ton of aluminum from raw materials than it does to make it from recycled material.

Prices. Opponents say that bottle laws cause soft-drink and beer prices to rise. Many beer and soda makers would have to convert to refillable bottling systems. And extra labor is involved in sorting, storing, and trucking the empty containers. These costs are passed on to the consumer.

Supporters say that any increase should only be a few cents per container, and that in the long run, prices may even decrease. Beverage makers would not have to buy as many new bottles as more and more refillable bottles are returned.

How do most people in states with bottle laws feel about the laws? In Michigan, 60 percent of the voters supported the bottle bill when it was voted on. A later survey indicated that 78 percent of the people were in favor of the law. In Maine, there was an attempt to repeal the bottle law, but voters overwhelmingly voted to keep it. Six years after a bottle bill was passed in Oregon, a poll showed that 90 percent of the people were in favor of it.

Under bottle-return laws, empty beverage containers will be recycled—not just thrown away.

FACE ᴛᴏ FACE

How would you feel if you were told that somewhere in the world there is a person exactly like you? This person not only looks like you but also likes the same clothes, food, and music that you do. Your look-alike even has the same allergies and may suffer from the same illnesses.

Strange as it may seem, such a person may exist—if you have an identical twin. Recently, researchers found several pairs of twins who had been raised apart from each other. The researchers reunited the twins, with very interesting results.

NATURE OR NURTURE?

The twins who took part in the study were special—they were identical twins. There are two types of twins, fraternal and identical. Fraternal twins develop when two eggs are fertilized by two sperm cells at about the same time. They account for about two thirds of all twin births. Fraternal twins resemble each other as much as (and no more than) any two children who are born to the same parents.

Identical twins develop from a single fertilized egg. They share the same genes—the chemical molecules that determine how they will develop. So at birth they are more or less exactly the same. Identical twins are always the same sex and have the same color eyes and hair. Looking at your identical twin would be like looking into a mirror—the features are the same but reversed. In fact, identical twins are sometimes called mirror twins.

It is this close similarity that makes identical twins so interesting to researchers. For years, scientists have been interested in the influences of heredity and environment—nature and nurture—on human behavior. Do people think and act in certain ways because they were born with set personality traits, inherited from their parents? Or are their personalities shaped by their surroundings and their way of life—their families, friends, schools, levels of income, and so on?

Thomas Bouchard, a psychologist at the University of Minnesota, decided to search for an answer. His method was to bring together identical twins who had been raised apart and study the similarities and differences between them. Because the twins had been identical at birth, any differences would have to be due to the different environments in which they were raised.

The study compared the twins' behavior, intelligence, personalities, interests, values, and even their physical characteristics. Some surprising similarities were revealed.

THE JIM TWINS

One of the first pairs of identical twins to be investigated were so strikingly alike that they amazed the scientists. Jim Springer and Jim Lewis have come to be known as the Jim twins. When they were 4-week-old infants, each was adopted by a different working-class family in Ohio. They didn't see or communicate with each other until they were 39 years old.

As the Jims got to know each other, they discovered eerie similarities. Not only had they been given the same first name by their adoptive parents, but they had each been married twice. Both their first wives were named Linda, and both their second wives, Betty. Lewis had three sons, one of whom was named James Alan. Springer had a son and three daughters. His son's name? James Allan. Each twin once had a dog with the unusual name of Toy.

When the Jim twins were reunited, they discovered that they both had similar workshops in their basements, made similar things, and chain-smoked the same brand of cigarette.

Both Jims enjoyed mechanical drawing and woodworking. Both had been average students, liking math and disliking spelling. They both had been deputy sheriffs and had even taken vacations at the same three-block-long beach on Florida's Gulf coast. Both chewed their fingernails, liked stock-car racing, disliked baseball, drove the same make of car, and chain-smoked the same brand of cigarette. Their scores on tests to measure personality traits were so close that researchers wondered if one person had taken the tests twice. Not only had both twins suffered severe headaches, but each used almost exactly the identical words in describing their symptoms to the researchers. They had identical pulse rates, blood pressure, and sleep patterns. And at about the same time in their lives, each had gained about ten pounds (4.5 kilograms).

What is it like meeting your twin image? Said Jim Lewis, "Right off the bat I felt close. It wasn't like meeting a stranger." His twin brother said, "It was like we'd known each other all our lives and we'd just been gone a long time."

DIFFERENT BACKGROUNDS

Another pair of twins had backgrounds that were dramatically different. Oskar Stöhr and Jack Yufe, 47 when they were reunited, were born in Trinidad. Their father was Jewish; their mother, German. Shortly after their birth, their mother took Oskar back to Germany. There he was raised by his mother and grandmother as a Catholic and a Nazi. Their father raised Jack in the Caribbean as a Jew.

At the time of their reunion, the twins were leading totally different lives. Oskar was married and worked as an industrial supervisor in Germany. His brother was separated from his wife and ran a clothing store in California.

But, although the twins had never corresponded, there were remarkable similarities. When they met, both were wearing wire-rimmed glasses and two-pocket shirts with epaulets. And each was sporting a mustache. The twins found they both enjoyed spicy foods and sweet liqueurs. They were both absentminded and were likely to fall asleep in front of the television. They both thought it was funny to sneeze in a crowd of strangers. They read magazines from back to front, dipped buttered toast in their coffee, flushed the toilet before using it, and stored rubber bands on their wrists.

Although the two were raised in different cultures, the researchers were impressed by the similarities in their personalities and mannerisms. The twins also seemed to supply evidence against the theory that children's personalities are shaped by the sex of those who rear them. Oskar was raised by women, and Jack, by men.

THE GIGGLE TWINS

Another pair of twins were nicknamed the giggle twins. One twin was always saying things that made the other twin giggle. But the twins said they didn't giggle with their adoptive families. The twins, Daphne and Barbara, were in their 30's. They had been separated during World War II and brought up in Britain.

What interested the researchers about the giggle twins was the fact that they both handled stress in the same way—by ignoring it. And when faced with a conflict or controversy, the twins did their best to avoid it. The scientists were particularly interested in this shared aspect of behavior because avoiding conflict is usually thought of as something people *learn* to do. The giggle twins' common response to conflict suggested that some aspects of behavior are influenced more by genetic factors than environment.

Another curious similarity that surprised the researchers was the twins' handwriting. The twins had learned to write in different schools, miles apart. But their handwriting appeared almost the same.

THE RING TWINS AND OTHERS

Bridget and Dorothy, also in their 30's, were another pair of British twins reunited after being separated as babies. When they met, each was wearing seven rings. The researchers were interested in the "ring twins" because they were raised in very different social and economic situations. The differences in upbringing, however, turned out to be practically meaningless. The class difference was evident only in the fact that the twin raised in modest circumstances had bad teeth. Their ability and intelligence test scores were about the same. The twin raised in the lower-class neighborhood had a slightly higher score.

The curious circumstance of twins giving their children the same names also occurred with Bridget and Dorothy. One twin had a son named Richard Andrew. The other twin named her son Andrew Richard. Each twin also had a daughter. Their names? Catherine Louise and Karen Louise!

Jeanette and Irene were identical twins in their mid-30's. One was raised in England; the other, in Scotland. Both were afraid of being in closed rooms. During the research project, they didn't want to enter a closed booth to take some scientific tests. But each sister agreed to enter the booth if the door was left open. Both were also leery of swimming in the ocean, and both resolved this fear by backing into the surf slowly. Neither liked escalators. And both had a habit of

Although raised apart, Daphne and Barbara (the giggle twins) had handwriting that was astonishingly similar.

counting such things as the number of wheels on a truck, people in a line, and houses on a block. They even counted to get to sleep.

Other twins reared apart had other unusual similarities. Two 57-year-old women, for example, had developed diabetes at the same time in their lives. In several cases, one twin wore eyeglasses while the other didn't. But when the eyes of each twin were examined, it was found that both needed glasses.

There have been other studies of identical twins, in the United States, Britain, and Denmark. The Minnesota study was one of the most thorough ever done. What have scientists learned? Most researchers are not ready to say that nature plays a greater role than nurture in shaping behavior. But many scientists think the study of twins reared apart shows that far more behavior is determined or influenced by heredity than has ever been supposed.

BENEDICT A. LEERBURGER
Editor in Chief, *Gateways to Science* (3rd edition)

THE HEART OF THE MATTER

The most popular exhibit at the Franklin Institute in Philadelphia, Pennsylvania, is a human heart. But it's no ordinary heart. It's 125,000 times the size of a real heart. It's so big that you can walk through it, pretending that you are a blood cell that passes through and out of the heart.

The giant pinkish-red heart is 18 feet (5.5 meters) tall and 28 feet (8.5 meters) wide. You enter through the right atrium. This is the chamber that blood enters as it returns to the heart from the arms, legs, head, and most other parts of the body.

From the right atrium, you pass through a narrow opening into the right ventricle. This is the chamber that pumps blood to the lungs. From there, you walk up into a hallway to see what happens in the lungs. You will learn how blood releases carbon dioxide and picks up oxygen in the lungs. Then, just like a blood cell, you return to the heart.

Now you move on to the left side of the heart. You enter the left atrium and then go into the left ventricle. The left ventricle is the most muscular part of the heart. It pumps blood to every part of the body except the lungs. Blood leaves the left ventricle through a very large blood vessel called the aorta. This is the same way that visitors leave the Franklin Institute heart—through a giant aorta.

As you look back, you can see the openings to the coronary arteries. These first branches of the aorta go to the walls of the heart itself. The muscles that make up the walls of the heart need a constant supply of food and oxygen.

Near the giant heart is an exhibit that shows how hard the heart works as it continuously supplies blood to all parts of the body. The exhibit has a hand pump that allows you to compare your hand muscles to the heart muscles. Attached to the hand pump is a scale that shows how much body weight your hand muscles could support if they were pumping blood. Some people's hand muscles can keep up with the heart—for a short time. But the hand muscles soon tire, while the heart muscles keep pumping. They pump every second of your life.

As you walk through this popular exhibit at the Franklin Institute, you can pretend that you are a blood cell passing through a human heart.

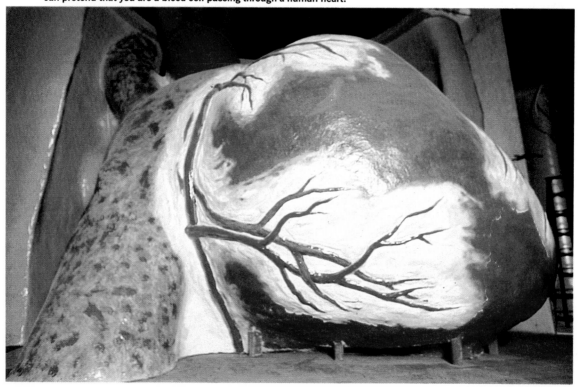

DID YOU KNOW...

The symbol of Valentine's Day is a human heart. But the heart used on Valentine's Day doesn't look like a healthy heart. It looks like a very sick heart. If it were a healthy heart, the left side would be bigger than the right side.

Big people have bigger hearts than small people. The normal weight of a human heart is about 0.5 percent of the total body weight. For example, if you weigh 100 pounds (45 kilograms), your heart weighs about a half pound (0.2 kilograms).

Athletes have heavier hearts and stronger heart muscles than people who do not exercise a lot. This is true for animals, too. A very active dog has a larger, stronger heart than a lazy dog.

Different people have different heart rates. Athletes usually have lower heart rates than nonathletes. Their hearts use fewer beats to pump the same amount of blood.

The heart rate of the average person is about 72 beats per minute. Many athletes, especially those who are long-distance runners or swimmers, have heart rates of about 45 beats per minute.

The heart rate slows down when you sleep. It speeds up when you get excited or angry. It also speeds up when you exercise.

At an average rate of 72 beats per minute, the heart contracts (beats) about 4,320 times in one hour, about 103,680 times in one day, and about 37,843,200 times in one year.

Small hearts beat faster than big hearts. A baby's heart beats faster than an adult's heart.

The shrew is the smallest mammal on earth. It has a heart rate of 1,000 beats per minute. The blue whale, the largest animal on earth, has a rate of only 5 or 6 beats per minute.

Each time the heart beats, blood is pumped out of the heart. In one minute, at least 4 quarts (3.8 liters) of blood leave the heart. The blood travels through 60,000 miles (96,500 kilometers) of blood vessels. If all your blood vessels were placed end to end, they would form a tube more than long enough to circle the world twice.

Many chemicals affect the heart rate. Nicotine, a chemical in cigarettes, increases the heart rate. So does caffeine, which is found in coffee, tea, and many soft drinks.

Temperature affects the heart rate. The heart beats faster on warm days than on cold days.

Noise increases the heart rate. The greater the noise, the greater the increase. This is true even if you are sleeping.

New electronic equipment, like this videodisc machine, is giving the TV set uses once only dreamed of.

THOSE FABULOUS VIDEO MACHINES

Until recently, the family TV served only to pick up programs that were broadcast from television stations. But now people are finding new uses for their TV sets. More and more people are attaching special electronic equipment—video-cassette and videodisc machines—to them. These machines use cassettes or discs to play movies and other programs. Cassette machines can even record programs. And these machines are giving the TV set uses only dreamed of not long ago. For example:

• Joanne is going on a trip and will miss her favorite TV show. She sets up the video-cassette machine to record the program. When she returns home, she'll be able to watch it.

• Tony buys a videodisc of his favorite movie. He puts the disc in the videodisc machine and watches the movie on his TV.

• Sandra is having trouble with her tennis serve. A friend records her serve on a video cassette. Then Sandra watches the playback on her TV to see what she's doing wrong.

• Frank borrows a videodisc on bicycle repair from the public library. Soon after he gets home, he learns enough to fix his bike.

• Maria uses a video camera to record her brother's birthday party. That evening, her uncle and aunt view the party on the TV set.

• Tom wants to watch two TV programs, but both are being broadcast at the same time. He watches one program while his video-cassette machine records the other program—using one TV.

Video cassettes and videodiscs are much like standard tape cassettes and phonograph records. You can play them whenever and as often as you like. There are several different systems, and each has advantages and disadvantages. And because the video systems are so new, the machines that will be sold even a few years from now may be quite different from those being sold today.

VIDEO-CASSETTE MACHINES

These machines are called video-cassette recorders, or VCR's. They are similar to

112

tape-cassette recorders in that they play programs that have been recorded on magnetic tape. But the tape used in a tape cassette carries only sound. The video-cassette tape carries both sound and pictures.

A VCR can play prerecorded programs that are sold in stores—such as movies, sports events, and do-it-yourself instructions. A VCR can also *make* recordings. It can record TV shows as the shows are being broadcast. (In 1981, a federal court ruled that recording TV programs may violate copyright laws. VCR manufacturers said they would appeal the decision.)

A VCR is attached to the television set, and it is easy to operate. Drop a cassette into the VCR. Turn on the TV. Then push a button to record a TV show or to play a prerecorded program. The program appears on the TV screen. A cassette about the size of an average paperback book can play for three to six hours.

If you are going away, you can set the machine to record your favorite program—a VCR can be set to turn on and off automatically. And if you want to record programs from more than one channel, your VCR can be set to do that too.

A VCR can also be hooked up to a video camera to create instant home movies. Both black-and-white and color video cameras are available. Unlike the film used in regular movie cameras, the magnetic tape in the VCR doesn't need to be processed. The tape is also less expensive than film. And if you don't like what you shoot, you can rewind the tape and use it again to record something else.

If you have a video camera, it's possible to transfer home movies and color slides onto a video cassette. Then you can watch the movies or slides on your TV, instead of having to set up a projector and screen. With some VCR's you can even record a sound track to go with the pictures.

There are two VCR systems—Beta and VHS (Video Home System). The two systems use different recording methods, so cassettes made for one machine cannot be played on the other machine.

VIDEODISC MACHINES

Like VCR's, these machines play movies and other sight-and-sound programs. But videodisc machines cannot record. This is their main disadvantage.

A video-cassette machine is easy to operate. One cassette can play for three to six hours.

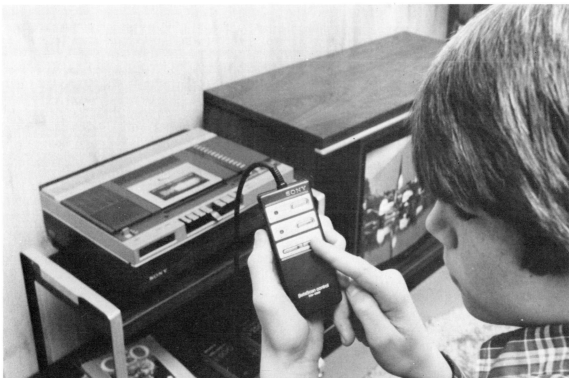

A video-cassette machine can be hooked up to a video camera to create an instant home movie.

Videodisc machines are similar to phonographs. They play discs that are about the same size and shape as records. And like records, the discs are spun on a turntable.

Operating the videodisc machine is as easy as operating a VCR. The machine is connected to the TV. A disc is placed into the machine, and the program on the disc appears on the TV screen. Each side of the disc can play for up to an hour.

Videodisc machines cost less than VCR's because they are simpler machines. And the discs cost less than video cassettes. The plastic used to make discs is less expensive than magnetic tape.

A videodisc machine has another advantage. You can move to any part of the disc in a short time, just as you can with a phonograph record. The machine can go directly to a certain part of the program, and in seconds, it will appear. (This is called random access.) In contrast, the program on a video cassette may be spread through hundreds of feet of tape. To reach any part of it, you must play through all the tape prior to the desired part. Even if the VCR is operating at high speed, this takes a fair amount of time.

By the end of 1981, three videodisc systems were available. Different methods were used to record and play the discs, so a disc from one system would not play on a different system.

One system—which was being sold under the names Magnavision and Laser Disc—uses a beam of light from a laser to put the program on the disc. The program is embedded in the disc in billions of tiny pits. If you look at one of these discs, its surface appears to be smooth. There are no grooves.

A laser beam—not a needle—is used to play the disc. The pits reflect the laser light back into the machine. The returning flashes are changed into electrical impulses, which are sent to the TV set. The TV converts the electrical impulses into pictures and sound.

The laser can focus on one picture, or it can speed forward or backward to locate a specific scene. It can repeat any section of a program. Discs read by a laser should last indefinitely because the light beam doesn't damage the surface. And even if the disc is dusty, the laser can still read it clearly.

Another system, the VHD (Very High Density) system, also uses a laser beam to put the program on the disc. But a needle, or stylus, is used to play back the programs. The discs don't have grooves. Instead, electronic sensing circuits guide the needle

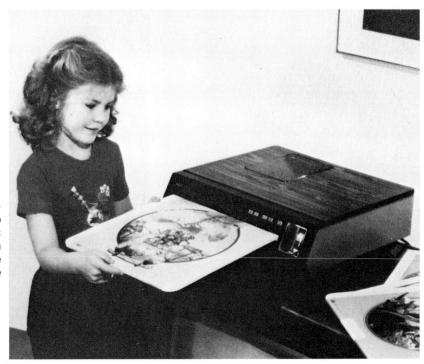

A videodisc looks like a phonograph record. It is inserted into the machine inside its plastic sleeve. When the disc has been deposited on the turntable, the sleeve is removed from the machine.

across the disc. The system can find parts of the program at random.

A third system—being sold under the name SelectaVision—uses an electron beam to record a program on a disc. The program appears on the disc in microscopic grooves. A diamond needle is used to play the disc. The needle moves over the surface of the disc much in the same way that the needle of a phonograph moves over the surface of a phonograph record.

A needle has one disadvantage—it can wear out much-played discs. Another disadvantage of SelectaVision is that a part of the program cannot be selected at random.

HOW POPULAR WILL THEY BE?

In 1981, relatively few families had these video systems. The least expensive system cost about $500. But some experts believe that prices will drop and that many families will one day own the systems.

Schools and businesses are also finding uses for video machines. Programs can be made anywhere in the world, thus bringing distant places and events into a classroom. A program can be put together from a variety of materials—film, slides, drawings, and graphs. Or the equipment can record a talk

by an expert. A video program can be viewed by hundreds of people at a time—or by just one person. It can be stopped at a particular place, for a discussion or question, and then continued.

Businesses, too, use video programs to educate people. Automobile and aircraft companies use videodiscs to teach mechanics how to repair equipment. Hospitals show nurses video programs on how to care for patients. Companies that sell office equipment use video programs to show customers how to use the equipment.

Video programs can also be used to help sell products. One car manufacturer has more than 10,000 videodisc players in its showrooms. Insurance salespeople show possible customers video programs that explain the benefits of insurance. Builders show programs that describe new resorts and housing projects.

In fact, just about anything that can be seen and heard can be put on a video cassette or a videodisc. The new technology is making TV more useful and more exciting than ever.

JENNY TESAR
Series Consultant
Wonders of Wildlife

Foxglove

Seedpod of a cat's-ear

WILD FLOWERS OF THE SAN JUANS

Nothing so clearly signals the end of winter than the appearance of the first wild flowers. They are the very essence of springtime. But what are wild flowers, and how are they different from the flowers that grow in our gardens?

To define a wild flower is not as easy as it seems. A wild flower to one person may be just a weed to another. However, we may say that a wild flower is any flowering plant that grows without the help of people. And from wild flowers have come all our cultivated flowers—those that we grow in gardens and greenhouses.

Camas lily

Indian paintbrush

Shooting star

Wild flowers are found nearly everywhere —from cracks in city sidewalks to parched desert expanses, from flat plains to rocky coasts, from mountain meadows to dark forests. They come singly, like rare treasures. Or they come in great masses, like wild splashes of paint.

On these pages are some of the wild flowers that grow in the San Juans, a group of small islands nestled in the sea north of Seattle, Washington. The islands contain many different natural habitats—bogs, marshes, lakes, creeks, open meadows, dense forests, and the seashore. And in these habitats bloom an extraordinary variety of beautiful wild flowers.

PETER D. CAPEN
Terra Mar Productions

Fawn lily

117

This color-enhanced photo of Saturn's rings was taken by Voyager 2.

SPACE BRIEFS

A hamburger-shaped moon . . . clouds of hot gases . . . huge storms . . . ammonia rain. These were some of the things that Voyager 2 found when it kept its date with Saturn on August 25, 1981. The U.S. space probe had taken four years to travel the long distance from Earth. It was the last of three U.S. spacecraft to fly past Saturn since 1979, and it sent back to Earth a wealth of new information about the large ringed planet.

Voyager 2 flew much closer to Saturn than had the earlier space probes. It also got much closer to some of the planet's 17 known moons. One unusual moon it photographed was Hyperion. Most orbiting bodies are spherical in shape. But Hyperion looks like a squat cylinder. Its shape is so strange that scientists have likened it to a hamburger patty, an Idaho potato, and a hockey puck.

Another moon, Tethys, was found to have an extraordinarily large, deep crater. Tethys is only 650 miles (1,050 kilometers) wide. The crater is 250 miles (400 kilometers) wide and 10 miles (16 kilometers) deep.

Saturn's weather is not pleasant. Instruments aboard Voyager 2 detected electrical discharges at least 10,000 times stronger than Earth's lightning. Some photographs suggested that ammonia rain was falling over much of the planet. Other photographs showed a huge storm in the northern hemisphere. The storm was 6,000 miles (9,650 kilometers) long and 4,000 miles (6,440 kilometers) wide. Smaller storms and many clouds were also seen. One curious feature was a white cloud in the shape of the numeral 6.

Scientists also detected a doughnut-shaped cloud consisting of electrified gases. The cloud, which orbits Saturn, is the hottest spot ever found in the solar system. It is 300 times hotter than the outer regions of the sun.

Much interest was focused on Saturn's rings. It appears that the rings are much thinner than previously believed. Saturn's A-ring, one of the largest of the planet's rings, appears to be only 500 feet (152 meters) thick. It also seems that the rings are very different from one another. They differ in size and density. They may also have different compositions. The B-ring, for example, is the only ring with dark spoke-like features. Photographs taken by Voyager 2 suggest that the spokes may be made up of snowflake-sized particles.

As Voyager 2 began moving away from Saturn, the platform that held three scientific instruments and the two television cameras became stuck. For three days, until the problem was solved, the spacecraft didn't take pictures and was unable to make certain scientific measurements. Nonetheless, project scientists said that they had an "overwhelming amount of new data." It will take years to study and understand all the data and pictures.

Voyager 2 is now following a path that will take it past Uranus in 1986 and Neptune in 1989. Neither of these planets has yet been visited by any spacecraft.

DIAMONDS IN THE SKY

Uranus and Neptune have been seen only through telescopes, and we don't know a great deal about them. Most scientists believe that the planets have a rocky core surrounded by a layer of ice, ammonia, and methane (natural gas). Outside this layer is a layer of hydrogen and helium.

Temperatures and pressures on Uranus and Neptune are very high. The temperatures may reach 21,500°F (12,000°C). The pressures range from 200,000 to 6,000,000 times the pressure of Earth's atmosphere. Dr. Marvin Ross of the Lawrence Livermore National Laboratory in California believes that these conditions may cause diamonds to form.

Dr. Ross believes that the high temperatures and pressures rip apart the methane, separating it into carbon and hydrogen atoms. He says that under these conditions, the carbon atoms are squeezed together to form diamonds. The diamonds could drift through the atmosphere of the two planets or fall to the planets' surfaces.

Is Dr. Ross correct? Perhaps Vogayer 2 will find out.

FOUR NEW GALAXIES

Astronomers at the University of California in Berkeley announced the discovery of four new galaxies in 1981. The galaxies are estimated to be 10,000,000,000 (billion) light years away. That is, it took that many years for the light of these galaxies to reach Earth.

The galaxies are the most distant galaxies discovered to date. The next most distant galaxy, which is about 8,000,000,000 (billion) light years away, was discovered in 1975 by the same research team.

The newly discovered galaxies are much bigger and much older than the Milky Way (the galaxy in which we live). Each contains many billions of stars. And each is thought to be about 16,000,000,000 (billion) years old. The Milky Way is only about one fourth as old. By studying the older galaxies, scientists may learn about the future of our own galaxy.

FINAL MISSIONS TO SALYUT 6

Salyut 6 is a Soviet space station that was launched in September, 1977. During the following years, many manned spacecraft docked with the station, which orbits Earth. The final missions to the space station were conducted in 1981. On March 13, Soyuz T-4 linked up with Salyut 6. Aboard were two Soviet cosmonauts. They stayed in the space station for 75 days, conducting experiments and doing repair work before returning to Earth on May 26. Twice during their stay, they had visitors for about a week. The first visitors, a Soviet and a Mongolian, arrived aboard Soyuz 39 on March 23. On May 15, Soyuz 40 brought another Soviet cosmonaut and an officer of the Rumanian Air Force. Like the Mongolian, the Rumanian was the first person from his country to travel into space.

COMPETITION FROM THE EUROPEANS

Until recently, the United States and the Soviet Union have had space pretty much to themselves. But the European Space Agency has shown that it will soon offer important competition. In June, 1981, the agency launched an Ariane rocket that put a payload of two satellites into Earth orbit. One satellite was a European weather satellite. The other was a communications satellite built by India.

Eleven nations are members of the European Space Agency: Belgium, Britain, Denmark, France, Ireland, Italy, the Netherlands, Spain, Sweden, Switzerland, and West Germany. Unlike the U.S. space shuttle launched in 1981, Ariane is not re-usable. It has three stages, which can be used only once. The first two stages lift the rocket and its payload into space. The third stage puts the payload into orbit.

QUICKER THAN A WINK

It takes you about $\frac{1}{40}$ of a second to wink. You may think this is an extraordinarily short period of time. Yet in $\frac{1}{100,000}$ of a second, it's possible to snap a photograph. This type of photography is called ultra-high-speed photography. It enables us to capture motion that is too fast for the human eye to record.

With ultra-high-speed photography, motion can be frozen in time. We can see what happens when a bullet passes through an apple (*above*). The bullet is traveling at a speed of about 3,000 feet (900 meters) per second. Yet in the photo it appears to be standing still.

A jet of water is captured as a series of "flowers" connected by a thin stem of water (*left*). A picture such as this helps scientists learn how water behaves. It shows that a falling column of water—like the flow from

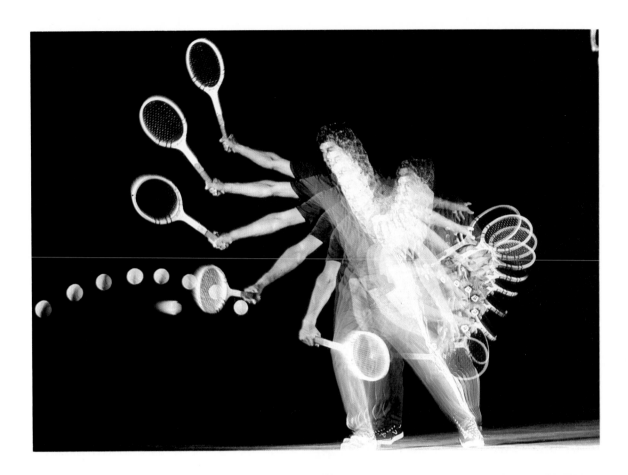

your kitchen faucet—quickly loses its streamlined shape. It breaks up into drops that are evenly spaced, with narrow threads of water between.

Continuous motion can be shown by rapidly making a number of exposures on one piece of film. The whole flowing motion of a tennis stroke is caught as a player hits a tennis ball (*above*). The graceful arc of a back dive can be seen in the multiple exposure at the right. Photos such as these help athletes improve their form and technique.

The term ultra-high-speed photography usually refers to exposures of $\frac{1}{10,000}$ of a second or faster. In ordinary photography, the exposure is determined by the opening and closing of the camera's shutter. When the shutter opens, light enters the camera and makes an image on the film. In ultra-high-speed photography, exposure is determined by a flashing light. The light can flash on and off much more quickly than any shutter can open and close.

Single-Exposure "Stills": The group of photos below shows what happens when a drop of milk splashes on a plate. When the drop hits the plate, it spreads outward to form a crown. The crown collapses into a thin film of milk and a ring of tiny drops. All this happens in a fraction of a second.

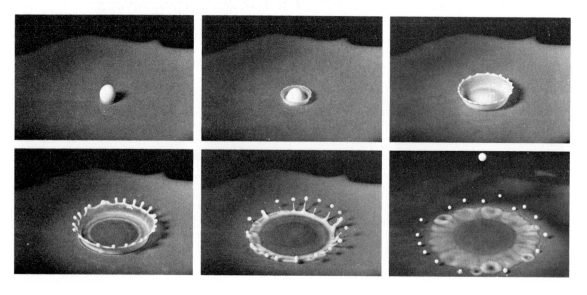

Multiple-Exposure Continuous Motion: Follow the bouncing ball above. See how the ball's movement changes as it nears the top of a bounce. The time interval between each exposure is the same. But the distance traveled by the ball changes. The photo of a golf swing at the right contains 8 exposures. They were taken in 8/1,000 of a second. Look at the writing on the ball. You can see that the ball is rotating as it moves forward.

This bristlecone pine, in California, is the oldest living thing in the world.

THE OLDEST LIVING THING

On a dry, rocky slope in the White Mountains of California, there's a tree that's almost 5,000 years old. It's the oldest living thing in the world.

The tree is a bristlecone pine. It sprouted from a seed about 2800 B.C.—before the great pyramids of Egypt were built. By the time of Moses it was already 1,500 years old. When Jesus was born it was close to 3,000 years old. When Columbus came to America it was more than 4,000 years old.

The tree hasn't had an easy life. It lives high on a mountain where it is exposed to fierce winds and winter storms. Sometimes the temperature falls below freezing. At other times the hot sun bakes the land. There is very little rain.

The tree shows its age and the results of its hard life. Its trunk and branches are bent and twisted. The wind has worn away much of the bark on its trunk and the soil from its roots.

Nevertheless, each year the tree grows a ring of new wood. The rings tell us how old the tree is. Scientists use a tool called a borer to remove a core of wood from the tree. The core is like a long, thin pencil. Scientists look at the core under a microscope so they can see and count the rings. The rings are very, very thin because the tree grows very

slowly. It may take a bristlecone pine 100 years to grow 1 inch (2.5 centimeters) wider, and 20 years to grow 1 inch taller.

There are several other bristlecone pines in the White Mountains that are more than 4,000 years old. And scientists have found very old bristlecone pines in Utah, Colorado, Arizona, and New Mexico. Wind and weather have taken their toll on these trees, too. In many cases, only a small part of the tree is alive—perhaps just a narrow band of wood leading from the soil to a few living branches. But this actually helps the tree survive. Because the living branches are so few, the tree needs very little water.

Bristlecone pine trees are named after their cones, which are dark brown and about 3 inches (7.5 centimeters) long. Each of the cone's thick scales ends in a long bristlelike spine. The trees have short, dark green needles (leaves) that grow in bundles of five. The bark is reddish-brown. The cones, needles, and bark are often covered with a sticky sap, or resin. The resin protects the trees from insect pests and diseases. It helps the trees live for thousands of years.

No one knows how much longer the oldest bristlecone pine will live . . . or which trees of today will still be alive 5,000 years from now.

THIS TREE HAS KNEES

The bald cypress is a curious tree. First of all, it lives in water. Its favorite home is a swamp forest in Mexico or in the southeastern United States. There, in quiet, shallow waters, it rises to great heights. A full-grown bald cypress may be 120 feet (37 meters) tall.

Second, the bald cypress is one of the few coniferous (cone-bearing) trees that sheds all its leaves in the autumn. Most of its relatives—such as pines, spruces, and firs—are evergreens, with at least some leaves on their branches all year round.

But perhaps most curious of all are the tree's big, knobby knees. These structures rise up above the swampy water—2, 3, even 4 feet (more than 1 meter) into the air. The knees are more or less cone-shaped. That is, they are bigger at the base, where they attach to the roots, than at the top. They consist of soft, spongy wood and are covered with a spongy bark. As they get older, they tend to become hollow.

A bald cypress tree may have many knees. Some of the knees grow quite close to the trunk of the tree. Other knees may be several feet away from the trunk.

What is the purpose of the knees? The most popular theory says that the knees help provide underwater parts of the tree with oxygen. But the internal structure of the knees doesn't seem to support this theory.

Another theory says that the knees help the bald cypress stand firmly in the soft, swampy ground. The root system that anchors the tree in the ground is certainly strong. Bald cypress trees stand firm even in hurricanes. The root system has two kinds of roots. Thick horizontal roots radiate in all directions from the base of the trunk. From the horizontal roots, large vertical roots—called anchor roots—go deep down into the ground. The knees usually rise up from the points where the anchor roots join the horizontal roots.

Scientists are still studying the knees and trying to determine their function. But for now, their value to the curious bald cypress tree remains a mystery.

The bald cypress is one of the few conifers that sheds its leaves in autumn. It also has strange, knobby knees.

BODY TRICKS

FOOL YOUR MOUTH . . .

For this trick you need a piece of raw, peeled potato and a piece of raw, peeled apple or radish. Shut your eyes and hold your nose. Taste each one. You won't know which food is which. Why?

When we eat something, we use both our sense of taste and our sense of smell. As you discovered, the tongue alone is not enough. There wasn't enough information for your brain to tell what you were eating.

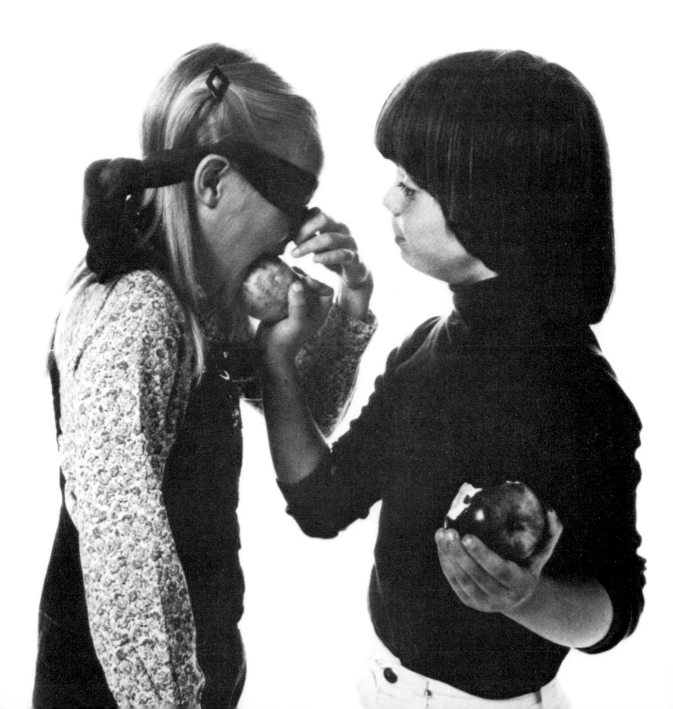

FOOL YOUR EARS . . .

Turn on the radio or play a record. Stand in the middle of the room, making sure that there are no tables or chairs nearby. Close your eyes, cover one ear, and spin yourself around ten times. Keeping your eyes closed, stop; try to point to the radio or record. Chances are you not only got dizzy but were fooled as to where the sound was coming from. But why?

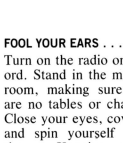

When you spin with your eyes closed, naturally you become disoriented. But losing your balance and locating sound have to do with your ears as well as your eyes. Our ears have two groups of nerves to send messages to the brain. One group of nerves senses balance; the other group of nerves senses sound. These nerves are affected by a liquid in the inner ear. When we spin, this liquid spins too, and thus the messages that go to our brain are all mixed up.

TOO HOT, TOO COLD, TOO WET, TOO DRY

- Too warm in Colorado.
- Too cold in Florida.
- Too much rain in British Columbia.
- Too little rain in Connecticut.

Did the weather go wild in 1981? It certainly seemed that way. While people in one place were dealing with floods, people elsewhere were worrying about empty reservoirs. Frost killed crops in some regions, and heat and drought killed crops in others. And in some places the weather was just the opposite of the previous year's. In 1980, Indiana farmers lost crops to drought. In 1981, they lost crops to heavy rains and flooding.

Although the weather usually co-operates with people, what we remember longest are the times when it doesn't.

BAD WEATHER IS BAD BUSINESS

Farmers are often the first to feel the effects of bad weather. Freezing winter temperatures cut New York's 1981 apple crop by nearly one third, and the state's apple growers lost $40,000,000. But bad weather in one area can also affect people who live far away. Freezing temperatures killed most of Florida's winter vegetable crop and much of its orange crop in 1981. As a result, people

Freezing temperatures killed much of Florida's citrus crop in 1981.

128

Some areas of North America received far too little rain . . . and other areas received far too much.

all over the United States and Canada paid more for these items. The price of orange juice concentrate rose 30 percent.

Bad weather affects more than food. As one person observed: "Bad weather is bad business." In early 1981, warm temperatures and a lack of snow in Colorado forced many ski businesses to close. In British Columbia, where rain fell instead of snow, ski instructors had no students and resort hotels were vacant. Across the continent, in Vermont, there was plenty of snow. But it was so cold that many skiers stayed indoors. And New England merchants complained that people weren't spending money in stores—because they were spending so much money on fuel to heat their homes.

Not everyone suffers from bad weather. Fuel companies sell lots of fuel in cold weather. Stores sell more boots and heavy coats. Heavy snows mean more sales of sleds, snowblowers, and snow tires. And poor harvests in one place mean a bigger market for crops from another place. Citrus-fruit growers in Texas found a greater demand for their oranges and grapefruits after much of Florida's citrus crop was lost.

Periods of unfavorable weather are nothing new. And we can't get rid of bad weather. But we can try to prepare for it. By making sure that buildings are well insulated, we can cut down on the amount of fuel needed for heating during cold spells. By using artificial snowmaking equipment, ski resorts can survive periods of low snowfall. By establishing grain reserves, we can provide food for people during years when grain harvests are poor.

Among the hardest problems to solve are those caused by periods of drought. These are difficult problems that involve not only a lack of rain but also the activities of people.

THE WATER CRISIS

People use vast amounts of water in their homes, in agriculture, and in industry. This water begins as rain and other forms of precipitation. It is collected in four main kinds of reserves, or sources—rivers, lakes, reservoirs, and the ground. In 1980 and 1981, low precipitation and high water use lowered the levels of all these sources in most of North America. Perhaps most alarming of all was the drop in the levels of groundwater.

Groundwater is held in natural underground reservoirs called aquifers. Think of them as sponges. They are made of sand, gravel, and other rock that is porous enough to hold water, sandwiched between two layers of nonporous rock. To obtain the water, people drill wells.

Some aquifers are huge. One of the largest aquifers in the world is the Ogallala aquifer, named after a band of Sioux Indians who once lived in the American Midwest. This aquifer stretches from western Texas to northern Nebraska. It provides much of the water needed by the farms in the Great Plains.

The water trapped in the Ogallala and other aquifers has collected over thousands of years. But today, people are removing the water much faster than it is being replaced by precipitation. If this continues, many of the aquifers may soon be dry. The consequences could be disastrous. As one Texan pointed out, taking too much groundwater is like taking money out of a bank account faster than you put it in. Sooner or later, there's not going to be any money left in the account.

In some parts of the Ogallala the water level is falling as much as 3 feet (90 centimeters) a year. Farmers in the region have already had to decrease the amount of irrigated farmland. Many have had to switch from growing corn, which needs a lot of water, to growing crops such as cotton and sorghum, which need less water.

It's hard to believe how much water is used to produce food and other products. It takes almost 15,000 gallons (56,780 liters) of water to grow one bushel (35 liters) of wheat. It takes 3,500 gallons (13,250 liters) of water to produce a steak (this includes the water needed to grow the corn that is fed to the steer). It takes 120 gallons (454 liters) to produce an egg. And it takes 60,000 gallons (227,000 liters) to produce a ton of steel.

Could people use less water? For people living in North America, the answer is yes. Much water is wasted. People could conserve water in their homes. They could use more efficient methods of irrigation. They could recycle water used in industry.

In many places, people have already begun practicing water conservation. The drought of recent years caused alarming drops in the water levels of many reservoirs and other surface bodies of water. Suddenly some communities found themselves with less than a month's supply of water. States of emergency were declared in these communities, and using water to wash cars and water lawns became illegal. The amount of water people were allowed to use was rationed. For example, in eastern Pennsylvania, a person was allowed to use only 40 gallons (150 liters) of water a day. People who used more could be fined or even sent to jail.

Forty gallons isn't much when you consider that a shower uses about 8 gallons (30 liters) of water a minute . . . that flushing a toilet uses about 5 gallons (20 liters) . . . and that a clothes washer uses about 35 gallons (130 liters) per load.

Drought and low water levels have made many people aware of the fact that oil is not the only precious fluid on which we depend. Water, too, is precious—and limited. It must be protected from pollution, and it must be used wisely. People should remember Benjamin Franklin's proverb: "We know not what the well is worth till it is dry."

This sinkhole in Winter Park, Florida, swallowed up a house when it formed in 1981.

PLOOP! THERE GOES FLORIDA

Imagine that you are quietly paddling around a swimming pool on a rubber raft. What would happen if the water were suddenly drained out of the pool? Ploop! You'd find yourself down at the bottom of the pool.

This is pretty much what happened one day in May, 1981, in Winter Park, Florida. But it wasn't a kid on a raft that fell. It was the ground—and everything on it.

Mae Rose Owens was in her home in Winter Park when she heard "a queer swishing noise" coming from the land next to her house. Then there was a "ploop" as a large sycamore tree fell into the earth.

Mrs. Owens called the police, but there was nothing that they—or anyone else—could do. As people watched, the ground just sank away, leaving a hole that grew bigger and bigger. It gobbled up the Owens' house, five expensive cars that were at a neighboring repair shop, a truck, a parking lot, parts of two streets, and part of a large swimming pool.

What caused this disaster?

Most of Florida sits on top of a thick layer of limestone. This layer is more than 100 feet (30 meters) beneath the surface of the earth. It contains cavities that range in size from small holes to gigantic caverns. These cavities were formed when rainwater trickled through the ground and came in contact with the limestone. Rainwater contains carbonic acid. The carbonic acid reacted with the limestone and dissolved it. Over thousands of years, more and more of the limestone was dissolved, and bigger and bigger cavities were formed.

Usually, the cavities are filled with water. The water helps hold up the overlying layers of clay, sand, and soil. But Florida has been suffering from a drought, which has lowered the water level. And the water has gradually drained from the limestone caverns. Without the water, the caverns can collapse. As a cavern collapses, the overlying layers of clay, sand, and soil fall in—forming what is called a sinkhole. This is what happened to Mrs. Owens. And it is not an unusual event in Florida. In fact, many of the lakes in the state began as sinkholes.

MAKE AND DO

These presents are all wrapped up and ready to go. And the lucky people who receive them will enjoy them all the more because of the specially designed wrappings. Try decorating your own gift packages. It's fun!

ALL WRAPPED UP

It's always fun to give presents. It's even more fun when the presents are covered in special wrappings designed by you. These pages show some of the ways you can decorate a package. Each has a theme. Some give hints to what's inside the packages. Others use pictures to say "this is especially for you!"

Before you begin, gather all the materials you want to use to decorate the package. These can include construction paper, wrapping paper, crayons, paints, markers, ribbons, yarns, lace, buttons, gold seals . . . the list is almost endless. You will also need scissors, a ruler, a compass, glue, and tape.

Begin by neatly wrapping the box. The kind of decoration will depend to some degree on the design of the wrapping paper. It's best to use solid-colored paper because it gives you more flexibility than paper with designs.

MAKE MINE VANILLA

This is a fun wrapping to use in hot summer months. The cones are triangles cut from brown construction paper. The ice cream scoops are circles of colored paper made with a compass. Can you guess all the flavors on the box?

Use markers to add nuts and sprinkles to your cones. If you wish, write a message in one or more of the ice cream scoops.

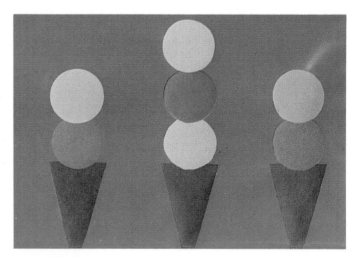

CREATIVE CANDLES

Pieces of ribbon, lace, and embroidery can be used to give an elegant appearance to a package. Cut the materials to the desired length. They can be placed on the top of the box, or they can be made long enough to wrap down the side and onto the back. Carefully determine where each will be placed, then glue it onto the box. Next, cut out flames from yellow paper. Or make the flames out of sequins, gold sprinkles, or bright red nail polish.

A COOL TREAT

Here's another idea for a gift that is meant to be used during the hottest months of the year. This watermelon slice is most effective on big boxes. First cut out the "flesh" from a piece of bright pink or red paper. Then cut out the rind from green paper. Glue the flesh and rind onto the box. Use markers to make the seeds—or glue on real watermelon seeds. Use extra seeds to decorate corners, to make a border, or to write out a message.

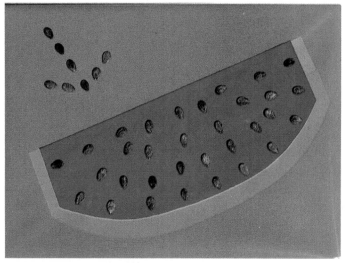

FUNNY FRIEND

Decorate a present with a caricature of the person who will receive the gift. Begin by cutting out a face from construction paper. This can simply be a large circle drawn with a compass. Use a different color for the shirt or blouse. Glue the face and clothing onto the box. Make hair from yarn. Glue each strand of yarn in place individually. Add a bow or hat. Next, draw on eyes, a mouth, and other facial details. Add a collar, necklace, necktie, or other decoration to the clothing.

A caricature can be made even more personal by adding objects related to the person's job or hobby. If your father likes to play baseball, make a picture of him complete with bat and ball. If your brother is a cook, add a rolling pin and a bag of flour. If your mother is a teacher, add a report card (with all A's, of course).

BON VOYAGE!

You don't have to wrap a gift in expensive paper. A brown grocery bag can be used. Newspaper can be used. Even an old road map can be used. This is an especially good idea if the gift is for someone leaving on a trip. If possible, use a map of the place the person will be visiting. If the person is touring by car, use a marker to highlight the route the person will be taking. Add a ribbon and bow for some extra color.

GARDENER'S DELIGHT

Worms are beloved by all who enjoy gardening. So if you're giving someone seeds, bulbs, garden tools, or a plant, decorate the package with Willy the Worm. Cut a wiggly body from brown paper and glue it onto the package. Add stripes and other markings to the body. Give Willy a jazzy hat and a bow tie. And add a few flowers for him to sniff.

CARD CRAZY

If you're giving a gift to someone who enjoys playing card games, decorate the wrapping with old playing cards. Or make felt cutouts of a spade, heart, diamond, and club. Use cookie cutters to help you make the design. Simply place each cookie cutter on the felt, trace its edge with pencil or chalk, then cut out the design and glue it onto your box.

WHERE WILL YOU TRAVEL?

It's time to board a spaceship for a journey into outer space. Where will the ship take you?

To answer this question, you will need a pencil and a sheet of tracing paper. Place the tracing paper over this page. Carefully follow all the directions given below. They will lead you to the spaceship's destination. Hint: It will be easier if you rewrite the complete word at each step.

The solution is on page 381.

1. Print the word SPACESHIP. _____

2. Remove the first vowel from the right; replace it with an A. _____

3. Insert an I in the first position at the left. _____

4. Place a T after every S and every A. _____

5. Remove the third consonant from the left; replace it with an N. _____

6. Remove the last letter and replace it with an O and an E. _____

7. Remove the fifth consonant from the left and the fifth letter from the right. _____

8. Place an R in the eleventh position from the left. _____

9. Place an S in the fourth position from the right. Then insert a D before the first vowel from the left. _____

10. Locate the fifth and sixth letters from the left; reverse their order. _____

11. Move the letters from the last three positions at the right to the first three positions at the left. _____

12. Remove all the E's. _____

THERE'S A ROOT IN YOUR SOUP!

The next time you eat vegetable soup, look closely. You'll find roots and stems and maybe even fruit in it. This is because we eat different parts of different plants.

Most plant foods are grouped as fruits or vegetables. But this does not necessarily tell us what part of the plant is being eaten. We eat the underground stem of a potato plant; the seeds of a pea plant; the fruit of an orange tree; the bark (stem covering) of a cinnamon tree; and the leaves of an onion plant. (Most people don't know that onions are leaves wrapped around one another, forming a bulb.)

The names of 45 plants are listed below. Match each to the part that we normally eat.

a. leaf or leafstalk
b. stem
c. root
d. flower
e. fruit
f. seed

1. almond
2. apple
3. artichoke
4. asparagus
5. banana
6. beet
7. blueberry
8. broccoli
9. cabbage
10. carrot
11. cauliflower
12. celery
13. cherry
14. coconut
15. collards
16. corn
17. cucumber
18. date
19. eggplant
20. fig
21. green pepper
22. lettuce
23. lima bean

24. onion
25. parsley
26. parsnip
27. peach
28. peanut
29. pear
30. pecan
31. pineapple
32. plum
33. potato
34. pumpkin
35. radish
36. rhubarb
37. rice
38. rutabaga
39. spinach
40. squash
41. strawberry
42. tomato
43. turnip
44. walnut
45. watermelon

ANSWERS: 1.f; 2.e; 3.d; 4.b; 5.e; 6.c; 7.e; 8.d; 9.a; 10.c; 11.d; 12.a; 13.e; 14.f; 15.a; 16.f; 17.e; 18.e; 19.e,f; 20.f; 21.e; 22.a; 23.f; 24.a; 25.a; 26.c; 27.e; 28.f; 29.e; 30.f; 31.e; 32.e; 33.b; 34.c; 35.c; 36.a; 37.f; 38.c; 39.a; 40.e,f; 41.e,f; 42.e,f; 43.c; 44.f; 45.e.

138

Next, go on a hunt. All 45 plants are hidden in this search-a-word puzzle. To find them, read forward, backward, up, down, and diagonally. If you wish, cover the puzzle with a sheet of tracing paper. Then you can draw a neat line through each plant as you find it. One plant has been shaded in for you.

Some letters will be left over after you have found all the plants. Circle all the unused letters. If you read them from left to right, you will find a hidden message.

B	R	A	B	U	H	R	W	A	T	E	R	M	E	L	O	N
R	O	S	E	A	E	G	A	B	B	A	C	T	I	N	G	I
O	T	P	R	Y	R	E	L	E	C	L	O	N	I	O	N	K
C	A	A	G	A	A	T	N	H	E	E	T	U	N	A	E	P
C	T	R	R	S	E	R	U	T	A	B	A	G	A	E	G	M
O	O	A	E	F	C	P	T	P	L	U	M	T	O	P	G	U
L	P	G	E	C	A	U	L	I	F	L	O	W	E	R	P	P
I	T	U	N	O	C	O	C	O	C	R	T	A	P	P	L	E
D	T	S	P	E	C	I	R	U	R	H	C	B	F	D	A	H
N	U	S	E	E	T	A	D	A	M	H	O	I	E	N	N	S
O	R	S	P	I	N	A	C	H	I	B	G	K	A	E	T	I
M	N	Q	P	I	N	E	A	P	P	L	E	N	E	S	T	D
L	I	U	E	V	Y	R	R	E	B	W	A	R	T	S	N	A
A	P	A	R	S	L	E	Y	E	R	B	C	O	R	N	A	R
Y	G	S	O	O	D	F	O	S	D	R	A	L	L	O	C	R
Y	C	H	E	R	R	Y	N	A	E	B	A	M	I	L	E	O
B	L	U	E	B	E	R	R	Y	P	I	N	S	R	A	P	U

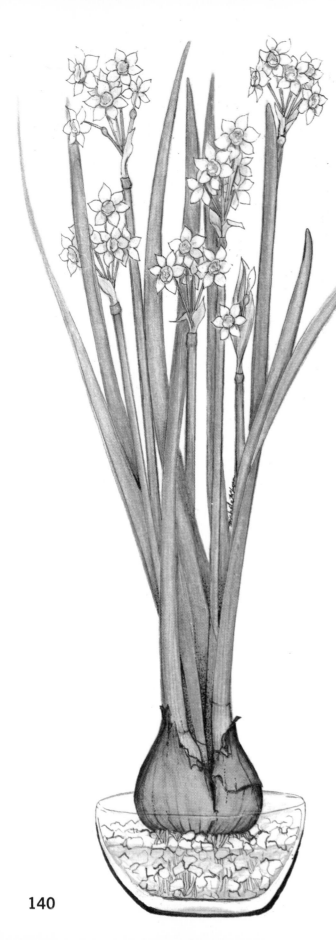

HOW TO FOOL FLOWERS

In cold climates, winter can be a dull time of year. The bright leaves and colorful flowers that adorn the other seasons are missing. But it's very easy to bring this color into your home in winter. You do it by fooling the flowers. You make plants think it's spring by bringing them into the warmth of the house. The plants respond by blooming early. This process is called forcing.

Hyacinths, tulips, crocuses, and other bulb plants can be forced, either in water or soil. First, the bulbs must be stored in a cold place for two to three months. During this time they grow a root system, and tips of green leaves begin to poke up at the top. Then, when the bulbs are given warmth and light, the leaves and stem shoot up. Soon the plant blossoms. Some bulbs, such as the paper-white narcissus, have been especially developed for indoor forcing—they are ready to grow even without the cold period.

Budded branches from trees that flower in the spring can also be forced. Forsythia, pussy willow, flowering quince, cherry, and apple blossoms are especially easy to force. The closer to spring you cut the branches, the quicker they will blossom.

Here are directions for forcing three kinds of flowers. Try these—and then experiment with others.

PAPER-WHITE NARCISSUS

Fill a shallow bowl with about a cup of clean pebbles. Place one or more bulbs on the pebbles so that the pointed ends are up. Spread more pebbles around the bulbs, and then arrange the bulbs so that they will stand up straight. Add water to the bowl. The water should barely touch the bottoms of the bulbs. Add water as necessary to keep it at this level.

Put the bowl in a cool, light place such as a windowsill. When the leaves are several inches high, move the bowl to a warmer spot. (Avoid putting the bulbs in a very warm room or near a radiator. The heat may cause the flower buds to dry up.) A few weeks later, clusters of fragrant white flowers will burst forth. (Paper-whites also come in yellow, but they take longer to force.)

HYACINTHS

Choose a vase or jar with a narrow opening. You want the bulb to sit on the opening. Fill the vase with room-temperature water. Set the bulb, pointed side up, so that its bottom barely touches the water.

Put the vase in a cold, dark place, but one where the temperature won't fall below freezing. When a good root system has developed—about eight weeks—bring the vase into a cool place in the house. A few days later, move the vase into a warm, light room and wait for the flowers to blossom.

FORSYTHIA

By early February you can cut branches from a forsythia bush and bring them indoors. Cutting should be done on a day when the temperature is above freezing. Choose branches with plump, well-developed buds. Cut off the branches with a sharp pair of clippers. Never try to pull or break off branches. This can hurt the bush. Arrange the branches in a vase filled with room-temperature water. Change the water every few days. Put the branches where they will get a lot of light. In a few weeks, the branches will be wreathed with bright yellow flowers.

141

STAMP COLLECTING

The year 1981 was a special one for stamp collectors. A royal wedding in Britain caused lovely stamps to be issued in many countries. In the United States, two postal rate increases produced a flood of new U.S. stamps. And for the first time, a single stamp sold for $1,000,000.

The million-dollar stamp was sold in May to a European collector. It is a 5-cent stamp issued in Alexandria, Virginia, and used on a letter sent in 1846 to Richmond, Virginia. It belongs to a "provisional" U.S. issue that is of high value because it dates from before the first official U.S. stamp was issued in 1847. Collectors call this stamp the "blue boy" because it carried a love letter written in a sad, or "blue," mood.

THE ROYAL WEDDING

In honor of the wedding of Prince Charles and Lady Diana Spencer, stamps were issued in Britain and in 22 Commonwealth countries closely related to Britain. A number of countries with no ties to Britain also issued royal wedding stamps.

Britain issued a pair of stamps showing the happy couple in their official portrait. Prince Charles posed for the portrait standing on a box, so he could be a head taller than Lady Diana. The reason for this pose was not vanity but to make room for the silhouette of Queen Elizabeth, which appears on all British stamps in the upper right-hand corner.

The Commonwealth countries marked the marriage with a special series of three stamps each. One design, common to many of the countries, showed the engagement photograph of the Prince and Lady Diana. The second stamp showed the Prince in military uniform or dressed as a sportsman—a polo player by Barbados and a sailor by Fiji, for example. The third stamp pictured either a wedding bouquet made of local flowers or a British royal residence or historic building —Buckingham Palace by the Maldives, for example.

YEAR OF THE DISABLED

"Full participation and equality" was the theme of the United Nations International Year of Disabled Persons, which was observed in 1981. The U.N. issued a set of six stamps showing, in symbols, the need to include the disabled in all phases of life. And nearly 100 nations also issued stamps to mark the fact that disabled people must be treated with respect and dignity and given equal opportunities. The stamp issued by the United States showed a scientist seated in a wheelchair, working with a high-powered microscope. The stamp bore the words, "Disabled doesn't mean Unable."

In Canada, there were plans to issue a stamp honoring the heroic 1980 long-distance run of Terry Fox, who had lost a leg to cancer. The issue would officially mark the Marathon of Hope, a Cancer Fund drive, in which 22-year-old Fox nearly made it from the east coast to the west before his illness stopped his progress. (Terry Fox died in June, 1981.)

A WEALTH OF U.S. STAMPS

In the United States, postal rates were raised in March and again on November 1. The first rise in first-class postage was to 18 cents, and the second to 20 cents. Rates had never before risen twice in one year in the United States, and the stamp presses were kept busy issuing new stamps in new denominations. When the first increase came, the Postal Service released stamps carrying the letter "B," without denominations. These stamps, which had been stockpiled in case of a sudden rate rise, took care of immediate needs until the first 18-cent stamps could be printed. For the November increase, a "C" stamp went on sale.

An unusual 1981 issue was a block of eight stamps celebrating U.S. achievements in space exploration. In the center, four large stamps showed the space shuttle *Columbia* in four stages of its historic first flight: taking off, being boosted into orbit, circling Earth, and landing. At each end of the block were smaller stamps showing a U.S. astronaut on the moon, a Pioneer spacecraft, Skylab studying the sun, and the Space Telescope, scheduled to be carried by the space shuttle in 1985.

Canada 17

Suomi Finland 1,10

1981 STAMPS
FROM AROUND
THE WORLD

14P

Surrey 1890s
USA 18c

EUROPA 14F BELGIE-BELGIQUE

REPUBLIC OF CHINA 5

Exploring the Moon · Benefiting Mankind · Benefiting Mankind · Understanding the Sun · Probing the Planets · Comprehending the Universe · Benefiting Mankind · Benefiting Mankind · USA 18c

Save Wetland Habitats
USA 18c

Lily USA 18c

United Nations
International Year
of Disabled Persons
20c

A TOPICAL
COLLECTION OF
DANCES AND DANCERS

A lovely issue was a block of four flower stamps showing the camellia, the rose, the lily, and the dahlia, all against a pink background. Another block of stamps pictured wild creatures in their habitats—a great blue heron in the wetlands, a badger gazing over the grasslands, a grizzly bear in mountain surroundings, and a ruffed grouse perched on a log in a woodland.

Two legendary sports figures were honored in the first stamps of a new sports series: Robert Tyre (Bobby) Jones, Jr., the golfer who in 1930 won the four most important world titles in one year, and Mildred (Babe) Didrikson Zaharias, who was the foremost woman athlete of the century. Among other people honored on U.S. stamps was civil rights leader Whitney Moore Young, Jr. This stamp was part of the Black Heritage USA series. Rachel Carson, the writer and pioneer in efforts to protect the environment, and the popular poet Edna St. Vincent Millay were depicted on stamps in the Literary Arts series.

Another U.S. stamp featured a surrey "with a fringe on top," just like the one in the musical *Oklahoma!* This marked the start of a new transportation series. And the American Architecture series continued, with a block of four stamps showing buildings dating from the late 1800's and early 1900's.

STAMPS FROM AROUND THE WORLD

The year's Europa stamps, issued by the Conference of European Postal and Telecommunication Administrations, had folklore as their theme. The member countries contributed designs based on their folktales or customs. Britain, for example, submitted a Valentine's Day stamp and one depicting the Morris Dancers, folk dancers who traditionally herald spring.

Castles and other historic buildings made their usual welcome appearance on the world's stamps in 1981. Liechtenstein issued four stamps showing Gutenberg Castle, which dates from the mid 13th century. On one stamp the castle is seen perched on a hill; the other stamps showed interior scenes.

Many countries used growing things as stamp designs in 1981. The African country Malawi displayed its agricultural products on a series of stamps depicting corn, rice, millet, and wheat. The Republic of South Africa pictured four different orchid blossoms. The Falkland Islands, which lie off the southern tip of South America, showed six Antarctic plants, including Magellan club mosses and Antarctic bedstraw. And Greece featured fresh and canned vegetables, in a stamp issue devoted to Greek exports.

Many countries also depicted wildlife. Canada issued the final two stamps in an eight-stamp endangered wildlife series begun in 1977. One stamp showed the Vancouver Island marmot, a little burrowing mammal. The other showed the wood bison, a larger, woolier relative of the plains bison. Sweden issued a handsome stamp showing a falcon in flight. Taiwan pictured crabs from the waters around its shores. And Britain pictured butterflies.

In China and other Far Eastern countries, 1981 was the Year of the Rooster. A rooster appeared, accordingly, on the stamps issued to carry China's New Year's greeting cards. South Korea printed a pair of stamps for its New Year's issue. One showed a rooster in human form, wearing human clothing and holding religious objects in its hands. The other stamp depicted a pair of cranes, a symbol of long life.

Art remained a popular subject for stamps. An unusual series from Taiwan showed laser art, or lasography. Taiwan also used designs by children on a series of four stamps. In Canada, works by the Canadian painters Paul Emile Borduas, Frederick H. Varley, and Marc-Aurèle Fortin were reproduced on stamps. And Portugal began a series honoring one of the country's most beloved art forms, the ceramic tile.

A TOPICAL COLLECTION

Dance would be an excellent subject for a topical stamp collection (a collection built around a single theme). Folk dancers, jazz dancers, twirling ballerinas—all have been depicted on stamps. One British stamp even shows kilt-clad dancers from the Scottish Highlands. A collection that had dance as its theme would be certain to include some of the world's liveliest stamp designs.

CHARLESS HAHN
Stamp Editor, *Chicago Sun-Times*

The Grouch

LET'S FACE IT

Look closely. All these "faces" aren't faces at all. They are pieces of nature. The Barbershop Quartet singers are markings on a butterfly wing. The Grouch with the spiky hair is a common weed called a teasel. Curious Fish is part of a moth wing. A japonica shrub and an icicle created Runny Nose. And an orchid and droplets of water gave us

Runny Nose

146

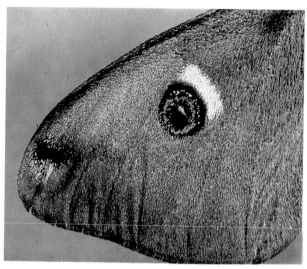

Curious Fish

Pop-eyed Pony. Sunny Smile, the grinning critter wearing a yellow bonnet, was formed by more than one organism—it's a beetle inside a flower.

If you're a good observer and have some imagination, you can find faces everywhere —funny ones, sad ones, scary ones. So pick up your camera and head outdoors. Look closely at that tree trunk and that tiger lily blossom. Is someone looking back at you? Quick—take a picture.

Sunny Smile

Pop-eyed Pony

Treasure Chests

Decorated egg cartons are perfect containers for your small treasures. Each egg compartment can hold one or several objects. A carton can be turned into a jewelry box, filled with rings, pins, and earrings. It can be used to hold collections of stamps or shells. It can be used as a desk organizer, to separate clips, pins, and erasers. What kind of treasure chest would *you* create?

1. You'll need a cardboard egg carton, spray paint, decorations, newspaper, and glue.

2. Cover your work area with newspaper to protect it from the paint.

3. Paint the entire outside of the carton. Wait until the first coat of paint is completely dry before applying a second coat.

4. You can also paint the inside of the carton, with the same or a contrasting color.

5. When the paint is completely dry, decorate the outside of the carton. Decide how you will arrange the trimmings before beginning to glue them in place. You may want to co-ordinate the decorations with the carton's purpose: If the box will be used to hold stamps, use stamps to decorate the box. If it will hold jewelry, trim it with lace and sequins, and use beads from jewelry that you no longer wear.

A MYTHICAL MAZE

The unicorn was a mythical creature that looked like a horse with a long horn in the center of its forehead.

Place a sheet of tracing paper over this mythical unicorn maze. Begin at the arrow on the bottom and try to find your way out (to the arrow at the top). If you come to a blind alley, try using a different-colored pencil and a different route.

The solution is on page 381.

POPULAR CRAFTS

The trend to "make-it-yourself" continued to grow in 1981. More and more people valued handmade items over manufactured ones. And people who had never before tried their hands at a craft eagerly completed one project after another. They discovered that crafts give us a chance to express ourselves with our hands and imaginations. And crafts are an exciting way to spend leisure time.

Do you have a favorite craft? Perhaps some of the following projects will appeal to you. Some are easy, some are hard. But each one will give a feeling of satisfaction at having created something both attractive and useful.

CLOISONNÉ

Cloisonné is a type of enamel work. On a metal backing, areas are partitioned off by thin strips of wire, forming a design. The areas between the wires—called *cloisons,* the French word for compartments—are filled with layers of finely ground glass enamels. After each layer is applied, the piece is fired (baked in a special oven called a kiln). The layers are applied until the enamel is flush with the tops of the wires. One simple piece may be fired as many as twenty times before it is completed.

Cloisonné is an art craft that demands great precision and patience. In ancient times, it was used to decorate jewelry, sculpture, bowls, vases, and religious articles. Today the technique is used mainly on jewelry. The metal backings are usually copper, brass, silver, and gold. The glass enamels come in a great variety of colors.

Cloisonné is a type of enamel work that is today used mainly on jewelry.

Folk painting can be used on a wide variety of wooden and metal objects.

FOLK PAINTING

Folk painting is a form of decoration that draws on interesting and unusual techniques from the past. It can be used on a wide variety of wooden and metal objects—trunks, plaques, trays, milk cans, cutting boards, and furniture. You can paint on new objects, or you can search attics, flea markets, and barns for old ones.

The designs that can be painted are almost endless. Try landscapes, fruits, flowers, portraits, or figures. And there are several techniques to choose from—stenciling, freehand, and traditional styles from other countries. For example, *rosemaling* ("rose painting") is a Norwegian peasant style that uses freehand floral designs. It is used on furniture and accessories and even on the walls of homes.

Folk painting is fairly easy to master. You need only learn the basic brushstrokes and coloring techniques. And since stencil patterns are often used, strong drawing talent is not essential.

151

A sock monkey is adorable. And if you add a bit of Velcro to the hands, it can perform some amusing tricks.

You can make beautiful silk flowers, "string" them, and wear them like a festive lei.

SOCK MONKEYS

Adorable monkeys can be made from a special kind of men's work socks—they are gray and white with a red wedge woven into the heel. The socks are cut out according to a pattern and then stuffed with fiberfill to make the monkey bodies. The monkeys come to life with a few extra touches—button eyes, an embroidered nose and mouth, a little scarf or bow tie. And if some Velcro is attached to the hands, your sock monkey will be able to perform some amusing tricks.

SILK FLOWERS

Beautiful silk or organdy flowers can be made in any season. They can be "strung" and worn like a festive lei. Or wire stems can be added to make a flower arrangement for your home. Put one on a special gift, or wear one in your hair.

Twelve petals are in each flower, and they are cut from a pattern. The petals are folded

152

These incredibly real-looking bread dough flowers *(above)* were made from a mixture of white bread and glue *(below)*.

and wired together and then fastened around pearled stamens. If you use white silk, you can dye the petals with batik dyes. Silk leaves can be bought, or you can cut them out from a piece of green silk.

BREAD DOUGH FLOWERS

Flowers can also be made from bread. By mixing measured amounts of white glue and fresh white bread, you will get a non-sticky, easy-to-shape dough that can be colored with acrylic paint or food coloring. The dough is then rolled and squeezed into petals, and the petals are overlapped to form flowers. Wire stems covered with green tape are inserted, and the flowers are dried at room temperature.

Bread dough flowers look incredibly real, and they last for years. Try making a vase of yellow roses for your mother.

WENDIE R. BLANCHARD
Managing Editor
Creative Crafts magazine

153

MANY FRIENDS COOKING

SOUTHERN PECAN PIE, from the United States

"What's for dessert?" is a common question in the United States, a dessert-minded country. In the North, it might be apple pie. In the Southern states, especially Louisiana and Georgia, pecan pie is a favorite. Nearly every Southern cook has a recipe for pecan pie. Here is a classic version. Serve it with freshly made whipped cream.

EQUIPMENT

mixing bowl
eggbeater
mixing spoon
measuring cups
measuring spoons
9-inch pie plate

INGREDIENTS

3 eggs
2 tablespoons sugar
2 tablespoons flour
2 cups dark corn syrup
1 teaspoon vanilla
¼ teaspoon salt
1½ cups pecans
1 unbaked 9-inch pie shell

HOW TO MAKE

1. Preheat the oven to 425°F.

2. In the mixing bowl, beat the eggs with the eggbeater until light and fluffy.

3. Add the sugar, flour, corn syrup, vanilla, and salt and beat well.

4. Break the pecans into small pieces and stir into the mixture.

5. Place the unbaked pie shell in a pie plate and pour in the filling.

6. Bake at 425° for 10 minutes. Reduce heat to 325°. Bake 40 minutes more. Cool and serve.

This recipe serves 6 to 8 people.

CHICKEN—LONG RICE SOUP, from Vietnam

Rice is the main food in the Vietnamese diet. Served boiled, fried, or made into noodles, rice appears at almost every meal. This dish consists of shredded chicken, bits of scallion, and a special cellophane noodle called "long rice," all served in a flavorful broth. You can buy "long rice" noodles in Oriental food stores. Or you can use Italian vermicelli.

INGREDIENTS

½ pound "long rice"
2 scallions
5 cups chicken broth
1 tablespoon soy sauce
    salt and pepper to taste
1 large chicken breast

EQUIPMENT

large serving bowl
knife
medium saucepan
measuring cups
measuring spoons
mixing spoon

HOW TO MAKE

1. Place the chicken breast in the saucepan and add enough water to cover it. Bring the water to a boil and cook for three minutes. Lower the heat, cover, and simmer for 20 to 30 minutes. Remove the chicken breast and let it cool. Then skin and slice into thin strips.

2. If using "long rice," soak in warm water for 10 minutes. Drain. Break into pieces. If using other noodles, cook until tender following package directions.

3. Pile the noodles in a large serving bowl.

4. Finely chop the scallions, both green and white parts.

5. Bring the chicken broth to a boil in the saucepan. Stir in the soy sauce. Season with salt and pepper. Add the cooked chicken strips and chopped scallions and cook for 1 minute over medium heat.

6. Pour the soup over the noodles. Serve hot.

This recipe serves 4 to 6 people.

155

COIN COLLECTING

The skyrocketing prices of gold, silver, and rare coins made headlines in recent years. As a result, the coin market was filled with investors and speculators, and coin collectors had to concern themselves with rapidly changing prices. But in 1981, with the prices of precious metals at more stable levels, coin collectors returned to the more traditional aspects of their hobby. And commemorative coins captured much of their interest.

Soviet coin marking the first piloted space flight

Many other commemorative coins were issued in 1981. Among the most significant was a 1-ruble coin from the Soviet Union, marking the 20th anniversary of the first piloted space flight. The Soviet coin featured a portrait of cosmonaut Yuri Gagarin and designs of space vehicles. The Soviet Union and its allies have issued a number of commemorative coins on space themes in recent years.

Railroads and music provided the 1981 designs for Canada's ongoing commemorative coin program. The silver dollar showed an antique steam locomotive, in honor of the Trans-Canada railway. The $100 gold coin featured the opening bar of the new national anthem, "O Canada," superimposed on a map of the country.

Britain's royal wedding commemorative

COMMEMORATIVE COINS

Commemorative coins have always been popular with collectors. These coins are minted by governments all over the world to mark important events and to honor famous people.

The principal commemorative event of 1981 was the July 29 wedding of Prince Charles and Lady Diana Spencer. As a way of showing respect for the British monarchy, more than 85 different commemorative coins were issued by 24 countries with past or present ties to the Commonwealth of Nations. The centerpiece of these was Britain's own wedding coin. It featured a double portrait of Prince Charles and Lady Diana, with a portrait of Queen Elizabeth II on the obverse. It was the first British coin to show both the reigning monarch and the heir to the throne. Two versions of the coin were struck —one in silver and one in copper-nickel. The most lavish wedding commemorative was the Bahamas' $500 gold piece. But all the coins gave collectors a new topic of interest.

Canada's $100 gold coin

The United States also issued gold commemoratives in 1981—but the U.S. commemoratives were medals, rather than coins. Continuing the American Arts Gold Medallion program into its second year, the Treasury released two medals. A half-ounce

United States gold medallions honoring writers Willa Cather (*above*) and Mark Twain (*below*)

gold medal honored writer Willa Cather, and a one-ounce medal commemorated the work of Mark Twain. In all, ten medals are planned.

Not counting the Bicentennial coins of 1975–76, the United States' last commemorative coins were issued in 1954. In that year Booker T. Washington and George Washington Carver were honored. But in 1981, Congress was considering proposals for new commemoratives. One proposal concerned coins to mark the 1984 Summer Olympic Games in Los Angeles. Another was a plan to issue a silver half dollar in 1982, in honor of the 250th anniversary of the birth of

A 1932 design, being considered for a new commemorative half dollar honoring George Washington

George Washington on February 22, 1732. Collectors were hopeful that this coin would be minted. The familiar Washington quarter was first issued in 1932 as a commemorative marking the bicentennial of Washington's birth. He has also been honored on a commemorative silver dollar (1900) and a commemorative half dollar (1926).

U.S. COIN NEWS

The year 1981 seemed to be the last for the Susan B. Anthony dollar coin. More than 800,000,000 Anthony dollars were minted in 1979 and 1980. But the coins, which are about the size of quarters, were unpopular from the start, and most of them still rest in Treasury vaults. Admitting defeat, the Treasury dropped plans to redesign the coin and issued only a few 1981 Anthony dollars, for inclusion in special proof and uncirculated coin sets. This meant that the 1981 issue, which would probably be the final version of the mini-dollar coin, was scarce. Thus collectors who had ordered the special sets were fortunate.

The year was also the last for specially packaged "mint" sets—sets of uncirculated coins of all denominations from the Philadelphia and Denver mints. This program was begun in 1947. It was phased out because orders had declined while the cost of assembling and packaging the sets had gone up.

An important change in the U.S. one-cent coin was scheduled to take place at the end of 1981. The Mint planned to begin producing cents made of a new alloy. The new coins would have a core of over 99-percent zinc, electroplated with a copper coating. They would replace cents made of an alloy that was 95-percent copper and 5-percent zinc. Mint officials said the high cost of copper was the reason for the change.

Some 13,000,000,000 (billion) one-cent coins are struck by the U.S. Mint each year. The mint plans to issue both types of cents through 1982, in the hope that people will not try to hoard the doomed 95-percent copper version. Experts say that the only way to tell the two versions apart will be by weight—the copper-coated zinc coins will be lighter.

ROBERT F. LEMKE
Numismatics News

PRETTY POTS

Your special plants deserve special pots. Even ordinary plants will look brighter and more cheerful if they are placed in pots that have been designed just for them.

To make these decorative pots, you can use almost any kind of watertight container—a regular clay or plastic flowerpot, a coffee can, an old bucket, or the bottom half of a large plastic bleach bottle.

Match or blend the containers with the decor of the room in which they will be placed. Perhaps there is some fabric left over from a tablecloth made for the kitchen table. Use the leftover fabric on pots that will be in the kitchen. Flower pots that will be kept in your bedroom might be covered with cartoon decals or pictures of racing cars.

Before you begin, make sure that the container is clean and dry. And plan your design on a piece of paper first.

CRAZY CALICO

You'll need a plastic container, scraps of calico or other printed fabrics, scissors, and white glue.

Cut a strip of fabric wide enough to cover the top edge of the container. Cut a second strip wide enough to circle the bottom few inches of the container. Glue the strips in place.

Now cut out a number of triangles of different patterns and sizes. If you use pinking shears, the triangles will have notched edges.

Arrange the triangles in an interesting overlapping design. Try not to put two triangles of the same fabric next to each other. When the arrangement pleases you, glue the triangles onto the container.

PAINTED POTS

You'll need tin cans, acrylic spray paint and poster paints, a paint brush, and decals.

Cover the entire outside of each can with spray paint. After the paint has dried, add painted designs or decals—or both.

Unlike clay and plastic containers, coffee cans and other tin cans should not hold plants directly. The cans, which consist mainly of steel, will rust after a while. It's better to use the tin cans as "jackets" for clay or plastic pots. In fact, this is a good way to hide your old chipped or stained pots.

Put a thin layer of pebbles in the bottom of each tin can before inserting a flowerpot. This makes it easier for excess water to drain away from the plant's roots.

Tin containers can also be decorated with holiday designs. A white can with a green and red holly design painted on it would add a charming touch to any room at Christmastime. A green can with bright red heart decals would be attractive for Valentine's Day. It's easy to substitute these containers for the plants' regular containers for a while.

CLAY CACTI

You'll need a clay (terra cotta) pot and felt-tipped markers in several colors.

Ordinary clay flowerpots can be turned into exciting works of art. They can be covered with many different kinds of designs. Perhaps you might create a group of pots that will hold cactus plants. The pots could be decorated with desert scenes and patterns like those on Indian blankets.

Or design a city street scene, a country meadow, or big bold flowers. Geometric patterns look especially good on clay.

Some colors will work better than others on clay. Browns, bright reds, and dark greens are good. Pale pinks and blues tend to look washed out. Test various colors on the underside of the pot before drawing on the designs.

FELT FUN

You'll need a plastic container, printed fabrics, pieces of felt, scissors, and white glue.

Cover the container with the fabric. You can use one kind of fabric or several kinds with different designs. This will form the background for the felt cutouts that you will paste on.

You can make your own designs for the felt cutouts, or you can trace designs from books. Felt cutouts of your home and some trees could be placed on green polka dots. Bright red felt horses could gallop across a field of yellow flowers. A black felt cat or two could sit on an orange-striped background.

Use felt-tipped markers to add details, such as windows and a door on a house. Green sequins could be used for the cat's eyes.

WRAPPED IN YARN

You'll need a plastic container, yarn in several colors, scissors, and glue.

Draw a line from the top of the container to the bottom. As you wrap the yarn around the container, begin and end all pieces along this line. This side of the container should be placed toward the wall so that people won't see the yarn ends. But try to cover each yarn end with the beginning of the next piece of yarn. This will keep the yarn from unraveling and will give a neater look.

Begin at the top of the container and work downward. Put a thin thread of glue on the container, then press and briefly hold the yarn in place. Keep the rows horizontal and evenly spaced.

HIDDEN ANTS

Some ants live in the ground, some ants live in houses . . . and some ants live in words. Lots of words contain ants. Here are 20 of them. On a separate piece of paper, try to figure out what the words are.

The solution is on page 381.

ANT WORD	DEFINITION
1. __ __ ANT	It has green leaves and flowers.
2. __ ANT __	People wear these on the lower part of their bodies.
3. ANT __ __ __ __	An animal that uses its long tongue to catch its food.
4. __ __ ANT	A very, very big person.
5. __ ANT	Desire; wish; long for.
6. __ __ ANT	He was the 18th president of the United States.
7. ANT __ __ __ __ __ __	The area around the South Pole.
8. __ ANT __	He visits children at Christmastime.
9. __ __ __ __ ANT	Firefighters draw water from it.
10. __ ANT __ __ __	A kind of lamp.
11. __ __ ANT	A slope or incline.
12. __ __ __ ANT	A child who stays away from school without permission.
13. ANT __ __ __ __ __	A graceful animal with horns.
14. __ ANT __ __ __ __ __	A kind of melon.
15. ANT __ __ __ __ __ __	A substance added to a car radiator to prevent freezing.
16. __ ANT __ __ __	A product of a person's imagination.
17. __ __ __ __ ANT	A long-tailed bird.
18. ANT __ __ __ __	A very old object.
19. __ __ __ __ ANT	Pleasing; very nice.
20. __ __ __ __ ANT	To put under a spell.

SPORTS

During 1981, the world's two finest tennis players continued their fierce rivalry. In the major showdowns—Wimbledon and the U.S. Open—John McEnroe defeated Bjorn Borg and became number one.

A three-run home run by Ron Cey helped propel the Los Angeles Dodgers over the New York Yankees in the World Series.

BASEBALL

Bizarre was the word for the 1981 baseball season. A 49-day strike by the players in mid-season interrupted the pennant races. As a result, the schedule was reduced from 162 games to an average of 105 contests per team. And there was an additional round of playoffs leading up to the World Series.

The strike ended when management and players reached an agreement after seven weeks of negotiations. Baseball executives decreed that the 1981 season would be a "split" season. The won-lost records of the teams as of June 12, the day the strike began, would determine the first-half champions in each division. The teams would then begin with clean slates when play resumed on August 10, and the teams with the best records in each division would be second-half champions. The first-half and second-half champs would then have intra-divisional playoffs prior to the normal East-West competition that determines the league champions.

Only the final act, the World Series, struck a familiar note, for the participants were the long-time adversaries, the Los Angeles Dodgers and the New York Yankees. It was

their eleventh Series confrontation in four decades, stretching back to the era when Brooklyn was the Dodgers' home base. The Yankees had won eight of the ten previous meetings. But this time the Dodgers prevailed, 4 games to 2.

The Yankees captured the first two engagements in New York with comparative ease. They took the opener, 5–3, and blanked the Dodgers, 3–0, in the second game. But the tide turned when the Series moved to Los Angeles. The Dodgers swept the three contests in their home stadium after trailing at some point in each game. They ultimately emerged with one-run decisions, 5–4, 8–7, and 2–1. That brought the teams back to the Bronx, where, including their losing Series efforts in 1977 and 1978, the Dodgers had been beaten six straight times. Again they were briefly behind, but they exploded for seven runs in the fifth and sixth innings for a 9–2 victory that gave them the Series.

Most Valuable Player honors in the Series were shared by three Dodgers: Ron Cey, who delivered a three-run homer in the first

Dodger victory (the third game); Steve Yeager, whose homer was the decisive factor in the fifth game; and Pedro Guerrero, whose double, triple, and homer accounted for five runs in the finale.

It was the first World Series title for the Dodgers since 1965, and their fourth overall. Their comeback from a two-game deficit was the climax of their performance throughout the post-season play.

In the five-game Western Division playoff, the Dodgers were down, 2 games to 0, but then won three straight from the Houston Astros. In the battle for the National League championship, the Montreal Expos, the Eastern Division titlists, led Los Angeles, 2 games to 1, before the Dodgers captured the final two contests for the necessary three victories.

In the American League's first half, the Yankees and the Oakland Athletics finished on top in the East and West, respectively. The National League's East and West leaders were the Philadelphia Phillies and the Dodgers. All four division battles in the second half were very close. The Milwaukee Brewers and the Kansas City Royals emerged on top in the American League East and West, and Montreal and Houston led the National League East and West.

Three of the four intra-divisional series turned out to be five-game battles, with the Yankees winning over Milwaukee, the Dodgers over Houston, and Montreal over Philadelphia, the winner of the 1980 World Series. Only Oakland had an easy time, sweeping Kansas City, the 1980 American League champions, 3 games to 0.

In the final playoffs before the World Series, the Yankees captured their 33rd American League pennant with a three-game sweep over Oakland. The Dodgers took three out of five from Montreal.

The split-season arrangement left considerable bitterness, particularly in St. Louis and Cincinnati. The Cardinals and the Reds had the best season-long won-lost percentages in their respective divisions. But neither led its division for the first half or the second half, and thus neither qualified for the playoffs.

Baseball's strangest season produced some remarkable individual performances.

First-year pitcher Fernando Valenzuela of the Dodgers pitched eight shutouts. This was a record for a rookie pitcher—and a really remarkable record, considering that the season was shortened by more than 50 games. Southpaw Valenzuela had a 13–7 record, and he led the major leagues with 180 strikeouts. The young Mexican citizen won the Cy Young Award as the league's best pitcher, the first rookie ever to do so. He was also named the National League's rookie of the year.

Mike Schmidt of the Phillies was the winner of the National League's Most Valuable Player award for the second year in a row. His major-league-leading 31 home runs and 91 runs batted in would be a good year's work for a regular 162–game season.

Ace relief pitcher Rollie Fingers of the Brewers won both the American League's Cy Young Award and the MVP award. The tall right-hander had a 6–3 record and a classy 1.04 earned run average (ERA). Most important for a reliever, Fingers was credited with 28 saves. He was the first relief pitcher ever to be the American League's MVP.

Other outstanding individual performances included: A record fifth career no-hitter by pitcher Nolan Ryan of the Astros; a third National League batting title for Pittsburgh Pirate Bill Madlock (.341); and the American League batting crown for Carney Lansford of the Red Sox (.336).

Dodger pitcher Fernando Valenzuela won the National League's Rookie of the Year and Cy Young awards.

MAJOR LEAGUE BASEBALL FINAL STANDINGS

FIRST HALF

AMERICAN LEAGUE

Eastern Division

	W	L	Pct.	GB
New York	34	22	.607	-
Baltimore	31	23	.574	2
Milwaukee	31	25	.554	3
Detroit	31	26	.544	3½
Boston	30	26	.536	4
Cleveland	26	24	.520	5
Toronto	16	42	.276	19

Western Division

	W	L	Pct.	GB
Oakland	37	23	.617	-
Texas	33	22	.600	1½
Chicago	31	22	.585	2½
California	31	29	.517	6
Kansas City	20	30	.400	12
Seattle	21	36	.368	14½
Minnesota	17	39	.304	18

NATIONAL LEAGUE

Eastern Division

	W	L	Pct.	GB
Philadelphia	34	21	.618	-
St. Louis	30	20	.600	1½
Montreal	30	25	.545	4
Pittsburgh	25	23	.521	5½
New York	17	34	.333	15
Chicago	15	37	.288	17½

Western Division

	W	L	Pct.	GB
Los Angeles	36	21	.632	-
Cincinnati	35	21	.625	½
Houston	28	29	.491	8
Atlanta	25	29	.463	9½
San Francisco	27	32	.458	10
San Diego	23	33	.411	12½

SECOND HALF

AMERICAN LEAGUE

Eastern Division

	W	L	Pct.	GB
Milwaukee	31	22	.585	-
Boston	29	23	.558	1½
Detroit	29	23	.558	1½
Baltimore	28	23	.549	2
Cleveland	26	27	.491	5
New York	25	26	.490	5
Toronto	21	27	.438	7½

Western Division

	W	L	Pct.	GB
Kansas City	30	23	.566	-
Oakland	27	22	.551	1
Texas	24	26	.480	4½
Minnesota	24	29	.453	6
Seattle	23	29	.442	6½
Chicago	23	30	.434	7
California	20	30	.400	8½

NATIONAL LEAGUE

Eastern Division

	W	L	Pct.	GB
Montreal	30	23	.566	-
St. Louis	29	23	.558	½
Philadelphia	25	27	.481	4½
New York	24	28	.462	5½
Chicago	23	28	.451	6
Pittsburgh	21	33	.389	9½

Western Division

	W	L	Pct.	GB
Houston	33	20	.623	-
Cincinnati	31	21	.596	1½
San Francisco	29	23	.558	3½
Los Angeles	27	26	.509	6
Atlanta	25	27	.481	7½
San Diego	18	36	.333	15½

PENNANT WINNERS

American League: New York Yankees
National League: Los Angeles Dodgers

MAJOR LEAGUE LEADERS

AMERICAN LEAGUE

Batting
(top 10 qualifiers)

	AB	H	Pct.
Lansford, Boston	399	134	.336
Gibson, Detroit	290	95	.328
Paciorek, Seattle	405	132	.326
Cooper, Milwaukee	416	133	.320
Henderson, Oakland	423	135	.319
Hargrove, Cleveland	322	102	.317
G. Brett, Kansas City	347	109	.314
Zisk, Seattle	357	111	.311
Oliver, Texas	421	130	.309
Remy, Boston	358	110	.307

Pitching
(top 5 qualifiers, based on ERA)

	W	L	ERA
McCatty, Oakland	14	7	2.32
Stewart, Baltimore	4	8	2.33
Lamp, Chicago	7	6	2.41
John, New York	9	8	2.63
Burns, Chicago	10	6	2.64

Home Runs

	HR
Armas, Oakland	22
Evans, Boston	22
Grich, California	22
Murray, Baltimore	22
Luzinski, Chicago	21
Thomas, Milwaukee	21

NATIONAL LEAGUE

Batting
(top 10 qualifiers)

	AB	H	Pct.
Madlock, Pittsburgh	279	95	.341
Rose, Philadelphia	431	140	.325
Baker, Los Angeles	400	128	.320
Schmidt, Philadelphia	354	112	.316
Buckner, Chicago	421	131	.311
Griffey, Cincinnati	396	123	.311
May, San Francisco	316	98	.310
Brooks, New York	358	110	.307
Concepcion, Cincinnati	421	129	.306
Hernandez, Saint Louis	376	115	.306

Pitching
(top 5 qualifiers, based on ERA)

	W	L	ERA
Ryan, Houston	11	5	1.69
Knepper, Houston	9	5	2.18
Hooton, Los Angeles	11	6	2.28
Reuss, Los Angeles	10	4	2.30
Carlton, Philadelphia	13	4	2.42

Home Runs

	HR
Schmidt, Philadelphia	31
Dawson, Montreal	24
Foster, Cincinnati	22
Kingman, New York	22
Hendrick, Saint Louis	18
Clark, San Francisco	17

1981 WORLD SERIES RESULTS

		R	H	E	Winning/Losing Pitcher
1	Los Angeles	3	5	0	Jerry Reuss
	New York	5	6	0	Ron Guidry
2	Los Angeles	0	4	2	Burt Hooton
	New York	3	6	1	Tommy John
3	New York	4	9	0	George Frazier
	Los Angeles	5	11	1	Fernando Valenzuela
4	New York	7	13	1	George Frazier
	Los Angeles	8	14	2	Steve Howe
5	New York	1	5	0	Ron Guidry
	Los Angeles	2	4	3	Jerry Reuss
6	Los Angeles	9	13	1	Burt Hooton
	New York	2	7	2	George Frazier

Rollie Fingers, the American League's MVP.

Chang Cheng-ching scores for Taiwan in the final game of the Little League World Series, as a Tampa, Florida, player looks on helplessly. Taiwan won the championship for the fifth consecutive year.

LITTLE LEAGUE BASEBALL

Taiwan's Little League teams come from various cities on that Far Eastern island. But when they reach the Little League World Series in Williamsport, Pennsylvania, the result is invariably the same—they win.

In 1981, a Taiwan entry (Tai-Ping from the city of Tai-Chung) captured the championship for the fifth consecutive year and for the tenth time since 1969. This record for consistent success is probably unmatched in any continuing sports competition.

For the second straight year, Taiwan's opponent in the championship game was Tampa, Florida. And the 4–2 victory was the only reasonably close decision of the three games involving the Taiwanese at Williamsport. In the first round of the tournament, they defeated Monterrey, Mexico, 10–0. In the semifinal, they overwhelmed Trail, British Columbia, Canada, 16–0. Each of those shutouts was achieved on one-hit performances, pitched by Chang Ming-pin and Tsai Chi-wan, respectively.

In the final against Tampa, the big hit for Taiwan was Chang Cheng-ching's fourth-inning triple, which drove in two runs. Chang subsequently scored on a wild pitch by Tampa's hurler Derek Bell.

Taiwan held a 4–0 lead after four innings behind pitcher Wang Yao-hsin. In the top of the fifth, Derrick Pedro walloped a two-run homer for Tampa. Chang Ming-pin, Taiwan's pitcher in the first round, replaced Wang and held the Floridians scoreless for the remainder of the six-inning game. Wang was credited with the victory.

Tampa had reached the final with victories over Stamford, Connecticut, 6–3, and Barrington, Illinois, 11–10. The other competitors in this 35th annual Little League World Series—Escondido, California, and SHAFE, Belgium—were both defeated in the first round. The SHAFE team was composed of sons of U.S. and Canadian personnel assigned to Supreme Headquarters for Allied Forces in Europe.

BASKETBALL

The National Basketball Association (NBA) has become noted for its continually changing champions. And 1981 was no different—for the twelfth year in a row, professional basketball got a new winner. But the 1981 champs, the Boston Celtics, were not strangers in the seats of power. When they defeated the Houston Rockets in the final playoff series, the Celtics became the titlists for the 14th time in the 35-year history of the NBA.

Boston defeated Houston 4 games to 2. The teams had been deadlocked at 2–2 before the Rockets were overpowered in the fifth and sixth games, 109–80 and 102–91.

The Celtics had survived a more difficult journey in their semifinal series against the Philadelphia 76ers, with whom they shared the honor of compiling the league's best regular-season record (62–20). In the seven-game playoff, the 76ers captured three of the first four engagements. This left the Celtics with a 3–1 deficit, which is difficult for teams in any of the major sports to overcome.

The Celtics then had to battle through three tense, close games to avoid being eliminated. In the fifth and sixth contests, they emerged with winning scores of 111–109 and 100–98. And in the final contest against the 76ers, the championship was decided by just one point, 91–90.

No one in the Boston cast, including Coach Bill Fitch, had been part of previous Celtic championships. Cedric Maxwell was chosen most valuable player (MVP) in the post-season competition. But he had such able colleagues as Larry Bird, Robert Parish, Chris Ford, and Nate Archibald.

The Houston Rockets reached the championship series for the first time in their 14 years of existence. This was especially astonishing in view of their regular-season record (40–42), a tie for low among the playoff entries. They provided a shocker by eliminating the 1980 champion Los Angeles Lakers in the first round, 2 games to 1. Then they defeated San Antonio and Kansas City to qualify for the meeting with Boston.

College Play. Indiana University captured the National Collegiate Athletic Association

Indiana University, spearheaded by Isiah Thomas (11), captured the NCAA title for the fourth time.

The Boston Celtics' Larry Bird (33) helped his team beat the Houston Rockets for the NBA championship.

(NCAA) title for the fourth time. The team was led by Coach Bobby Knight and spearheaded by All-American sophomore guard Isiah Thomas. The Hoosiers had entered the post-season tournament with a modest 21–9 record. But they overwhelmed their five opponents, defeating 31-game winner Louisiana State, 67–49, in the semifinal, and North Carolina University, 63–50, in the championship contest.

Indiana's nine defeats were the most by any team that subsequently won an NCAA title. But in their five tournament games, the Hoosiers' average margin of victory was 22.6 points.

Louisiana Tech won the championship of the Association for Intercollegiate Athletics for Women (AIAW), defeating the University of Tennessee in the tournament final, 79–59. The victory was the 34th of the season for the Louisiana girls, who were undefeated. As champion, Louisiana Tech succeeded Old Dominion University, the titlist the previous two years.

NBA FINAL STANDINGS

EASTERN CONFERENCE

Atlantic Division

	W	L	Pct.
Boston	62	20	.756
Philadelphia	62	20	.756
New York	50	32	.610
Washington	39	43	.476
New Jersey	24	58	.293

Central Division

	W	L	Pct.
Milwaukee	60	22	.732
Chicago	45	37	.549
Indiana	44	38	.537
Atlanta	31	51	.378
Cleveland	28	54	.341
Detroit	21	61	.256

WESTERN CONFERENCE

Midwest Division

	W	L	Pct.
San Antonio	52	30	.634
Kansas City	40	42	.488
Houston	40	42	.488
Denver	37	45	.451
Utah	28	54	.341
Dallas	15	67	.183

Pacific Division

	W	L	Pct.
Phoenix	57	25	.695
Los Angeles	54	28	.659
Portland	45	37	.549
Golden State	39	43	.476
San Diego	36	46	.439
Seattle	34	48	.415

NBA Championship: Boston Celtics

COLLEGE BASKETBALL

Conference	Winner
Atlantic Coast	Virginia (regular season) North Carolina (tournament)
Big Eight	Missouri (regular season) Kansas (tournament)
Big Ten	Indiana
Ivy League	Princeton
Mid-American	Toledo (regular season) Ball State (tournament)
Missouri Valley	Wichita State (regular season) Creighton (tournament)
Pacific Ten	Oregon State
Southeastern	Louisiana State (regular season) Mississippi (tournament)
Southwest	Arkansas (regular season) Houston (tournament)
West Coast Athletic	San Francisco
Western Athletic	Utah/Wyoming (tied)

NCAA: Indiana

National Invitation Tournament: Tulsa

FOOTBALL

A resurrected quarterback and a quick-handed linebacker were the stars of Super Bowl XV, played in the New Orleans Superdome on January 25, 1981. Quarterback Jim Plunkett, "reborn" after his career had been considered finished, threw three touchdown passes in leading the Oakland Raiders to a 27–10 victory over the Philadelphia Eagles. And Oakland linebacker Rod Martin, he of the fast hands, picked off three of Eagle quarterback Ron Jaworski's passes, setting a Super Bowl record for interceptions.

With his blockers giving him excellent protection, Plunkett completed 13 of 21 passes for 261 yards. The longest was an 80-yard touchdown play, with Kenny King on the receiving end. Plunkett's other two touchdown passes were to Cliff Branch, on plays of 2 and 29 yards. It was an exciting victory for the Raiders, who had entered the playoffs as one of the wild-card teams in the American Conference. The Raiders' triumph marked the first time a wild-card team had won the Super Bowl.

But if Oakland finished the 1980–81 season in ecstasy, they finished their 1981–82 season in dismay. They wound up with a 7–9 record, and they did not make the playoffs. And Oakland fans were upset by the management's desire to move the team to Los Angeles.

Things were far brighter on the other side of San Francisco Bay. The 49ers had an outstanding season in 1981–82. Led by quarterback Joe Montana, they won the National Conference Western Division title with a record of 13–3, best in the National Football League. Montana's favorite target was Dwight Clark, who caught 85 passes, a 49er team record. San Francisco was not only an offensive team, though. Its defense was one of the stingiest in the NFL.

The other division titlists were Dallas (12–4) and Tampa Bay (9–7) in the National Con-

Tony Dorsett (33) gained 1,646 yards, second in the NFL, to lead the Dallas Cowboys to a division title.

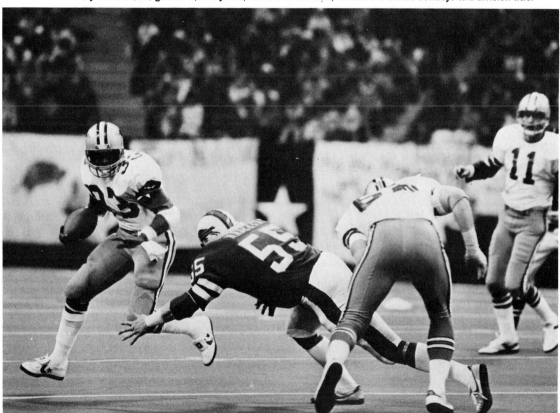

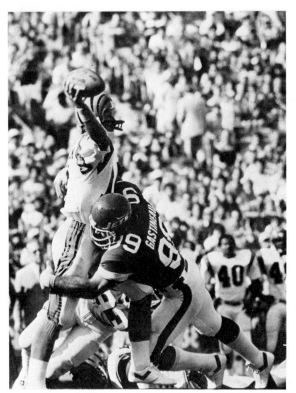

Cincinnati Bengal quarterback Ken Anderson led the American Conference in passing.

ference and Cincinnati (12–4), Miami (11–4–1), and San Diego (10–6) in the American Conference. The other National Conference teams in the playoffs were Philadelphia (10–6) and the New York Giants (9–7); the other American Conference teams were the New York Jets (10–5–1) and Buffalo (10–6).

Tony Dorsett's fine season helped the Dallas Cowboys to their excellent record. He gained 1,646 yards rushing, second in the NFL to New Orleans Saints' rookie George Rogers. Rogers' total of 1,674 was an NFL record for rookies.

The Cincinnati Bengals roared into the playoffs behind the passing of Ken Anderson, whose statistics led the American Conference. He completed 62.6 percent of his passes for a total of 3,754 yards.

Quarterback Dan Fouts of San Diego surpassed the 4,000-yard mark for the third year in a row. His total of 4,802 in passing yardage broke his year-old record of 4,715.

New York City football fans were over-joyed when both the Jets and the Giants made the playoffs—the first time they had done so in the same year. At the other end of New York State, the Buffalo Bills also made the playoffs—thus three of the four wild-card teams were from the Empire State.

In the Canadian Football League, the Edmonton Eskimos won the Grey Cup championship for the fourth straight year. Trailing 20–1 at halftime, they surged back to beat the Ottawa Rough Riders 26–23. Dave Cutler kicked the winning field goal with three seconds left in the game to break a 23–23 tie. Ottawa quarterback J. C. Watts, who played college football at Oklahoma, was named the game's outstanding offensive player.

College Play. Southern teams stood at the top of the rankings as the regular season ended. Clemson, of South Carolina, went undefeated and untied, finishing 11–0–0, and was ranked number one in the country. Georgia (10–1–0) was second, and Alabama (9–1–1) was third.

The winner of the Heisman Trophy, as the nation's outstanding college player, was Marcus Allen of the University of Southern California. A senior, Allen set an NCAA rushing record of 2,342 yards—no one before him had topped 2,000. Allen averaged 5.8 yards per carry, scored 23 touchdowns, and rushed for more than 200 yards in a record eight games.

Second in the balloting for the Heisman was Herschel Walker of Georgia. Walker, the powerful running back with the world-class sprinter's speed, had finished third in 1980. Only a sophomore, he would have two more chances to win the Heisman, unless he decided to enter the NFL before graduating.

Alabama's coach, Paul "Bear" Bryant, became the "winningest" coach in college football history. When the Alabama Crimson Tide beat Auburn in the last game of the regular season, Bryant had his 315th victory, surpassing by one the total of legendary coach Amos Alonzo Stagg.

Alabama met Texas (9–1–1) in the Cotton Bowl; Georgia faced Pittsburgh (10–1–0) in the Sugar Bowl; Iowa (8–3–0) played Washington (9–2–0) in the Rose Bowl; Clemson took on Nebraska (9–2–0) in the Orange Bowl; and Arkansas (8–3–0) faced North Carolina (9–2–0) in the Gator Bowl.

Marcus Allen of Southern California won the 1981 Heisman Trophy.

COLLEGE FOOTBALL

Conference	Winner
Atlantic Coast	Clemson
Big Eight	Nebraska
Big Ten	Iowa, Ohio State (tied)
Ivy League	Yale, Dartmouth (tied)
Mid-American	Toledo
Pacific Ten	Washington
Southeastern	Georgia, Alabama (tied)
Southern	Furman
Southwest	Southern Methodist
Western Athletic	Brigham Young

Cotton Bowl: Texas
Gator Bowl: North Carolina
Orange Bowl: Clemson
Rose Bowl: Washington
Sugar Bowl: Pittsburgh

Heisman Trophy: Marcus Allen, Southern California

NFL FINAL STANDINGS

AMERICAN CONFERENCE

Eastern Division

	W	L	T	Pct.	PF	PA
Miami	11	4	1	.719	345	275
N.Y. Jets	10	5	1	.656	355	287
Buffalo	10	6	0	.625	311	276
Baltimore	2	14	0	.125	259	533
New England	2	14	0	.125	322	370

Central Division

	W	L	T	Pct.	PF	PA
*Cincinnati	12	4	0	.750	421	304
Pittsburgh	8	8	0	.500	356	297
Houston	7	9	0	.438	281	355
Cleveland	5	11	0	.313	276	375

Western Division

	W	L	T	Pct.	PF	PA
San Diego	10	6	0	.625	478	390
Denver	10	6	0	.625	321	289
Kansas City	9	7	0	.563	343	290
Oakland	7	9	0	.438	273	343
Seattle	6	10	0	.375	322	388

NATIONAL CONFERENCE

Eastern Division

	W	L	T	Pct.	PF	PA
Dallas	12	4	0	.750	367	277
Philadelphia	10	6	0	.625	368	221
N.Y. Giants	9	7	0	.563	295	257
Washington	8	8	0	.500	347	349
St. Louis	7	9	0	.438	315	408

Central Division

	W	L	T	Pct.	PF	PA
Tampa Bay	9	7	0	.563	315	268
Detroit	8	8	0	.500	397	322
Green Bay	8	8	0	.500	324	361
Minnesota	7	9	0	.438	325	369
Chicago	6	10	0	.375	253	324

Western Division

	W	L	T	Pct.	PF	PA
*San Francisco	13	3	0	.813	357	250
Atlanta	7	9	0	.438	426	355
Los Angeles	6	10	0	.375	303	351
New Orleans	4	12	0	.250	207	378

*Conference Champions and Super Bowl Contenders

Nineteen-year-old Nathaniel Crosby (son of the late Bing Crosby), after winning the U.S. Amateur golf championship.

GOLF

PROFESSIONAL		AMATEUR	
	Individual		Individual
Masters	Tom Watson	U.S. Amateur	Nathaniel Crosby
U.S. Open	David Graham	U.S. Women's Amateur	Juli Inkster
Canadian Open	Peter Oosterhuis	British Amateur	Phillipe Ploujoux
British Open	Bill Rogers	British Ladies Amateur	Belle Robertson
PGA	Larry Nelson	Canadian Amateur	Richard Zokol
World Series of Golf	Bill Rogers	Canadian Ladies Amateur	Jane Lock
U.S. Women's Open	Pat Bradley		
Ladies PGA	Donna Caponi		
	Team		Team
Ryder Cup	United States	Walker Cup	United States

HOCKEY

In 1981, the New York Islanders captured the Stanley Cup—the symbol of the National Hockey League (NHL) championship—for the second straight season. Their triumph over the Minnesota North Stars, 4 games to 1 in the final playoff series, was the climax of a campaign during which the Islanders had consistently displayed awesome power.

It was in sharp contrast to their first success, in 1980. At that time, the Islanders emerged as champions after only a modest regular-season performance. But in 1981, they finished at the top of the standings after the 80-game schedule—with 48 victories, 18 defeats, and 14 ties for a total of 110 points.

From mid-February until the end of the regular season, the Islanders lost only three games. They were just as impressive during the post-season competition, with 15 victories in 18 engagements. They swept through the Toronto Maple Leafs, 3 games to 0, in the preliminary playoff. They eliminated the Edmonton Oilers, 4 games to 2, in the quarterfinals. They then qualified for the championship round with Minnesota by routing the New York Rangers, 4 games to 0.

On the way to their Stanley Cup triumph, the Islanders won eight consecutive playoff contests—the last of the Edmonton series, four in a row against the Rangers, and the first three against Minnesota (with scores of 6–3, 6–3, and 7–5). The North Stars delayed the inevitable by winning the fourth game, 4–2, before succumbing in the finale, 5–1.

Robert (Butch) Goring, the Islanders' center, was awarded the Conn Smythe Trophy as the most valuable player in the Stanley Cup competition. Goring repeatedly played well while other Islander stars, such as Bryan Trottier and Denis Potvin, performed somewhat below their normal abilities because of injuries.

Goring's major contribution was two goals in the last contest of the final series. But he was a fiery, aggressive skater throughout the playoffs. There were other impressive individual achievements: Mike Bossy's 17 goals and an NHL playoff record of 35 points; Trottier's record streak of 18 playoff games in which he scored at least one point; and Potvin's 25 points in the playoffs, a record for a defenseman.

Minnesota, while understandably the underdog against the defending champion Islanders, nevertheless achieved a success by reaching the Stanley Cup finals for the first time. The North Stars were ninth in the NHL's final standings, but they were impressive in the competition leading to the

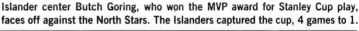

Islander center Butch Goring, who won the MVP award for Stanley Cup play, faces off against the North Stars. The Islanders captured the cup, 4 games to 1.

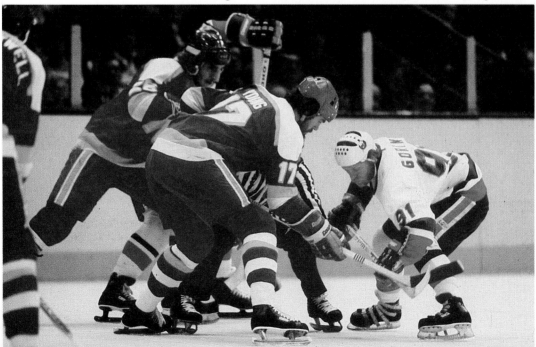

confrontation with the Islanders. They swept the Boston Bruins, 3 games to 0, in the preliminary playoff; then defeated the Buffalo Sabres, 4 games to 1, and the Calgary Flames, 4 games to 2.

The most surprising result in the post-season skirmishing was the defeat of the Montreal Canadiens by the Edmonton Oilers in three straight games of a preliminary playoff round. The Canadiens, who had the third highest regular-season record, thus failed to reach at least the semifinals for the second successive season.

Edmonton's Wayne Gretzky won the Hart Trophy as the NHL's most valuable player. He was the league's high scorer during the season with a record 164 points, the result of 55 goals and 109 assists.

The Canada Cup Tournament. The second Canada Cup tournament was played in 1981, with some of the world's best hockey players participating. Six nations competed in the international event—Canada, Czechoslovakia, Finland, Sweden, the Soviet Union, and the United States.

Team Canada, which had won the Cup in 1976, was the strong favorite to win. Its all-star squad was loaded with top NHL talent—including Bossy, Potvin, Trottier, and Gretzky. But in an astonishing championship game, the national team of the Soviet Union scored an overwhelming 8–1 victory over the Canadians. The one-sided result was even more surprising in view of Canada's defeat of the Soviets in an exhibition game prior to the Canada Cup, its four victories and one tie in the tournament's preliminary round (including another triumph, 7–3, over the Russians), and its easy 4–1 defeat of the U.S. squad in the semifinals.

With the silver trophy and a claim to world hockey supremacy at stake in the finale, the Canadians were able to hold the Soviets in check only during a scoreless first period, and briefly during a 1–1 deadlock in the second period. Thereafter, the Soviets riddled the Canadian goaltender, Mike Liut, the NHL's premier goalie, with two more tallies in the second period and five in the third. Meanwhile, the Soviet goaltender, Vladislav Tretyak, was giving a superlative performance, blocking 26 of the 27 shots fired at him by the Canadian team.

NHL FINAL STANDINGS

CAMPBELL CONFERENCE

Patrick Division

	W	L	T	Pts.
N.Y. Islanders	48	18	14	110
Philadelphia	41	24	15	97
Calgary	39	27	14	92
N.Y. Rangers	30	36	14	74
Washington	26	36	18	70

Smythe Division

	W	L	T	Pts.
St. Louis	45	18	17	107
Chicago	31	33	16	78
Vancouver	28	32	20	76
Edmonton	29	35	16	74
Colorado	22	45	13	57
Winnipeg	9	57	14	32

WALES CONFERENCE

Adams Division

	W	L	T	Pts.
Buffalo	39	20	21	99
Boston	37	30	13	87
Minnesota	35	28	17	87
Quebec	30	32	18	78
Toronto	28	37	15	71

Norris Division

	W	L	T	Pts.
Montreal	45	22	13	103
Los Angeles	43	24	13	99
Pittsburgh	30	37	13	73
Hartford	21	41	18	60
Detroit	19	43	18	56

Stanley Cup: New York Islanders

OUTSTANDING PLAYERS

Hart Trophy (most valuable player)	Wayne Gretzky, Edmonton
Ross Trophy (scorer)	Wayne Gretzky, Edmonton
Vezina Trophy (goalies)	Richard Sevigny, Denis Herron, Michel Larocque, Montreal
Norris Trophy (defenseman)	Randy Carlyle, Pittsburgh
Selke Trophy (defensive forward)	Bob Gainey, Montreal
Calder Trophy (rookie)	Peter Stastny, Quebec
Lady Byng Trophy (sportsmanship)	Rick Kehoe, Pittsburgh
Conn Smythe Trophy (Stanley Cup play)	Butch Goring, N.Y. Islanders

In 1981, Phil Mahre became the first American to win a World Cup skiing championship.

ICE SKATING

FIGURE SKATING

World Championships

Men	Scott Hamilton, U.S.
Women	Denise Biellmann, Switzerland
Pairs	Irina Vorobieva/Igor Lisovsky, U.S.S.R.
Dance	Jayne Torvill/Christopher Dean, Britain

United States Championships

Men	Scott Hamilton
Women	Elaine Zayak
Pairs	Peter Carruthers/Caitlin Carruthers
Dance	Judy Blumberg/Michael Seibert

SPEED SKATING

World Championships

Men	Amund Sjoebrend, Norway
Women	Natalya Petruseva, U.S.S.R.

SKIING

WORLD CUP CHAMPIONSHIPS

Men	Phil Mahre, U.S.
Women	Marie-Theres Nadig, Switzerland

U.S. CHAMPIONSHIPS

ALPINE

Men's Downhill	Doug Powell, New York
Men's Slalom	Steve Mahre, Washington
Men's Giant Slalom	Phil Mahre, Washington
Women's Downhill	Holly Flanders, New Hampshire
Women's Slalom	Cindy Nelson, Minnesota
Women's Giant Slalom	Tamara McKinney, California

NORDIC

Men's 15k Cross-Country	Bill Koch, Vermont
Men's 30k Cross-Country	Bill Koch
Men's 50k Cross-Country	Tim Caldwell, Vermont
Women's 5k Cross-Country	Allison Owen-Spencer, Washington
Women's 10k Cross-Country	Allison Owen-Spencer
Women's 20k Cross-Country	Lynn Spencer Galanes, Vermont

High-scoring New York Cosmo Giorgio Chinaglia (9) was named MVP for the 1981 season of the North American Soccer League. But he was thwarted in the Soccer Bowl *(above)*. Chicago Sting defender Frantz Mathieu (7) stayed close to Chinaglia and helped prevent him from scoring. The Sting won the Soccer Bowl, 1–0, in an overtime shootout. Mathieu was named the game's MVP.

SOCCER

NORTH AMERICAN SOCCER LEAGUE
FINAL STANDINGS

Eastern Division

	W	L	GF	GA	Pts.
New York	23	9	80	49	200
Montreal	15	17	63	57	141
Washington	15	17	59	58	135
Toronto	7	25	39	82	77

Southern Division

	W	L	GF	GA	Pts.
Atlanta	17	15	62	60	151
Fort Lauderdale	18	14	54	46	144
Jacksonville	18	14	51	46	141
Tampa Bay	15	17	63	64	139

Central Division

	W	L	GF	GA	Pts.
Chicago	23	9	84	50	195
Minnesota	19	13	63	57	163
Tulsa	17	15	60	49	154
Dallas	5	27	27	71	54

Western Division

	W	L	GF	GA	Pts.
San Diego	21	11	68	49	173
Los Angeles	19	13	53	55	160
California	11	21	60	77	117
San Jose	11	21	44	78	108

Northwest Division

	W	L	GF	GA	Pts.
Vancouver	21	11	74	43	186
Calgary	17	15	59	54	151
Portland	17	15	52	49	141
Seattle	15	17	60	62	137
Edmonton	12	20	60	79	123

Soccer Bowl-81: Chicago Sting

SWIMMING

WORLD SWIMMING RECORDS SET IN 1981

EVENT	HOLDER	TIME
	Men	
100-meter freestyle	Rowdy Gaines, U.S.	0:49.36
400-meter freestyle	Vladimir Salnikov, U.S.S.R.	3:45.10
1,500-meter freestyle	Vladimir Salnikov, U.S.S.R.	14:44.09
100-meter butterfly	William Paulus, U.S.	0:53.81
200-meter butterfly	Craig Beardsley, U.S.	1:58.01
200-meter individual medley	Alex Baumann, Canada	2:02.78
	Women	
100-meter breaststroke	Ute Geweniger, E. Germany	1:08.60
100-meter butterfly	Mary T. Meagher, U.S.	0:57.93
200-meter butterfly	Mary T. Meagher, U.S.	2:05.96
200-meter individual medley	Ute Geweniger, E. Germany	2:11.73
800-meter freestyle relay	U.S. team	8:07.44

Alex Baumann of Canada swims to a world record in the 200-meter individual medley.

Tracy Austin recaptured the U.S. Open championship, which she had won as a 16-year-old in 1979.

TENNIS

John McEnroe of the United States was recognized as the world's outstanding tennis player after he captured the two most prestigious tournaments of 1981. He won the men's singles titles at Wimbledon, in July, and at the U.S. Open, in September.

In the final matches of both tournaments, 22-year-old McEnroe defeated Bjorn Borg of Sweden, who had previously been considered the world's best. When McEnroe won at Wimbledon (4–6, 7–6, 7–6, 6–4), he snapped Borg's record string of 5 successive championships and 41 straight victorious matches on the historic British grass courts.

The U.S. Open is the only major tournament that Borg has failed to win—in ten tries. And when McEnroe triumphed in 1981, again in four sets (4–6, 6–2, 6–4, 6–3), he became the first player to win as many as three straight U.S. championships since Bill Tilden captured six in a row between 1920 and 1925. McEnroe's win also marked his third consecutive success in a final match against Borg, whom he defeated twice at the U.S. Open and once at Wimbledon. Borg was thus left with one major crown, in the French Open, which he had swept four years in a row.

Glory in the women's division was shared by Chris Evert Lloyd and Tracy Austin, both of the United States. Lloyd won her third Wimbledon title in eight years. Austin recaptured the U.S. Open championship, which she had won as a 16-year-old in 1979.

Lloyd, who had lost three straight Wimbledon finals, emerged with the honors this time by defeating Hana Mandlikova of Czechoslovakia (6–2, 6–2).

Austin, sidelined for several months due to a nerve injury, was eliminated at Wimbledon. But she made a strong comeback in the U.S. final after losing the first set to Martina Navratilova (1–6). Austin was the victor in two tingling tie-breaking sets (7–6, 7–6).

TOURNAMENT TENNIS

	Australian Open	French Open	Wimbledon	U.S. Open
Men's Singles	Brian Teacher, U.S.	Bjorn Borg, Sweden	John McEnroe, U.S.	John McEnroe, U.S.
Women's Singles	Hana Mandlikova, Czechoslovakia	Hana Mandlikova, Czechoslovakia	Chris Evert Lloyd, U.S.	Tracy Austin, U.S.
Men's Doubles	Mark Edmondson, Australia/ Kim Warwick, Australia	Heinz Gunthardt, Switzerland/ Balazs Taroczy, Hungary	Peter Fleming, U.S./ John McEnroe, U.S.	Peter Fleming, U.S./ John McEnroe, U.S.
Women's Doubles	Betsy Nagelsen, U.S./ Martina Navratilova, U.S.	Rosalyn Fairbank, South Africa/ Tanya Harford, South Africa	Martina Navratilova, U.S./ Pam Shriver, U.S.	Kathy Jordan, U.S./ Anne Smith, U.S.

Davis Cup Winner: United States

Renaldo Nehemiah of the United States flies over a hurdle and sets a record in the 110-meter event.

TRACK AND FIELD

WORLD TRACK AND FIELD RECORDS SET IN 1981

EVENT	HOLDER	TIME, DISTANCE, OR POINTS
	Men	
800-meter run	Sebastian Coe, Britain	1:41.72
1,000-meter run	Sebastian Coe, Britain	2:12.18
1-mile run	Sebastian Coe, Britain	3:47.33
5,000-meter run	Henry Rono, Kenya	13:06.20
25,000-meter run	Toshihiko Seko, Japan	1:13:55.80
30,000-meter run	Toshihiko Seko, Japan	1:29:18.80
110-meter hurdles	Renaldo Nehemiah, U.S.	0:12.93
Pole vault	Konstantin Volkov, U.S.S.R.	19' 2"
	Women	
1-mile run	Ludmilla Veselkova, U.S.S.R.	4:20.89
5,000-meter run	Paula Fudge, Britain	15:14.51
Javelin throw	Antoaneta Todorova, Bulgaria	235' 10"
Heptathlon	Ramona Neubert, E. Germany	6,716 pts.

SPORTS BRIEFS

A man called Sugar, a woman with a "windmill," an international tug-of-war, and several other interesting people and events made sports news in 1981.

A CONTROVERSIAL INDY 500

At the Indianapolis 500 auto race, the winner is usually determined by guts, stamina, brains, luck, and simply who has the best car. But in 1981, the winner was determined by a panel of judges from the U.S. Auto Club—four and a half months after the race was run. The May 24 race was marred by several accidents, and more than a third of the 200 laps were run under the yellow caution flag. Under the caution flag, racers must slow down and may not pass each other. On lap 149, Bobby Unser re-entered the race from the pit area and merged with the line of cars. In doing so, he passed at least seven cars. Unser eventually won the race by 5.3 seconds over Mario Andretti. But after the race, Unser was given a one-lap penalty for passing under a yellow flag. He was dropped to second, and Andretti was declared the winner. Unser appealed to the U.S. Auto Club. The panel of judges decided in Unser's favor, giving him his third victory at Indy.

A COED COXSWAIN

On a chilly April day in England, Oxford University's eight-man crew team outrowed its rival Cambridge along the Thames River. But as the muscular young men stroked their way along the 4¼-mile (6.8-kilometer) course, all eyes were on the Oxford coxswain—22-year-old Susan Brown. It was the first time in the race's 152-year history that a woman took part in the competition. The 92-pound (42-kilogram) Brown steered her teammates to an eight-length victory, Oxford's sixth win in a row.

Oxford coxswain Susan Brown holds the trophy while her crewmates raise her aloft in celebration of their victory over Cambridge. She was the first woman ever to take part in the famous race on the Thames River.

TUG-OF-WAR?

Santa Clara, California, was the site of the first World Games, an international competition involving sixteen non-Olympic sports. About 1,000 athletes from 58 nations took part in such sports as bowling, karate, fin swimming, waterskiing, body building, badminton, baseball, and softball. Some spectators were awed and others were merely amused as teams of young men, grunting under the July sun, tried to outpull each other in tug-of-war. Most of these sports have attempted but failed to get into the Olympics. The World Games were set up to provide a showcase for athletes who might otherwise go unrecognized. By the end of the games, one thing was certainly clear: even in non-Olympic sports, the best in the world are pretty good indeed.

MARATHON MILESTONES

Ideal running weather and a strong field spurred on Toshihiko Seko, 24, to a record in the Boston Marathon. Seko, from Japan, ran the April 20 race in 2 hours, 9 minutes, 26 seconds, beating by one second the record set by Bill Rodgers in 1979. The women's winner over the 26.2-mile course (42.2 kilometers) was Allison Roe, 24, of New Zealand. Her time, 2:26:46, was also a Boston record.

Alberto Salazar was only one of 14,500 runners in October's New York Marathon. But he was the one who thrilled the spectators. The 23-year-old from Massachusetts won the race for the second year in a row, and, in the process, he ran the fastest marathon ever run, anywhere, anytime: 2 hours, 8 minutes, 13 seconds. The women's winner also set a world record: 2:25:29. Her name? Allison Roe—the same New Zealander who had won at Boston.

THREE TIMES ACROSS

Swimming across the English Channel has always been considered a difficult feat. Naturally, people were astounded when the first round trip was made—back and forth across

Toshihiko Seko breaks the ribbon at the finish line and sets a record in the Boston Marathon.

the Channel nonstop. In August, 1981, John Erikson of Illinois went one better: a three-way nonstop Channel swim. The waterway is 21 miles (34 kilometers) wide between Dover, England, and Cap Gris Nez, France. Erikson's total time for the historic 63-mile (101-kilometer) journey was about 38½ hours.

THE SOAP BOX DERBY

It rained hard in Akron, Ohio, on August 15, the day of the finals of the 44th All-American Soap Box Derby. But two young people from Ohio muddled through in fine fashion to become the 1981 champions. Tonia Schlegel, 13, won the senior division with a time of 28.33 seconds over the nearly 954-foot (290-meter) course. (Tonia had gone even faster before the final round.) The junior division winner was 11-year-old Howie Fraley, who took his title with a time of 28.90 seconds.

CHAMP VS. CHAMP

When two welterweight boxing champions meet in the ring, you can be sure you'll see a pretty good fight. This took place in September, when Sugar Ray Leonard, the World Boxing Council titleholder, and Thomas (Hit Man) Hearns, the World Boxing Association champ, took each other on. Hearns, the heavy hitter from Michigan, jabbed away at Leonard through the early part of the fight. But Leonard, from Maryland, outboxed his opponent, blasting him through the ropes for a nine-count in the 13th round. In the 14th, Hearns was so badly hurt that the referee stopped the fight. It was the first loss for Hearns in his professional career. The welterweight (147-pound) division now has one champ only: the classy Sugar Ray Leonard.

THE NATIONAL SPORTS FESTIVAL

More than 30 sports, Olympic and non-Olympic, were featured at the third U.S. National Sports Festival. The festival took place in Syracuse, New York, in July. Hometown favorite Mark Caso, 20, was a big winner in men's gymnastics, with a gold medal in the still rings, plus three bronzes in other individual events. Caso showed that he

Howie Fraley, 11, and Tonia Schlegel, 13, were the champions of the 1981 Soap Box Derby.

Gymnast Ron Galimore, who scored a perfect 10 in the vault, shows his form on the rings at the National Sports Festival.

inches (188 centimeters) tall. Her fastball, thrown with her "windmill" delivery, has been timed at 95 miles (153 kilometers) per hour. Her pitches "move" a lot, too. She throws "risers," "drops," and curveballs. She averages better than two strikeouts per inning, and she has pitched many no-hitters. At the festival, Arendsen overpowered some of the best women's teams in the United States. Her goal is to be the "best pitcher ever."

YOUTH SOCCER

The third Youth World Cup soccer tournament, for players aged 20 and under, took place in Australia in October. For the first time, a team from the United States qualified for the tournament, which is held every two years. Among the U.S. players were both college and professional athletes. But the talented U.S. team was eliminated in early play. The championship went to West Germany, which beat Qatar in the final by a score of 4–0. Third place was taken by Rumania, and the team from England came in fourth.

Another star at the National Sports Festival was Kathy Arendsen, an overpowering softball pitcher.

had completely recovered from the broken neck he had suffered a year and a half earlier —he had been temporarily paralyzed from the neck down. The men's gymnastics competition also featured a score of a perfect 10 in the vault by Floridian Ron Galimore. Another big winner at the festival was David Halpern of Washington, who won six medals, including four golds, in men's kayak competition. Halpern had taken up the sport less than a year before. Other multiple winners included Chris Seufert of Michigan, with two golds in women's diving, and Denise Wood of New Jersey, who won two golds in women's track and field.

A WINDMILL WHIZ

One of the big attractions at the National Sports Festival was Kathy Arendsen, a softball pitcher for the Raybestos Brakettes of Connecticut. Arendsen, 22, stands 6 feet 2

MARBLEOUS MARBLES

There is a little world in which you'll find some odd creatures —*aggies, commies, puries, immies, steelies,* and *glassies.* There may also be some *alleys,* and if you're lucky, you may even see a *black beauty.* Into this little world steps a *mibster,* who shoots a *taw,* hoping for a *stick.* A stick means that the mibster may shoot again!

What little world has such creatures in it? Can you guess? It's the world of marbles, a game that has been played for centuries in many different countries and in many different ways. Marbles —those tiny, smooth spheres of glass or stone or steel—are delightful to play with, to look at, and to hold.

Have you ever stuck your hand into a bag of marbles and grabbed a bunch? They are smooth and round and cool to the touch. When you shake a couple in your closed palm, they rattle around with pleasing clicks.

Some marbles may be as small as peas, others as large as golf balls. But most are middle-sized, about as big as a sour ball candy. Glassies—glass marbles—may be clear or opaque. A purie is clear (pure) glass, without a pattern running through it. Aggies are made of polished agate, or they may be made of marble or limestone. Commies are small marbles that are shot at in various marbles games. Immies get their name from the fact that they are imitation aggies, made of glazed or fired clay. An immie may be used as a commie.

Steelies are usually ball bearings. They are often quite heavy because they are made from steel, iron, or brass. Alleys are made of alabaster. Of all these different types of marbles, aggies are thought to be the best, though some people prefer alleys, and a shining purie is lovely indeed. But above all, a collector of marbles will cherish a black beauty. It's a heavy marble, usually made of black agate or obsidian. Black beauties, like priceless gems, are quite rare.

MIBSTERS, TAWS, AND STICKS

Ancient peoples played with marbles. They used sheep's knucklebones, small stones, polished wood, and even tiny nuts. Some of these types of marbles exist today in various countries around the world.

There are many different ways to play with marbles, and the game has many different names. In the United States it's called Marbles or Immies or Mibs. English, Irish, and Scottish youngsters play Boss or Taw or Span. In Africa it is Jorrah, and in Brazil it is Gude. Call it what you will, any mibster (marble-player) would surely agree that the game is a lot of fun.

Although there are many variations, there are only three basic ways in which the game is played.

1. Hole games, in which marbles are shot into, out of, or near holes in the ground or in boxes.

2. Chase games, in which players shoot their marbles at opponents' marbles as they follow a winding course.

3. Enclosure games, in which players shoot their marbles at other marbles within an enclosure such as a circle or a square.

A popular enclosure game is Ringer. In Ringer, 13 marbles are placed in the shape of a cross in the middle of a 10-foot (3-meter) circle. If you are the mibster, you take your shooting marble (called a shooter or taw), and you try to knock each of the commies (target marbles) out of the circle (ring). When your taw stays inside the ring, that is called a stick, and you shoot again. But if you miss, it's your opponent's turn. The mibster who knocks out the most marbles is the winner.

The key to winning is in the shooting. There's a special way to hold your shooter for best results. The shooter should be nestled inside the crook of your index finger. But some champions insist that it's better to have the marble resting between the index finger and the second finger, right at the first joints. Hold the shooter there tightly with your full thumb nail pressing against it. When you flick your thumb, the marble shoots out. It sounds easy, but it's difficult to do well, especially when you're trying to hit another marble with your shooter. It takes practice. And in a game like Ringer, you have to learn how to put spin on your shooter so that it stays (sticks) in the ring after it knocks the commie out. If it doesn't stick, you lose your turn. Without spin, you can't win.

THE NATIONAL MARBLES TOURNAMENT

Every June, in Wildwood-by-the-Sea, New Jersey, the National Marbles Tournament is held for mibsters aged 8 to 14. About 60 boys and girls gather for the event. Most

Joelle Guiles, 14, was the girls' champ of the 1981 National Marbles Tournament . . .

A MARBLES GLOSSARY

Aggies, glassies, puries, alleys, immies, and **steelies**—Various types of marbles.

Black beauty—An extremely rare, heavy marble, usually made of black agate or obsidian.

Ringer—One of many marbles games. Ringer is played every year at the National Marbles Tournament.

Shooter—A marble used for shooting, usually an aggie or a glassie. Also called a **taw.**

Mibs—Target marbles. Also called **commies.**

Mibster—A marbles player.

Stick—A stick occurs when a mibster's shooter stays inside the ring after knocking a mib out of the ring. The mibster gets the chance to shoot again.

are state and regional champions. During a week of furious Ringer competition, each contestant plays some 80 games, until a girls' national champion and a boys' national champion are finally crowned.

The tournament began in 1922, and it is now sponsored by the children's television program "Big Blue Marble." (The name of the show comes from the idea that Earth, viewed from a rocket ship several thousand miles up, looks like a beautiful, big blue marble.)

In 1981, the girls' champ was 14-year-old Joelle Guiles, from Pennsylvania. The boys' winner was 13-year-old Jeff Kimmell, from Maryland. Each won a $500 college scholarship. But neither mibster will be back in 1982. Champions are not allowed to repeat. New marbles champs will be crowned!

WHAT OTHER USES DO MARBLES HAVE?

Not all marbles games involve rolling, shooting, or throwing. Chinese Checkers is a game in which marbles are the pieces. They are moved from hole to hole on a board as each player tries to outwit the others.

And marbles are not only used in games. Have you ever picked up an aerosol can and heard something clicking inside? It's a marble. The marble is used to agitate the contents of the can. This helps the contents come out more easily when you press the button.

In the printing industry, marbles are used to make a smooth finish on copper engraving plates.

In fish hatcheries, you will see marbles on the bottom of spawning pools. They help increase the number of fish eggs that are laid.

If you are ever in an automobile at night, you will probably see a roadside sign reflect the glare of your headlights. What is doing the reflecting? Marbles, which have been inserted in the sign.

And sometimes marbles are just collected —simply because they're beautiful.

and Jeff Kimmell, 13, was the boys' champion.

LIVING HISTORY

The Vikings are usually thought of as ruthless plunderers and fearless seafarers who sailed the seven seas in search of new lands. But the Vikings were also traders, farmers, artisans, and colonizers. To present a more balanced picture of the Norsemen, a major exhibition of Viking objects was assembled and toured several countries. Below is a replica of the famous Viking longship, on display in New York City.

The large, sprawling city of Los Angeles celebrated its 200th birthday in 1981.

L.A.'S THE PLACE!

"L.A.'s the Place," said the 3,000,000 people who call themselves Angelenos.

"L.A.'s the Place," said bumper stickers, buttons, T-shirts, and radio announcers.

"L.A.'s the Place," said a giant birthday cake. The cake was eaten at a party that began a year-long celebration ending on September 4, 1981—the 200th birthday of the city of Los Angeles.

The celebration was marked by a wide variety of events, activities, and permanent projects. Special art exhibits showed the city's cultural heritage. A photography exhibit included pictures of Los Angeles and its residents at various stages of the city's growth. There were neighborhood improvement projects, such as landscaping and tree plantings. There were special marathons, bicycle races, and a golf tournament. And the Los Angeles Dodgers sported bicentennial patches on their uniforms.

The Los Angeles of today is a large,

sprawling city covering 464 square miles (1,202 square kilometers). It is very different from the tiny *pueblo,* or town, founded on September 4, 1781. At that time, California was part of Mexico, which was under Spanish rule. The Spanish founded *El Pueblo de Nuestra Señora la Reina de Los Angeles de Porciuncula* ("the town of Our Lady the Queen of the Angels of Porciuncula") mainly to provide food for the Spanish soldiers. There were eleven founding families, consisting of eleven men, eleven women, and twenty-two children. Each family was given a plot of land to cultivate and a home facing the Plaza, a square that still exists. It is located not far from today's Civic Center.

For a long time, Los Angeles remained a small, quiet town. Some of the residents turned from farming to raising cattle, and huge ranches began to surround the town. Outsiders rarely visited. The first English-speaking person to settle in Los Angeles arrived in 1818. His name was Joseph Chapman. He was a carpenter and helped to build a church facing the Plaza—a church that still exists.

In 1821, Mexico became independent of Spain. During the following years, small groups of American settlers began arriving from the East. But the town remained primarily Mexican and Spanish.

In 1846, at the beginning of the Mexican War, fewer than 2,000 people lived in Los Angeles. As a result of the war, California became part of the United States. At the same time, gold was discovered north of Los Angeles. The hordes of miners who flocked to the goldfields needed beef and other food. This was provided by Los Angeles, then known as the Queen of the Cow Counties.

It was about this time that Los Angeles became a hangout for outlaws. For a while, the town was so filled with violence that people began calling it *Los Diablos* ("the devils"). Almost every night there were fights, and outlaw gangs, cattle thieves, murderers, and drunks roamed the streets. Finally, the city realized that it had to re-establish law and order, and gradually Los Angeles became a peaceful place once again.

As the years passed, more and more "Yankees" moved to Los Angeles. In the 1880's, after two railroad lines reached the city, thousands of people arrived to build new lives in this place of sun and year-round warmth. The first of the city's real-estate booms began after the railroads offered fares of as little as $1 from the Midwest to Los Angeles. In less than three years, the population grew from 12,000 to 50,000.

In 1892, oil was discovered. This drew even more people, and by the turn of the century the population had passed 100,000. Other large migrations occurred after World War I, during the Depression of the 1930's, and after World War II. By its 200th birthday, the city had the third largest population in the United States.

People are still moving to Los Angeles. But many of today's newcomers arrive not from the eastern and midwestern parts of the United States but from other countries.

Olvera Street is a brick-paved lane filled with Mexican shops. It is in the old area of Los Angeles where the *pueblo* was founded in 1781.

193

A PLACE OF CONTRASTS

Los Angeles has always been a melting pot—a place where people of different ethnic backgrounds live and work together. The original settlers were Spaniards, blacks, and Indians. Today, people of European descent make up almost half the population. People from Latin America are the next largest group, and Spanish is heard almost as frequently as English. But if you walk down a Los Angeles street you'll hear other languages, too—Korean, Vietnamese, Russian, Arabic, Japanese, Chinese. Some 83 languages are spoken in Los Angeles!

The city is dotted with ethnic neighborhoods. More than 100,000 Koreans live in a neighborhood called Koreatown. New Chinatown is the center of the city's Chinese population. Little Tokyo is the center of the Japanese population. In wealthy Bel Air, there are hundreds of Iranians, who fled their country when Ayatollah Khomeini came to power.

This ethnic variety has influenced L.A.'s art and culture. It also played an important role in the city's bicentennial activities. A day-long fiesta featured Mexican food and dancing. A three-day pow-wow included demonstrations of Indian arts and crafts, dancing, and foods made from recipes that had been handed down from mother to daughter for generations.

A jazz festival featured Caribbean music. A concert series presented Japanese musicians, dancers, and actors. A folk festival paid tribute to the residents of the Furlong Tract, the city's first major black residential area. And a dance series presented more than 40 dance companies, including the Ballet Mexicapan, the Middle Eastern Dance Company, and the Korean Classical.

The city's architecture also presents exciting contrasts. The houses include Victorian homes decorated with fancy woodwork, brownstones, tiny wooden bungalows, and stucco Spanish-style houses with tiled roofs.

L.A. has always been a melting pot, and the city is dotted with colorful ethnic neighborhoods. This is New Chinatown, the center of the Chinese population.

L.A.'s vast freeway system (seen here through a fish-eye lens) is very different from the crooked, muddy streets of 200 years ago. Then, people walked or used horses to get from one place to another. Today, there are more cars per person in the city than in any other place in the world.

In the San Fernando Valley, where about a third of Los Angeles' residents live, most of the homes are ranch houses, with backyard patios and swimming pools.

In the past 20 years, land has become scarcer and more expensive. As a result, apartment houses are becoming common, and tall sleek skyscrapers are replacing low office buildings.

Another architectural feature of Los Angeles is its freeway system. This vast network of high-speed, multilane roads crisscrosses the city. The wide roads, with their on-and-off ramps and their overpasses, are very different from the crooked, muddy streets found in the *pueblo* of 1781. Two hundred years ago, people walked or depended on horses to get from one place to another. Today's Angelenos depend almost entirely on cars. There are more cars per person in Los Angeles than in any other place in the world.

PAST, PRESENT, FUTURE

In celebrating its bicentennial, Los Angeles could look with pride not only at its past but also at its present. The city had grown from a tiny *pueblo* into one of North America's more important business centers. Its port is the busiest port on the West Coast. And its motion-picture and television industry is world famous. Tourists come from all over the world to visit L.A.'s many places of interest and to enjoy the wonderful climate.

Los Angeles does, of course, have problems. All communities do. There is a need for low-cost housing and for a good mass transportation system. Automobile exhaust and factory smoke create serious air pollution problems. Violent crime is a problem. And the area is constantly threatened with natural disasters, particularly earthquakes, fires, and floods. In fact, on its September 4 birthday, the strongest earthquake in ten years shook the city—and quickly became dubbed the "birthday quake."

L.A.'s problems are minor in comparison to its riches. The sun, warmth, and wonderful mixture of people promise to continue to make L.A. "the Place."

CLARA BARTON: ANGEL OF THE BATTLEFIELD

The television newscaster looked grim as he announced: "Severe storms ripped through the Southwest today, leaving a trail of destruction in their wake. Thousands have been driven from their homes because of flooding. Red Cross workers are on the scene, providing shelter and medical care for victims of the disaster . . ."

This type of story is familiar to anyone who watches the evening news. And the tag line is almost always the same—"Red Cross workers are on the scene." Whether it's a volcano erupting in Washington, a flood along the Mississippi River, or an earthquake in California, the American Red Cross—like its counterparts all over the world—is always there to lend a helping hand.

Today we may take the Red Cross for granted. We know we can count on that organization whenever disaster strikes. But if it hadn't been for the determination of a woman named Clara Barton, there might not be an American Red Cross.

In 1981, the American Red Cross celebrated its 100th anniversary. And friends of the Red Cross recalled the tireless efforts of the frail but strong-willed woman who made it all possible.

Clarissa Harlowe Barton was born in Mas-

In war and peace, the Red Cross is always there to aid the victims of disasters. In 1981, the American Red Cross celebrated its 100th birthday.

sachusetts on Christmas day in 1821. The youngest of five children, she began her career of caring for others by nursing her invalid brother David. In her mid-teens, she became a schoolteacher. This remained her career until the 1850's, when ill health forced her to give up teaching.

In 1854, she went to Washington, D.C., where she got a job as a clerk with the U.S. Patent Office. When the Civil War broke out in 1861, Barton watched as Union soldiers streamed into the capital, often without proper clothing and equipment. She set out to remedy this situation, advertising in newspapers for provisions. Contributions poured in, and she quickly set up a center to distribute clothing, bandages, and other supplies to the soldiers.

She became more involved as the war went on, and she began to bring her supplies and nursing skills straight to the battlefield. Soldiers would see her leading a supply-laden wagon through mud up to her knees. At the bloody battle of Antietam, she was nearly killed helping a wounded soldier. She was nicknamed the "Angel of the Battlefield." And her courage, sympathy, and resourcefulness became legendary.

After four years of war service, she spent four more years of government work searching for missing Union soldiers. In 1869 she went to Europe for a much-needed rest. While there, she heard about the International Red Cross, which had been established a few years earlier by a Swiss man named Jean Henri Dunant. She learned of the group's activities to aid wounded soldiers in wartime. And she stayed to work with them during the Franco-Prussian War.

Red Cross officials encouraged her to return to the United States to set up an American chapter of the organization. But before an American Red Cross could be truly effective, the United States would have to ratify the Geneva Convention of 1864. This was an international treaty providing for the humane treatment of wounded soldiers and civilian relief workers in times of war.

Back in the United States in 1873, Barton worked hard to get the United States to ratify the treaty. Her long campaign included writing pamphlets and visiting government officials. By the spring of 1881, support for the treaty had grown. Clara Barton and her supporters met on May 21 to organize the American branch of the Red Cross. The Geneva Convention was ratified a year later.

Barton became the first president of the American Red Cross. She held that position for 23 years. Throughout those years, she changed the organization from one that served only during wartime to one that served at all times. She personally supervised Red Cross operations during almost every major disaster in the United States. When Johnstown, Pennsylvania, was nearly wiped off the map by a great flood in 1889, she organized a massive relief effort. In 1900, Barton, nearly 80 years old, took charge of relief activities during the Galveston Flood.

If Barton had a flaw, it was that she tried to do too much herself. She always had to be in charge. By the early 1900's, opposition to her leadership of the American Red Cross had grown. She was accused of mismanagement and improper business procedures.

There was no evidence that she had done anything illegal. Barton was not dishonest—only a poor administrator and bookkeeper. But the controversy led to her resignation in 1904 and to the reorganization of the Red Cross.

Somewhat embittered, Barton was still eager to serve. She formed a group called the National First Aid Association, which she noted would "supplement" the programs of the Red Cross. She also wrote several books about the Red Cross. And so Barton remained active until her death in April, 1912, at the age of 90.

Since then, the American Red Cross has continued to grow and expand its activities. Today the Red Cross runs programs to train people in first aid. It sponsors a blood donor program. And it has junior Red Cross chapters for young people. All this, of course, is in addition to its traditional work of aiding the victims of disasters in war and peace.

Although the American Red Cross has changed and expanded since its creation in 1881, it is firmly rooted in the humanitarian ideals of its founder—Clara Barton.

Clara Barton was the founder of the American Red Cross. Her courage and sympathy became legendary, and she was nicknamed the "Angel of the Battlefield."

W.M.Allison

Music boxes, like this newly made carousel and antique birdcage, are enjoyed by people everywhere.

THE MECHANICAL MUSIC MAKER

Once upon a time a portable radio who was strolling along a seaside beach struck up a conversation with a little music box. "I hope you won't be offended if I ask you a personal question," said the radio, "but how do you music boxes manage to survive in today's electronic world? Shouldn't you be extinct by now?"

Thorens Treasury of Music Boxes

At one point in history, for a period of about 100 years, the music box reigned supreme as a source of automatically made music. Music boxes could be found in taverns, ice cream parlors, and in almost every home. And they played all kinds of songs, even the melodies of famous composers such as Beethoven, Haydn, and Mozart. Today, in our electronic world of radios and stereos, the gentle music box has survived very well, and it is still enjoyed by people everywhere.

LITTLE BOXES OF SOUND

A music box is a mechanical, self-playing instrument that plays tunes when it is wound up like a clock. The sounds it produces are usually soft, delicate, and high pitched.

The first music boxes were made by Swiss watchmakers in the late 1700's. They were tiny mechanisms that were encased in luxury items such as watches, snuff boxes, perfume bottles, and walking sticks. They played only simple tunes, and often the mechanism created such a loud noise that the little melody was drowned out. In these early music boxes, the music was secondary to the use of the item.

As the mechanisms were improved, music boxes began to be made as entertainment items in their own right. By the early 1800's, music boxes that were operated by a cylinder mechanism had become popular musical instruments. At first they were made for

198

Colored wood and brass were used as inlay on some antique boxes.

their musical qualities rather than for appearance, and they were enclosed in simple wood boxes.

In the mid-1800's, the art of the cabinet-maker joined that of the music box maker, and elaborate cases were designed. Mother-of-pearl, colored wood, and precious metals were used as inlay on the tops and fronts of the boxes. They were often worked into designs with musical motifs, such as mandolins and harps. Birds and flowers were also popular designs. Larger music boxes were often custom-made in the form of writing desks, ladies' cabinets, and other pieces of furniture for the home.

Around 1850, little drums and bells were added to the mechanisms of some music boxes. These were the forerunners of the spectacular orchestra boxes. Orchestra boxes included a set of bells, a snare drum, a wood drum that produced the sound of castanets, and sometimes a triangle or a gong.

Automata were elaborate music boxes that were very popular during Victorian times. These music boxes had figures of people and animals that played little instruments, danced, and clacked castanets while the music played. Magicians, monkeys, and acrobats performed tricks. Miniature birds in cages flapped their wings and whistled songs. Horses and riders galloped as miniature carousels spun around. The music did

This bell-and-drum box shows "castanets" on the left, bells in the center, and a drum on the right.

not come from the figures but from a tiny cylinder mechanism in the base of the box.

Despite continuing improvements, most cylinder music boxes could play only a few melodies. And interchangeable cylinders were very expensive. In the late 1800's, the cylinder music box was replaced by the disc music box. The discs were a standard size and interchangeable—they could be changed like records. They were immensely popular. At the beginning of the 20th century, an automatic disc-changing device was introduced.

Thomas Edison invented the phonograph in 1877. But it was more than 25 years before this instrument, with its scratchy, squeaky music, was so improved that it overtook the

Automata music boxes had figures of people or animals that played little musical instruments while the music played. The music came from a tiny cylinder mechanism in the base of the music box.

In the late 1800's, the cylinder music box was replaced by the disc music box. The discs could be changed like records. (The bar across the disc is holding the disc in place.)

LOOK INSIDE A MUSIC BOX

If you open a music box and look inside, you will probably see a cylinder mechanism. The cylinder has small metal pins sticking out of it. The pins may look as if they are helter-skelter, but they have been arranged in a certain order to produce a melody. Parallel to the cylinder is what looks like a steel comb. The teeth of the comb are of varying lengths, and they are tuned to the musical scale.

Now, when you turn the key of the music box, you wind up a spring. The spring sets gears in motion, and the gears turn the cylinder. As the cylinder rotates, the pins pluck the teeth of the comb. The teeth vibrate and produce delicate, tinkly sounds. The longer teeth on the comb produce the lower notes of the melody, and the shorter teeth produce the higher notes.

Cylinders in old music boxes were usually programmed to play several tunes. And some boxes contained more than one cylinder.

A disc music box contains a metal disc instead of a cylinder, and a steel comb. The disc, which looks like a record, has punched-out projections on the underside. The projections are arranged to produce a melody. As the disc rotates, the projections cause small star-shaped wheels to turn, which pluck the tuned teeth of the comb.

Large disc music boxes, with interchangeable discs, were very popular in the late 1800's and early 1900's.

music box in popularity. Gradually, music boxes disappeared from taverns, ice cream parlors, and living rooms. They went into attics, cellars, and barns.

Over the years, collectors have been digging out old music boxes from their hiding places and restoring them. Why don't you go on a treasure hunt? If you're lucky, you just may find an antique music box that your parents or grandparents stored away. If you find one, wind it up and listen to the sweet, tinkling tune. You may hear anything from *The William Tell Overture* to "Gently Over the Pimples, John," a favorite played in barber shops when men were getting a shave.

Perhaps you would like to start a collection of music boxes—both old and new ones. Although the elaborate orchestra boxes are of a past era, it's easy to find fascinating new music boxes in the form of jewelry cases, toys, birds, and Swiss chalets. It's even possible to buy a do-it-yourself music box kit. This includes a musical movement, with tunes of your choice, and rotating or stationary bases for mounting figurines and craftwork. By creating your own music box, you may enjoy all the more the gentle tunes from the little boxes of sound.

HARRY GOLDSMITH
Former patent counsel

The old and new Court Houses in London, Ontario, where the present blends with the past.

ANOTHER LONDON

Do you know that without even crossing the Atlantic you can visit London? You can stroll down Piccadilly, hear the bells of Saint Paul's Cathedral, and snack on a ripe, red apple at Covent Garden Market. Then you can board a boat and take a trip on the sparkling Thames River.

"Impossible!" you may say. But this London is not in England. It's in Ontario, Canada, southwest of Toronto. London, Ontario, was named after London, England. It borrowed many place names from the Old World city. But Canadian London is a very different place.

London, Ontario, was built on land that was once inhabited by Attiwandrian Indian tribes. In 1792, an English colonel, John Graves Simcoe, arrived at the place where London now stands. As he gazed at the peaceful valley at the forks of the Thames River, he decided that it should be the site of the capital of Upper Canada (the old name for Ontario). But Toronto became the capital, and the valley remained unsettled until the 1820's.

Because of its location on the Thames River, London prospered. It grew from a pioneer village to a town in 1848 and then a city in 1855. Today it is a manufacturing and financial center with sleek, modern buildings and a population of more than 250,000.

If you visit London you will find that it is a city of unexpected surprises, where the present blends with the past. You might start with Fanshawe Pioneer Village, a community that preserves the country life of 100 years ago. Many of the old log and frame houses were moved from the surrounding area to form the village. And you can see horse-drawn farm machines ploughing a field, cutting hay, and harvesting grain.

London's past and present meet again at Covent Garden Market, a colorful farmer's market that dates back to 1845. Modern trucks have replaced the horse-drawn farm wagons that once brought fruit and vegetables from the countryside. But you can still feast on the area's abundant produce, as well as on all kinds of delicious specialities.

As you wander through the city, you will notice that it is filled with parks—so many, in fact, that London has become known as Canada's "forest city." Some of the parks are lush, some are wild. The biggest and most beautiful is Springbank Park. It has hills and dales for exploring, a merry-go-round, a miniature train, and boat rides. But the most wonderful part of this park is. . .

Walk through an enchanted castle and come upon . . .

. . . the Old Woman's Shoe . . .

Storybook Gardens. Walk across a drawbridge and through an enchanted castle, and you will enter a "once upon a time" land of nursery rhymes, fairytales, and childhood stories. You will come upon Jack and Jill Hill, the Trojan Horse, Peter Pan Fountain, the Old Woman's Shoe, and the Jolly Miller's House.

All kinds of real animals mingle with the make-believe characters. Barnyard animals are on Old MacDonald's Farm. White mice play in the Hickory Dickory Clock. Monkeys live on Robinson Crusoe's Island. The Gingerbread House is the home of tropical birds. There are lambs in Mary's Schoolhouse. And you can even see little bear cubs playing with their porridge bowls—just waiting for Goldilocks.

. . . the Jolly Miller's House . . .   . . . and the Trojan Horse.

The 13th-century castle at Segovia, Spain, casts a spell of legend and romance.

ONCE UPON A CASTLE

Castles make us think of fairy tales and enchanted lands. They bring to mind romantic stories of bold knights, fair maidens, and legendary kings and queens. But in fact, most castles were not romantic at all. They were built for defense in a violent age, and life in them was harsh by today's standards.

The castles you are probably most familiar with were built in Europe during the Middle Ages. But at different times in history, castles were built in many places—in the Middle East and the Far East as well as in Europe. Like forts, they defended strategic places such as mountain passes and river crossings. But while both forts and castles housed troops, a castle was also the home of its owner—a king or a lord.

EARLY EUROPEAN CASTLES

Castles developed along with feudal systems. In these systems, powerful lords owned large areas of land, called fiefs. A lord might serve a king, but he was master of his fief. To help him defend his fief—from his neighbors as well as from foreign raiders—he could call on the men who were under his rule: his vassals. And a lord could build castles. A lesser lord might rule his fief from one castle. But the more powerful lords scattered castles throughout their lands, and they moved with their families from one castle to the next.

Motte-and-Bailey Castles. Early European castles were modeled on the forts of the Roman Empire. But they were a far cry from the solid walls and towers of the Romans. A typical castle of the year 1000 was built of earth and wood, in a form called motte and bailey.

The outer defense of a motte-and-bailey castle was a deep ditch, or moat, often filled with water. Usually, the moat took the form of a figure eight. In one half of the eight, the *motte*—a tall mound of earth—would be raised. On top of the mound the lord would build a wooden tower, in which he lived. A stockade of pointed logs surrounded it.

A long, sloping bridge led down from the motte and across the moat to the other half of the eight, the *bailey*. The bailey was simply a flat area enclosed by a wooden stockade, with stables and other buildings for work and storage. The main entrance to the castle was usually at the end of the bailey farthest from the motte. There, a drawbridge could be lowered to admit friendly visitors.

Motte-and-bailey castles were most common in England and France, but they were built in other parts of Europe as well. They could be put up quickly and cheaply. But the wood they were built of could rot or burn or be smashed by attackers.

The solution to these problems was the stone castle. Some stone castles were built in France in the early 1000's. Because of the great weight of the stone, they stood on natural hills or level ground, rather than on artificial mounds.

When the Normans conquered England in 1066, they established their rule by quickly putting up motte-and-bailey castles everywhere. But by the 1100's, they were replacing these early castles with stone ones. One of the first stone castles to be built in England was the White Tower of the Tower of London, so called because it was painted white. It was begun in 1078.

Norman Castles. A typical Norman castle was enclosed by a stone wall, called a *curtain wall,* and ringed by a moat. The entrance to the castle—across a drawbridge—was defended by a stone gatehouse. And the gate itself could be blocked with a heavy iron grill called a *portcullis,* which dropped into place from above.

The massive curtain wall was thickest at the base, to withstand battering rams and to make it hard for attackers to sap (collapse by removing the base stones). Towers were placed at intervals along the wall.

The area inside the curtain wall was often divided by another wall, to form an inner and an outer bailey. In the outer bailey were barns and other buildings, a garden, and an exercise yard for the men-at-arms. The inner bailey contained storehouses and kitchen buildings, and perhaps a chapel. But its main feature was the *keep,* or *donjon*—a massive square tower in which the lord and his family lived.

Wooden stockades enclosed the two parts of a motte-and-bailey castle—the courtyard (bailey) and the raised mound (motte).

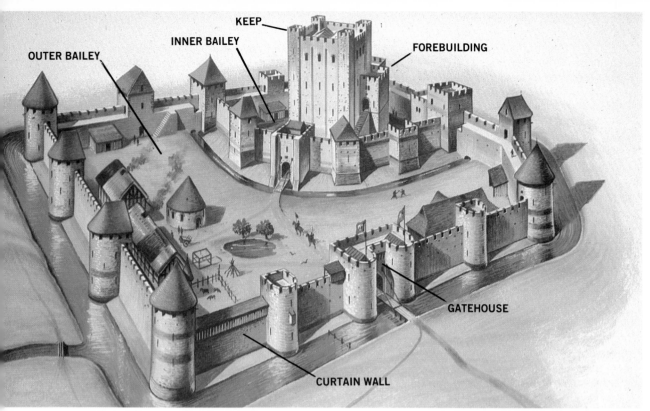

KEEP

INNER BAILEY

FOREBUILDING

OUTER BAILEY

GATEHOUSE

CURTAIN WALL

A typical Norman castle of the 1100's.

The keep was uncomfortable—cold, damp, and drafty. The ground floor was used for storage. The entrance, at the second floor, was reached by a flight of stone steps that led to a small side tower called the fore-building. The second floor provided living quarters for the castle's garrison.

The lord's quarters were on the third floor. Most of this floor was taken up by the Great Hall, a large room where meals were served and official business was carried on.

Meals were served in the Great Hall, the center of castle life and the most important room in the keep.

The lord's *solar,* where he received important visitors and often slept, was here, too. Other sleeping chambers were on the fourth and final floor. *Garderobes,* or bathrooms, were cut into the thick stone walls of the keep. They were simply latrines that emptied into the moat.

Suppose you could go back to the 1100's and visit a Norman castle. What would it be like?

LIFE IN A NORMAN CASTLE

Your first impression might be one of bustling activity. As you enter the outer bailey, soldiers are practicing with long, heavy swords in the exercise yard. The sound of a smith's hammer rings out from a low building nearby, where the armorer is repairing a broken shield. Some men are adding thatch to the roof of a storehouse. A stableboy is drawing water from a well in the center of the court, and others are rubbing down the horses of a recently returned hunting party. In a pen beyond the stable, pigs grunt and squeal. Geese and chickens scatter as you walk through to the inner bailey.

Here, delicious smells pour from the kitchen building. Eating and drinking are an important form of entertainment in the castle, and today a feast is being prepared. Cooks and helpers scurry this way and that in the kitchen. Great cauldrons of stew bubble over the fire, and chickens are roasting on a spit. One cook makes pastry for a meat pie. And in one corner, a lowly scullion cleans cups and wooden platters. In the buttery, next to the kitchen, the butler rolls out a cask of ale to be tapped.

You pass by and go up the stairs to the keep, pausing to let your eyes adjust to the dim light. Then you go up a narrow spiral stairway to the Great Hall. This is a huge room, with a high wooden ceiling. Tapestries hang on the stone walls, and rushes are strewn on the floor. The few narrow windows and the fire burning in the great fireplace do little to dispel the darkness or the chill.

Near the fire, two squires are having a game of tables, which is rather like backgammon. Near them, the lady of the castle is giving instructions to a seamstress. Servants are moving rough wooden tables and benches into place for the feast. The lord's table is on the dais, a raised platform at one end of the hall. His is the only chair.

Off the Great Hall is the solar, the lord's private room. There the lord is conferring with his steward, who is in charge of managing the estate. The lord sits on the bed while the steward, standing, goes over a list of rents due from tenant farmers. In comparison to the rest of the castle, this room seems bright and comfortable. A large arched window looks out over the bailey. The walls are covered with rich hangings, and there are fur throws on the floor. Two hunting dogs sprawl in front of the solar's large hooded fireplace.

On another visit, you might find the lord in the Great Hall, hearing the complaints of his vassals and administering justice. Or he might be riding out to hunt or hearing services in the chapel next to the keep. But whenever the lord is at the castle, the staff —anywhere from a dozen to a hundred people—will be hard at work. Servants bring in food from surrounding farms, carry wood for fires, do laundry and mending, heat water for baths, bake bread, brew ale, make medicines, and carry out dozens of other household chores. Clerks write letters and keep accounts. The chapel priest gives lessons to the lord's children. Traveling minstrels may be on hand to provide entertainment.

If the lord's household is large, food supplies will be used up in a few weeks. The moat will be fouled with wastes. Then the lord and most of his retainers will move on to another of his castles. The permanent staff—a small garrison of men-at-arms and a few servants—will stay behind and clean up.

Your visit would be quite different if you found the castle under attack. The lord's enemies would try to take the castle by laying siege to it. They would surround the castle to cut off its supplies. Then they would move toward the walls under the cover of wooden screens and begin to attack the castle at all points.

Some enemy soldiers would begin to fill in a section of the moat so that a tall wooden tower called a *belfrey* could be rolled up to the walls. If they succeeded, archers could shoot down into the bailey from the top of

Soldiers manned the walls when the castle was attacked.

the belfrey. Soldiers might even be able to enter the castle by dropping a bridge across to the top of the wall. Or the attackers might bring across a battering ram and begin to pound on the main gate or the walls.

Others would set wooden bridges across the moat and try to scale the walls with ladders. Meanwhile, catapults would send their missiles soaring over the walls and raining down into the bailey—spears, stones, and flammable liquid called Greek fire.

Many castles were so bristling with defenses that they might well withstand such an onslaught. Defenders could shoot arrows through narrow slits, called *loopholes,* in the tower walls. They could also defend the castle from the wall-walk, or *allure.* This was a narrow walkway near the top of the wall. Archers could shoot from evenly spaced gaps, called *crenels,* at the top of the wall. And when the castle was attacked, wooden galleries called *hoardings* were hung out over the walls. Defenders stood in the hoardings and dropped stones and boiling liquids down on the attackers.

Of course, any castle could be taken if the attackers waited long enough. The defenders would run out of food and be forced to surrender or starve. But often the attackers couldn't wait. Under the feudal system, men-at-arms were usually required to serve their lords for a period of only 40 days. If the castle hadn't surrendered in that time, the attacking army was likely to disband and go home.

Krak des Chevaliers, in Syria, was built by Crusaders in the 13th century. It is a concentric castle, with an outer, lower ring of walls.

DIFFERENT CASTLE DESIGNS

Feudal society was common to most of Europe in the Middle Ages, and so was the basic castle design. But there were many variations. In Germany and some other parts of Europe, the keep was a place of refuge when the castle was attacked, but the lord and his family lived in a low building next to it in times of peace. Such keeps were taller and slimmer than the Norman ones, and the residences were more spacious.

In France, some keeps were made up of separate towers. These towers were linked by walls to enclose a courtyard. The French were also the first in Europe to replace wooden hoardings with permanent stone galleries called *machicolations.*

As time went on, there were many other changes in castle design. Some came about as a result of the Crusades, which began in the 11th century and continued into the 13th century. When the European Crusaders traveled to the Middle East, they saw different kinds of defenses, and they brought back new ideas.

One of the most important ideas was that of the concentric castle. The main feature of a concentric castle was an extra ring of walls. Attackers who managed to break through the outer ring would be faced with a second ring, taller than the first. And they would be trapped in the open space between.

Another important change was the round keep. The corners of the square keep had always been a weak point because it was fairly easy for attackers to pry out a cornerstone and bring the keep down. A round keep was much more difficult to sap.

The main gate was strengthened by the addition of a gatehouse, called a *barbican,* that stood like an island in the moat. Attackers would have to take the barbican before they assailed the main gate. And the barbican was like a miniature castle. It had two portcullises, and stones could be dropped on intruders through *murder-holes* in the ceiling of the main passage.

As the outer defenses became stronger, the keep became less important. In later castles, the lord and his family often lived in a hall that stood in the central courtyard. Instead of a single solar, the family might have a suite of rooms.

This castle in Limousin, France, was built in the 1400's. The round towers are topped with machicolations—projecting galleries supported by stone brackets. Between the brackets are holes through which defenders could drop stones.

By the late 1200's, castles had become the ultimate military defenses of their day. But gradually, they became less important. Kings became more powerful and kept large standing armies, which could wait as long as necessary for a castle to surrender. Strong rulers also put an end to much of the squabbling between local lords that had made fortress homes necessary in the early Middle Ages. Castles continued to be built in parts of Europe through the 1500's, especially in areas such as Italy where many small states fought among themselves. Many of these later castles had gunports for cannon. Or the walls might be low so that cannon could be mounted on top to fire out at attackers.

THE CASTLES OF JAPAN

Japanese castles were more elaborate—and more comfortable—than those of medieval Europe. But they had some of the same features. Many of the Japanese castles were built at the end of the 1500's, a time when local lords were fighting for control of large sections of the country. Each *daimyo,* as a lord was called, built castles to defend the territory he held.

The daimyo often picked a hilltop as the site for his castle. As in Europe, the outer line of defense was a moat, with a wall just inside it. Sometimes this outer wall was built of grass-covered earth, but more often it was faced with massive stones. Built to withstand earthquakes as well as enemies, some walls were 50 feet (15 meters) thick at the base. On top was a parapet, built of wood, clay, and plaster and roofed with tile. Defenders on the parapet could shoot arrows through loopholes, or they could drop stones and boiling water through chutes called *ish-iotoshi*. Towers, one to three stories tall, stood at the corners of the wall.

Usually the moat was crossed by a permanent bridge or causeway, rather than a drawbridge. Gates were often complicated. For example, visitors might enter through an outer gate into a small court. Then they would turn at right angles to pass through a second, larger gate, which was defended by a gatehouse.

Beyond the gatehouse was a maze of courtyards. They were arranged so that if one courtyard fell to attackers, the rest could still be defended. The courtyards were often beautifully landscaped, and their gardens helped the defense. Evergreens grew up to hide the walls, so that attackers could not see what the defenders were up to. The trees also provided an extra screen against enemy arrows. And when the castle was under siege, oak and bamboo from the gardens could be used for spear and arrow shafts, and garden pools provided an extra source of water.

The chief retainers and *samurai* (men-at-arms) lived in the inner courtyards. In the central courtyard, on the highest ground, were the keep and the palace of the daimyo. The keep, or *tenshu-kaku*, was three to seven stories tall, wider at the base than at the top. Many keeps were painted black. Like the other castle buildings, the keep had a tile roof with curved gables. A pair of mythical dolphins called *sachi* were placed at each end of the ridgepole as a charm against evil.

The keep was the castle's chief command

White Heron Castle at Himeji is one of the best-preserved castles in Japan. Figures of mythical dolphins, called *sachi*, top its graceful, curving roofs.

post and its final line of defense. Sometimes a courtyard near it was set aside for the purpose of committing suicide, in the event the castle was taken. In times of siege, the daimyo and his retainers lived in the keep.

Most of the time, the daimyo lived in the palace. This building might be decorated with elaborate carvings and fine works of art. The wood floors were often laid in a pattern called *uguisu-bari,* or nightingale boarding, so that they would make noise when people walked on them. This made it difficult for enemies to sneak into the palace at night.

By the early 1600's, most of Japan had been united under a *shogun,* or military ruler. The daimyos became less important. Gradually their castles were abandoned and fell into disrepair.

RUINS AND RESTORATIONS

In Europe, too, the end of the feudal system made castles obsolete. Nobles were less interested in defense and more interested in comfort. They moved out of their damp castles and into stately manors, or they remodeled the castles with an eye to comfort. It wasn't until the 1800's that castles took on the romantic appeal they have today.

By then, most of the medieval castles were crumbling into ruins. Many were restored—sometimes accurately, sometimes fancifully. Wealthy people built homes that looked like castles, with crenellated rooflines and narrow slits of windows.

What may be the most lavish imitation castle anywhere is Neuschwanstein Castle, built by Ludwig II, king of Bavaria, in the late 1800's. Ludwig got so carried away with this castle—and spent such vast sums of money on it—that the Bavarian Government declared him insane and deposed him. Neuschwanstein is perched on a spur of rock, with the Alps towering behind it and a lake at its feet. Its white spires and towers and beautifully furnished interior are nothing like the rough, damp castles of earlier days.

Many restored castles are open to the public, in Japan as well as in Europe. If you visit one, you can step into the pages of history and see what life was like in feudal times. But if you visit Neuschwanstein, you can step straight into a fairy tale.

Neuschwanstein Castle, in the Bavarian Alps, may be one of the most fanciful castles ever built.

THE VIKINGS ARE COMING

It's a summer morning more than a thousand years ago. A half dozen long and slender sailing ships glide quietly up a narrow inlet on the coast of France. The sails are furled, and muscular oarsmen bend their backs in unison as they row their longships close to the shore. Up ahead, through the early morning mist, a castle is visible on its hilltop perch.

A lookout in the castle's tower spots the serpent-headed ships as they suddenly break out of the mist. He shouts the alarm, but it's already too late.

With a final effort, the sturdy oarsmen run their shallow-draft ships right up onto the shore. Shouting battle cries, three hundred fierce Norsemen swarm out of their ships. Swords and battle-axes at the ready, they charge up the hill toward the castle gate.

Inside the castle, cries of terror can be heard. "The Vikings are coming! Run for your lives!" The women and children rush to escape, while the soldiers try to hold back the invaders.

A battering ram smashes through the gate. Ladders breach the walls. The tide of Vikings sweeps over the battlements and quickly overwhelms the defenders.

In less than an hour, the fighting is over. The soldiers in the castle have been slaughtered. The women and children are dragged off to be sold into slavery. And everything of value has been hauled back to the longships. As swiftly as they had come, the Vikings depart, having won another bloody victory.

Scenes like this were repeated often during the Viking Age, which lasted from roughly A.D. 800 to A.D. 1050. It was the sort of thing that the Vikings were best known for—a swift surprise attack followed by killing and looting.

Until recently, our view of the Vikings has mainly been limited to their activities as savage pirates and fearless seamen. We remember them as ruthless seafarers who plundered their way from the British Isles and northern France to the Mediterranean and Caspian seas. And we romanticize them as fearless navigators who braved the dangerous and uncharted Western seas to discover new lands from Iceland to present-day Canada. In fact, the Vikings arrived in North America 500 years before Columbus.

Certainly the Vikings were ruthless fighters. And they were probably the best seamen and shipbuilders of their day. But

In the Viking exhibit: A silver-encrusted sword hilt . . .

. . . a box-shaped brooch of gold, silver, and bronze . . .

. . . a warrior's head carved from an elk antler . . .

the Vikings were also traders, farmers, craftsmen, and colonizers. Overseas, they opened up trade routes with Russia and with the Arab lands of the Mediterranean. Viking ships carrying furs and slaves returned loaded with silk, spices, pearls, and jewels from Arabia and the Byzantine Empire. The Vikings also colonized parts of England, Ireland, and France. Some of their settlements became important commercial centers.

It was also during the Viking Age that the three Scandinavian countries—Denmark, Norway, and Sweden—were united into kingdoms. In these Viking homelands, towns were created, roads were built, and woodlands were cleared to make way for farming settlements.

To provide a more balanced picture of the Norsemen, a major exhibition of Viking objects was recently put together. It went on display at the British Museum in London, the Metropolitan Museum of Art in New York City, the Minneapolis Institute of Arts in Minnesota, and the Museum of National Antiquities in Stockholm, Sweden.

The exhibition included important archeological finds of the past ten years. It featured hundreds of objects, showing all

. . . and a reconstruction of a Viking house.

aspects of Viking life. There were actual tools used by silversmiths, woodcarvers, weavers, and other Viking artisans; hoards of gold and silver coins from Arabia; models of Viking ships and houses; and magnificently fashioned brooches, pendants, rings, and other gold and silver ornaments made by the Vikings.

THE LAND OF THE VIKINGS

Let's visit Scandinavia—the land of the Vikings. There you will find many interesting historical sites and museums that give the feeling of what it must have been like back in the days when the Norsemen went a-Viking—that is, on seagoing adventures.

Take the old Viking fortress called Fyrkat, for example. In the 900's, Fyrkat was a bustling military post in what is now the part of Denmark known as Jutland. Today all that remains of the fort is the partly reconstructed circular rampart (wall) and four gaps where timber-lined gateways once stood. There are also neat lines of cement-filled holes, which once held heavy timber posts used to support the walls of houses.

The precise way the fort was laid out and its strategic location on a hill overlooking a river tell us that the Vikings were clever people—especially when it came to planning towns and settlements. Fyrkat is one of four such forts unearthed in Denmark. They are believed to date from the reign of the Danish King Harald Bluetooth, who united Norway and Denmark into one kingdom.

If Fyrkat tells a lot about the Vikings' skill as builders and planners, a visit to the nearby Moesgaard Museum, just outside the city of Aarhus, tells much about the way they lived. There you can see a reconstructed Viking village, complete with a typical middle-class family house.

The re-creation includes a working hearth and clay oven. For its day and age, the house was quite comfortable and spacious. Central heating and light were provided by the hearth fire in the center room. Low benches made of earth surround the hearth, providing a place for the family to sit while eating and also serving as a sleeping area. If you look around, you can see a loom in one corner, and many wooden bowls and spoons, along with iron skillets and pans.

Moesgaard's Viking Village is truly a "living history" museum. You may even be startled by the smell of fresh-baked bread. Peeking into the main room, you will see a group of Danish schoolchildren sitting around the hearth toasting pieces of flat bread on long-handled iron pans—just as their Viking ancestors might have done. Groups of schoolchildren are regularly given a taste of Viking life and food this way.

Above all, however, we remember the Vikings as people of the sea. Their ships were the best constructed and most modern of their day. Only a few Viking ships have survived. The best preserved of these are housed in Oslo's Viking Ship Museum, on the outskirts of the Norwegian capital.

Near the entrance of the museum, you will see the majestic Oseberg ship. Like its sister ships in the museum, it was dug up from one of the Viking burial mounds discovered along the Oslo fiord. Standing in the shadow of its high prow, an observer can't help but be impressed by the power and grace of this example of the Viking art of shipbuilding.

The prow rises to form the coiled head of a snake—the closest thing to a dragon's head found on any of the surviving Viking ships—and the stern bears the serpent's tail. It is an appropriate symbol for a vessel that could snake its way through narrow fiords and riverways. The beautifully decorated Oseberg ship was most likely a coastal freighter or a royal yacht belonging to the Norwegian Queen Asa, whose remains were found in the Oseberg burial mound.

A more seaworthy vessel is the Gokstad ship, which sits in a neighboring wing of the museum. It has no decorative frills, only the simple, functional lines of a ship of war. The sturdy hull is made of oak planks, riveted together "clinker style"—that is, one plank overlapping the other—and then lashed to the ribs of the ship. This construction technique gave the vessel more flexibility when battling its way through rough North Atlantic seas.

Because the Gokstad ship, and others like it, required only a few feet of water to stay afloat, it could go where other European ships would have run aground. This explains how the Vikings could appear—as if by magic—in the unlikeliest of places. They could maneuver their longships up shallow waterways to settlements thought to be safe from attack by seaborne raiders.

The Viking Ship Museum also has many fine examples of hand-crafted objects found in the burial mounds. One of these is a large, four-wheeled wooden cart decorated with carvings that form a storybook of legends and folktales. One shows a Viking being prevented from striking an enemy warrior by a woman who has a firm grip on his sword hand. It reminds us that in Viking times, Scandinavian women often had a degree of freedom and influence that would not be seen again until our own century.

The richness of the treasures found in the burial mounds also tells us a lot about Viking burial customs. In the case of powerful chieftains, burials were magnificent affairs. A large pit was dug, big enough to hold the chief's longship. The ship was placed with its bow pointing toward the sea so it could take him on his journey to Valhalla—the Viking warrior's heaven. Then the chief was laid out amidship, with his helmet, shield, sword, and other favorite possessions surrounding him.

For most Vikings, however, burial was simple and practical. Some years back, archeologists unearthed a large Viking ceme-

The Gokstad: A Viking ship of war.

tery in northern Jutland, with about 60 gravesites. Most of those buried there were cremated, and their ashes were spread over a piece of ground marked off by stones. Sometimes the stones were grouped to form the familiar shape of a Viking longship.

Today the Vikings live on in memory and in daily life in Scandinavia. Wherever one goes in Denmark, Norway, and Sweden, there are reminders that Scandinavians are proud of their Viking heritage. There are hotels, restaurants, and other businesses that bear the name Viking, or have as their symbol a bearded Viking warrior or sleek Viking longship. SAS, Scandinavia's major airline, has named all its aircraft after Viking kings and warriors. Emblazoned on the sides of SAS jets are such names as "Huge Viking," after a mythological warrior, who, it was said, could run "as fast as thought," and "Dan Viking," in honor of the Viking king who supposedly gave Denmark its name.

What could be more appropriate. For the sleek jetliners that carry passengers all over the world are the modern equivalent of the Viking longships that once sailed the seven seas to trade, to plunder, and to discover and colonize new lands.

HENRY I. KURTZ
Author, *John and Sebastian Cabot*

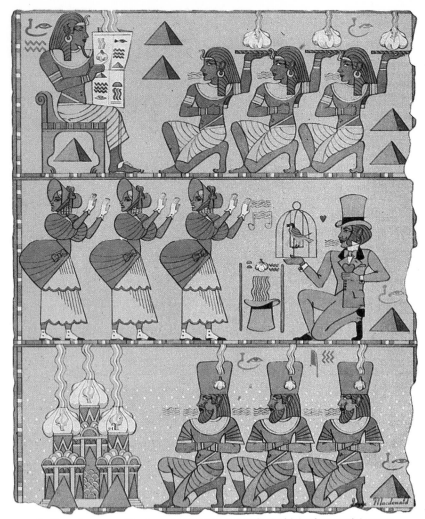

Garlic, a strong-smelling herb, has long been credited with having special powers.

IN LOVE WITH GARLIC

• In ancient Greece, athletes ate garlic to increase their strength.

• In ancient Rome, soldiers ate garlic to give them courage on the battlefield. They also used it to cure a long list of ailments, including snakebites, scorpion stings, and asthma.

• In 16th-century France, people wore garlic around their necks to keep vampires away and to ward off the plague.

• Medieval women believed that garlic made their skin beautiful.

• During World War I, the British used garlic as an antiseptic in treating wounded soldiers.

• Garlic has been said to prevent baldness and to cure rheumatism, leprosy, tuberculosis, and smallpox.

• In the 20th century, people are claiming that garlic helps to prevent heart attacks and that it may even cure cancer.

Since ancient times, garlic has been credited with having special mystical and medicinal powers. It has sometimes even been called the "heal-all" herb. But how much truth is there to the power of garlic? It is difficult to say for sure. Scientists have done very little research on garlic. None of the beliefs have been proved true. But on the other hand, none have been proved false.

And there *is* some evidence that garlic can fight bacteria and fungi, although not nearly as effectively as penicillin.

Most people who eat garlic today don't do so for health reasons. They eat it because they love its strong, unusual flavor.

Gilroy is a town in California where the love for garlic can readily be seen. Gilroy is the garlic capital of the United States. More garlic is grown there than anywhere else. For the past few years, the town has held an annual garlic festival, attracting thousands of people. There are bands, jugglers, and balloon rides. But the main reason people go to the festival is to smell and eat garlic. There are booths selling garlic sausage, snails in garlic butter, spaghetti with garlic sauce, and many other dishes. There is also a contest for the best garlic recipe. One year, someone entered a recipe for garlic ice cream.

There is one drawback to eating garlic—it does terrible things to your breath. So after you eat garlic, eat a few sprigs of fresh parsley. This will help fight bad breath. And it will let you enjoy garlic without chasing your friends away!

COOKING WITH GARLIC

Garlic is related to the onion, and both plants are members of the lily family. The part of the garlic that we eat is the underground bulb. The bulb is made up of pieces called cloves. An average-sized bulb will have ten to twelve cloves. Each clove is enclosed in a crisp whitish skin.

To use garlic, remove the skin from the cloves. Usually, a cook minces or crushes the cloves before using them. This releases the flavorful oils. Some people use garlic powder instead of fresh garlic. Garlic powder is made by grinding up dried garlic.

Garlic is used in many dishes. And garlic bread is one of the most popular. Here is a recipe for garlic bread. It's delicious and easy to make. For one loaf, you need:

  1 8-ounce loaf French or Italian bread
  ¼ pound butter or margarine, softened
  2 cloves garlic
    knife
    aluminum foil

1. Remove the dry whitish skin that encloses each clove.

2. Carefully chop each clove very finely. The smaller the pieces, the better.

3. Mix the chopped garlic with the butter or margarine. Let the mixture stand at room temperature for about a half hour.

4. Preheat the oven to 350°F.

5. Cut the bread lengthwise. Spread the mixture on the inside of both the top and bottom pieces. (Optional: In addition to the garlic mixture, spread Parmesan cheese and a little paprika on the bread.)

6. Put the two pieces together. Cut the bread into serving pieces.

7. Wrap the bread in aluminum foil. It should be completely sealed in the foil.

8. Put the bread in the oven for about 15 minutes.

THE FRENCH FOREIGN LEGION

Every year on July 14, hundreds of thousands of Parisians turn out for a great parade celebrating Bastille Day—the French national holiday. Many splendid military units march down the broad boulevard called the Champs-Elysées.

But there is one military unit that gets the biggest applause from the crowd. Most of the soldiers in this unit are not even French. They include Swiss, Russians, Germans, Americans, Belgians, and Poles. Over the years, men from more than 50 nations have served in the ranks of this famed fighting corps. As they march by in their stately slow step, wearing their traditional *kepis blancs* (white caps), there is a great cheer. Many of the onlookers shout, *"Vive la Legion!"* ("Long live the Legion!")

For these are the men of the French Foreign Legion, the elite of the French Army and one of the toughest military units in the world. And in 1981, this gallant fighting force celebrated its 150th anniversary.

The Foreign Legion! The name itself has a glamorous ring. It brings to mind scenes from Hollywood action films like *Beau Geste* and *Outpost in Morocco*—columns of dust-covered troops trudging across the hot sands of the Sahara . . . a handful of brave Legionnaires holding a mud-brick fort against hordes of fierce desert warriors, fighting to the last man and the last bullet.

It is legends such as these—of exotic locales and brave deeds—that have given the Legion its romantic quality, its mystique. The Legion is, in fact, noted for its heroism. And it *has* served in exotic lands, in all corners of the globe. Legionnaires have fought as far north as Norway and as far south as Madagascar. They have shed their blood in the rice paddies of Indochina and on battlefields in North Africa, Spain, Italy, France, Germany, Syria, and Mexico.

But conditions in these romantic places have not always been pleasant. Discipline has always been tough, the pay low, and living conditions often primitive. Especially in the days of France's colonial empire, disease, starvation, and death were what the Legionnaire could look forward to.

Despite these conditions, the Legion has never been short of recruits. Adventurers and criminal and political fugitives have flocked to serve under its colors. But it is mainly poverty and personal problems that drive men to join the Legion. For these uprooted men, the Legion is a homeland. And that explains the corps' unofficial motto: *Legio Patria Nostra* (The Legion Is Our Country).

Members of the French Foreign Legion, one of the toughest military units in the world, raise the flag at the Legion's headquarters in Aubagne.

The ranks of the Foreign Legion have included lawyers, doctors, mechanics, tradesmen, priests, princes, and poets. A Danish prince made the Legion his career. Prince Rainier, the current ruler of the tiny country of Monaco, served briefly in the Legion during World War II. Alan Seeger, an American poet, fought with the Legion in World War I and died in the Battle of the Somme.

It is mainly the fighting spirit of the Legion that has made the corps a living legend. The willingness to fight to the last man is a trademark of the corps. The classic example of this tradition is the Battle of Camerone. It occurred on April 30, 1863, during the unsuccessful French effort to conquer Mexico. A company of 65 Legionnaires under Captain Jean Danjou was sent out to protect a convoy of ammunition and other supplies on its journey to Mexico City.

Near the village of Camerone, the Legion company was attacked by a large force of Mexican cavalry and infantry. Captain Danjou and his men fought their way through to an abandoned farmhouse. There, the Legionnaires dug in and battled heroically throughout the day. By evening, two-thirds of the Legionnaires had been killed or wounded. Shortly before he was fatally shot, Captain Danjou asked his remaining soldiers to take an oath to die rather than surrender. Each of the Legionnaires gave his word—and kept it.

Camerone was not an important battle—it was really just a minor skirmish. But the courage of that small band of Legionnaires, fighting against overwhelming odds, was epic. The conduct of the men who fought and died at Camerone is considered a model to be followed by all Legionnaires.

For this reason, Camerone Day (April 30) is celebrated as the official holiday of the Legion. No matter where Legion units are stationed, they pay tribute to the spirit of Camerone. There are parades and banquets, and the story of Camerone is read aloud to the troops.

YEARS OF COMBAT

The French Foreign Legion was founded on March 10, 1831, by a royal decree of King Louis Philippe. The decree authorized the creation of ''a legion composed of for-

Beau Geste, a film classic, starred Gary Cooper, Ray Milland, and Robert Preston as Legionnaires.

eigners . . . between the ages of 18 and 40'' for service outside of France.

The French king's main reason for creating the corps was to provide troops to help in the conquest of Algeria, which France was trying to colonize. By the end of 1831, some 3,000 Legionnaires had been recruited and shipped off to Algeria. In the beginning, however, the Foreign Legion was not the elite unit it was later to become. Many of the first recruits were in bad health. They were poorly trained and equipped. And when they arrived in Algeria, they were laughed at by regular French soldiers. But after a few months of toughening up, the Foreign Legion began to prove itself. In a series of battles against the Algerians, the Legionnaires showed they could be effective fighters.

Algeria was the first of many tests for the Legion. During the Spanish civil war of 1835–38, the King of France sent the Legion to fight on the side of Queen Isabella II against a pretender to the throne named Don Carlos. There were many bloody battles, including one in which the French Foreign Legion fought against a foreign legion recruited by Don Carlos. Of the 4,000 French Legionnaires who started the campaign, only 500 were left at the end.

The Legion was so badly mauled that it had to be reorganized from scratch. The "New Legion" was soon back in the thick of the fighting in Algeria, establishing its headquarters at a town called Sidi-bel-Abbès. (The Legion's headquarters remained there until the French withdrew from Algeria in the early 1960's. Headquarters are now at Aubagne, in France.)

Legion units also fought gallantly in the Crimean War (1854–56), in the Italian Campaign of 1859, during the French attempt to colonize Mexico in the 1860's, and in the Franco-Prussian War of 1870–71.

Throughout the late 1800's and early 1900's, the Foreign Legion fought colonial wars in Algeria, Indochina, Dahomey (where Legionnaires battled against fierce women warriors called Amazons), Madagascar, and Morocco. The Legion also participated in many of the battles of World War I, becoming the most decorated French military unit of that war.

The Legion's exploits in battle have been matched by equally heroic feats building roads and tunnels and doing other construction work. In the 1920's, while fighting the Riffs in Morocco, a Legion unit was ordered to build a tunnel through a large mountain. The Legionnaires had no bulldozers, tractors, or other heavy equipment. So they used shovels, picks, other hand tools, and plenty of muscle power. In six months, 40 Legionnaires did what was thought impossible. They built a tunnel through the mountain. Then they proudly chiseled the Legion's insignia and the following inscription over the entrance:

> The mountain barred the road to us.
> The order was given to pass nonetheless.
> The Legion executed it.
> November 1927–May 1928.

World War II saw the Legion hotly engaged against the Nazis. At Sedan, in the early days of the war, 2,000 Legionnaires held back the German Army for 48 hours, until they were wiped out to the last man. But their valiant rearguard action enabled the rest of the French Army to re-form. Later, a Legion battalion fought at Narvik, Norway, during an attempt by the British and French to establish a foothold in that Nazi-occupied country.

The Legion fought colonial wars in Morocco and other countries of North Africa.

These Legionnaires wear leather aprons and carry axes to symbolize their role as military builders.

Legionnaires fought with the British Eighth Army in the North African campaign against the German Afrika Corps. In one bitter moment, during the fighting in Syria, a force of Legionnaires in the Free French Army fought against a Legion unit loyal to the French Vichy government (the puppet government set up by the Nazis during their occupation of France). It was the only time in war that Legionnaires fought against Legionnaires.

After World War II, the Legion went back to policing France's colonies in North Africa and Indochina. There they met with frustration and defeat. At Dienbienphu, the last major battle of the French Indochina War, Legionnaires fought to the bitter end.

The end was equally bitter in Algeria. After years of bloody guerrilla warfare by Algerian nationalists, France gave that country its independence. Angered by this, a group of French generals, aided by several thousand French troops including a Legion paratroop regiment, attempted a coup. The revolt was crushed, and the Legion paratroop regiment was disbanded.

The years since the Algerian war have generally been quiet ones for the Legion. Today the Foreign Legion consists of about 10,000 men, mostly foreign volunteers, organized in motorized and paratroop regiments. Helicopters and armored vehicles have replaced the camels and mules of yesterday. The majority of the units are stationed in France or on the islands that are controlled by France in the Pacific and Indian oceans. But some things are still the same. The pay is still low—about $200 a month for a recruit—and discipline is still tough.

So in spirit this crack military unit is not too different from what it was years ago when a Legion officer told a would-be recruit: "The Legion! Hard work, hard knocks, hard discipline!"

And many of those who have served in its ranks would probably shake their heads and say—as Legionnaires have been saying for 150 years—"C'est la Legion!" ("That's the Legion!")

HENRY I. KURTZ
Author, *Captain John Smith*

WHAT DO YOU MEAN BY THAT?

Did you spill the beans? Are you in hot water? Do you have feet of clay?

These questions might not make sense to someone who is not very familiar with the English language. That's because they contain idioms—expressions with special meanings that can't be figured out from the individual words in them. Like many idioms, these expressions rose out of stories and situations that are hundreds and sometimes thousands of years old. Today the stories and situations are often forgotten, but the idioms live on.

SPILL THE BEANS

You "spill the beans" when you tell a secret to someone who's not supposed to know. This idiom goes back to ancient Greece. The Greeks had secret societies that were like very exclusive clubs. When someone wanted to join one of these societies, the members would vote. Each member would put a bean into a pottery jar—a white bean for a "yes" vote, a brown bean for a "no" vote. The vote was kept secret so that the person's feelings wouldn't be hurt if there were a lot of brown beans. Only the leaders were supposed to look in the jar. But sometimes a member would knock the jar over and spill the beans—and the secret would be out.

PULL THE WOOL OVER SOMEONE'S EYES

To "pull the wool over someone's eyes" is to fool that person. This idiom is thought to date from the 1700's, when fashionable gentlemen wore elaborate wigs. The human or animal hair that was used to make the wigs was generally called wool. Practical jokers (and sometimes thieves, too) would sneak up behind a gentleman and tip his wig down over his eyes, so that he couldn't see. The joker would run off laughing—but the thief would steal the gentleman's money!

LION'S SHARE

If you take the "lion's share" of something, you take the largest part—or perhaps all of it. The expression comes from a story in *Aesop's Fables*. In the story, several animals join a lion for a hunt. But when the time comes to divide up the kill, the lion claims one fourth as his right, one fourth for his bravery, and one fourth for his lioness and cubs. He offers to fight the other animals for the final share, and they slink away, leaving him with the entire kill.

IN HOT WATER

When you're "in hot water," you're in trouble. This expression is thought to have come from a test that was used hundreds of years ago to show innocence or guilt. A person accused of a crime would be told to reach into a pot of boiling water. People were judged guilty if they were burned (which, of course, they always were).

COLD SHOULDER

If you get the "cold shoulder" from someone, you've been snubbed and treated rudely. In this expression, "shoulder" refers to a cut of meat for roasting, not a part of the rude person's body. The saying is thought to have originated in medieval times, when it was the custom for nobles to offer a hot meal and a bed to any weary traveler who knocked on the castle gate. But unwelcome travelers would be offered only a meal of leftovers —perhaps a few slices from a cold shoulder of mutton—in the hope that they would go away.

FEET OF CLAY

"Feet of clay" are a weakness. This idiom comes from the Old Testament of the Bible. In the Book of Daniel, King Nebuchadnezzar dreams of a statue with a head made of gold, chest and arms of silver, stomach and thighs of brass, legs of iron, and feet partly of iron and partly of clay. A stone strikes the feet, and the whole statue shatters. Daniel interprets the dream to mean the decline of the King's realm. Nowadays, the expression is used to refer to a weak point in the character of a person who is otherwise strong.

YOUTH

Sunset Volleyball, *by David Wagenknecht, 16, of York, Pennsylvania: A winner in a 1981 photography awards program for young people.*

Peacock, by Lesa Duran, 17, Fairview Park, Ohio

YOUNG PHOTOGRAPHERS

Here's proof that something as ordinary as a bunch of colored pencils can be just as beautiful as an exotic subject—like a proud peacock. All that's needed to make the transformation is a camera and the imaginative eye of a photographer.

The photographs on these and the following pages were among the winners in the 1981 Scholastic/Kodak Photo Awards program, which was open to junior and senior high school students in the United States and Canada. The contest shows how popular photography has become with young people. And the pictures show what excellent photographers young people have become.

Long John, by Marla Cohen, 17, Park Ridge, Illinois

A Rainbow of Color, by Charlene Burroughs, 17, Burbank, California

Surreal Produce Reach, by Jeffrey Plansker, 17, Grosse Pointe Farms, Michigan

Tennis Ball,
by Peter Loisibeas, 17,
Burbank, California

Atomic Sunrise, by David Waitz, 16, Orangeburg, New York

Rooftop Overlook, by Doug Brodke, 17, Avon, Ohio

Canadian Blue Heron,
by Gerald Hare, 18,
Allison Park, Pennsylvania

Slide to the ground . . .

Climb up the outside . . .

FANTASY PLAYHOUSES

Imagine all the wonderful things you could do in one of these playhouses. Play a game of hide-and-seek. Act out an adventure story. Dance. Climb. Sit and daydream.

Does one of the playhouses remind you of a castle? If so, be its king or queen. Is one like a spaceship? Be an astronaut headed for distant stars. Is one a ship? Be its captain, guiding it through a stormy sea.

These playhouses were created by artists who wanted to give children places in which to use their imaginations. Children even helped to build some of the playhouses. They mixed concrete, dug holes, hammered nails, and painted. And they gave their ideas on how to design the structures.

Even before the playhouses were completed, children were using them. They knew that they had a play place—and a fantasy world—of their own.

Hide under the stairs . . .

. . . or crawl along a ledge.

YOUNG HEADLINERS

In 1981, petite **Amanda McKerrow** became the first American to win a gold medal at the Moscow International Ballet Competition. Soviet dancers had always dominated the event, which is held every four years. But in June, 17-year-old Amanda captivated the judges and the audience with her lyrical dancing. She shared top honors in the junior women's division with Natalya Arkhipova of the Soviet Union. Amanda, who lives in Rockville, Maryland, and dances with the Washington Ballet, has been devoted to dancing since she was 7.

Have you ever given a "wrong" answer on a test—and been *sure* you were right? **Daniel Lowen,** a 17-year-old from Cocoa Beach, Florida, outsmarted a panel of college professors with one answer on the 1981 Preliminary Scholastic Aptitude Test. Students were expected to answer "7" to the question below—by adding up the 9 faces of the pyramids and then subtracting 2, for the faces that would be hidden when the pyramids were put together. But Daniel answered "5." He reasoned that 4 of the faces would blend together to form 2 new faces, and he made a model that proved his point. As a result, his test score was raised—and so were the scores of most of the 240,000 other students who took the test.

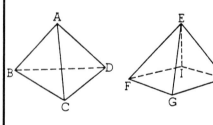

IN PYRAMIDS ABCD AND EFGHI SHOWN ABOVE, ALL FACES EXCEPT BASE FGHI ARE EQUILATERAL TRIANGLES OF EQUAL SIZE. IF FACE ABC WERE PLACED ON FACE EFG SO THAT THE VERTICES OF THE TRIANGLES COINCIDE, HOW MANY EXPOSED FACES WOULD THE RESULTING SOLID HAVE?

(A) FIVE   (B) SIX   (C) SEVEN
(D) EIGHT   (E) NINE

The best-selling puzzle Rubik's Cube made **Patrick Bossert** a best-selling author at the age of 13. The cube is named for its inventor, Ernö Rubik, a Hungarian professor. It has six sides, each in a different color and each made up of nine smaller cubelets. The object is to scramble the cubelets and then twist and turn them until all the sides are solid colors again—a feat that has baffled millions. But Patrick, who lives near London, can solve the cube in under 90 seconds. He wrote a 112-page book, *You Can Do the Cube,* that became a best seller. His advice: "Don't despair, and don't give up."

Amy Sue Reichel, a 17-year-old high school senior from New York City, won first prize—a $12,000 scholarship—in the 1981 Westinghouse Science Talent Search. The science contest is the largest and most competitive in the United States. Amy, whose hobbies include French cooking and playing classical piano, said she would use the award to study biochemistry at Harvard. Her winning project involved five months of research into the genetic structure of yeast cells. She was the third girl to win the top award—and the third member of her family to win a prize of some kind in the contest.

THE SKATING BOOM

Figure skating has been around since the 1700's. But only in recent years has it become a "hot" sport in North America. If people aren't watching it on TV or going to live ice shows, they're out on the ice themselves. Why has figure skating suddenly become so popular?

Much of the new interest has to do with television. During the 1960's and 1970's, people were able to watch the Winter Olympics right in their own living rooms. They saw the beauty and theatrics of figure skating and the skill and grace of the competitors. In time, the world and national championships, skating exhibitions, and ice shows were televised. People saw different techniques and more complicated routines. And the more people learned about figure skating, the more fascinated they were by the sport.

The individual skating styles and personalities of the young competitors added to the new wave of interest. Names like Peggy Fleming, Dorothy Hamill, John Curry, Tai Babilonia, and Randy Gardner were recognized by almost everyone, and fans avidly followed the careers of their favorites.

In 1981, several new skaters attracted the public's attention—among them, Elaine Zayak and Peter and Caitlin Carruthers.

Elaine Zayak. Fifteen-year-old Elaine Zayak, from Paramus, New Jersey, won the 1981 U.S. women's figure-skating championship. Not only did she win, but she stunned the world by doing something that no other female skater had ever done before in competition: She made seven triple-revolution jumps during a four-minute routine. In a triple jump, the skater leaps up from the ice and whirls around three times in the air before touching down on the ice again.

Just a month after the U.S. championships, Elaine placed second in the world championships, winning the silver medal. Once again, she completed seven triple jumps. But she also became the center of a controversy.

Figure skating is partly an athletic sport and partly a graceful art form because its

Elaine Zayak

Caitlin and Peter Carruthers

movements are a lot like ballet. There have always been some acrobatic routines in figure skating, but nothing as daring as Elaine's jumps. Some critics say that Elaine's style doesn't have enough grace. They worry that she may begin a trend in which women's figure skating will lose its dancelike qualities and become too acrobatic. But Elaine has said, "People have said what I do isn't figure skating, but they're into ballet. I think the sport is changing, becoming more athletic. I think people like my way better."

Elaine's "way" has been developing since she was about 4 years old, when she began to skate. Then her parents bought a trampoline, and she learned to jump. Elaine put these two skills together and has become the "jumpingest" figure skater ever known. And in case anyone has any doubts, Elaine has announced that she wants to be the next Olympic champ. It's certain that her fans will be rooting for her at the 1984 Winter Olympics, at Sarajevo, Yugoslavia.

Peter and Caitlin Carruthers. Twenty-one-year-old Peter and 19-year-old Caitlin also excelled at the 1981 U.S. figure-skating championships: They won the gold in the pairs event.

They suffered a setback just a short time later, when they placed only fifth in the world championships. But they skate so well together that many experts feel they will become a top twosome in the sport.

Pairs skating involves a team of a man and a woman. The style is athletic, rather than acrobatic or balletic. Pairs skating involves something else, too—a special relationship, a special closeness, between the partners. They must think and act in the same way.

Peter and Caitlin (or Kitty, as she is often called) certainly have that special relationship. They are brother and sister, although not by birth—as babies they were adopted into the same family. They grew up in Burlington, Massachusetts. When their father built a backyard ice rink, Peter played hockey, and Caitlin skated. Peter then switched to figure skating, and from then on, they worked together and developed the energetic style of figure skating that they have become known for.

Their hard work began to pay off when they skated to fifth place in the 1980 Winter Olympics. And they, like Elaine Zayak, are looking forward to skating to first at the 1984 Games.

SCOUTING

Electronics was one of more than 70 career fields that Boy Scouts explored in merit-badge programs during 1981. Others ranged from agriculture and computers to theater and woodworking.

This Cadette Scout studies a scale model of a building to learn about architecture. Her project is part of the Girl Scout career-exploration program.

The four age groups of the Girl Guides of Canada are represented here. From left to right are a Ranger (15 to 18 years old), a Pathfinder (12 to 15), a Guide (9 to 12), and a Brownie (6 to 9).

The Boy Scouts of Canada held their 1981 Jamboree in Alberta, July 1—10. Here, Scouts at the Jamboree are learning the finer points of archery.

Two Brownie Girl Scouts concentrate on an art project—one of many activities that are part of the Brownie program.

Lunch, anyone? These Girl Scouts have made a portable solar oven and are about to cook some grilled cheese sandwiches in it.

The Oak Ridge Boys, a country and western music group, entertained U.S. Scouts at the 1981 National Scout Jamboree at Fort A.P. Hill, Virginia.

Here's one way to keep your head above water. These Canadian Boy Scouts are practicing walking through water on stilts—one of several activities in the "waterlogging" program at the Jamboree.

International Street, a fascinating place for shopping and eating.

CANADA'S WONDERLAND

What is your secret dream? To visit a foreign land? To travel back in time? To bring an imaginary world to life?

Such fantasies are the themes for Canada's Wonderland, a new park that opened in 1981 in Vaughan, just north of Toronto. The park features sights, sounds, and experiences from places around the world, from times past, and from some places that never existed anywhere.

The heart of the park is Wonder Mountain, an artificial peak that is 150 feet (46 meters) tall. It was created for the park from steel, concrete, and other materials. If you climb the twisting path that leads to the summit, you'll have a view of the park's five theme areas.

International Street. The park's front gate opens onto International Street. The focal point of this theme area is a long reflecting pool with a series of fountains. The pool is fed by a waterfall that tumbles down the side of Wonder Mountain. The fountains are most thrilling after dark, when lighting makes them look like diamond showers. The street itself is a fascinating place for shopping and eating. Each of the street's four main buildings is designed in a different style —Latin-American, Scandinavian, Mediterranean, and Alpine.

International Festival. Spread out around the base of Wonder Mountain is International Festival. The highlight of this theme area is the International Showplace, a Greek-style amphitheater. The show "Singing to the World," staged here, is one of several live shows at the park. The performers are Canadian students.

Grande World Exposition of 1890. This area aims to carry you back in time, to the 1890's. And it leads you to some distant lands as well. For example, there's a small version of the Crystal Palace, a glass building that was the main feature of a British fair of 1851. You can also visit a Moroccan bazaar and try a scary African boat ride called the Zumba Flume. Perhaps the most wonderful ride is the old-fashioned carousel, or merry-go-round, which was built in the 1920's. It has 64 horses and 2 chariots, all brightly painted and hand carved. After this gentle ride, walk to the edge of the exposition to see something very different—the Mighty Canadian Minebuster, one of the largest, fastest roller-coaster rides in North America.

Medieval Faire. Cross over a castle drawbridge and find yourself in the Middle Ages. Court jesters stroll about the streets juggling. A knight in shining armor escorts his lady fair. Also in this section is the scariest of the

Canterbury Theatre, in the Medieval Faire theme area.

The Hanna-Barberry-Go-Round.

park's four roller coasters—the Dragon Fyre. It will turn you upside down four times if you dare to ride on it.

A pirate ship floats on a lake at the center of this area. It's the scene of a stunt show called "Plight of the Land Locked Pirates." And in Canterbury Theatre, a castle not far from the Dragon Fyre, a live show is held that's not medieval at all. It's called "Those Magnificent Movies," and it gives the student performers a chance to act and sing in scenes from great movies of the past.

Happyland of Hanna-Barbera. This is the home of Yogi Bear, Scooby Doo, Fred Flintstone, and other TV cartoon characters. Here they are out of the TV set and walking around in the street, ready to give you a hug or have their pictures snapped with you.

This theme area has rides that are especially for young people—including the Hanna-Barberry-Go-Round and the Ghoster Coaster. At the Saltwater Circus, dolphins and sea lions cavort. Macaws and parrots perform at the Woodland Theatre in Yogi's Woods. At Yogi's Cave, Yogi and the other characters can be seen in animated films.

It's hard to leave this fantasyland. But when you come back, Canada's Wonderland will greet you with yet another theme land: Frontier Canada—coming soon!

Young artists can develop their talents at a special museum in the Soviet Union.

Improvisation, by a 7-year-old Soviet artist, was created from colorful yarns.

Circus, by a 13-year-old artist, is formed of colorful scraps of fabric.

YOUNG ARTISTS

The pictures on these pages are on display in a special museum—one of the few museums in the world devoted completely to children's art. The museum is in the city of Yerevan, in the Armenian Soviet Socialist Republic in the Soviet Union. It was founded over ten years ago, and it has a collection of more than 100,000 works of art. The museum also has a studio, where young people can use new art materials and learn new techniques. Thus the museum is really an art center, with two goals. One is to help young artists develop their talents. The other is to study children's art as a separate branch of art—art that is expressive and closely linked to fantasy.

Children made all the works of art at the museum.

CREATIVITY

244

The artist Joseph Cornell selected various objects and uniquely arranged them in small wooden boxes. Each of his creations, such as A Pantry Ballet, *below, is a little dreamworld of delight and mystery.*

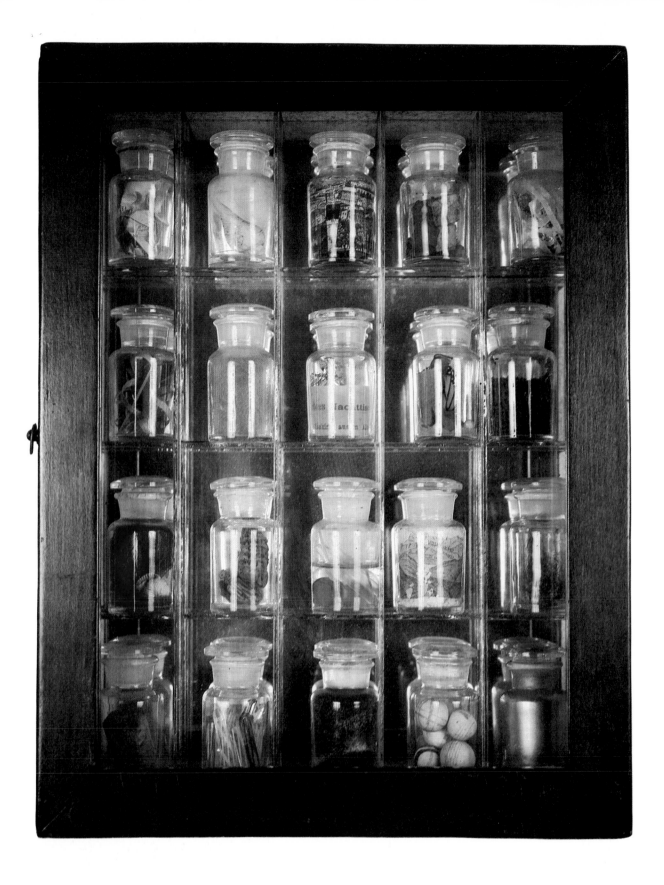

JOSEPH CORNELL'S MAGICAL BOXES

Joseph Cornell was an artist who lived in two worlds. One was the ordinary, everyday world in which we all live. The other was a magical world that existed only in his imagination. But because of his creations, all of us can see his magical world.

Cornell constructed hundreds of small wood boxes. He filled these boxes with familiar objects—seashells, marbles, twigs, cutouts of people and animals, clock springs, bird feathers. His magic lies in the unique way he selected and arranged these common objects. Cornell was able to make each box a little dreamworld of delight and mystery.

COLLECTING "LOOT"

Cornell was born in 1903. For most of his life he lived in Flushing, an area of New York City. He would travel by subway into Manhattan, where he would spend many hours looking for materials for his boxes. He visited old bookshops, record stores, souvenir shops, and five-and-dime stores. He collected all sorts of "loot," as he called it. Postage stamps, photographs, ballet programs, magazines, driftwood, sequins, clay pipes, toys, and coins were found and saved.

None of these cost a lot of money. Cornell couldn't afford to buy expensive things. But although they were inexpensive, Cornell thought of them as treasures. They were the raw materials of his work.

It took Cornell a long time to make one of his boxes. He wanted to create a feeling of age. He polished the wood so that it would look old. If the wood was painted, he might put it in the oven. The heat would make the paint peel and crack. Sometimes he would paste pages from old books and magazines on the back of a box.

Tilly Losch

Opposite page: *Pharmacy*

247

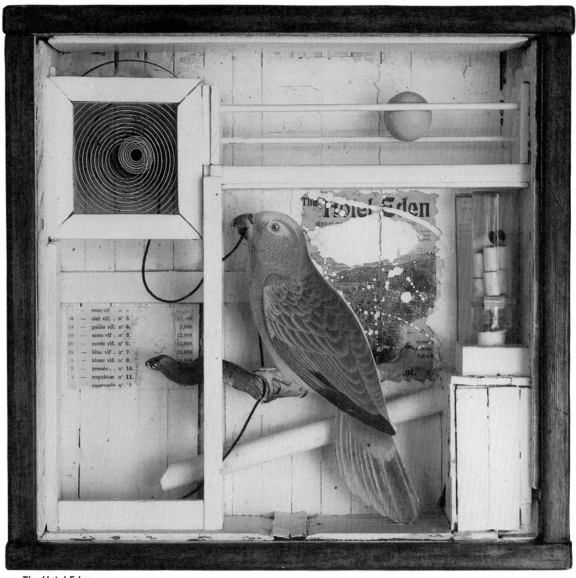

The Hotel Eden

The most time-consuming part was arranging his treasures in the box. This could take weeks. Cornell moved things around and added or removed items, until he felt "a sense of rightness."

Each of the objects in a box had a special meaning—it was a symbol. A seashell was a symbol of the sea. A feather on the floor of a box symbolized a bird that had flown away. A spiral watch spring symbolized time.

Often, Cornell's works showed unexpected connections between very different objects. He showed the similarity between the seams in a ship's sails and the threads of a spider's web. He showed connections between soap bubbles and planets, and between butterflies and ballerinas.

Cornell died in 1972, but his work lives on. His magical boxes are exhibited all over the world, enchanting people everywhere.

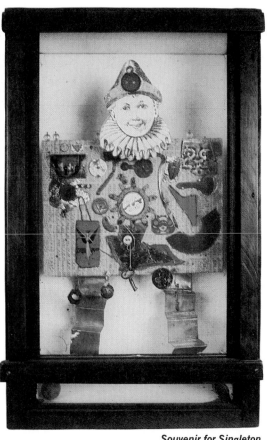

Souvenir for Singleton

Medici Princess

Paul and Virginia

LISTEN TO THE HANDS

"Language and mood shimmer in their movements. They use their hands, their faces, their whole bodies to convey an idea that the spoken word can barely suggest. They are like sculptors, carving language in the air."

This is a description of a remarkable group of people—the deaf actors and actresses of the National Theatre of the Deaf. They "speak" to their audiences in a language that can be seen but not heard. The key to their dramatic art is in the beautiful hand language of the deaf, which is called "signing." The hand gestures, or signs, represent words and ideas. To help them communicate the language that is flashing from their hands, the performers use mime, dance, and all the expressive powers of body language.

Most of the audience usually consists of people who can hear. So that the hearing audience can better understand the sign language, one or more narrators speak the words as the other performers are signing them. What results is a unique interplay of sound and sight. The spoken words interpret the sign language. And the signing broadens the meanings of the words. The communication is so total that hearing people actually believe they can understand the signing.

If you ever get the chance to attend a production, be sure to notice how alert the deaf performers are. If you can hear, you rely on both your ears and your eyes to receive information. But deaf people must rely completely on their eyes. For this reason, the performers have learned to be extremely observant. On stage, this creates an aliveness that you may not see in a production that has all hearing performers.

HOW IT BEGAN

The National Theatre of the Deaf (NTD) was founded by David Hays. Hays, a hearing person, had visited Gallaudet College for the Deaf in Washington, D.C., in 1958. A stage designer, he had gone to Gallaudet with other show people who were seeking advice about a play they were producing on Broadway. The play, *The Miracle Worker*, was about the life of Helen Keller, a famous and talented woman who was both deaf and blind. While at Gallaudet, Hays attended some student theatrical productions. He was captivated by the performers and the way they expressed themselves with their hands. He began to work on setting up a professional theater of deaf actors and actresses. Nine years later, in 1967, the NTD was established, at the Eugene O'Neill Memorial Theater Center in Waterford, Connecticut.

Since that time, the NTD has performed in countries throughout the world—including Canada, France, Sweden, Australia, Japan, and Korea. And everywhere the performers

---

THE LITTLE THEATRE OF THE DEAF

The popularity of the NTD quickly led to the establishment of the Little Theatre of the Deaf (LTD), which performs for young people in schools and children's theaters everywhere. The LTD program consists of stories, playlets, poems, fairy tales, and fables. Young people respond enthusiastically, excitedly laughing and screaming, yet all the while paying very close attention to the talented deaf performers and their remarkable language. Audience participation plays a great role. Sometimes the youngsters are invited to join in and imitate the performers. And at the end of each show, the performers do improvisations based on suggestions from the children.

---

have gone, their dramatic artistry has won great acclaim. Attractive and talented, they keep their audiences enthralled. At the end of the show, the performers cannot hear the audience's appreciative applause. But they can see the reaction that they have evoked. And they, better than anyone, know how much can be said without spoken words.

In *Parade*, a play performed by the National Theatre of the Deaf, characters imagine a make-believe place where deaf people can live as they wish. There, they have Mr. Silence *(left)*, the deaf version of Superman, and their own soap operas, such as "As the Hand Turns" *(below)*.

Mary Tyler Moore and Timothy Hutton (best supporting actor) in *Ordinary People* (best motion picture).

1981 ACADEMY AWARDS

CATEGORY	WINNER
Motion Picture	*Ordinary People*
Actor	Robert De Niro *(Raging Bull)*
Actress	Sissy Spacek *(Coal Miner's Daughter)*
Supporting Actor	Timothy Hutton *(Ordinary People)*
Supporting Actress	Mary Steenburgen *(Melvin and Howard)*
Director	Robert Redford *(Ordinary People)*
Foreign Language Film	*Moscow Does Not Believe in Tears* (U.S.S.R.)
Song	"Fame" *(Fame)*
Documentary Feature	*From Mao to Mozart: Isaac Stern in China*
Documentary Short	*Karl Hess: Toward Liberty*
Cinematography	Geoffrey Unsworth and Ghislain Cloquet *(Tess)*

Sissy Spacek (best actress)
in *Coal Miner's Daughter.*

Robert De Niro (best actor)
in *Raging Bull.*

Alexander the Great, King of Macedonia, was one of the most famous warriors of ancient times. He also helped to spread Greek culture to millions of people under his rule.

This marble head of Alexander was found in Pella, the capital of ancient Macedonia and the birthplace of Alexander.

THE SEARCH FOR ALEXANDER

Alexander the Great was one of the most famous people who ever lived. His fame is well deserved. By the time he was 18 he was commanding troops in battle. At 20 he became king of Macedonia, a country north of the ancient Greek city-states. In the next twelve years he conquered a vast amount of territory. He extended his kingdom as far east as India and as far south as Egypt. But Alexander was more than a great warrior. He introduced new ideas for governing conquered countries. And one of his major contributions to world history was the spread of Greek culture to millions of people living in the countries under his rule.

The culture and civilization of Alexander's time—the 4th century B.C.—was brought alive by a stunning exhibit that toured the United States from late 1980 through early 1982. Called "The Search for Alexander," the exhibit showed the objects that the ancient Greeks had used in their homes, for adornment, and for worship. There were also more recent items that were inspired by the legends of Alexander.

Alexander's Time. Alexander was born in Pella, Macedonia, in 356 B.C., some 2,300 years ago. His father was Philip II, king of Macedonia from 359 to 336 B.C. When Alexander was 13, he

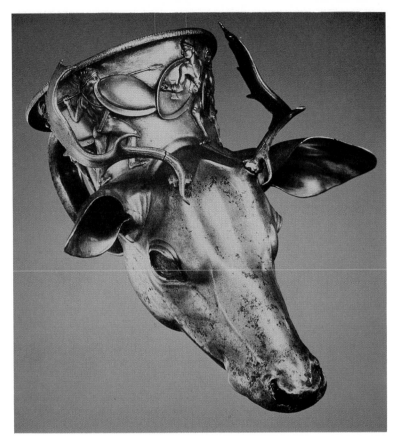

These ancient objects—a silver drinking horn and a silver container decorated with a portrait of Heracles—were included in an exhibit that brought alive the culture and civilization of Alexander's time.

became a pupil of the Greek philosopher Aristotle. From this great teacher, Alexander learned much about Greek culture, and he became deeply attached to it.

Alexander's father was also a great warrior. Philip developed a superb army and used it to make Macedonia the most powerful country in Europe. He conquered most of the city-states of Greece and ruled over much of the land to the north and northwest of Macedonia as well. Philip was assassinated as he prepared to invade Greece's main enemy, Persia.

With Philip's death and Alexander's ascension to the throne, southern Greece tried to break away from Macedonian rule. Alexander led his troops south and crushed the rebellion. He reunited the cities of Greece and became their leader. Then he turned to the countries of Asia and Africa. He conquered Persia and Egypt and began an invasion of India. He never lost a battle. His military successes fulfilled the desires of his father, who had once said, "My son, look for a kingdom worthy of yourself. Macedonia is too small for you."

When Alexander was only 32 years old, he died of a fever. His body was wrapped in gold cloth and placed in a beautiful coffin. He was buried in Alexandria, a city he had founded in Egypt. At the time of his death, he had been the leader of the largest Western empire of the ancient world. And throughout this empire, he

Philip II, Alexander's father, was also a great warrior-king.

had spread the Greek way of life—language, customs, art, games, philosophy, and education.

The Exhibit. Many of the ancient treasures in the exhibit had been found in graves. Graves are a major source of archeological material. Objects buried in graves are protected and are less likely to decay or break than objects kept above ground.

The people of ancient Greece believed in an afterlife—a life after death. Thus they buried with a dead person those things that might be needed in the afterlife: weapons, armor, containers for food and drink. These objects tell us a lot about life during Alexander's time.

From the exhibit, we can see that the people of Alexander's time took great pride in the containers created by their artisans. These included huge bowls, storage jars, drinking cups, pitchers, and vases. The containers are made of metal—gold, silver, iron, and bronze. Some of the containers are decorated with designs and portraits, often of mythological beings. Heracles, a mythical hero known for his strength, was a popular subject.

An outstanding example of metalwork is a huge bronze krater, or vase, found in a grave at Derveni in northern Greece. The vase is 3 feet (90 centimeters) tall. It was used for mixing wine and water. Its decorations show the wedding of Dionysus and Ariadne. (In Greek mythology, Dionysus was the god of wine, and Ariadne was the daughter of King Minos of Crete.)

The highlights of the show were magnificent objects found in a tomb in Vergina, a Greek village in what was once ancient Macedonia. The tomb was uncovered in 1977 by Greek archeologist Manolis Andronikos. It was filled with armor and beautiful ceremonial objects made of precious metals.

When Andronikos opened the marble coffin in the main cham-

Also in the exhibit was this huge bronze vase, showing the wedding of Dionysus and Ariadne. It is an outstanding example of the metalwork made by the artisans of Alexander's time.

The highlights of the show were magnificent objects found in a tomb that may be that of Philip II. This solid gold casket is decorated with a sunburst, the symbol of all the Macedonian kings. Inside the casket was a . . .

ber of the tomb, he found a solid gold casket decorated with a sunburst, the symbol of the Macedonian kings. Inside the casket were the remains of a man, covered with a gold wreath of oak leaves and acorns. (The oak tree was the sacred tree of Zeus, the most important god in ancient Greece.) There was also a gilded silver diadem. This adjustable hoop was worn on the head to indicate that the wearer of it was a ruler. Archeologists had known of diadems from portraits of kings on coins. But this was the first time that an actual diadem had been found. Obviously, the tomb was no ordinary tomb. It was the tomb of a very special person.

Andronikos believes that Vergina was once the ancient burial place of the kings of Macedonia. He believes the tomb is that of Philip II, Alexander's father. There is no absolute proof that this is true, but the evidence supports the belief. The richness of the objects in the tomb suggests a royal owner. All the objects date from between 350 and 325 B.C. During this time only one king, Philip II, was buried in Macedonia. The bones in the casket were those of a man of approximately 46, Philip's age at the time of his death. And the greaves, or leg armor, found in the tomb consist of two unequal pieces. The greave for one leg is shorter than the other. Philip, who was lame, probably would have needed unequal greaves.

If it is true that the objects found in Vergina belonged to Philip II, then they are the objects that Alexander actually lived with too. But even if they weren't Philip's, they belonged to Alexander's time. So while the vast empire created by Alexander no longer exists, we still have many of the beautiful treasures that were created when that young man was the most important person of the Western world.

A terra-cotta statuette of Aphrodite (the Greek goddess of love) playing an ancient lyre called a cithara.

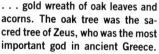

. . . gold wreath of oak leaves and acorns. The oak tree was the sacred tree of Zeus, who was the most important god in ancient Greece.

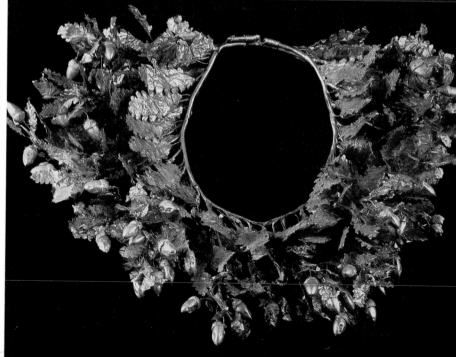

SLEEP IN AN ELEPHANT

Let's sleep in an enormous elephant . . . or in a cement tepee. Let's snap a photo of the Santa Maria House, a copy of one of Christopher Columbus' ships with a mast going right through the ceiling. And let's take a gander at the marvelous Mother Goose House.

These are just some of the many unusual buildings that people have created. They are used as homes, hotels, motels, or restaurants. They can be found everywhere—from big cities to small towns. There's a teapot-shaped building, complete with handle and spout, in Washington. There's the Pig House in Texas. And in Pennsylvania, there's the Shoe House. Next to it is a smaller shoe house for the family dog. Even the mailbox is in the shape of a shoe. Who built this wonder? Why, a shoemaker, of course.

THE MUSIC SCENE

As the year 1981 opened, the music world was still mourning the tragic death of John Lennon, who had been killed in late 1980. Lennon's last album, *Double Fantasy,* moved quickly to the top of the charts and remained there for a long period of time. Fans rushed to record stores to buy his final artistic achievement—and to honor the memory of a musical great. The album, recorded with his wife, Yoko Ono, featured the best-selling single, "Just Like Starting Over."

By the end of 1981, the Rolling Stones were the talk of the music scene. They hit the charts with a new album, *Tattoo You,* and embarked on their first U.S. concert tour in several years. The tour drew hundreds of thousands of loyal Stones fans in Philadelphia, Los Angeles, and New York, and 22 other stops in between. The tour was hailed as a genuine "happening." Perhaps more than anything, it proved the popularity and staying power of a rock group that had been on the music scene for more than fifteen years.

Aside from these two highly charged events, the music world continued the trends set in 1980, and the airwaves echoed the sounds of the past. No great superstars appeared on the scene, and those newcomers who did record seemed to base their styles on earlier popular personalities and groups.

SOMETHING FOR EVERYONE

A wide variety of styles were presented by a number of artists during the year. The heavy metal sound continued to command a sizable following. The rasp and roar of synthesizers and giant amplifiers produced sales and fans for REO Speedwagon ("Take It on the Run" and "Keep on Loving You" from *Hi Infidelity*); Foreigner ("Urgent" from *4*); Journey ("Who's Crying Now" from *Escape*); Air Supply ("The One That You Love" from the album of the same name); AC/DC *(Back in Black);* and Styx ("The Best of Times" and "Too Much Time on My Hands" from *Paradise Theater*).

Pop-oriented music also received its share of the audience. The Commodores produced

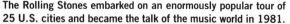

The Rolling Stones embarked on an enormously popular tour of 25 U.S. cities and became the talk of the music world in 1981.

The Commodores hit the charts with *In the Pocket*, featuring the single, "Lady (You Bring Me Up)."

In the Pocket, featuring "Lady (You Bring Me Up)"; the Carpenters hit the charts with "Touch Me When We're Dancing" from *Made in America;* and the Doobie Brothers scored with *One Step Closer.* Rick Springfield excited his fans with "Jessie's Girl" and *Working Class Dog.* And George Harrison recorded "All Those Years Ago," a tribute to his former sidekick, John Lennon. This hit single came from Harrison's *Somewhere in England* album.

Still different sounds were heard from other artists. Joey Scarbury landed on the charts with "Greatest American Hero," the title song of the TV series. Manhattan Transfer sang "Boy from New York City" to the delight of their fans. Pablo Cruise ("Cool Love"), Rick James ("Super Freak" and "Give It to Me Baby"), Tom Petty and the Heartbreakers ("The Waiting"), and Juice Newton ("Angel of the Morning" and "Queen of Hearts") also made the record-buying public happy.

MAINSTREAM COUNTRY

The "new" country music—a mixture of mellow rock and Western twang—was enormously popular during the year. An example

Eddie Rabbitt followed in the footsteps of Kenny Rogers as the best country-pop crossover.

of the new country sound was provided by the Oak Ridge Boys, a 20-year-old down-home country group. Their first Top-Ten hit, "Elvira," was a light pop tune with the oom-pah-pah-mow-mow sound.

The mainstream acceptance of the country sound was so extensive that Las Vegas, long the home of only middle-of-the-road singers, became a stopping place for country artists. The Vegas clubs that usually featured stars like Frank Sinatra and Barbra Streisand made room for Mickey Gilley and Johnny Lee of *Urban Cowboy* fame, Dolly Parton, Kenny Rogers, Dottie West, Larry Gatlin, Crystal Gayle, and Waylon Jennings. Eddie Rabbitt, following in the footsteps of Rogers as the best country-pop crossover, also starred in Las Vegas and vaulted to the top of the pop charts with "Step by Step," a follow-up to his "I Love a Rainy Night" hit.

THE YEAR OF THE WOMAN

Male singers and musicians had to make a lot of room for female company in 1981. This was the year that the women challenged the men of the music world by zooming to the top of the charts with resounding hits.

Dolly Parton, originally from the Smoky Mountains of Tennessee, successfully kept up with her musical career. At the same time, however, she also became a film star. She combined her many talents and wrote and recorded "9 to 5," the hit record from the film of the same name, in which she starred. "I'm not leaving country music," she told her Nashville colleagues when she went to Hollywood, "I'm just taking it with me."

For many years, Kim Carnes had re-corded albums that didn't sell while she wrote hit songs for other singers. In 1980, Kenny Rogers invited Carnes to duet with him on the popular "Don't Fall in Love with a Dreamer" disc. This was one of the songs in an album that Carnes and her husband had written for Rogers. But in 1981, Kim Carnes came into her own. She exploded as an artist in the pop field with a song she did *not* write. "Bette Davis Eyes," sung in a husky, raspy monotone reminiscent of Rod Stewart's, was a six-year-old ballad written by Donna Weiss and one-time recording star Jackie DeShannon. The record zoomed to the top

Kim Carnes's "Bette Davis Eyes" was a strong hit.

of the charts and took hold of the number-one position for many weeks. And the rest of Carnes's *Mistaken Identity* album was headed in the same direction.

Pat Benatar, with a multi-octave, classi-cally trained voice, became another of the year's success stories with the popular "Hit Me with Your Best Shot," a cut from her *Crimes of Passion* album. Benatar kept the momentum going with "Fire and Ice" from *Precious Time*.

Deborah Harry of Blondie fame continued on her successful path. Although Blondie had three platinum albums and four num-ber-one singles (including *Autoamerican*, which featured "The Tide Is High" and "Rapture"), Harry decided to strike out on her own. Her first solo effort, *KooKoo*, caused excitement throughout the musical world with its controversial album cover and selection of songs. For the most part, the songs were a mix of reggae, rock, and funk over a disco beat. "The title *KooKoo*," she explained, "stems from the 'cu' syllable in acupuncture," a medical procedure in which Harry was involved.

Stevie Nicks of Fleetwood Mac fame also took a brief vacation from the group to try a solo fling. Denying rumors that she was leav-

Pat Benatar was another success story with "Hit Me with Your Best Shot" and "Fire and Ice."

ing Fleetwood Mac permanently, Nicks cut *Bella Donna,* and topped the single charts with "Stop Draggin' My Heart Around," a duet with Tom Petty.

LONG-TIME FAVORITES

Diana Ross continued to display disc power in 1981. Her biggest hit, however, had some excellent help. Ross and Lionel Richie, the lead singer and songwriter of the Commodores, teamed up to record the popular "Endless Love." Ross and Richie held the number-one position on the charts for months with their rendition of the theme from the motion picture of the same name. Richie was also the writer of "Lady," the Kenny Rogers' smash recording of 1980–81. And he produced Rogers' next big hit of the year, "I Don't Need You."

Singer and songwriter Neil Diamond added to his long list of hits with "Love on the Rocks," "America," and "Hello Again." All these songs were from the film score of *The Jazz Singer,* in which Diamond starred.

Carly Simon, of folk/rock fame, changed her tune to nostalgia and brought out *Torch.* The album featured "sad" songs from the 1930's, '40's, and '50's.

Britain's Cliff Richard, who first became known in 1959 for his "Living Doll" single, reappeared on the charts with "A Little in Love" from *I'm No Hero.* And he and Olivia Newton-John teamed up to duet on "Suddenly" from the soundtrack of the film *Xanadu.* The English group Moody Blues, remembered for years for their hit "Nights in White Satin," recorded *Long Distance Voyager,* which featured "Gemini Dream." Marty Balin, a member of the Jefferson Airplane (now Jefferson Starship) group, took off on a solo flight with "Hearts," a cut from his *Balin* album.

Smokey Robinson, who had left the Miracles in the early 1970's, returned to the charts with "Being with You," the title song from his new album. Steve Winwood, formerly of the Spencer Davis and Traffic groups, produced *Arc of a Diver,* his first album since 1976. It went straight to the top of the album charts.

Daryl Hall and John Oates appear to have spent the entire year in the recording studio. They recorded the Righteous Brothers' famous standard "You've Lost That Lovin' Feeling" (from *Voices*); *Private Eyes* (featuring the hit title song); and the very popular "Kiss on My List."

The reunion of Simon (*right*) and Garfunkel (*left*) at a concert in New York City's Central Park drew more than 400,000 people.

ODDS AND ENDS

In 1981, newcomer Christopher Cross was the surprise winner of five Grammy awards for his very first single, "Sailing," and his debut album, *Christopher Cross*. He also scored a solid hit with his follow-up recording of "Arthur's Theme" from the soundtrack of the film *Arthur*.

Every now and then an unusual or strange song will take the public by storm. Its popularity may be short-lived, but it does make an impression. The year 1981 saw two such odd hits. "Shaddup You Face," by Joe Dolce, actually hit the top of the charts of radio stations around the country. And "She's Got Papers on Me," sung by Richard (Dimples) Fields and Betty Wright, reportedly sold over half-a-million copies before stations began to ban the rhythm-and-blues marriage woes disc. ("Papers" is black slang for a marriage license.)

"Rapping" established itself as a trend in 1981, branching out from disco disc jockeys who popularized the style to street corners and best-selling records. Rapping is a style in which street slang is chanted at a jaw-breaking speed to a simple rhythmic background. In the wake of the Sugar Hill Gang's success in 1980 with "Rapper's Delight," Kurtis Blow, a champ rapper from New York City, came up with "The Breaks." Tom Waits produced "Heartattack and Vine," and the Sugar Hill Gang created *The Adventures of Grandmaster Flash on the Wheels of Steel*.

The film *American Pop* was the work of Ralph Bakshi, the creator of the popular full-length cartoon film *Fritz the Cat*. *American Pop* was described as "an epic journey through American music." It employed a cartoon technique using the recordings of Bob Seger, Jim Morrison, Jimi Hendrix, and Janis Joplin, among other rock superstars.

Central Park in New York City was the scene of two unusual events connected with the music world. An area of the park, just across the street from John Lennon and Yoko Ono's apartment, was officially named Strawberry Fields in Lennon's honor. It was a favorite walking place of the Lennons.

1981 GRAMMY AWARDS

Record of the Year	"Sailing"	Christopher Cross, artist
Album of the Year	*Christopher Cross*	Christopher Cross, artist
Song of the Year	"Sailing"	Christopher Cross, songwriter
New Artist of the Year		Christopher Cross
Pop Vocal Performance—female	"The Rose"	Bette Midler, artist
Pop Vocal Performance—male	"This Is It"	Kenny Loggins, artist
Pop Vocal Performance—group	"Guilty"	Barbra Streisand, Barry Gibb, artists
Rhythm and Blues Vocal Performance—female	"Never Knew Love Like This Before"	Stephanie Mills, artist
Rhythm and Blues Vocal Performance—male	*Give Me the Night*	George Benson, artist
Country Vocal Performance—female	"Could I Have This Dance"	Anne Murray, artist
Country Vocal Performance—male	"He Stopped Loving Her Today"	George Jones, artist
Original Score for a Motion Picture	*The Empire Strikes Back*	John Williams, composer
Score from an Original Cast Show	*Evita—Premier American Recording*	Andrew Lloyd Webber, composer; Tim Rice, lyricist
Classical Album	*Berg: Lulu (Complete Version)*	Pierre Boulez conducting the Orchestre de l'Opera de Paris
Recording for Children	*In Harmony/A Sesame Street Record*	The Doobie Brothers, James Taylor, Carly Simon, Bette Midler, Muppets, Al Jarreau, Linda Ronstadt, Wendy Waldman, Libby Titus & Dr. John, Livingston Taylor, George Benson & Pauline Wilson, Lucy Simon, Kate Taylor & the Simon/Taylor Family, artists

The Great Lawn in Central Park was the location of a surprise reunion of Paul Simon and Art Garfunkel. The two artists reunited (if only momentarily) to give a free concert benefiting the parks department of New York City. Money was raised through the sale of mementos of the concert. The crowd was estimated at over 400,000 people, all eager to see and hear the two popular singers who had gone their separate ways eleven years earlier.

A MIXED BAG

Perhaps the status of popular music in 1981 was best described by a rock critic who reviewed the Styx's album *Paradise Theater*. The critic described it as a "combination of European-styled art rock, Midwestern heavy metal assault, and softer piano-based ballads." Whether one views fusion as a healthy phenomenon or as a lack of direction, the styles of many 1981 rock groups were a mix.

ARNOLD SHAW
Author, *The Rock Revolution*
and *The Rockin' 50s*

Newcomer Christopher Cross won five Grammy awards for his first single, "Sailing," and his debut album.

Daniel J. Travanti, at left, (best actor, drama series) and Michael Conrad (best supporting actor, drama series) in "Hill Street Blues" (best drama series).

1981 EMMY AWARDS

CATEGORY	WINNER
Comedy Series	"Taxi"
Actor—comedy series	Judd Hirsch, "Taxi"
Actress—comedy series	Isabel Sanford, "The Jeffersons"
Supporting Actor—comedy series	Danny DeVito, "Taxi"
Supporting Actress—comedy series	Eileen Brennan, "Private Benjamin"
Drama Series	"Hill Street Blues"
Actor—drama series	Daniel J. Travanti, "Hill Street Blues"
Actress—drama series	Barbara Babcock, "Hill Street Blues"
Supporting Actor—drama series	Michael Conrad, "Hill Street Blues"
Supporting Actress—drama series	Nancy Marchand, "Lou Grant"
Special—drama or comedy	"Playing for Time" (drama)
Children's Program	"Donahue and Kids" (Project Peacock)

Isabel Sanford, at far right, (best actress, comedy series) in "The Jeffersons."

Judd Hirsch (best actor, comedy series) in "Taxi" (best comedy series).

GET LOST!

You might wonder why anyone would think that getting lost is fun. But getting lost —and finding your way again—is the whole idea behind a maze.

A maze, or labyrinth, is an intricate pattern of passages. It can be a drawing, or it can be something you actually walk through. The goal is to find your way through the passages and come out again. But wrong turns and dead ends fool you all along the way.

People have been fascinated by mazes since ancient times. The Egyptians and the Greeks built underground mazes that may have been used to store treasure (and befuddle any would-be thieves). Some of these mazes may have been prisons. But whatever their actual use, mazes played an important role in the myths of the ancient world.

The most famous mythological maze was the labyrinth of Crete. Legend says that Daedalus, the master craftsman, built the labyrinth for King Minos of Crete. In the labyrinth Minos confined the Minotaur, a half-man, half-bull monster who devoured anyone who entered. And no one who entered ever came out—until Theseus, the legendary hero of Athens, arrived. Theseus unrolled a spool of thread behind him as he went deep into the labyrinth. Then he slew the Minotaur and followed the thread to find his way out.

In Europe during the Middle Ages, maze patterns were built into the tiled floors of churches and cathedrals. These mazes may have symbolized the difficult path of a Christian pilgrimage. Mazes were also carved into the earth of village greens, just for fun.

Mazes became a favorite amusement of European royalty and nobility. Nobles often planted hedges in the form of mazes in their gardens. Many hedge gardens were planted in geometric patterns that were not at all hard to walk through. But others were truly confusing.

One of the best-known hedge mazes was planted in the late 1600's at Hampton Court, near London, by the English King William

The labyrinth of Crete, the most famous mythological maze, as imagined by an 18th-century artist.

The well-known hedge maze at Hampton Court, near London, was planted in the late 1600's.

III. There the members of the court held races to see who could find the way to the center of the maze and back in the fastest time. Today this maze still confuses and delights visitors to Hampton Court.

What may be the most complicated hedge maze anywhere opened in 1978 at Longleat, one of Britain's most famous estates. The Longleat maze covers an area larger than a football field. More than 16,000 waist-high yew trees were planted to form it. As the trees grow to form a towering hedge, the Longleat maze will become the most impenetrable in the world.

It's already confusing enough. The maze has two parts. The first section can be figured out in about half an hour. But the challenging second part will keep the daring befuddled for a much longer time. Six bridges add to the confusion. And the maze's four resting spots have been designed to look exactly alike. Coming on one, you're certain you've passed that way before . . . or have you?

The Longleat maze in Britain, which opened in 1978, may be the most complicated hedge maze in the world.

Alan Alda, who plays Hawkeye Pierce on the series "M*A*S*H," has been one of television's most popular actors ever since the program first appeared in 1972. He has also succeeded as a scriptwriter and a stage and screen actor. And in 1981, he combined three jobs—actor, director, and scriptwriter—for the movie *The Four Seasons.* Born in 1936, Alda was stricken by polio at age 7 but recovered after several years of physical therapy. He earned a degree in English literature at Fordham University and then followed in the footsteps of his father, Robert Alda, in choosing acting as a career. Friends say that the "nice guy" image Alda projects on screen is a true one—he's considerate, generous, concerned about social issues, and devoted to his wife, Arlene, and their three college-age daughters. The Aldas divide their time between Los Angeles and the New Jersey home where their children were raised.

Faster than a speeding bullet, *Superman II* set box-office records within a week of its release in June, 1981. The film's star, 28-year-old **Christopher Reeve,** has been acting since the age of 9. When he isn't busy leaping tall buildings in a single bound, Reeve skis, sails, flys a glider plane, and plays the piano.

At 20, **Timothy Hutton** won the 1981 Academy Award for best supporting actor for his role in *Ordinary People.* The role was his first in a major motion picture—Hutton did not decide to become an actor until he was 17. He then landed parts in a number of TV specials, including the TV movie "Friendly Fire."

"Writings marked by a broad outlook, a wealth of ideas, and artistic power" earned **Elias Canetti** the Nobel prize for literature in 1981. Canetti was born in Bulgaria in 1905 and was educated in Switzerland, Germany, and Austria. He left Austria for England in 1939, and he now divides his time between London and Switzerland. His writings, all in German, include plays, memoirs, and works of fiction.

A 21-year-old senior at Yale University was the surprise winner of a national contest to design a memorial honoring veterans of the Vietnam War. **Maya Ying Lin**'s design was chosen over more than 1,400 other entries, and it will be built in Washington, D.C. It features two long walls of polished black granite, set to form two sides of a triangle and carved with the names of Americans killed in the war. Lin plans to use the $20,000 contest prize to complete her education as an architect—education that includes graduate school and several years of apprenticeship.

The 100th anniversary of the birth of **Anna Pavlova,** one of the greatest ballerinas of all time, was celebrated in 1981. There were exhibits and special performances in many countries. In the United States, two dance companies were formed to re-create her most famous roles. Pavlova, who was born in Russia, had toured the world in programs designed to appeal to general audiences. Her grace and talent popularized ballet and made her a legend.

A lost symphony by **Wolfgang Amadeus Mozart** turned up in a pile of old letters in Germany and was given its first performance in May, 1981. Mozart was 5 years old when he composed his first piece of music. He was only 9 when he wrote this symphony (probably his third) in 1765. Scholars had known the work existed, but it had been lost for 216 years. It is one of hundreds of musical pieces that Mozart composed before his death in 1791, at the age of 35.

FUN TO READ

Petrouchka, by Elizabeth Cleaver, is a beautifully illustrated story about three puppets. It was awarded a Children's Literature Prize by the Canada Council.

Karen's New System

Karen pedaled her bike down Spruce Street. She held the handlebar with one hand and leaned back. With her other hand she reached into one of the baskets that hung over the rear wheel. She pulled out a rolled newspaper and, with a flip of her wrist, flung it at Mr. Watson's porch.

It was a neat trick. Without stopping once, or even slowing down, Karen could do her whole route from her bicycle.

She reached back and grabbed another paper and flipped it toward Mrs. Bennett's porch. The paper sailed over the lawn and landed neatly on the porch. Then it slid across the porch and disappeared over the edge, next to a big juniper bush.

"Oh well, she'll find it," Karen said aloud. She couldn't stop now. That would ruin the whole game.

Karen flipped Mr. Jacob's paper, and then started down the other side of Spruce Street.

That was it. She was finished. Only her extra emergency paper was left. She had finished her route in record time!

Karen ran inside for her collection tickets. This was Wednesday, and on Wednesday of the last week of the month she collected on Pine Street. That was part of Karen's new system.

A successful newspaper route, according to Karen, was run by a system. She delivered her papers quickly and promptly each day. During the last week she collected. On Monday she collected Aspen Street; Tuesday, Willow Street; Wednesday, Pine Street; and Thursday, Spruce Street. On Friday she turned her money in. Her customers could count on her.

Just as she reached the front door, the telephone rang. Nobody else was home, so Karen answered it.

"Hello! May I speak to Karen, please?" a woman's voice asked.

"This is Karen."

"Karen, this is Mrs. Bennett. I saw you go by on your bicycle. Did you forget me?"

"Oh no, Mrs. Bennett. I wouldn't do that! I threw the paper on the porch. It just slid off. It's next to the porch by the juniper bush."

"Oh, Karen, not again! We never know where to find the paper! Last week it was in the rosebushes. The week before it was under the porch. Once it even landed in the maple tree, and Mr. Bennett had to climb up to get it."

"I'm sorry," said Karen. "It's my new system. I'm getting better, though. I got it on the porch today, but it slid off into the bush."

Mrs. Bennett hung up without saying good-bye.

The next day, Karen was determined to beat her own forty-three-minute record. She rolled her papers two minutes faster than Wednesday, and she was five minutes ahead of schedule when she came to Mrs. Bennett's house on Spruce Street.

Karen reached into the basket and flipped the paper before she looked up and saw the sprinkler. The paper hit the corner of the porch and bounced back, landing on the grass just under the sprinkler.

"Why do people sprinkle their lawns in the afternoon?" mum-

bled Karen. "If she did it in the morning, her paper wouldn't get wet." Karen didn't stop. "Mrs. Bennett should have a system for watering." She pedaled home for her collection tickets.

It was Thursday—the day to collect on Spruce Street.

When Karen came to Mrs. Bennett's house, the sprinkler was still going. And the paper was still under it.

She rang the doorbell. Mrs. Bennett was smiling when she came to the door. "Hello, Karen," she said. "I was expecting you. I have the money ready."

"Good!" said Karen. Her customers could count on her.

"I put fifty cents in five separate envelopes, and I put the envelopes where I've found the papers." Mrs. Bennett was still smiling. "It's part of my new system for paying the newspaper bill. Don't worry, you'll find them." She closed the door.

Karen could hardly believe what she had heard. She turned around. She looked at the soggy newspaper under the sprinkler. There was a white envelope under the rubber band on the paper.

The surprised girl ran quickly under the sprinkler. She grabbed the paper and ran back to the porch. Her sweat shirt and hair were dripping wet. She pulled the wet envelope from under the rubber band. There was fifty cents.

Karen looked around the yard. Dangling from a branch high in the maple tree was another white envelope. She quickly climbed the tree.

Just before she reached the envelope, her right knee slipped and caught on an old branch. She heard the rip.

When she got down, Karen examined a tear in her new jeans.

She had found one dollar now. But the bill was two dollars and fifty cents. She would turn in two dollars. The fifty cents was her pay.

Karen remembered Mrs. Bennett's Wednesday night telephone call. "Last week it was in the rosebushes. The week before, it was under the porch," she had said.

The girl walked toward the rosebushes. When she reached in for the white envelope, she scratched her arm on the thorns. Karen crawled under the porch for the fourth envelope. It was muddy from the sprinkler. Now Karen's hands and jeans were muddy. Her jeans were torn. Her arm was scratched, and her sweat shirt and hair were wet.

She had two dollars now, but where was the last envelope? The desperate girl looked around the yard. There were no white envelopes. Mrs. Bennett had said there were five. Karen was beginning to wish that she'd gotten the papers on the porch each week. This searching was no fun.

Should she ring the doorbell and say she was sorry? Maybe Mrs. Bennett would tell her where the last envelope was. And maybe she wouldn't.

Should she just forget her fifty cents pay for this month? Karen sat down on the bottom step of the porch. She put her chin in her hands and her elbows on her knees. She thought and thought.

Just as she was about to give up and go home, Karen suddenly remembered yesterday's paper. It had hit the porch and slid off next to the juniper bush.

Karen walked across the porch to the juniper bush and looked down. There on the ground under the bush was the last white envelope. The sharp juniper needles scratched her face. She couldn't reach the envelope. Karen leaned farther. A small dead branch broke off and stuck in her hair. She had it! The last envelope was hers!

Karen stood up and brushed the branch from her hair. She stuffed the envelope in her pocket. Then she picked up the soggy newspaper from the porch and put it back into her bicycle basket. She took out her extra emergency paper and carried it up to the porch and rang the doorbell.

When Mrs. Bennett opened the door, Karen handed her the paper. "I found the five envelopes," she reported. "And I have something new in my system." Karen brushed the wet hair from her eyes with a mud-covered hand. "It's called service, and it means that your paper will always be on your porch."

LOOKING AT BOOKS

Petrouchka

This book retells the story of the Russian ballet *Petrouchka,* which is about three puppets—the clown Petrouchka, a ballerina, and a Moor. While performing at a winter carnival, Petrouchka falls in love with the ballerina. He becomes jealous when the Moor flirts with her. Petrouchka tries to win the ballerina's love but fails. Later, mistakenly thinking that the Moor is harming the ballerina, Petrouchka attacks the Moor. The Moor draws his sword, chases Petrouchka through the fairgrounds, and kills him. But Petrouchka's spirit lives on, finally free of his straw-filled puppet's body. This book, written and illustrated by Elizabeth Cleaver, was awarded a 1981 Children's Literature Prize by the Canada Council.

FABLES

Fables, written and illustrated by Arnold Lobel, won the 1981 Caldecott Medal for excellence in illustration. It contains 20 fables, each accompanied by a wonderful drawing. A fable is a brief story that teaches a lesson about how people behave, and it usually ends with a moral. Consider the ostrich who falls in love with a young lady but is too shy to talk to her. Although he doesn't have the courage to share his feelings with her, his love makes the ostrich feel very happy and alive. The moral: Love can be its own reward. Then there is the rhinoceros who buys a dress that looks awful on her because a salesperson told her that the dress made her look glamorous. The moral: Nothing is harder to resist than a bit of flattery. Other fables in this book tell of a pig who flies through marshmallow clouds to a marzipan moon and a crocodile who spends his life smiling at the bedroom wallpaper. The book ends with a story about a mouse who undertakes a dangerous journey to see the ocean. The moral: All the miles of a hard road are worth a moment of true happiness.

JACOB HAVE I LOVED

The title of this book comes from a biblical quotation: "Jacob have I loved but Esau have I hated." The book is the story of twin girls who grow up on an island in Chesapeake Bay in the 1940's. Caroline is delicate, charming, loved by all. Louise—usually called Wheeze—should have been the boy her father wanted. Then she could have followed in her father's footsteps. She could have been a waterman, tonging for oysters from November to March, crabbing from April into the fall. Did God love Caroline and hate Louise? Louise thought so. But once she realized that she, too, was loved, she was able to begin building a life of her own, free from the shadow of her twin. This memorable book by Katherine Paterson was awarded the 1981 John Newbery Medal, the highest award for a book for young people.

HENRIETTA
and the Gong from Hong Kong

Evelyn is a Perfect Little Lady. Henrietta, her younger sister,
isn't—and doesn't want to be. She loses scarves and gloves,
carries lots of junk in her pockets, and much prefers dungarees
to dresses. One day the two girls and their parents go to their
grandparents' home for lunch. Everyone fusses over Evelyn.
Henrietta is ignored by her father and criticized by her mother.
Worst of all, her grandfather won't ring the fabulous brass
Chinese gong he brought back from Hong Kong. But this story
by Winifred Rosen, with drawings by Kay Chorao, has a happy
ending. Henrietta hears the gong—and also learns some surprising things about her family.

AND THE SLEEPY

THE DAY BEGINS

HOURS OF NIGHT

ARE OVER

284

MASQUERADE

Within the pages of this book there is a story told
Of love, adventures, fortunes lost, and a jewel of solid gold.
To solve the hidden riddle, you must use your eyes,
And find the hare in every picture that may point you to the prize.

This verse introduces *Masquerade*—a story, a series of puzzles, and a guide to buried treasure. The story tells of Jack Hare's mission to bring a beautiful jewel from Lady Moon to her love, the Sun. Jack's many adventures take him through earth, air, fire, and water. But when he finally reaches the Sun, he discovers that he has lost the precious treasure. If you can figure out all the clues (riddles, puzzles, and especially the pictures), you will know where Jack lost the jewel. You may also be lucky enough to find a *real* treasure.

For there *is* a real treasure, buried somewhere in Britain. The author of *Masquerade,* an artist named Kit Williams, made a golden figure of a hare, adorned with precious stones. He put the jewel in a hare-shaped, ceramic container and buried it—on a night of the full moon, of course. Anyone who deciphers the clues in the story and finds the jewel can have it. So can anyone outside Britain who sends the correct solution to the author. Williams has said that a child of 10 could solve the puzzle as easily as a college graduate and that no knowledge of British geography is required. People have been digging all over Britain. So read carefully—the jewel "lies waiting safe . . . for you or Eternity."

POETRY

UNTITLED

We will watch the Northern Lights
playing their game of ball
in the cold, glistening country.
Then we will sit in beauty on the mountain
and watch the small stars
in their sleepless flight.

ABANAKI INDIAN SONG

TREES

The Oak is called the king of trees,
The Aspen quivers in the breeze,
The Poplar grows up straight and tall,
The Peach tree spreads along the wall,
The Sycamore gives pleasant shade,
The Willow droops in watery glade,
The Fir tree useful timber gives,
The Beech amid the forest lives.

SARA COLERIDGE (1802–1852)

UNTITLED

''Hope'' is the thing with feathers—
That perches in the soul—
And sings the tune without the words—
And never stops—at all—

And sweetest—in the Gale—is heard—
And sore must be the storm—
That could abash the little Bird
That kept so many warm—

I've heard it in the chillest land—
And on the strangest Sea—
Yet, never, in Extremity,
It asked a crumb—of Me.

EMILY DICKINSON (1830–1886)

WHERE GO THE BOATS?

Dark brown is the river,
    Golden is the sand.
It flows along for ever,
    With trees on either hand.

Green leaves a-floating,
    Castles of the foam,
Boats of mine a-boating—
    Where will all come home?

On goes the river,
    And out past the mill,
Away down the valley,
    Away down the hill.

Away down the river,
    A hundred miles or more,
Other little children
    Shall bring my boats ashore.

ROBERT LOUIS STEVENSON (1850–1894)

LOGICAL ENGLISH

I said, ''This horse, sir, will you shoe?''
    And soon the horse was shod.
I said, ''This deed, sir, will you do?''
    And soon the deed was dod!

I said, ''This stick, sir, will you break?''
    At once the stick he broke.
I said, ''This coat, sir, will you make?''
    And soon the coat he moke!
                  UNKNOWN

CATERPILLAR

Brown and furry
Caterpillar in a hurry,
Take your walk
To the shady leaf, or stalk,
Or what not,
Which may be the chosen spot.
No toad spy you,
Hovering bird of prey pass by you;
Spin and die,
To live again a butterfly.
     CHRISTINA ROSSETTI (1830–1894)

OLD NOAH'S ARK

Old Noah once he built an ark,
And patched it up with hickory bark.
He anchored it to a great big rock,
And then he began to load his stock.
The animals went in one by one,
The elephant chewing a caraway bun.
The animals went in two by two,
The crocodile and the kangaroo.
The animals went in three by three,
The tall giraffe and the tiny flea.
The animals went in four by four,
The hippopotamus stuck in the door.
The animals went in five by five,
The bees mistook the bear for a hive.
The animals went in six by six,
The monkey was up to his usual tricks.
The animals went in seven by seven,
Said the ant to the elephant, ''Who're ye shov'n?''
The animals went in eight by eight,
Some were early and some were late.
The animals went in nine by nine,
They all formed fours and marched in a line.
The animals went in ten by ten,
If you want any more, you can read it again.
            AMERICAN FOLK RHYME

MIDSUMMER VIGIL

Dawn already, after the shortest night,
Has dimmed the harbour lanterns, still alight.
           SHIKI (1866–1902)

DISCOVERY

I walked by chance
Into the western courtyard.
There I saw
A single orchid
Newly blown.

Who will spread
The tidings?
What bee
Will learn the secret first
And hasten
To the spot?
        YUAN MEI (1716–1797)

WHISPERS

Whispers tickle through your ear
Telling things you like to hear.
Whispers are as soft as skin
Letting little words curl in.
Whispers come so they can blow
Secrets others never know.

CANDY FIELDS
age 10
West Lafayette, Indiana

I WAS SITTING AT HOME . . .

I was sitting at home watching TV one night.
I saw a very interesting sight.

Spaceships left and spaceships right,
Straining their motors with all their might.

I ran into the house with lots of hope,
Needing to find my long lost telescope.

There it was in my dresser drawer,
Under my banana and apple core.

I went outside, telescope in hand,
And watched the spaceships zoom across the land.

I went inside to call my son-in-law's niece,
Because my son-in-law was with the police.

She answered the phone like a frightened mouse.
I said, "There are spaceships flying outside of my house."

"You're lying!" she said and hung up the phone,
And all I heard was the dial tone.

Then I realized how hard it would be,
To convince the people about the spaceships and me.

I went outside, I knew they couldn't stay.
I yelled out loud: "Why don't you go away?"

Then all of a sudden the noise of the engines cleared,
And they were gone, they had disappeared.

I am sad they are gone, I said to myself.
I was beginning to like them as much as myself.

DAVID DAUMIT
age 11
Kamuela, Hawaii

THE MISTRESS' PRAISE OF HER CAT

You are cat.
Your ancestors were worshiped,
Idolized by their Egyptian owners.
Feared by the superstitious.
You are sleek, graceful,
You are cat.
As you sit in the window, you
watch passers-by and you are proud.
For you are slender, alert, quick,
intelligent, beautiful.
    You are cat.

AMY NORDAHL
age 12
South Weymouth, Massachusetts

SPRING

Spring, spring!
What a wonderful thing!
Leaves are uncurling,
The cool wind is swirling,
Warm April showers,
Blooming of flowers!
Small bleating woolly lambs,
Beavers are building dams!
The sun's shining bright
with God's profound light!
A husband and wife
bring new life!
Bees are buzzing in the leaves,
Birds are singing in the trees!
Ah, yes!
Spring is a beautifully wonderful
thing, full of new life!

JENNIFER BROOKS
age 11
Sault Ste. Marie, Ontario, Canada

THE RAIN, I RAIN

I love to rain,
It's fun.
I meet lots of things
On the way down.
I take rests on umbrellas,
Then I slide to the ground.
I get eaten by many plants
But never die.
I've had lots of fun on earth,
So I'll disappear back to the sky.

JASON JOY
age 8
Lake Placid, New York

A CORAL REEF

A foreign world,
A changing world,
A world that lies deep
And shallow amidst
Warm waters.
Eerie sounds and
Swiftly moving shadows
Outline this colorful place.
People have no place
Amongst this race
Of corals and fishes.
Priceless; timeless,
This place has
Infinite beauty and grace.
Golden and blue,
Alien but true,
A reef of coral
Is beautiful.

MEGGEN WATT
age 12
Danville, California

FAWN

A fawn nibbling leaves,
Its speckled back of sunshine,
Young and still so shy.

SHELLEY WALTZ
age 11
Denver, Colorado

THE MOON

floating
moon
in
the
sky
looks
ashwhite,
hovering
handsomely
about
the
sky,
feels
soft,
feels
hard,
silky
white
cordially
looking
over
our
Earth.

CLINTON GOINS
age 10
Lewes, Delaware

TO THE GIRAFFE

I'd like to write a poem to the giraffe
But I can't think of a rhyme, except ''one half.''
Half a giraffe is no good at all.
I like giraffes because they're tall.

Still . . .
I suppose
A silly rhyme
Is better than no valentine.

So here's to you, my fond giraffe,
A little verse to make you laugh.

Roses are red
Violets are blue
You got the best neck
In the whole zoo.

BROWN

Brown is the color of nature itself.
Brown is the color of an oakwood shelf.
Brown is the road or the dirt.
Brown is the rootbeer that we squirt.
Brown is the trunks of the trees
Or the rusty and worn-down keys.
Brown is a table.
Brown is the ground.
Brown is the penny that I found.

ALEX SAFFORD
age 11
Bozeman, Montana

DEVIN HURD
age 7
Lake Oswego, Oregon

Riders in the Night

The year 1981 marked the 200th anniversary of the last major battle of the American Revolutionary War. On October 19, 1781, the siege of Yorktown came to an end. The British Army commanded by Lord Cornwallis marched out of the Virginia town and surrendered to General George Washington's troops and their French allies.

The surrender of Lord Cornwallis' army brought to an end the bitter fighting that had begun more than six years earlier in Massachusetts. It was in April, 1775, that British troops clashed with American militia—called Minutemen—at Lexington and Concord, the opening skirmishes of the Revolutionary War.

Massachusetts, and particularly the city of Boston, was the center of American resistance to what the colonists regarded as unfair tax laws and other acts passed by the British Parliament. The trouble simmered and finally boiled over in a series of violent events. In March of 1770, a mob of Bostonians—protesting the presence of British troops in the city—attacked a British sentry at the Customs House. Other British soldiers came to his aid. And when the mob began to hurl rocks and bricks at the soldiers, they fired into the crowd, killing five Americans. The incident became known as the Boston Massacre.

Three years later, in 1773, Boston Patriots dressed as Indians raided British merchant ships carrying cargoes of tea. To show their anger over Parliament's tax on tea, the raiders dumped several hundred chests of tea into Boston Harbor. The British Government quickly retaliated. Among the repressive measures passed by Parliament was the Boston Port Bill, which closed the city's harbor to all shipping. The port was to stay closed until the people of Boston paid for the tea they had destroyed. More troops were called in, and the city was put under martial law. But the resolute Bostonians refused to give in. Food and other supplies sent by neighboring colonies kept the citizens of Boston from facing starvation and sickness.

Meanwhile, Patriot groups like the Sons of Liberty—spurred on by their leaders, John Hancock, Samuel Adams, and Joseph Warren—began stockpiling arms and munitions and organizing for war. Matters came to a head on the night of April 18, 1775, when Sir Thomas Gage, the British governor-general of Massachusetts Colony, sent a detachment of troops to Lexington and Concord to capture the Patriot leaders and seize their military supplies.

But the American rebels had an efficient network of spies and couriers. When Boston Patriots learned of Gage's plan, they sent riders to sound the alarm and rouse the Minutemen in the surrounding towns and villages. One of the night riders was Paul Revere, a silversmith, engraver, and staunch Patriot. Paul Revere's ride was immortalized by Henry Wadsworth Longfellow's stirring poem, which begins with these familiar lines: "Listen, my children, and you shall hear / Of the midnight ride of Paul Revere . . ."

But Longfellow's poem, though lively and romantic, was not quite accurate. Revere did not ride alone on that fateful night. There were two other men who rode with him to "spread the alarm through every Middlesex village and farm." One was a Boston man named William Dawes. The other was a 24-year-old Concord physician named Samuel Prescott. According to Longfellow's account, it was Revere who galloped into Concord on the morning of April 19 and roused the Patriot militia. As Longfellow's poem records it:

"It was two by the village clock,
When he came to the bridge in Concord town.
He heard the bleating of the flock,
And the twitter of birds among the trees,
And felt the breath of the morning breeze
Blowing over the meadows brown."

That's not true. Paul Revere heard neither bleating sheep nor twittering birds in Concord. He never got there. Revere was captured by a British patrol a few miles outside of Lexington. William Dawes was unhorsed while being chased by British soldiers and had to return to Lexington on foot. Only one of the night riders reached Concord. And that was young Samuel Prescott.

What follows is a dramatized account of that historic night ride.

The moon had broken through the clouds, casting a pale glow over the city of Boston. Church bells had just sounded the hour of ten as a stocky man wrapped in a cloaklike overcoat and wearing riding boots walked briskly through the cobbled streets.

Only a short while before, the ruddy-faced man who now hurried toward the waterfront had met with Dr. Joseph Warren, a leader of the Patriot group called the Sons of Liberty. Warren had told the man that a force of elite British grenadiers and light infantry was being sent by boat across the Charles River for a quick night march to surprise the American Patriots at Lexington and Concord.

"You must warn Sam Adams and Hancock that they are in danger," Warren had told him. "Then press on to Concord and alert the Minutemen. Tell them they must take precautions to prevent the British from capturing the guns and supplies we have hidden there. I'm sending Billy Dawes by another route in case you are taken by the Redcoats. Remember, our cause may well be lost if you do not get through."

So Paul Revere had hastily returned to his house in North Square to put on his riding boots and coat. Then he had made his way to the North Church, where as a boy he had served as a bell ringer to summon worshipers to church services. He instructed the church sexton to light two lanterns and place them in the steeple.

"That will tell our people in Charlestown that the British are coming by water and not by land," he told the sexton.

Now, on this crisp and clear night of April 18, 1775, Revere headed for the north end of town, where he had concealed a boat. He made his way through back alleys and side streets, sloshing through puddles of water left from the afternoon rain. Finally he

arrived at the river's edge. His boat had already been pushed into the water and made ready by two friends.

"Is that you, Paul?" one of them called out in a loud whisper.

"Yes, Jack," Revere answered. "I've just come from Dr. Warren. The Redcoats are out in force. Gage is planning to send them by boat across Back Bay to Cambridge so they won't be detected."

"Aye, we know," said the second man. "We saw the lanterns in the North Church belfry."

Revere nodded. "Let's hope our friends in Charlestown have seen them as well. Now lads, let's make haste and get across to Charlestown."

Swiftly they clambered into the longboat and hoisted oars. Moments later, they were gliding quietly across the moonlit waters of the Charles River. Off to the right they could see the shadowy hulk of the British man-of-war *Somerset,* its tall masts, like leafless trees, etched against the star-speckled sky. Tied to the ship's stern were a dozen rowboats, which would soon be used to ferry the British troops across the river.

Revere and his comrades slipped by the British warship without being spotted. Once on the other side, they hopped out and headed for Charlestown. There they were met by Colonel William Conant and a small group of Patriots.

"We saw the signal from North Church," Conant reported. "I figured they would send a good horseman like you to carry the word."

Revere swept a hand back in the direction of Boston. "Billy Dawes is riding as well, by the long route from Boston Neck. As for me, I shall need a fast horse."

Conant nodded. "Deacon Larkin has the swiftest mount. I'll send a man to fetch him."

While they waited for the horse to be saddled and brought up, another man rode up.

"Why, that's Richard Devens," Colonal Conant said. "What news have you, Dick? Our friend Mr. Revere is about to ride for Lexington."

Hastily dismounting, Devens shook the dust from his clothes and reported: "If you are heading for Lexington, you had best be on your guard. I met up with ten British officers, mounted and well armed. They asked me for directions to Lexington and if I knew the location of Mr. Clark's house."

Revere glowered. "Then they must know that Hancock and Adams are hiding there."

"I fear so," said Devens. "I told them I knew of no such house and then pointed them the wrong way. When they were out of sight I doubled back to a friend's home and asked him to get word to Jonas Clark that he might have Redcoat visitors."

"You did well, Mr. Devens," Revere said approvingly. "And I shall take care to avoid the British patrols."

By now the horse had been readied and stood waiting. Revere tightened the girth and mounted.

"Good luck and Godspeed," Conant called out.

Revere tipped his hat and laughed cockily. "Have no fear, my friends. Those Lobsterbacks won't catch me. I'll ride like the wind."

Then he put spurs to his horse and galloped off. It was eleven o'clock as Revere rode through the darkened streets of Charlestown and across the narrow neck connecting Charlestown Peninsula with the mainland. The waters of the Mystic glistened on his left, and those of the Charles on his right. Once across the neck, Revere turned left toward Cambridge and the main road to Lexington. He rode along a narrow sandy trail, through scrubland and clay marshes. At a point where the road narrowed, near a clump of trees, Revere spotted two mounted men.

He slowed his horse as he got nearer, trying to make out who they were. Suddenly he spotted their army holsters and the cockades on their tricorn hats. Redcoats!

One of the officers trotted toward him, shouting, "Halt and make yourself known!"

The other British officer cantered onto the road to block his way. Revere yanked the reins and swiftly wheeled his horse around. Hunching over the animal's neck, he brought his whip down hard on its flanks and raced off. He could hear the British officer shout a curse as he galloped after him.

Revere sped back toward Charlestown Neck, hoping to elude his pursuer and reach the Mystic Road. For a few minutes it was a close race. But as the British officer circled to cut him off, his horse stumbled into a clay pond, allowing Revere to make good his escape. Soon the Patriot courier was clattering across the Medford Bridge. Then he turned left and headed down the Mystic Road toward Lexington.

At the same time that Revere was avoiding capture by the pursuing Redcoats, a quieter scene was taking place in Lexington, some 10 miles away. There, in the home of the Mulliken family, 24-year-old Samuel Prescott of neighboring Concord was visiting his friend Lydia Mulliken. Like his father and grandfather before him, young Prescott had chosen to become a doctor. Lydia Mulliken, two years his junior, was the daughter of a master clockmaker who had died a few years earlier. She lived with her widowed mother and three brothers and two sisters.

As the tall wooden clock in the corner struck the hour of midnight, the two young people sat at a small table in the parlor sipping tea. They spoke softly to avoid disturbing the other members of the Mulliken family, who were asleep.

"You look troubled tonight, Sam," Lydia observed, an expression of concern on her pretty face.

Prescott swept a loose strand of sandy brown hair from his forehead and replied: "You're right, Lydia, I'm worried. There is talk that Governor Gage is preparing to send troops to Concord to seize the weapons the Minutemen have hidden there. They will probably also come here, to Lexington, and arrest John Hancock and Sam Adams."

Lydia patted his hand reassuringly. "But surely they will not bother law-abiding people who are not involved in all this talk of rebellion."

Prescott frowned. "It isn't that simple, Lydia. If the British march on Lexington and Concord, the Minutemen will surely stand up to them. There's bound to be fighting and many innocent people will be hurt. Musket balls do not respect the rights of civilians."

"Well, I don't understand all this anger at the British Government. Surely King George has a right to demand loyalty from his subjects."

Prescott leaned forward, his eyes narrowing. "It isn't the King, Lydia, but the Parliament. They tax us without our consent or concern for our feelings. Why, even this cup of tea has a tax on it. And look at the poor people of Boston. Fifteen thousand of our fellow colonists held prisoner in their own city. No ships allowed to leave or enter. It isn't right. I tell you . . ."

His words trailed off as the sound of horses' hooves striking gravel outside the house reached their ears.

Prescottt looked puzzled. "Riders at this hour," he mused. "Now who could they be?"

He rose quickly and went to the window. Outside, on the main road through Lexington, the dim shapes of half a dozen horsemen could be seen. They wore dark-colored capes, but as the wind blew back one of the garments, Prescott glimpsed the scarlet coat and silver epaulet of a British officer.

"Redcoats!" he announced, startled. "They're going through the town, down the road toward Concord!"

Lydia summoned him back to the table. "Come, Sam, finish your tea. This is no concern of ours. You are not involved with the Patriots, are you?"

A grim-faced Prescott returned to his chair. "No, I have not been active in any political group. But that does not mean I am without convictions. If the Redcoats mean to cause trouble in Concord, I will stand with my people."

Lydia Mulliken tried to calm her friend. But as the minutes ticked by, the young man fidgeted and paced the room. It was nearly one o'clock when the sound of horses again interrupted their talk. This time Prescott went outside to get a better look at the riders.

When he returned, Lydia asked: "Did you recognize them?"

Prescott nodded. "I believe one of them is Mr. Revere, the Boston silversmith. I have seen him often in these parts. He serves as a courier for the Committee of Safety in Boston."

And then, all at once, the realization of what was happening hit him. "Of course," he exclaimed. "Revere must be here to warn of the British troops. And those British officers—why, they are probably waiting up ahead, ready to snare any messengers from Boston. By God, Lydia, I must warn Revere and his companion that they are heading into a trap!"

Despite the young woman's protests, Prescott would not be deterred. Hastily pulling on his riding boots and grabbing his whip, he rushed out the door and mounted his large bay stallion.

As he rode off he called out, "God willing I will see you tomorrow, Lydia. If the Redcoats come, keep your family inside the house." And putting spurs to his horse, the young man sped up the road in pursuit of the two couriers from Boston.

It didn't take Prescott long to catch up with the Boston couriers. *Thank God,* Prescott thought to himself. *I've found them before the British.* The two messengers heard the pounding of his horse's hooves and turned to see who was following them. Prescott raised his right hand to show he was not armed and waved a salute.

Prescott reined in his horse as he came abreast of the night riders and was immediately challenged by the taller of the two men—a stocky fellow whom he recognized as Paul Revere.

"Well now, young sir, what brings you out at this late hour?"

Revere asked suspiciously. "And why have you chosen to come upon us in such haste?"

Prescott took a second to catch his breath, then blurted, "I am Dr. Samuel Prescott of Concord. I saw you ride through Lexington and reckoned you were messengers from Boston bringing word of the Redcoats. I came to warn you that a British patrol awaits you farther along this road."

The look of suspicion on Revere's face softened to one of friendliness. "We are much in your debt, sir. I am Paul Revere and my companion is William Dawes. We are spreading the word that the regulars are out and will probably march to Concord to seize the stores there."

Dawes leaned over and tugged Revere's sleeve. "No offense, but how do we know this young fellow is not a British spy who will deliver us into the arms of the Redcoats?"

Revere looked toward Prescott. "I think not. He seems an honest fellow. What are your politics, sir, Whig or Tory?"

"I belong to no party, Mr. Revere. But I am a loyal Concord man who opposes the tyranny of the British Government."

Revere smiled and placed a hand on the young man's shoulder. "Well said, Dr. Prescott. You must be a high Son of Liberty."

"Then let me join you," said Prescott. "I am well known to the people in this area. If I am with you, they will have more faith in your words."

Revere and Dawes agreed, and moments later the three men were cantering down the road to Concord. Along the way, Revere told Prescott how he had escaped capture outside of Charlestown and had then alerted every house and farm between Medford and Lexington. Revere explained that he had been the first to arrive in Lexington, where he had informed John Hancock and Sam Adams about the British movements. Dawes, who had been sent by the long route through Boston Neck, had arrived a half hour later. After a quick meal, the two men had started out for Concord, intending to rouse every household en route.

By now, the three were about halfway to Concord. Off to the right loomed a darkened farmhouse.

Revere motioned to Prescott and Dawes. "Go awake those people. I'll scout on up ahead."

Prescott and Dawes trotted over to the house and dismounted. The young doctor pounded loudly on the door. Moments later a flickering candle appeared in the window. Then the door opened cautiously. A tousled-haired man emerged in his nightshirt. "Why, Dr. Prescott, what brings you here at this hour? Is there some trouble?"

"Trouble enough, Mr. Blackwell. The British are marching on Lexington and Concord. Pass the word to your neighbors that the Minutemen are turning out to meet them, and there may be fighting on the morrow."

The sleepy-eyed man nodded his understanding. Prescott and

Dawes vaulted back into their saddles and trotted back to the road. Prescott spotted Revere about 100 yards ahead on the narrow highway. But he was not alone. Two British officers were standing in his way—and two more were in a pasture to his right to cut off any escape.

"By God, Redcoats!" Dawes exclaimed. "They'll get Paul for sure. Let's go to his aid."

But Prescott grabbed the bridle of Dawes's horse, pulling him up short. "No, Billy. I'll help Revere. You make good your escape. That way, at least one of us will reach Concord."

Before Dawes could protest, Prescott spurred up the road to where Revere had been halted by the British soldiers.

"Here comes another rebel," one of the scarlet-coated officers shouted as Prescott approached.

Revere was trying to push past the Redcoats, but the British officers used their sword blades to prod the American Patriot's horse through an opening in the fence bordering the pasture.

"Stop!" one of the officers commanded. "If you go an inch farther we will shoot you."

By now both Prescott and Revere had been forced into the pasture. The British officers drew their muzzle-loading pistols and cocked them menacingly. Suddenly one of the Redcoats spotted Dawes hightailing it back toward Lexington.

"Look, there's another one getting away," he called out to his companions. "Go after him."

The two British officers on the road wheeled around and charged off in pursuit of Dawes, while the remaining Redcoats grabbed at the bridles of Revere's and Prescott's horses.

Prescott saw an opportunity to get free. He reckoned that the British soldiers wouldn't dare fire their pistols for fear of alarming the countryside. Using the butt of his whip as a weapon, he struck out at the Redcoat officer nearest him, forcing him to duck to avoid the blow. Then Prescott cried out, "Now, Revere, run!"

Before the Redcoats could recover, both Americans whipped their horses and made a dash across the pasture. Prescott broke to the left and Revere to the right, with the two British officers hot on their heels.

A low stone wall blocked Prescott's way, but his horse jumped it nimbly and galloped off down a narrow path that led to a ravine. As Prescott neared the ravine, he glanced over his shoulder in time to see the British officer halt abruptly when his horse failed to jump the wall.

Prescott had gambled correctly. The Redcoats didn't fire their weapons. But Revere was not as fortunate. Prescott stopped long enough to see the Patriot courier ride smack into another group of Redcoats posted in a wood at the edge of the pasture. The British troopers quickly surrounded Revere. He was a prisoner.

They've got him, thought Prescott. *Well then, it's up to me to carry the alarm to Concord.*

And with that thought in mind, he dug his spurs into his horse's flanks and rode at full gallop through the ravine and past the swamp. Prescott continued through thickets and woods, heading north and then west down narrow country lanes.

He knew the area well and guided his horse skillfully through the backwoods. His eyes darted nervously at every turn. Would a Redcoat suddenly spring out of the shadows? he wondered. But the only sound as he rode through the dark forest was the pounding of his horse's hooves—and the thumping of his own heart.

At last he came to a clearing, beyond which he could see the fresh-plowed fields of the Hartwell farm. The wooden, two-story house was bathed in the gentle glow of the moon as Prescott cantered up to the rear of the dwelling. Hastily dismounting, he strode to the kitchen door and pounded loudly on it.

A few moments later, Samuel Hartwell, a sergeant in the local militia company, stuck his head out the door. "What in blazes is all that noise about—who's there?" he asked angrily.

"It's Samuel Prescott of Concord, and you'll have noise enough when the sun rises. The regulars are marching on Lexington, and I've come to spread the alarm."

Prescott quickly told Hartwell of Revere's capture and how he himself had narrowly escaped being snared by the British patrol. Hartwell assured the young man that he would pass the word on to the militia.

Wasting no more time, Prescott rushed back to his horse and continued on to Concord. He moved stealthily around a low hill and across a series of meadows, careful to avoid the main road until he was near enough to Concord village to make out the dim outlines of the houses.

It was just after two o'clock when Prescott, dusty and tired, rode into his hometown. Soon he was hammering on doors, rousing the sleepy village and giving word of the approaching British troops. Immediately, the bell was rung in the meetinghouse, summoning the militia. Prescott, exhausted, returned to his own house and stretched out for a few hours' sleep.

At daybreak, the young physician was roused from his slumber by the loud sound of voices in the nearby village common. Splashing some water on his face, he hurried outside to the common. He could see Colonel James Barrett giving orders to the hundred or so militiamen who had assembled to the sound of the alarm bell. He could also see carts hauling away supplies from the storehouses to places of concealment.

Walking up to Colonel Barrett, Prescott inquired, "What news from Lexington?"

"Bad news, Sam," Colonel Barrett responded somberly. "The British troops arrived at daybreak and were met by Captain Parker's Minutemen. There was fighting, and some of our people were killed. Reuben Brown saw it all."

Brown, standing nearby, nervously tugged on his hat. "Aye, it was a fearful sight. There were scarce a hundred Minutemen and against them fully six hundred or more regulars. I know not who fired first, but suddenly the whole line of Redcoats was firing their muskets."

Colonel Barrett interrupted. "But thanks to you, Sam, we were fairly warned. We have hidden spare flints, powder, and balls in attics and in the fields. Most of the stores are safe. Now we are preparing to march out to meet the British."

There were nods of approval from some of the other Minutemen leaning on their burnished muskets. "Aye," said one, "the bloody Lobsterbacks will learn that they cannot shoot Americans without paying a price."

Prescott shook his head from side to side. "I cannot believe the British are such fools," he said quietly, and then he looked over to Colonel Barrett. "Colonel, you will need a doctor to care for your wounded. I will go and fetch my bag."

"Then you will march with us, Sam?" asked Barrett.

"Yes," said Prescott. "I think the time has come for all of us to take a stand."

A few minutes later, his surgical bag in hand, young Sam Prescott joined the tradesmen and farmers as they marched out of Concord to the beat of a solitary drum. All around, the alarm bells in other villages were sounding. Soon Minutemen from every town in the area would be swarming about like angry hornets. As he marched, Prescott wondered if this would be the beginning of a real war. He thought it might be, and a chill of fear swept over him. Then, like the others, he marched on.

HENRY I. KURTZ
Author, *John and Sebastian Cabot*

THE PIRATES AND THE PUPPET

Treasure Island and *Pinocchio* are two books that are very different from each other. One is a rousing adventure tale of pirates and buried treasure. It was written by a romantic, venturesome Scot, who is well known as the author of many books for adults and young people. The other book is a fantastic fairy tale, quite different from most other fairy tales. It was written by an Italian government clerk, who is almost unknown except as the author of this book. But in 1981, *Treasure Island* and *Pinocchio* had something in common—an anniversary. Each in its own way had delighted people for 100 years.

TREASURE ISLAND

The story we know as *Treasure Island* was begun in the summer of 1881. Robert Louis Stevenson and his family were staying in a village called Braemar, in Scotland. The weather was terrible. It rained, it poured, it drizzled, and then it rained some more. Stevenson, whose health was poor, had to stay indoors, and nobody else went out very much. Stevenson's young stepson, Lloyd Osbourne, spent his time painting and drawing, and Stevenson sometimes joined him.

One of them—afterward, no one was sure which—painted a map of an island. They called it Treasure Island. As Stevenson looked at it, a story began to take shape in his mind, and he decided to write the tale. He wrote every morning, and after lunch he read what he had written to his family.

Young Lloyd was not the only one to be fascinated. Stevenson's father, a lighthouse engineer, knew the sea and seafaring men. This was his kind of story, and he listened with delight. It was he who suggested *Walrus* as the name of Flint's ship, and he drew up the list of what Jim and his mother found in Billy Bones's chest.

Stevenson wrote 15 chapters in 15 days at Braemar. Meanwhile, a friend had come to visit and had heard the tale. He had been asked to find stories for a magazine, *Young Folks*. When he left, he took with him as much of the story (then called *The Sea-Cook*) as Stevenson had written. The tale was later finished in Switzerland and appeared in *Young Folks* that autumn.

In 1883, *Treasure Island* was published as a book. Stevenson had sent the original map to the publisher, who was supposed to include it among the illustrations. But the publisher never got it, and Stevenson had to redraw it.

Treasure Island was Stevenson's first novel. It was enjoyed by readers and highly praised by critics. It has been translated into many languages, and many artists have illustrated it. And it has been filmed at least three times.

The Story of Treasure Island. The hero and narrator of this tale, Jim Hawkins, is the son of an innkeeper. Billy Bones, a "retired"

Ransacking the pirate chest.

Jim with Long John Silver.

pirate, comes to stay at the inn—and dies, in frightening circumstances. Jim and his mother ransack the pirate's chest for money that he owed them. They find a map showing the burial place of the treasure of the notorious pirate Captain Flint.

Flint's villainous men want the map, but Jim escapes them and brings the map to the leading men of the district, Squire Trelawney and Dr. Livesey. The squire and the doctor decide to seek the treasure. They charter the schooner *Hispaniola,* and Jim is to come along as cabin boy. But unknown to them, the pirates get wind of the expedition and sign on as crew members. The captain has doubts about some of the crew, but nobody suspects the jovial, kindly ship's cook, one-legged Long John Silver.

During the voyage, however, Jim is horrified to overhear Silver and some of the hands plotting to mutiny and steal the treasure. Jim warns his friends, but when they reach the island, the captain, the squire, the doctor, and some loyal men are besieged in an old stockade by Silver and the pirates.

Meanwhile, Jim slips off by himself. He meets up with old Ben Gunn, a rather harmless pirate who had been marooned on the island years before. Ben, promised a share of the treasure and passage home to England, agrees to help Jim and his friends.

Taking Ben's small boat, Jim manages to board the *Hispaniola* and to bring the ship to another anchorage. He returns to tell his friends this good news, but he finds that Silver and the pirates hold the stockade and that his friends have left. The pirates take Jim as a hostage and go to search for the treasure. But Ben Gunn has been there long before them, and all they find is an empty hole in the ground.

In the end, Jim's friends come to the rescue. The treasure—except for some bars of silver that Flint had buried elsewhere—is loaded on the *Hispaniola,* and they sail for England. But Silver manages to escape on the way back.

Several authors have written sequels to *Treasure Island.* Some people think that Stevenson himself intended to write one, and that is why he left some of the treasure on the island and let Long John Silver escape.

Sighting the *Hispaniola.*

Taken hostage.

PINOCCHIO

As a young man, Carlo Lorenzini fought in the wars that created modern Italy out of a patchwork of small states. In his middle years, he settled down to working for the new Italian Government. But he had always done some writing on the side. In 1879, a friend who was an editor asked him to translate Perrault's fairy tales into Italian. Lorenzini's version was a success, and he tried writing some children's stories. They were more informative than entertaining, however, and they have long been forgotten.

Then, in 1881, another friend founded a magazine, *Giornale per i bambini* (''Children's Journal''). Lorenzini sent the friend a new story he had written, and the first installment of it was pub-

From log of wood to puppet.

Meeting a horrible serpent.

lished in the magazine's first issue. It was titled *Storia di un burattino* (''Story of a Puppet''). Lorenzini's name did not appear. Instead he used a pen name, C. Collodi. (Collodi was the name of the villa, or country estate, where young Carlo had grown up. It is now a town.) The puppet of the title was Pinocchio. Further episodes appeared in later issues. And when the original story was finished, children wrote in begging for further adventures. The author complied, and a second part began to appear in 1882. This time the story was titled *The Adventures of Pinocchio*. The next year, the two parts were put together, revised, and published as a book.

The book was a great success in Italy and sold over 1,000,000 copies. In time, it was translated into many languages—German, French, Polish, English, and even Esperanto and Latin. And, like *Treasure Island*, it has been illustrated by many artists.

In Italy, the 100th anniversary celebrations for Pinocchio were to be spread over three years: 1981 to 1983. A park in honor of the puppet was created in the author's hometown, Collodi. Special editions of the book were prepared. And films, cartoons, and puppet shows based on the book were presented.

The Story of Pinocchio. Pinocchio (his name means ''pine seed'') is a wooden puppet. But he is a most unusual one. Even while he is still just a log of wood, he speaks and cries—to the astonishment of the carpenter who owns the log. The carpenter gives the log to his neighbor, old Geppetto, who wishes to carve a puppet.

Before the puppet is even finished, he starts misbehaving. Once completed, he is in one scrape after another.

Despite the loving concern of old Geppetto, the sage advice of a talking cricket, and the kindness of a good fairy (the Beautiful Child with Blue Hair), Pinocchio continues on his wayward course. He is also selfish and lazy. And when he is caught in mischief, he lies. But his nose grows longer and gives him away.

In some of Pinocchio's many adventures, he is led astray by a pair of scheming villains—a fox and a cat; he is robbed of his money and then arrested for having been robbed; he meets a horrible serpent; and he finds himself transformed into a donkey. Finally, he rescues old Geppetto from the belly of the terrible Dogfish and achieves his goal—he becomes a real boy.

In 1940, a Walt Disney animated film of Pinocchio was released. This version may be even more familiar to many children than Collodi's original. Disney made several changes in the original story. For example, the helpful but nameless talking cricket became Jiminy Cricket, the faithful conscience of Pinocchio. And the Beautiful Child with Blue Hair became the golden-haired, but blue-robed, Blue Fairy. But the main lines of the story are the same: A heedless and mischievous puppet eventually learns to be brave, truthful, and unselfish—and becomes a real boy.

Led astray by two villains.

With Jiminy Cricket.

Song for a Princess

Once upon a time there was a princess who at birth had been given so many fine titles that she had forgotten them all. In fact, she was never called by any other name than Princess Rosen-knopp, which is Swedish for "rosebud." And this name suited her because she always wore a garland of fresh rosebuds in her hair.

She was the loveliest princess in the whole world, and after she became sixteen years of age, the castle was always full of emperors, kings, and princes who were trying to court her. But she only laughed at them, saying, "Don't you silly men know that I am quite too young to marry? Don't bother me anymore!"

Then she would run away, and as she went she would hum a little song that made no sense to anyone.

Nonetheless, all thought the song so lovely that they lingered to listen. Yet when any person asked her to sing the song out loud, she shook her head and replied, "I really don't know it well enough, for I can't remember the last line."

When asked who had taught her this song, she would answer, "The trees hum it, the wind whispers it, and the sea sings it."

The King, her father, became more and more worried about her as the years passed, but still she refused to marry. Now everyone knows that a princess is urged to marry earlier than other girls, and finally the King determined that the matter must come to a head. So one morning he stamped into her room, faced her, and pounded on the floor with his cane.

"Now all this nonsense must stop! For a long time you have been amusing yourself by saying 'No!' to your suitors. You'll have to change at once and say 'Yes!' "

Thereupon the Princess bowed her head and looked very thoughtful. "I shall do as you desire, Father dear," she replied, "but only on *one* condition."

"Let's hear what *that* is," grumbled the King.

The Princess smiled her most endearing smile and wound both arms around the King's neck.

"You see, Father dear, I *must* learn the ending of that song taught me by the trees, the wind, and the waves. Really I must hear that last line; and the man who can sing *that,* I'll marry at once!"

The King frowned, for he deemed her test a ridiculous way to decide upon a suitor.

"Silly girl! Who on earth can tell if this suitor sings the last line correctly?"

"Oh, *that* I'll feel at once—deep inside!"

"Hum!" growled the King. "But suppose it's not an emperor, a king, or a prince who guesses right—suppose the lucky suitor turns out to be a peasant lad?"

"Well, that can't be helped," answered Princess Rosenknopp.

"I want to warn you in time," the King went on, still frowning. "Your unknown suitor is not going to inherit half my kingdom. Your brother, the Crown Prince, will receive my whole realm. So if a peasant guesses the last line rightly and you marry him, you'll have to content yourself with becoming just a simple farmwife."

The Princess bowed her head and looked grieved at this dreary prospect.

"Even so, it can't be helped," she said at last, and this ended their interview.

So the King had to give in. And he sent throughout his whole realm royal messengers to proclaim that all young men who wanted to pay court to his daughter, and who dared take their turn at guessing, must appear in the throne room the following Sunday precisely at noon.

Upon the appointed day, exactly at twelve o'clock, the King, his Queen, and Princess Rosenknopp made their entrance into the Great Hall and seated themselves upon their thrones. That day the Great Hall was full of emperors, kings, and princes who had heard the announcement about the proposed choice of a husband for Princess Rosenknopp. Not only were the highest royalty present, but a horde of counts, barons, and ordinary noblemen were packed into the palace. Even peasant lads and kitchen hands had turned out. Since the choice would be determined by a guess, each man thought he might be just as lucky as the next. And everyone knows that emperors, kings, and princes are not always the cleverest at guessing.

When the Great Hall fell silent, the Princess rose and related the story of the song—how the trees, the wind, and the waves had taught it to her. Then she complained sadly that certain words were missing at the end. Thereupon she began to sing with such a lovely and clear voice that the music went straight to the heart of every man in the hall.

And this is what she sang:

> Woods are sleeping; fields are dreaming;
> Their dance forgotten, waves are whisp'ring.
>
> 'Neath trembling tree, the little bird
> Hides his head; no song is heard.
>
> Morning blesses field and mark;
> No foot falls in royal park.
>
> No eye greets the blooming rose,
> The buds unwakened still stay closed.
>
> See, upon the castle stairway,
> Wearing coat of silver sheen,
> In the springtime of his manhood
> Stands the Prince of handsome mien!
> From this youth all dreams have passed,
> . . . .

At this point the Princess fell silent and sat down. The King then arose and bade all the suitors leave the hall to ponder the solution to the riddle.

Slowly all the suitors squeezed themselves out of the hall and sought out corners and quiet nooks where they could ponder the end of the song. They thought so hard that most of them felt their heads would split, for many had not done any thinking in their whole lives. And those poor wretches who had not been able to push their way into the Great Hall asked to hear the song from those who had managed to get in. Soon, young men in the whole realm, and even in neighboring realms, were humming and singing this song in order to discover the last line—and win a princess in the bargain.

The very first person to come back into the Great Hall was a young emperor. He felt proud and sure of himself. He dropped to his knees before Princess Rosenknopp and began to sing her song from the beginning. Then he came to the last stanza:

> From this youth all dreams have passed,
> His ears have caught the cannons' blast.

When the young emperor got up from his kneeling position and gazed into the eyes of the Princess, she only shook her head.

"Alas," said she, "that ending is not correct."

Brokenhearted, the emperor stumbled out of the hall. So deeply did he feel his disappointment that the very feathers on his hat drooped.

The next suitor was a king, who looked solemn and majestic.

"I know that the last lines of that song must go this way," said he, and he began to sing in a very harsh voice:

> From this youth all dreams have passed,
> He sees his foes for battle massed!

Hearing these words the Princess shook her head even more times than she had shaken it at the emperor.

"No, no, no!" she cried. "It isn't like that at all!" Whereupon the king's face fell, and he seemed to shrink into a ball of fur and silk. Somehow he managed to roll out of the hall before anybody could start laughing at him.

Next came a prince, but not a prince without a song. This one waved his arms grandly and shouted the song in the following manner:

> From this youth all dreams have passed,
> The bugles blow, the hunt is fast!

Hearing this absurd ending, the Princess burst into laughter and covered her face with her hands. Then she said with a giggle, "No, no, no, certainly my song could not end that way!"

Now it was clear that it was much harder to solve the song-riddle than the King had thought. Every day young men came from far and wide, and they sang new endings for the song—but not one of them was correct.

It happened that one day when the Princess and her ladies-in-waiting were out in the nearby forest, taking their usual promenade, they lost their way. To return to the castle they had to cross a wide river, but nowhere could they find a bridge. They were getting frightened, for daylight was fading from the sky. Suddenly they caught sight of a boatman rowing a small craft along the river.

One of the court ladies called out to him that he should come ashore and take them across the river, and this he proceeded to do. When all the young ladies were seated, the Princess glanced at the young boatman. And all at once she found this stranger in the blue shirt more handsome than any emperor, king, or prince she had ever seen.

He gazed back at her, and suddenly he parted his lips and in a deep warm voice began to sing the song that had been made just for her but the ending of which she had never heard. When he came to the last line of the song, the Princess was seized with an excitement and expectation that she had never known in all her life.

> See, upon the castle stairway,
> Wearing coat of silver sheen,
> In the springtime of his manhood
> Stands the Prince of handsome mien!
> From this youth all dreams have passed,
> For now ....

But at this point he stopped suddenly and planted his oar on land. So of course the ladies had to step from his boat. When they were safe on land, he rowed away so quickly that the Princess had no chance to pay him.

All that night the Princess kept waking up and humming to herself the song to which the boatman had added two new words:

> From this youth all dreams have passed,
> For now ....

But no matter how long she thought about it, she could not add another word or bit of melody.

Then, of course, having seen the boatman, the Princess and the court ladies had to walk again in the forest; again they had to lose their way and not find a bridge over which they could cross back to the castle. Then, of course, they caught sight of the boatman, and they called to him, and he rowed to them quickly and took them all on board.

As the Princess sat in his little boat, she could not keep her eyes from him, nor could he hold his eyes from her, and presently he was singing in his deep rich voice:

> See, upon the castle stairway,
> Wearing coat of silver sheen,
> In the springtime of his manhood
> Stands the Prince of handsome mien!
> From this youth all dreams have passed,
> For now the buds ....

Again she found the boatman more handsome than emperor, king, or prince. And she was quite sure that he sang in the finest voice she had ever heard, but she was anxious because he did not finish the last line. Instead he came near shore, set the ladies on land, and rowed off so quickly it was quite impossible to say a word to him.

That night she was awake again trying to complete the song all by herself, to no avail.

So Princess Rosenknopp with her court ladies went out into the forest for the third time. And happily they lost their way, and joyously they caught sight of the mysterious boatman who took them on board. After he had rowed a little way, the Princess and the ladies realized that he was not crossing the river but was rowing down along the shore in the direction of the castle. From a distance the Princess could make out a train of people rushing down to meet them. These people were the King, the Queen, and the entire court, and they were all waving their hands frantically.

But the boatman would not hurry; instead, he began to sing the song for the Princess:

> See upon the castle stairway,
> Wearing coat of silver sheen,
> In the springtime of his manhood
> Stands the Prince of handsome mien!

Suddenly the boatman stopped and gazed at the Princess. A smile began to play about his lips. She felt her heart pounding and her whole body trembled with expectation and excitement.

The boatman went on:

> From this youth all dreams have passed,
> For the buds have bloomed at last!

Just then the boat touched shore, and in the most graceful way in the world, the boatman helped the Princess onto land. Meanwhile, the whole court and her parents were waiting for Princess Rosenknopp. When they came close around her, a great hubbub of astonishment rose from them.

"Look at the garland in her hair!" they cried in a chorus.

They stared at the Princess, and indeed something miraculous had taken place. All the buds of the garland had opened into full-blown roses!

"That's the very ending I have been waiting for all my life!" cried the Princess, and she clapped her hands joyously. Then she took the boatman's hand and walked with him slowly toward the King. Her father was frowning as she came near, but nothing could hold her back.

"Here is the man who of all the men in the world has sung the true ending of my song." The young couple stood before the King, the Queen, and the entire court. And such a silence fell on the company that one could have heard a leaf turn. Then one by one the Queen and all the ladies of the court put their handkerchiefs to their noses and began to sniff, for it was clear by the words and action of the Princess that she was determined to marry a mere boatman.

This is the sorriest fate in the world for my beloved daughter, the Queen was thinking. The King looked angry and forbidding for he was saying to himself, *What a fate for my daughter, who could have married an emperor, a king, or a prince, to fall to such a low estate as to marry a mere boatman.*

Princess Rosenknopp (this name no longer suited her, for all the buds were in full bloom) spoke up in a clear firm voice:

"I can guess what all of you are thinking. But I shall not change my mind. And since this is not an occasion for a big wedding, I want you to call the Court Chaplain at once, and let's get on with it."

The Chaplain was there in a trice. He placed together the hands of the young pair and read the marriage service over them. And before an hour had passed, the Princess and the boatman were joined in the bonds of matrimony.

The King ordered a wedding dinner at once. But it did not last long, for no one had prepared for it. The very next morning the Princess said farewell to her parents and relatives and to all her friends at court. Then she stepped into the little boat, and her husband rowed her away.

Despite her feeling of love for the young man, it was not easy for the Princess to leave her home behind.

"Don't be afraid, my love," said her husband. "Have faith and wait till we come home. Then you'll find it is not so bad there as you might suppose."

These words comforted her, and gazing at him, she found that he had the most beautiful eyes in the world.

After they had gone a fair distance up the river, their boat moved between two shores that seemed deserted and forlorn. Finally the bride caught sight of a little gray cottage that was so near the shore it was almost falling into the water.

"That's where we're going to live," cried the boatman as he steered the little craft toward land.

But the Princess felt miserable when he brought her to the

shore. With hands joined, they walked toward the broken-down little cottage, which was built on a small plot entirely covered with large weeds.

Her heart sank, and she was thinking, *How can this man think it possible for me to be happy in this hovel surrounded by ugly weeds?*

The young husband did not glance at her but took a key from his pocket and started to open the door.

Inside, they found a little entrance hall. Here her husband turned his back to the inner door and faced her. And he began to sing:

> See, upon the castle stairway,
> Wearing coat of silver sheen,
> In the springtime of his manhood
> Stands the Prince of handsome mien!
> From this youth all dreams have passed,
> For the buds have bloomed at last.

As he sang, the Princess saw that his clothes were changing. No longer did he wear his shirt of blue, but he was attired in a coat "of silver sheen." And on his head he wore a velvet beret topped with a dashing blue feather.

Indeed, he had become "the Prince of handsome mien" whom she had learned to know in the song made for her by the trees, the wind, and the waves.

No longer did he stand in a broken-down doorway, but instead upon a staircase of white marble. In place of the ugly little shack she had entered, behind him now rose a marvelous castle, and she could see the sun glittering in a thousand windows. Strangest of all, in place of the weeds, they were surrounded by a whole garden full of gentlemen and ladies-in-waiting, all bowing in the wind like plants.

Before the Princess could recover from her astonishment, the Prince sprang down the steps, took her hand in his, and led her through a castle gate. They wandered through long corridors of elegant rooms and finally to their own apartment, which revealed a long balcony upon which they stood together.

With her husband at her side, the beautiful bride gazed down on a spacious green park and beyond it a great city with green towers and golden cupolas shimmering in the sunset.

"This is my home; here is my kingdom," said the Prince, and he kissed her hand tenderly.

"But where in the world did all this come from?" asked his wife, still numb with astonishment.

"Here is the truth," answered her husband. "He who learns the song taught by the trees, the wind, and waves—in time is always rewarded by the good fairies."

a Swedish story from *Scandinavian Stories*
by MARGARET SPERRY

THE NEW BOOK OF KNOWLEDGE
1982

The following articles are from the 1982 edition of *The New Book of Knowledge*. They are included here to help you keep your encyclopedia up-to-date.

OSTRICHES AND OTHER FLIGHTLESS BIRDS

When we think of birds, we usually think of creatures that fly and sing. Yet some birds cannot fly, and most of these flightless birds do not sing. They usually hiss, snort, roar, boom, whistle, or grunt.

Of course, most birds can fly. They depend on flying to get food, to travel, and to flee when they sense danger. But some kinds of birds—a few dozen—are flightless. Some, like penguins and ostriches, have very heavy bodies with wings that are too small to support their weight in the air. A few parrots, ducks, and other birds in families of normally powerful fliers are also flightless.

Scientists believe that all the flightless birds living today are descended from birds that could fly. The reason for this belief is that the wing bones of flightless birds have the same structure as those of flying birds. But the wings of these birds are no longer used for flight.

Why should some birds have lost their ability to fly? The flightless parrots and ducks and some nearly flightless pigeons give us a clue. These birds have no need to fly. They live in places where they are not threatened by enemies, and they can easily find food by walking or swimming. The larger flightless birds, such as ostriches, also live in places where they have few or no enemies, or they can run fast enough to escape.

Once a bird no longer needs to fly, it may evolve into a form so large that it cannot fly. The ostrich, for example, feeds on plant material that requires a very long intestine for digestion. The intestine of an ostrich measures 14 meters (46 feet). If the ostrich had to fly, its body could not contain such a long and heavy intestine. Then, perhaps, it would not be able to eat the food that grows in some of the very dry areas where it lives.

The best known group of flightless birds is

Ostrich chicks are about 30 centimeters (1 foot) tall when they hatch. They are carefully guarded by their father at all times. When they are only a month old, the young birds can run about 55 kilometers (35 miles) an hour for short distances. Adult ostriches can run at speeds of almost 100 kilometers (60 miles) an hour. Ostriches have very keen eyesight. If they spot danger, they may crouch down—with their necks stretched out—and disappear from view. People who saw ostriches acting in this way once believed, mistakenly, that the huge birds were burying their heads in the sand.

made up of ostriches, rheas, emus, cassowaries, and kiwis. All live in the Southern Hemisphere. They are known as ratites, from the Latin word for raft (a boat without a keel). Ratites have a flat breastbone without the keel-like structure to which flight muscles are attached in flying birds.

Scientists cannot decide whether all the ratite families are truly related or whether they merely seem similar because they lead similar lives. But most ratite families share one form of behavior that is very unusual. The males build the nests, incubate the eggs (warm them by sitting on them until they hatch), and care for the young birds. The females usually lay their eggs, which are very large, in the nests that have been prepared for them. Then they leave and lay eggs in the nest of another male. If the females had to stay on the nests, they might not be able to look for the large amount of food that they need to produce more eggs.

▶ OSTRICHES

The ostrich is the largest living bird. It may be as much as 2.5 meters (8 feet) tall and weigh about 135 kilograms (300 pounds). It has long, bare legs; only two toes on each foot (fewer than any other bird); and a long, pink, featherless neck. Males are black with white wing and tail feathers. Females are grayish brown. Both have thick eyelashes of fine feathers.

Today ostriches are found in the wild only in the grasslands and some desert areas of eastern and southern Africa. They usually live in groups of one male and three to five females. But sometimes as many as 40 to 50 birds may be found together. Ostriches eat grasses, leaves, and fruits, as well as insects and lizards. They also swallow large amounts of sand and small pebbles to help digest their food. Ostriches make a loud, hissing sound. In the breeding season, the male produces a booming roar. In east central Africa these huge birds often gather with herds of zebras, antelope, and giraffes.

During the breeding season, several female ostriches lay eggs in the nest made by a male. The eggs are huge and creamy white in color. Each female lays about six to eight eggs, usually one every three days. Unlike other ratites, male and female ostriches

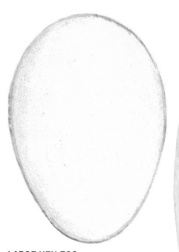

HUMMINGBIRD EGG

LARGE HEN EGG

Ostriches produce the largest eggs of any bird. One egg may weigh about 1,500 grams (53 ounces) and have the same volume as 26 hen eggs. Here you can see how an ostrich egg compares in size with a large hen egg and with a hummingbird egg, the smallest of all bird eggs.

OSTRICH EGG

share the incubation. The male sits on the nest at night, and the females take turns by day.

The long feathers of ostrich wings have been used as ornaments since ancient times. In the 1890's the feathers were often used to decorate women's hats. The establishment of ostrich farms, mainly in South Africa, reduced the killing of the wild birds. Today ostriches are still raised on farms for their feathers as well as for their hides, which are made into leather. But the demand for these products is not as great as in the past. On ostrich farms the feathers are clipped off the wings without hurting the birds. New feathers grow in later.

Ostriches have one of the longest life spans of any land animal. Some ostriches, especially those raised in captivity, may live to be 70 years old.

▶ RHEAS

Rheas are found only in South America. They are sometimes called South American

RHEA

CASSOWARY

EMU

KIWI

ostriches, or pampas ostriches. There are two kinds of rheas. The common rhea of Argentina and southern Brazil is about 1.5 meters (5 feet) tall. It may weigh more than 25 kilograms (55 pounds). The Darwin's rhea is somewhat smaller. It is found on the plains of western Argentina and high in the Andes mountains. Both the common rhea and the Darwin's rhea are brown in color. Unlike ostriches, rheas have feathers covering their heads and necks, as well as their bodies.

Rheas live in flocks of 20 or 30 and sometimes more. At times they mix with herds of deer or cattle. They eat leaves, roots, and seeds, as well as insects and lizards. When they run, rheas hold their necks stretched out in front of them. Often they make sudden

This scale shows how members of the ratite group compare in height with a human being. To the right of the human are two ratites that have been extinct for centuries. The elephant bird of Madagascar stood as high as 3 meters (10 feet). The moa of New Zealand was as much as 3.5 meters (12 feet) tall.

3.5 METERS
(12 FEET)

3 METERS
(10 FEET)

2.5 METERS
(8 FEET)

1.8 METERS
(6 FEET)

1.5 METERS
(5 FEET)

0.5 METER
(1¾ FEET)
LONG

KIWI   RHEA   CASSOWARY   EMU   OSTRICH   ELEPHANT BIRD   MOA

twists and turns. Their calls are whistling noises and a deep booming sound.

The shells of rhea eggs change color. When they are laid, the eggs are green. During incubation they become yellow, then blue. Finally, when the chicks hatch, the eggs are white. As the newly hatched birds begin to search for food, they and their father whistle to keep in contact.

Rheas are no longer hunted for sport as much as in the past. But their numbers continue to decrease for another reason. Fences have been built to enclose cattle on ranches. These fences limit the areas where the rheas can find the food they need to survive.

▶ EMUS

The tallest ratite after the ostrich is the emu, which lives in Australia. It may be as much as 1.8 meters (6 feet) tall and weigh up to 55 kilograms (122 pounds). Its feathers are brown or blackish brown. Like ostriches and rheas, emus live in open country. They feed on a wide variety of fruits and other plant material. They also eat insects. Emus make hissing, grunting, and booming sounds.

In some areas where wheat is grown, the emu is considered a pest because it knocks down fences and tramples crops. At one time, bounties (payments) were offered for shooting these birds. But today specially designed fences are used to keep the emus from entering the fields.

▶ CASSOWARIES

Cassowaries live in thick forests. Their feathers are black and shaggy. The long, white quills on their wing feathers are thought to show that the wings were used for flight long ago. Their heads and necks are bare of feathers and are brightly colored. The top of a cassowary's head has a casque, or bony helmet. The casque is thought to protect the bird as it runs at great speed, head first, through dense forest. Cassowaries may be more than 1.5 meters (5 feet) tall and weigh about 55 kilograms (122 pounds). The female cassowary is larger than the male.

The one-wattled cassowary and the Bennett's cassowary are found in New Guinea and on some of the nearby islands. The Australian cassowary lives in coastal forests in northeastern Australia.

Cassowaries usually live singly or in pairs. They are active day and night, feeding mainly on berries and fruit. In their forest homes they are more often heard than seen. The calls that they make sound like snorting, grunting, and bellowing.

Cassowaries are hunted for use as food. They are also valued for their feathers, which are used in headdresses. But these birds are difficult to hunt, and they can be very dangerous. Cassowaries will charge at people, feet first, often killing or badly wounding their victims with the long, sharp claws of their inner toes.

For hundreds of years the people of New Guinea have used cassowaries as a form of money. The government of Papua New Guinea has begun raising cassowaries on farms and selling them to the villagers so that more of these birds will be left in the wild.

▶ KIWIS

Kiwis are very small ratites. A kiwi is the size of a domestic hen and weighs between 1.5 and 4 kilograms (about 3 and 9 pounds). Kiwis have short legs and short necks. These give the body a rounded or hunched appearance. The tiny wings cannot be seen through the shaggy, brown feathers. A kiwi has a very sharp sense of smell. Its bill is long. And unlike the bills of other birds, a kiwi's bill has the nostrils at the tip. Female kiwis are larger than males.

There are three kinds of kiwis—the common, or brown, kiwi; the great spotted, or large gray, kiwi; and the little spotted, or little gray, kiwi. All are found in New Zealand and on its offshore islands.

A kiwi egg is white. It is 180 millimeters (7 inches) long. This is an extremely large egg for the size of the bird.

Kiwis live in burrows in thick forests. They hide by day but come out at night to feed on earthworms and insects. Their calls are shrill whistles or screams. To the Maori, the first people to live in New Zealand, the calls sounded like "kee-wee." At this time there is no threat to the survival of these shy birds because they are strictly protected by law in New Zealand.

ROGER F. PASQUIER
Author, *Watching Birds: An Introduction to Ornithology*

Then he fell on his head!
He came down with a bump . .
——*The Cat in the Hat*

And he puzzled three hours,
 till his puzzler was sore.
Then the Grinch thought of something
 he hadn't before!
"Maybe Christmas," he thought,
 "*doesn't* come from a store."
——*How the Grinch
Stole Christmas!*

If you wish
you may go
by lion's tail.
——*Marvin K. Mooney
Will You
Please
Go
Now!*

SEUSS, Dr. (1904–)

Have you met the Drum-Tummied Snumm, the wink-hooded Hoodwinks, and the Juggling Jot? Or the Lorax, the Sneetches, and the Yuzz-a-ma-Tuzz? Then you know Dr. Seuss, the author-illustrator who has created a fantastic menagerie of more than 40 children's books. Millions of copies of the Dr. Seuss books have been sold, in 17 languages.

Dr. Seuss's real name is Theodor Seuss Geisel. He was born March 2, 1904, in Springfield, Massachusetts, where his father was superintendent of the city parks and zoo. After graduating from Dartmouth College in 1925, Geisel studied at Oxford University in England. He had no formal art training, but after returning to the United States, he became an advertising illustrator known for his exaggerated cartoons and wacky wit.

His first children's book, *And to Think That I Saw It on Mulberry Street,* was published in 1937 with the author-illustrator listed as "Dr. Seuss." In this picture book, as in other Seuss creations, nonsense, exaggeration, and rhyme take over.

According to Dr. Seuss, all his books begin with doodles that turn into zany characters. Among the most popular are *The 500 Hats of Bartholomew Cubbins, Horton Hatches the Egg,* and *If I Ran the Zoo.*

The Cat in the Hat, published in 1957, uses only 175 different words to tell a smash-bang story easy enough for first graders to read on their own. The Beginner Books that followed use simple words to tell of hilarious situations. Two favorites are *Green Eggs and Ham* and *Hop on Pop.*

Dr. Seuss is also a designer and producer of animated cartoons and television specials. In 1951 he won an Academy Award for *Gerald McBoing-Boing.* And in 1977 he received an Emmy Award for *Halloween Is Grinch Night.*

For his "lasting contribution to literature for children," Dr. Seuss received the Laura Ingalls Wilder Medal in 1980. In some of his books he uses the name Theo LeSieg. "LeSieg" is "Geisel" spelled backwards.

NANCY LARRICK
Author, *A Parent's Guide to Children's Reading*

CASSATT, MARY (1844–1926)

Mary Cassatt was the foremost American woman painter of the 19th century. She was also the only American artist to exhibit paintings with the French impressionists—artists who revolutionized painting by using bright colors, small brushstrokes, and informal subjects.

Cassatt was born on May 22, 1844, in Allegheny City (now a part of Pittsburgh), Pennsylvania. She knew early that she wanted to be a painter. In 1861, she enrolled at the Pennsylvania Academy of the Fine Arts. Several years later, she went to Europe to study the old masters in churches and museums.

In 1872, Cassatt had a painting accepted for the Paris Salon, the official exhibition sponsored by the French Academy of Fine Arts. A year later, she settled permanently in Paris. She soon became aware of the impressionists, especially of Edgar Degas, who became her teacher and lifelong friend. The work of the impressionists was not ap-proved by the Academy. But it appealed to Cassatt. She stopped entering works for the Salon and exhibited with the impressionists.

Cassatt made women her main subject. In her work, we see women in their everyday lives. They take tea and talk. They go to the opera. They weave and knit and read quietly in the garden. And always, they enjoy and care for their children, especially the babies.

The taste of Cassatt's time was for highly idealized mothers and children. In contrast, Cassatt painted people as she saw them, often plain and awkward. But her truth reveals a beauty that has endured. Cassatt's work became popular in Paris, and she was the first impressionist to support herself by her art.

Mary Cassatt never married. She died in her country house outside Paris on June 14, 1926. In recent years, her work has gained increasing recognition in the United States.

FRANK GETLEIN
Author, *Mary Cassatt*

Mother About to Wash Her Sleepy Child (1880), by Mary Cassatt

RUBBINGS

Have you ever put a piece of paper on top of a coin and then rubbed a pencil over it until the pattern of the coin appeared? That is a very simple form of rubbing. Rubbing is an easy way to reproduce many designs and textures—even very complicated ones.

You can rub all kinds of things, from small coins to large wall carvings, manhole and sewer covers, and even stained-glass windows. In the United States old gravestones are often good subjects. The stones in New England graveyards are especially popular because of their interesting designs. In Britain the floors of churches are often set with brass plaques, some of which date back to medieval times. Many plaques mark the graves of important people. People enjoy doing rubbings of these plaques, with their designs of knights and ladies or religious subjects.

Rubbing is an exciting way to learn about history and architecture. It may help you to notice things in your town that you never noticed before. It is also a way to preserve, on paper, images of things that may one day be destroyed or worn away. Frame your rubbings and hang them on your walls, or use them as patterns for needlepoint, block printing, and other crafts.

There are two basic rubbing techniques. The wax method is used for rubbing flat surfaces or surfaces with designs carved into them. The graphite method is used on surfaces with raised designs.

▶ THE WAX METHOD

To do a rubbing with this method, first decide what you want to rub and get all your materials together. You will need a sheet of paper large enough to cover your subject. The paper should be fairly strong but not too thick. Brown wrapping paper, newsprint, and rice paper are all good. You will also need masking tape, scissors, a natural-bristle brush, and a crayon. Special rubbing wax is available in some art-supply stores. It is less likely to smear than crayons.

Go over your subject with the brush so that it is cleaned of dirt. (Never use a metal-bristle brush, as the bristles may damage the object.) Cut your paper to a size that will completely cover the design you want to rub. Then tape it down securely at the edges. Next, rub the colored wax or crayon lightly over the entire surface of the paper to block in the design. Feel around on the paper with your fingers to make sure you have covered all parts of the design. When you can see the whole design, decide where you want to darken the rubbing. If you press harder with the wax, the rubbing will become darker, and more details will show up.

Continue rubbing until you think you have all the details you want. To see if you have

To do a rubbing by the wax method, first get all your materials together. Use a natural-bristle brush to clean dust and dirt from the object you plan to rub.

The paper you use should be strong but not too thick. Cut the paper to a size that will completely cover the design, and then tape it down securely at the edges.

missed any, you can peek beneath the paper by lifting one section of tape. But make sure that the rest of the tape is tightly attached. Never lift the paper all the way off—it will be impossible to put it back exactly the way it was. When your rubbing is finished, gently remove the tape by peeling it toward the edges of the paper.

For a different effect, try metallic or white wax on black paper. Fabric may be used instead of paper, but you will need special fabric-dying crayons. These are available in some art-supply stores.

▶ THE GRAPHITE METHOD

In this method, rubbing is done with a paste of mineral oil and graphite. (Graphite is the soft, black carbon that is used in pencils.) Working with graphite is messy. You should wear old clothes and use utensils that can be thrown away. Cover your work area with newspapers or a plastic drop cloth.

You can buy mineral oil at a drugstore and powdered graphite at an art-supply or a hardware store. Find an old but clean can and a mixing stick. Put some graphite in the can and slowly stir in the mineral oil until the mixture is thick and pasty, like canned shoe polish. If the mixture gets too thin, add more graphite. Store the mixture in a covered plastic bowl to keep it from drying out.

You will also need scissors, masking tape, a natural-bristle brush, two small pieces of cloth, a spray bottle filled with water, and

The finished rubbing. Different colors of wax and crayon have been used to highlight the design.

Rub crayon or colored wax over the entire surface to block in the design. Then darken the rubbing and bring up details by going over it with the crayon again.

paper. The paper must be strong when it is wet, like the paper used in tea bags. Paper made with hemp or some other fiber is good.

To begin, brush the object clean, and tape the paper loosely but securely over it. Use the spray bottle to dampen the paper, but do not soak it. The idea is to soften the paper so that it will mold to the design underneath. Now wrap one of the small cloths around your finger, and dip it into the graphite mixture. Wipe most of the mixture off onto the second cloth. This will remove large clumps of graphite that might smear and spoil your rubbing. With the first cloth, apply the graphite to the dampened paper, blocking in the design lightly. Darken areas of the rubbing by going over them again in the same way. When the rubbing is completed, gently remove the tape by pulling it toward the edge of the paper.

CECILY BARTH FIRESTEIN
Author, *Rubbing Craft*

321

Eskimos on a whale hunt use a traditional open boat, or umiak, and modern snowmobiles.

ESKIMOS (INUIT)

The Arctic is a region of vast treeless plains, icy seas, and barren, rocky islands. This harsh, cold land is the home of the Eskimos, a people who live in scattered settlements in Greenland, Canada, Alaska, and Siberia. For thousands of years, the Eskimos were isolated from other peoples. They lived by hunting and fishing, and they developed a way of life well suited to their homeland.

Today the Eskimos are no longer cut off from the outside world. And their way of life has changed. If you were to visit an Eskimo community, you would find most people living in modern houses, going to work or to school, and taking part in a way of life not too different from your own. But the Eskimos are still a distinct ethnic group—a group of people who share the same ancestry and culture. Today most Eskimos blend the old ways with the new.

▶ THE PEOPLE

"Eskimo" is a word of American Indian origin meaning "eaters of raw meat." English explorers first used this name in the 1500's. Many Eskimos prefer to be called "Inuit," a word in their own language meaning "the people" or "the real people."

As a racial and cultural group, the Eskimos are quite distinct from North American Indians. The Eskimos are descended from an ancient Mongoloid people of Siberia, now a part of the Soviet Union in northern Asia. The Aleuts, who live in the Aleutian Islands and other islands in the North Pacific Ocean off the coasts of Alaska and Siberia, are closely related to the Eskimos.

Eskimos are of medium height, with a stocky body form. Their skin is a dusky yellowish brown. Their hair is black, heavy, and straight. The Eskimo face is rather square, with a sturdy jaw. Like others of Asian origin, many Eskimos have a fold of skin at the eyes. This fold gives them a slightly slanting, narrow eye opening.

Eskimo languages have been spoken for thousands of years, but they were not written down until modern times. These languages form the Eskimo-Aleut language family, a family that has no known connections with other language groups. There are three main languages in the Eskimo-Aleut family—Aleut, Yupik, and Inupik. Inupik, spoken from northern Alaska to Greenland, has the largest number of speakers, and it has many dialects. The differences among

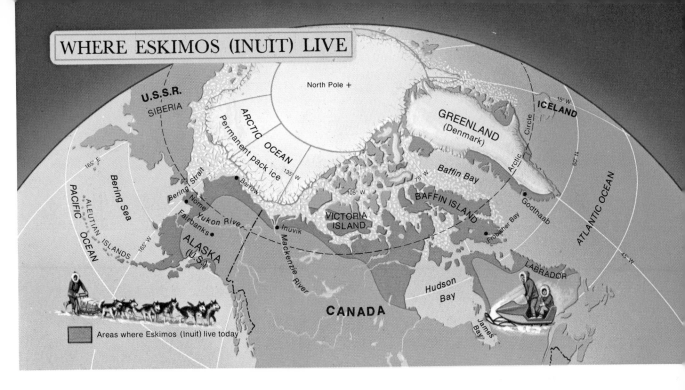

WHERE ESKIMOS (INUIT) LIVE

Areas where Eskimos (Inuit) live today

the dialects are small. Eskimos from northern Alaska can be understood by Eskimos from Canada and Greenland. Dialects of Yupik are spoken in southwestern Alaska and Siberia.

The Eskimos first entered North America about 5,500 years ago, crossing the Bering Strait from Asia. They moved rapidly across the Canadian North to Greenland. Some Eskimo groups then moved westward again, to the Bering Sea area. Today the Eskimo population is not large, but it is growing. About 2,000 Eskimos live in Siberia, 30,000 in Alaska, 22,500 in Canada, and 43,000 in Greenland. Some Eskimo communities are on the edges of the forests of the Far North. But most are on the treeless tundra, or Arctic plain, that lies north of the forests.

▶ **THE ESKIMO HOMELAND**

The tundra is a cold desert. Many areas within it receive less than 50 centimeters (20 inches) of snow throughout the long winter. But cold temperatures keep the snow from melting, and it stays on the ground. The Arctic seas, rivers, and lakes freeze hard by October. For much of the winter, daylight hours are brief, and in the northernmost areas the sun does not rise at all for months. In most areas, the ice breaks up in June. But in some it remains all year.

On the tundra, the top layer of soil is underlain by permafrost. This is a deep layer of permanently frozen subsoil. The top layer, where plants grow, thaws for a short time in summer. It is usually uneven and is poorly drained. Because of the rough ground and wet conditions, travel on the tundra is especially difficult in summer.

Summers are short and cool, but there is nearly continuous daylight from May to September. There may be warm days, with temperatures as high as 25°C (77°F). But the weather may change suddenly. In this bright, damp, and occasionally very warm Arctic summer, mosquitoes breed by the thousands. They are a major nuisance to both people and animals.

Slow-growing grasses, sedges, lichens, and low Arctic willows thrive on the tundra. The land animals most important to the Eskimos for food include several types of caribou, bear, musk-ox, and moose. In many coastal areas, the most important animals are seals of several types, walruses, sea lions, and belugas, narwhals, and other whales. But these animals are not always plentiful. Several kinds of waterfowl—geese and ducks—have their nesting areas in the Arctic. They provide valued food in spring and autumn.

Other animals are important to the Eski-

In winter, crabs are caught through holes in the ice in the Bering Sea, off the coast of Alaska.

Salmon, caught during the warmer months, are hung up to dry. Drying preserves the fish for later use.

mos for their fur. They include the white fox, marten, lynx, wolverine, and wolf. Many beavers and muskrats live in the deltas and lower parts of the mainland rivers. Small animals such as hares, muskrats, and beavers are also used for food.

▶ TRADITIONAL WAY OF LIFE

The Eskimos' traditional way of life developed to meet the challenges of the Far North. This section describes that way of life, which the Eskimos followed until recent times.

Group Life

The Eskimos lived in fairly small groups. There were villages of over 500 people on the northern Alaska coast. In the eastern region (Greenland, Baffin Island, and Labrador), a typical group might have 25 to 45 people. Eastern groups moved from place to place through the year, following a fairly fixed order of seasonal activities. They would spend winter near the coast, hunting seals and fishing. In summer, they would move inland to hunt caribou and gather berries. Sometimes they covered a circuit of more than 1,100 kilometers (500 miles). They crossed snow and ice in sleds pulled by dogs, and they traveled on water in open boats called umiaks.

Close co-operation was important if the members of an Eskimo group were to sur-

vive in their harsh land. Group members would work together in activities such as hunting. For example, in eastern groups ten to twelve hunters would be needed to harpoon seals at their breathing holes in the winter sea ice. Much larger groups—over 100 people—would work together to hunt caribou and large sea mammals such as whales. A few activities could be carried on by individuals and small family groups—tracking bears, fishing with nets, and gathering berries.

In eastern Arctic groups, there were no official leaders or chiefs. Each group would seek the opinions of respected members who had special skills. Such a person, called *issumataq* ("one who thinks much"), was a leader only for the time it took to complete a specific activity, such as a hunt.

In the northern Alaska coastal villages, organization was more formal. An example is the organization of boat crews for hunting large whales. These crews were made up of seven or eight men, related to one another through a male ancestor. The crew captain owned the boat. He had complete authority over the crew. He decided how each hunt was to be conducted and how the meat should be shared. He was a skilled hunter, with knowledge of animal behavior and of weather and ice conditions. He also knew the secret rituals, or ceremonies, that were thought to be necessary for good hunting.

Hunting and Fishing

Because they depended on hunting and fishing to live, Eskimos became highly skilled at these activities. Caribou hunting was essential for nearly all Eskimo groups. Caribou were hunted some distance inland in the summer and early autumn. In some places caribou were driven by lines of people into lakes or narrow streams, where they could be speared, shot with bows and arrows, or even harpooned. Sometimes Eskimos set up piles of stones in long lines. To the caribou, the stones looked like people in the distance. The caribou would turn away from the lines of stones and be caught in a convenient hunting spot.

For some groups, fishing was nearly as important as hunting. Fish were netted in deep muddy waters or through holes in the ice. They were speared in shallow, clear waters at weirs—low dams of stones placed across streams. Fish were chased into the weir by people wading in the stream and were caught by skilled hunters with three-pronged spears. Eskimos also used barbless bone hooks on short lines to fish through holes in the ice in winter or from the edge of the ice in spring. Seals were harpooned from the edges of ice floes or from kayaks—small canoelike boats made of animal skin stretched over a wooden frame.

Food Preparation

Meat, fat, and fish made up a large part of the Eskimo diet. Vegetables were scarce. Very little food was wasted. But because the Eskimos depended on hunting and fishing, hunger and even starvation were common when fish and game were not plentiful. Meat and fish caught in summer were stored in shallow cache pits. These pits were dug down to the permafrost and covered with piles of stones to keep out hungry animals.

Wood to make fires for roasting or baking was scarce in most of the Eskimo areas. Meat and fish were often eaten raw. Raw meat or fish was frozen and cut into thin strips, which were dipped in whale or seal oil. Some meat, especially meat from large sea mammals, was eaten in a partly decayed state. The decay made tough meat more tender and easier to digest. If food was cooked, it was almost always boiled, using the heat from oil lamps.

Shelter

The Eskimo word "igloo" means "shelter." It can refer to any kind of house, not only the dome-shaped snow houses that many people associate with the word.

In summer, most Eskimos lived in tents made of animal skins. In western Alaska, very large winter tents were made by placing

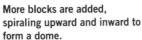

BUILDING A SNOW HOUSE

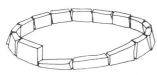

Snow houses were once built in parts of Canada and Greenland as winter homes. Today they are sometimes built for temporary shelter.

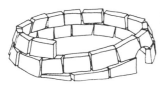

The house begins with a circle of blocks of snow (not ice). The blocks are set on edge, slanting inward, and shaped as shown in the diagram.

More blocks are added, spiraling upward and inward to form a dome.

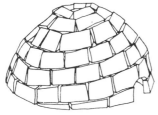

A small air hole is left at the top of the dome. The original entrance is closed, and an entrance tunnel is dug below floor level, as shown in the photograph at the right.

A cotton garment called a *kuspuk* covers this Eskimo girl's warm fur parka.

large snow houses were joined together by tunnels. Some snow houses were lined with sealskins that were sewed together and suspended from the top of the dome.

Clothing and Crafts

The Eskimos wore boots called mukluks, trousers, and hooded jackets called parkas —all made of animal skins. There were differences in details of clothing for men and women. The man's parka was thigh-length. The woman's parka had long flaps in front and behind. In winter, the Eskimos wore two layers of clothing. Caribou fawn skin was preferred in winter because it was soft and warm. Coastal groups preferred sealskin in late spring and summer. It had the advantage of being waterproof, although it was very stiff. Clothing was often embroidered and had decorative fringes. Cutouts of different-colored animal skins were pieced together to form patterns on parkas.

The Eskimos decorated tools and objects for everyday use. Such decoration made people's possessions very personal. Bone, ivory, wood, and a soft stone called soapstone were used to make small figures of people and animals, as well as weapons and tools. Tools were carefully carved to fit the hand of the user. In the Pacific and far western areas, masks were carved of wood, painted, and decorated with feathers and animal skins.

Religious Beliefs

Eskimo religion showed a deep concern with life, health, sickness, starvation, and death. The Eskimos believed that spirits controlled these things. All Eskimo groups believed in a supernatural power called Sila. They shared belief in a small number of spirits (such as Sedna, the goddess of life, health, and food), and they believed that people and animals had souls that lived on after death. But each group had certain beliefs and rituals of its own. Each person, family, or group had taboos, or bans, forbidding certain actions, such as eating a particular kind of food. Each group had a few major ceremonies, performed at births and deaths or when hunting was either very poor or very successful. Shamans (persons skilled in performing rituals) were believed to help

heavy walrus skins over wood frames. On the northern coast of Alaska, dome-shaped houses were built of logs and whale ribs. The dome was raised over a depression in the ground and was covered on the outside with frozen turf. In Greenland, houses were built of stone slabs.

Snow houses were used only in the eastern and central regions. They were made from blocks of packed snow (not ice), built into a dome. Small snow houses with short tunnel entrances were used while traveling. Larger snow houses were used as winter residences. Long tunnel entrances provided storage space in these larger homes. The entrance tunnel opened into the house below floor level.

In the rear half of the house and on both sides of the door, there were snow benches about 1 meter high. The rear bench was covered with animal skins and used for sleeping. The side benches supported racks for drying clothes, food supplies, and seal-oil lamps that provided light and heat. Sometimes two establish and keep contact with the spirit world. Shamans used trances, drama, and magic tricks in their performances, which were often frightening and awe-inspiring.

Recreation

Wrestling, racing, harpoon-throwing contests, and other vigorous athletic activities were popular. Games of skill were sometimes essential parts of religious rituals, as were storytelling, singing, drumming, and dancing. They were major sources of entertainment, too. Parties and social visits were occasions for huge feasts of meat and fat whenever possible.

▶ CONTACTS WITH THE OUTSIDE WORLD

The first Europeans to be seen by Eskimos were Vikings from Iceland, who established a settlement in Greenland. Contact between the Eskimos and the Icelanders began about A.D. 1200 and continued until about 1400.

Other Europeans began to explore deeper into the Eskimo area after 1576–78, when the English mariner Martin Frobisher visited Baffin Island. Danish, Norwegian, and English explorers sailed into the seas of the Far North to find the fabled Northwest Passage to China. By 1728, the Russians had arrived in Siberia and northern Alaska. Contact with the Europeans began in earnest as explorers tried to find the Northwest Passage from the Pacific Ocean as well as from the Atlantic. But some Eskimo groups in the northern Arctic islands did not have much contact with outsiders until the late 1800's and early 1900's.

After 1850, the arrival of European and American whalers and fur traders brought many changes. Eskimos worked for the whalers and sold furs to the traders. The outsiders, in turn, provided a steady source of metal tools and rifles. Because of the new tools and weapons and the new demand for furs, animals were hunted and killed in greater numbers. In some areas, animals such as caribou and seals were hunted almost to extinction.

The outsiders brought new diseases to which the Eskimos had no immunity, or natural resistance. Smallpox, tuberculosis, influenza, whooping cough, pneumonia, mumps, scarlet fever, and diphtheria were the most dangerous of these diseases. After the late 1800's, larger numbers of Europeans began to live year-round in the Arctic. And these diseases became very serious.

The pattern of relations between the Eskimos and outsiders has been described as "boom and bust." Waves of outsiders have brought brief periods of wealth, education, and employment. These times have been followed by periods of poverty and disorganization. Peak periods have been those of whaling (1850 to 1910), the modern fur trade (1925 to about 1950), the building of military and defense bases (mid-1950's), the building of urban centers (the 1960's), and oil exploration and development (the 1970's).

Each wave of activity has drawn the Eskimos into contact with different social and economic forces. The once isolated northlands have been opened up by air travel, highways, powerful modern ships, and satellite communications. These changes have produced great strains on the Eskimo way of life.

▶ THE ESKIMOS TODAY

No Eskimos now live as their ancestors did. Few—perhaps 10 percent—live off the land, following a way of life based on hunting, fishing, and trapping. Another 10 to 15

A husky watches an Eskimo boy fishing. Snowmobiles are popular, but dogs still pull sleds in winter.

Eskimo children delight in all kinds of active sports
and games—from blanket toss (*above*) to basketball.

percent have full-time, year-round jobs. But
most Eskimos work and live in a settlement
for part of the year and hunt, trap, and fish
the rest of the time.

In the settlements, most houses are simple
wood-frame buildings. But they have heat,
electricity, radios, telephones, color television sets, and other modern conveniences.
In Greenland, many Eskimos live in high-
rise apartment buildings of modern style.
Most settlements have schools providing
instruction up to the eighth grade. Many
Eskimos have adopted Christianity, and a
settlement usually has a church. Other
public buildings include general stores,
health care facilities, and a post office. Only
a few communities do not have an airstrip.
Places such as Nome and Fairbanks
(Alaska), Inuvik and Frobisher Bay (Canada), and Godthaab (Greenland) provide a
wider range of goods and services.

The Eskimos who live off the land use
canvas tents. In winter, log houses with turf
(sod) roofs are used in Alaska, the western
Canadian Arctic, and the Soviet Union. Traditional Eskimo snow houses are occasionally used in the eastern and northern Arctic,
usually only as temporary shelter while traveling. Snowmobiles are popular for crossing
the tundra in winter.

Apart from traditional-style parkas and
mukluks—now made of factory-produced
materials—the people have adopted European and American dress. Flour, sugar,
canned foods, dried milk, tea, coffee, and
tobacco are supplied by trading centers and
supermarkets. The Eskimos buy some meat
from stores. But caribou, seals, whales, and
fish are still widely hunted. Many people
who live and work in towns hunt and fish on
weekends and vacations. Those who do not
hunt much acquire at least some ''country
food'' as gifts and in exchanges with friends.
Vegetables are expensive and not widely
used. Wild blueberries, cranberries, and
young Arctic willow roots are still collected
and enjoyed. Fats—especially lard, butter,
and margarine—are still important to the Eskimo diet, especially in winter.

Most Siberian Eskimos now live and work
in government-organized collective groups.
Their main activity is the hunting of sea
mammals.

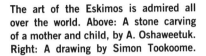

The art of the Eskimos is admired all over the world. Above: A stone carving of a mother and child, by A. Oshaweetuk. Right: A drawing by Simon Tookoome.

▶ CONTEMPORARY PROBLEMS

As more and more Eskimos have changed their way of life, they have been drawn into low-level, low-paying jobs. Many are unemployed or do not earn enough money to buy what they need and want in life. About half of the Eskimos are considered poor by Western standards. And many Eskimos have felt that the routines of employment are an invasion of their dignity, independence, and self-reliance. An increase in violence, crime, alcoholism, and mental stress among Eskimos seems to have been the result. In addition, disease and malnutrition have made life difficult for many Eskimos right up to the present day. Infant deaths are over ten times as frequent among Eskimos as among other people in North America.

Since the 1960's, Eskimos have become more and more involved in seeking solutions to these problems. They have concentrated on claims to Arctic lands, rights to hunt and fish over these lands, and the choice of a way of life that preserves their culture. Eskimos have formed a number of political groups. The Alaska Federation of Natives is one of these. In Canada, the Inuit Tapirisat (Eskimo Brotherhood), the Committee for Original Peoples Entitlement, and the Northern Quebec Inuit Association have been active.

Each of these associations has reached agreements on land issues with the governments concerned. The first agreement was the Alaska Native Claims Settlement Act (1971). Under it, land and money were divided among 200 Eskimo, Aleut, and Indian villages. This agreement provided the model for similar agreements in Canada. The Northern Quebec Inuit Association signed the James Bay Agreement in 1975, and the Committee for Original Peoples Entitlement has signed an agreement regarding the Mackenzie River Delta.

Eskimos have also been concerned about hunting rights. Many of the animals on which they once depended—including polar bears, walruses, and bowhead whales—are now scarce. Commercial and sport hunting of these animals has been banned or limited. But in many cases, the Eskimos are permitted to kill a number of the animals for their own use.

In the eastern Canadian Arctic, Eskimos have formed several co-operative economic associations. These associations provide Eskimos with a way to market valuable soapstone carvings and other arts and crafts, which are in great demand. Eskimos have also worked to preserve their language and culture. In Greenland, the Eskimo language has been declared an official language equal in status to Danish. The Eskimo language is taught in schools in Alaska and Canada.

Eskimo life is much changed. But today the Eskimos are making a place for themselves in the modern world.

DEREK G. SMITH
Carleton University

329

This portrait of Queen Victoria was painted in 1842, five years after she came to the British throne.

VICTORIA, QUEEN
(1819–1901)

In the reign of Queen Victoria—from 1837 to 1901—Britain reached the height of its power and prosperity. The British Empire extended to India, the tip of Africa, and the coast of China. British ships dominated the seas and kept watch over vast trade and financial interests. Clocks around the world were set by Greenwich (London) time.

Under Victoria, too, the British monarchy became a powerful unifying force. Before she came to the throne, the British rulers had lost the respect of their subjects by behavior that offended many people. The monarchy had become highly unpopular. Victoria had a strong sense of duty, and her personal conduct was above reproach. She won back the respect and devotion of her subjects.

Victoria (Alexandrina Victoria, in full) was born on May 24, 1819, at Kensington Palace in London. She was the only child of Edward, the fourth son of King George III, and Victoria Mary Louisa, the daughter of a German duke. She came to the throne in 1837 after the death of her uncle, the child-less William IV. Victoria was then a young woman of 18, high-spirited and fun-loving. In 1840, she married her distant cousin Albert, a German prince. His ideas about queenly dignity changed her outlook. She became a proper, dignified wife and the mother of nine children. After Albert's untimely death in 1861, she continued to live by his standards, as he would have wished. The Queen represented the middle-class taste in art and music, fashion and style, and religious observance. Above all, she stood for a stern morality.

Victoria ruled for almost 64 years—longer than any other British monarch. She was served by powerful prime ministers who were men of outstanding ability. They included Robert Peel, William Gladstone, and Benjamin Disraeli. Victoria's place in government was largely as a symbol. But the respect for her was so complete that she needed no legal authority to exert her influence. To be sure, her ministers were occasionally difficult. Victoria once fretted that Gladstone "speaks to me as if I am a public meeting." But she knew that genuine respect lay behind his formal speech. Disraeli was her favorite prime minister. He concluded negotiations that made her empress of India and that added the Suez Canal to her dominions. And he wisely treated his Queen with the charm of a model courtier.

In 1897, Britain honored the 60th year of Victoria's reign with a great celebration, the Diamond Jubilee. The affection that poured in for the "little gray lady" pointed up the respect that she had won from people of all classes and political beliefs. Because of marriages with other European royal families, the guests at the celebration included monarchs and princes and princesses who were children and grandchildren of Victoria. When her eldest son succeeded her as Edward VII, he could in a real sense be called the "uncle of Europe."

Britain was soon to lose its place as the leader of the world. But when Victoria died —on January 22, 1901, at the age of 81—she could close her eyes in peace, believing with her proud subjects that the British Empire was secure.

ABRAM L. SACHAR
Chancellor, Brandeis University

CASTRO, FIDEL (1926–)

Fidel Castro Ruz, a fiery speaker and firm believer in the idea of revolution, took power in Cuba in 1959. Under him, Cuba became the first socialist country in the Americas.

Castro once said that he was a "professional revolutionary" because he could not stand injustice. Yet he was not personally a victim of injustice. He was born on August 13, 1926, at Mayarí, in eastern Cuba. His parents were well-to-do farmers, and he was free to roam the family plantation. He attended the Mayarí parish school and Jesuit schools in Santiago de Cuba and Havana. At school, he excelled in debating, and he won a national award in athletics.

At 19, Castro entered the University of Havana to study law. He quickly became involved in politics. In 1947 he took part in an unsuccessful attempt to overthrow Rafael Trujillo, the dictator of the Dominican Republic. The following year, he married Mirta Díaz Balart, a fellow student. Their son, Fidelito, was born in 1949. The marriage ended in divorce about five years later.

Castro became a lawyer in 1950, and he ran for parliament in 1952. But on March 10, before the election, Fulgencio Batista seized power in a military coup. Castro began to organize opposition to Batista. His plan was to storm the Moncada army post, on the outskirts of Santiago, and launch a revolution.

The attack on Moncada—on July 26, 1953—failed. Most of Castro's followers survived but were captured and later killed by Batista's police. Castro was tried and jailed. But his defense speech (later published under the title "History Will Absolve Me") was so eloquent that he became the symbol of the opposition. He was set free in 1955, under a general amnesty, and went to Mexico. There he formed a group called the 26th of July Movement and planned his return to Cuba—as head of an army of liberation.

That "army," made up of about 80 men, landed on Cuba's southeastern coast on December 2, 1956. They met immediate resistance from Batista's forces. The rebels who survived fought hit-and-run battles for almost two years, until they had enough recruits to face Batista's forces in the open.

Fidel Castro, the leader of Cuba and the head of its Communist Party. He is known as a powerful speaker.

When they did, they won. Batista fled Cuba on January 1, 1959.

Castro became prime minister in February. Most Cubans supported him, but many, especially the wealthy, fled. Castro had come to power as a nationalist, but he soon began to move toward Communism. The United States had extensive business interests in Cuba, and Castro opposed this. He nationalized foreign companies and signed a trade agreement with the Soviet Union. In 1961 the United States ended trade and diplomatic relations with Cuba and also backed a group of Cuban exiles in an unsuccessful attempt to overthrow Castro, at the Bay of Pigs.

As head of government and of the Communist Party, Castro transformed Cuba into a socialist state. The government runs industry and agriculture. Health services and education are free, and illiteracy has been almost wiped out. But Cuba depends on Soviet aid, and food and consumer goods are in short supply. The press is censored, and dissent is not allowed. Hundreds of thousands of Cubans have left the island. To his opponents, Castro is a tyrant. But to his supporters, he remains a great revolutionary leader.

Castro's open support of revolution in other countries has made him a figure in world politics. Cuba has trained revolutionaries from countries in Africa and Latin America, and Cuban troops have fought in conflicts in several African countries.

JOHN GERASSI
City University of New York, Queens College

KARATE

It seems impossible that people could punch through bricks with their bare hands. But for masters of karate, that would be easy.

Karate is a spectacular and powerful method of unarmed self-defense. It combines kicking and punching with knowledge of weaknesses in the human body. Karate students can fight back against muggers and bullies with their hands, feet, elbows, knees, fingers, and other parts of the body—even the head. Using karate, it is possible to overcome an attacker with a single blow.

Besides being a means of self-defense, karate is a popular sport. It is also a system of exercise that builds agility, flexibility, and strength.

Karate masters place great importance on controlling their fighting ability. They live by a strict code of morals and do not fight unless attacked.

▶ HISTORY OF KARATE

In ancient times, a method of fighting began to develop on Okinawa. Around 1600, Japanese warriors invaded the island. To maintain control of the Okinawans, the Japanese made it a crime to own any weapon. From that time on, secret training in unarmed fighting increased among Okinawan farmers and their families. The Okinawans were also helped by Chinese visitors who knew many different ways to fight. They taught the Okinawans the points on the body that could be easily hurt—the eyes, the spine, the groin, the joints, and so on. The Okinawans toughened their hands by hitting hard posts and punching sand or gravel.

The Okinawans also invented ways to use their farm tools as weapons. Some karate schools still teach students how to fight with the *kama* (sickle), the *nunchaku* (flail), the *tonfa* (a short stick), the *bo* (a long wooden staff), and the *sai* (a short pitchfork).

These Okinawan fighting arts were taught secretly for over 300 years. Then, about 1920, an Okinawan, Gichin Funakoshi, first taught karate to the Japanese. Funakoshi, who is known as the "father of karate," started to learn the different Okinawan ways of fighting at the age of eleven. He combined those methods into one style before he began teaching in Japan. He also taught the idea that karate students do not attack anyone. They use karate only to defend against wrongdoers.

Today, karate is taught worldwide. Karate was introduced to the United States in the early 1950's, and many people have become highly skilled in this martial (fighting) art.

▶ LEARNING KARATE

A karate student is called a **karate-ka.** The practice gym is called a **dojo.** Most dojos have mats on the floor for barefoot practice and mirrors on the walls so that the students can check their form as they practice their punches and kicks.

A lesson usually begins with stretching exercises. Other exercises, including push-ups and sit-ups, are for strength and stamina.

As students progress, they learn **katas.** These are complex, dancelike patterns of imagined attacks and defenses, often performed with great speed. Like shadowboxing, katas are performed alone and are an excellent way of maintaining overall fitness. A well-performed kata—with its flowing, rhythmic movements—is also an art form, like ballet dancing or gymnastic routines.

Just as boxing does, karate stresses keeping one's balance during movement and coordinating one's breathing with punching.

▶ SPARRING

A beginning student is taught to punch or kick at a certain spot on a partner's body. The partner practices by blocking the attack. This kind of sparring is done carefully and slowly to prevent injuries. More advanced students spar more freely, at almost full speed, but without actually hitting each

---

What Is the Difference Between Karate and Judo?

Karate uses a variety of blocks, kicks, and punches for self-defense. Judo basically depends upon the use of balance and leverage to pull, push, or throw an opponent to the ground. Both words come from the Japanese. Karate means "empty hand," and judo means the "gentle art."

Karate was originally developed in Okinawa, an island hear Japan. Other Asian fighting methods that resemble karate have their own names. Kung fu is Chinese; tae kwon do is Korean.

Left: A black-belt karate-ka demonstrates a high front kick. Right: A black-belt karate-ka tests the power of his blows by breaking a wooden board with his bare hands.

other hard. They learn to pull the punch or kick at the last instant so that their practice partners do not get hurt.

▶ SPORT KARATE

In sport karate, two contestants spar with each other. Sometimes the rules allow only light contact. But sometimes they allow the fighters to spar with full contact. In this case they wear padded gloves and footwear. Points are scored by landing blows.

Karate tournaments may also have kata competitions. Kata competitors are judged on such things as form, correct focus of kicks and punches, power, and proper rhythm and breathing.

▶ BREAKING

The kicks and punches of a trained karate-ka are dangerously powerful. For this reason, students never strike each other bare-handed with full force. Those who wish to test the power of their blows do so by hitting objects. Boards, bricks, rocks, concrete slabs, and roofing tiles are commonly broken by karate-kas to test strength—or just to provide a show.

▶ THE BLACK BELT

Beginning students wear white belts in the dojo. The instructor keeps track of the students' progress by the color of their belts. A new belt is awarded after every test and promotion. The white belt is usually followed by a yellow belt, then a green belt, then a brown belt. It might be necessary to pass five tests to earn a green belt, then perhaps nine tests to earn the brown belt.

After passing the tenth test, students would be allowed to wear a black belt, the symbol of mastery of the basic skills and ideals of karate. To earn a black belt, students must be able to perform a number of katas well and to spar confidently with a number of trained attackers. They must also have developed the ability to control themselves and their fighting techniques. After earning a black belt, a student may become an instructor and teach other students.

Earning a first-degree black belt usually takes two to four years of hard practice. There are ten degrees of black belts. Second- and third-degree belts are awarded to conscientious karate-kas who have been dedicated in their training and teaching. Higher rankings are given to honor advanced martial artists who demonstrate exceptional dignity and dedication to the art of karate.

JOHN H. STEWART
Media consultant, martial arts subjects

333

OTTAWA

Ottawa was born an army brat, grew up as a lumberjack, and matured as a politician. The business of modern Ottawa, the capital of Canada, is government. But lumber, not politics, ruled the city until the late 1800's. And it was the British Army that founded the town, in 1826.

Location, rivers, and resources were basic to the start of the early town and to its growth. Today natural beauty is a more important feature of the site. It provides a magnificent setting for the national capital. Ottawa is in Ontario, on the south bank of the Ottawa River, where it narrows and tumbles over the massive Chaudière Falls. Below the falls, the river is joined by two smaller streams—the Rideau River, on the south (Ontario) side, and the Gatineau River, on the north (Quebec) side. The Ottawa then sweeps eastward for nearly 160 kilometers (100 miles) to join the St. Lawrence River near Montreal.

Until about 1800, the Ottawa River—or Grand River, as it was called—was the chief canoe route to the interior of North America. Since that time, it has carried untold numbers of logs to market from the vast forests of its valley. Later, its waterpower was used to run sawmills that cut the timber. And in the 1900's, it was dammed in many places to generate hydroelectric power.

▶ OTTAWA AND THE RIDEAU CANAL

The first settlement in the Ottawa River valley was Wright's Town, now Hull. It was begun in 1800 on the north shore of the river. But activity shifted in 1826 to a point on the south shore opposite Wright's Town. This site was chosen as the place to begin the Rideau Canal, which would link the river to Lake Ontario. Two men were responsible for the choice—Lord Dalhousie, the British governor of Upper and Lower Canada, and Lieutenant Colonel John By, of the Royal Engineers.

John By stayed on until 1832. He established a military garrison, and he designed and organized a town. At first the town had no name. Then it was called Bytown, after By. Finally, in 1855, it was named Ottawa. John By also supervised the design, construction, and operation of the canal. The canal, cut through an almost unpeopled wilderness, took some six years to build. Hundreds of workers, mostly Irish immigrants, were stricken with "swamp fever" in the Rideau marshes or lost their lives in accidents. The canal was intended to ferry troops and supplies from Montreal to Kingston, on Lake Ontario, in case of war with the United States. It also became a trade route.

The canal still slices through modern Ottawa. But its old military and commercial

The Rideau Canal was built in the early 1800's. Today, bordered by parks, it slices through modern Ottawa.

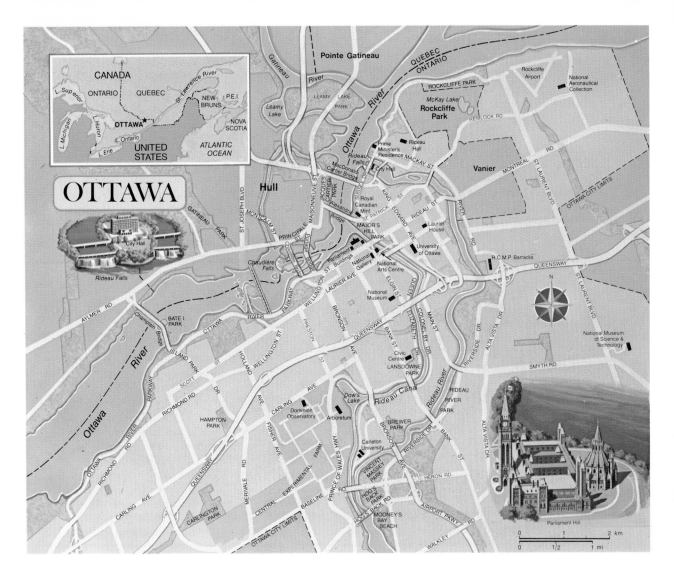

OTTAWA

Parliament Hill

roles have given way to recreation. The canal is flanked by scenic drives and parks, rather than by docks and railways. Each spring, during the city's Tulip Festival, millions of flower bulbs bloom along its banks. In summer, the canal is filled with pleasure boats. And in winter, it becomes a skating rink. Lansdowne Park, at the canal's edge, is the site of the Civic Centre, where professional sports are played. The Central Canadian Exhibition of agriculture and industry is held in this park each summer.

John By's home was at the entrance to the canal. This area is now Major's Hill Park, the site of open-air concerts in summer. The stone storehouse he built beside the headlocks of the canal is the oldest building in the city. It houses Bytown Museum. Rideau Hall, now the residence of the governor-general of Canada, began as the home of a contractor made wealthy by the canal. And Barracks Hill, where By housed his garrison, is now Parliament Hill.

▶ UPPER TOWN AND LOWER TOWN

John By set the social character of his town by organizing it in two parts. Upper Town, west of the canal, was reserved mainly for the gentility, who were mostly British Protestants. Lower Town, east of the Canal, was the commercial district. The homes of the tradespeople and the lumber workers (mainly Roman Catholic French Canadians and Irish) were also there.

Parts of the two sections remain, especially in Lower Town. The Mile of History, on Sussex Street, is a strip of restored 19th-century commercial buildings. Nearby is the Byward Market, an open-air farmers' and artisans' market that has been operating in much the same place for 150 years. Artisans' cottages dating from the 1800's can be found on the back streets. And Lower Town's Roman Catholic roots can be seen in such institutions as the Basilica of Notre Dame, with its beautiful wood carvings.

The two-part nature of the original town is reflected in other ways. More than 300,000 people live in Ottawa. About half the people are Roman Catholic, and about a third speak French or French and English. The educational system is divided into French and English and Catholic and non-denominational schools. The University of Ottawa is bilingual and has a Roman Catholic heritage. Carleton University, founded after World War II, serves a mainly English-speaking community. Newspapers, radio, and television are available in English and in French. Signs are in both languages, and the business of government is carried on in both.

▶ LUMBERTOWN OTTAWA

By about 1840, timber had replaced the canal as a focus for Bytown. Heavy winter snows were ideal for skidding logs through the woods to the rivers. In the spring, the logs were formed into rafts and floated downstream to market on the flooding waters. By the 1850's, a lumber industry had also developed. The valley supplied the trees, and the river the power to saw the logs into lumber. Large mills sprang up at Rideau Falls and Chaudière Falls. By 1860, Ottawa was the center of the largest lumber industry in North America. Fortunes were made and lost by the lumber barons of the valley.

Much evidence of the lumber era remains —including a layer of sawdust more than 6 meters (20 feet) deep at the bottom of the Ottawa River. At Chaudière Falls (now dammed to produce hydroelectric power), the old mills of the 1800's are being restored. The lands from which timber was cut have been reforested, and many areas have become parks. One of these is Gatineau Park, a 20-minute drive north of the city. Most of this park has been developed by the federal government's National Capital Commission as a year-round recreational and conservation area.

The timber heritage is also preserved in summertime raft festivals, and log drives can still be seen on the Gatineau and Ottawa rivers. But the great homes of the lumber barons are perhaps their greatest legacy to the city. One of these homes, Earnscliffe, became the residence of John A. Macdonald, Canada's first prime minister. It is now the home of the British ambassador. Another is the mansion at 24 Sussex Drive, the official residence of Canadian prime ministers since the 1950's.

▶ OTTAWA AS CAPITAL

Ottawa's role as capital resulted from rivalry among the cities of the Province of Canada. The Province of Canada was formed in 1841 by the union of Upper Canada and Lower Canada. But no one could agree on a site for a capital. For 20 years, the role of capital passed, in turn, among Kingston, Montreal, Toronto, and Quebec City. To end the argument, Queen Victoria was asked to pick a permanent site. In 1857 she chose Ottawa, the most central city.

The arrival of government had important effects on the city. It brought new people and new business opportunities. It also brought a new sophistication to the brawling lumber town. Government's impact was perhaps greatest on Upper Town, which benefited most from nearby Parliament Hill. Since the 1860's, this area has become the major shopping and office area of the city.

The buildings of Parliament Hill were finished in 1866, in time for only one legislative session of the province. In 1867, Ottawa was made capital of the independent Dominion of Canada.

The Parliament Buildings—center block, east and west blocks, and library—are now the centerpiece of a network of dozens of government buildings. The center block burned down in 1916 and was rebuilt in a somewhat altered form. It is home to the House of Commons and the Senate. The center block faces a large parade ground that is the site of many colorful ceremonies—including, in summer, the changing of the

The Parliament Buildings look out over the city and the Ottawa River from Parliament Hill.

guard. Its tall central tower, the Peace Tower, is a memorial to Canada's war dead. The 53-bell carillon in the tower often rings out over the city.

Many of the nation's treasures are gathered in Ottawa under the safekeeping of federal cultural agencies. There is a network of national museums with collections covering military history, technology and science, anthropology, natural history, and air transportation. The National Gallery has collections of Canadian art and art from other countries. Also in Ottawa are the National Library, the Canada Archives, and the Royal Canadian Mint. The National Arts Centre is home to a national orchestra and French- and English-language theater companies.

Especially since 1900, the national government has created many parks, memorials, and similar projects in the city. One of the largest open areas is not a park but a working farm—the Central Experimental Farm—complete with beef and dairy herds. Many parts of the farm, including an arboretum, are open to the public.

The government has a major influence on Ottawa's economy. It owns about one third of the land in the city, and it employs about 30 percent of the workers. Next in size to government, and related to it, is the tourist and convention industry. In recent times the electronics industry has grown rapidly.

Ottawa is the heart of the national capital region, which includes Hull and nearby towns on both sides of the Ottawa River. It has a population of about 800,000. The growth of government and the government's decisions about the location of buildings have made great changes in the region. Much activity has shifted out of Ottawa's center. Suburbs have grown.

This trend led the province of Ontario to create a regional government for Ottawa and its suburbs. (Quebec has set up a similar government for the Hull area.) City government is headquartered in Ottawa's modern City Hall, which stands on an island at the mouth of the Rideau River. Local activities, such as road building and social services, are divided between the city and regional governments. And the city and regional governments confer with the National Capital Commission in planning the future of the capital region.

JOHN H. TAYLOR
Carleton University

337

The Beatles in 1966. Clockwise from left: John, Paul, George, and Ringo.

BEATLES, THE

During most of the 1960's, the Western world seemed to move to the beat of four young rock musicians from the city of Liverpool, in England. They called themselves the Beatles.

John Lennon (1940–80), a guitarist and singer, was the original leader of the group. He explained the name Beatles in this way: "When you said it, it was crawly things [beetles]; when you read it, it was beat music." The other members were Paul McCartney (1942–) and George Harrison (1943–), also guitarists and singers, and the drummer and singer Ringo Starr (1940–), whose real name was Richard Starkey.

Each Beatle brought different strengths to the group. John had a strong personality and a sharp wit. Paul was a showman, who charmed audiences with his melodic voice. George was known as a gifted and serious musician. Ringo was adored for his "goofy," down-to-earth personality.

Brian Epstein, a young record dealer, became their manager. He was a major force in their success. With great difficulty, he found a record company willing to sign the Beatles. Their first single recording, "Love Me Do" (1962), quickly became popular. Their second record, "Please Please Me" (1963), was a big hit. Teenagers—in a frenzy known as "Beatlemania"—struggled to get close to their new heroes.

The Beatles appeared in New York for the first time in 1964. Their engaging personalities and energetic sound turned Britain's most popular rock group into an overnight success in the United States. Within weeks, the top five best-selling records there were all by the Beatles.

Before long, adults found it hard to ignore the Beatles' wide-ranging talents. John Lennon's first book, *In His Own Write,* and the group's first movie, *A Hard Day's Night,* won enthusiastic reviews. Beatles tunes like "Yesterday" were recorded by hundreds of other artists in many musical styles. In 1965, Queen Elizabeth II honored the Beatles by making them members of the Order of the British Empire.

As time went on, the words of their songs, written mainly by Lennon and McCartney, became more poetic. The subjects ranged from the haunting loneliness of "Eleanor Rigby" to the fantasy of "Yellow Submarine" (which became the theme song for the full-length cartoon of the same name). Their music changed, too. The Beatles began experimenting with electronic effects and instruments from around the world. And they invited jazz and classical musicians to perform on their recordings.

The Beatles made their last stage appearance in 1966. They produced their masterpiece, the album *Sergeant Pepper's Lonely Hearts Club Band,* in 1967, the year of their manager's death. Later that year, the four wrote and directed a film, *Magical Mystery Tour,* in which they toured the English countryside by bus in search of wonder, magic, and fun.

But the members gradually became involved in separate interests and individual careers, and the group disbanded in 1970. All four continued to enjoy some success as solo artists during the 1970's. Many fans hoped for a reunion. But in 1980, John Lennon was assassinated in New York City. The "magical mystery tour" was truly over.

NICHOLAS SCHAFFNER
Author, *The Boys from Liverpool*

MINT

A mint is a place where coins are made. Today mints are nearly always under government authority and supervision.

Coins were made in the ancient kingdom of Lydia, in Asia Minor, in the 8th century B.C. From there the art of coining spread throughout the Mediterranean world and into Persia and India. Somewhat later, coining began independently in China. It spread from there to Japan and Korea.

The foundations of modern minting, or coin making, were laid by the Romans. They minted silver coins in the Temple of Juno Moneta as far back as 269 B.C. In Latin, *moneta* came to mean mint or coin. The English words "money" and "mint" developed from this Latin word.

Gold and silver coins existed in Britain before Roman rule. During the Middle Ages, the chief mint in Britain was located in the Tower of London. The British Royal Mint was founded in 1810.

The first coins minted in Britain's North American colonies were made by John Hull in Massachusetts Bay Colony. In 1652, the Boston mint began to make coins that showed a pine tree. Pine-tree shillings and similar six-penny and three-penny coins were widely circulated in New England.

▶ THE UNITED STATES MINT

The states were permitted to coin money immediately after the Revolutionary War, but they do not have that right today. Under the Constitution, only Congress has the right to coin money and to regulate its value.

The first United States mint was established at Philadelphia, Pennsylvania, in 1792. At first the secretary of state supervised the mint. In 1799 it became an independent agency, under the president. Then, in 1873, Congress created the Bureau of the Mint, as part of the Department of the Treasury at Washington, D.C. The director of the mint is appointed by the president.

The bureau mints 1-cent, 5-cent, 10-cent, 25-cent, 50-cent, and 1-dollar coins. It also makes the dies (engraving stamps) and tools used in minting. The bureau mints coins for some foreign countries and sells coin sets and commemorative medals to the public.

An inspector at the Royal Canadian Mint checks blanks that will be stamped to make pennies.

The Bureau of the Mint is in charge of the mint at Philadelphia and another mint at Denver, Colorado. Coins made at Denver bear a mintmark—the letter D. The bureau also keeps the government's holdings in silver and gold bullion (bars). Gold is kept at Fort Knox, Kentucky, and silver is kept at West Point, New York. There are assay offices, which judge the value of ores and bullion, at New York City and at San Francisco, California. Also at San Francisco is the Mint Museum.

The nation's paper money is designed and printed by the Bureau of Engraving and Printing. This bureau is also a part of the Department of the Treasury.

▶ THE ROYAL CANADIAN MINT

Canada's mint began operation in 1908, as a branch of the British Royal Mint. It was called the Ottawa Mint until 1931, when it became the Royal Canadian Mint. It is headed by a seven-member board of directors, who report to Parliament. Coins for general circulation are produced at a plant in Winnipeg, Manitoba. The mint also buys and sells precious metals and produces medals, plaques, and the like.

STELLA HACKEL SIMS
Former Director, United States Mint

ORGANIZATION OF PETROLEUM EXPORTING COUNTRIES (OPEC)

The Organization of Petroleum Exporting Countries (OPEC) is made up of 13 countries that produce petroleum (oil). The members control about 75 percent of the world's known reserves. Usually they meet twice a year to set the prices that buyers must pay for oil produced in their countries.

▶ HISTORY OF OPEC

OPEC was founded in 1960. Venezuela and the Middle Eastern countries of Iran, Iraq, Kuwait, and Saudi Arabia were the first members. Qatar, Indonesia, Libya, Algeria, Ecuador, Gabon, Nigeria, and the United Arab Emirates joined the group later in the 1960's. Many of these countries had few resources other than petroleum. They hoped that by banding together, they could begin to control the price they were paid for their oil. Up to this time, large international oil companies, operating in these countries, produced the oil and set prices.

When world oil supplies were plentiful, OPEC had little influence in setting prices. But a world oil shortage began to develop by the late 1960's. The shortage gave the OPEC nations a chance to begin negotiations with the big oil companies for an increase in price. As a result, the average price of OPEC oil was increased from $1.80 a barrel in 1970 to $3.01 in 1973. By this time, the OPEC members had set up national oil companies and had begun to take part in running the oil industries in their countries.

In 1973, the Arab nations of the Middle East fought a war with Israel. OPEC immediately raised the price of oil, without negotiating with the international oil companies. The Arab members also began to withhold oil from the United States and other nations friendly to Israel. A world oil crisis developed. OPEC took advantage of this situation and increased the price of its oil nearly fourfold in 1974. The control of oil pricing by the international oil companies was destroyed. Since then, OPEC has set world oil prices.

From 1974 until early 1979, increases in oil prices were small. But by the end of 1980, the minimum price per barrel reached $32. Prices did not rise in 1981 because there was an oil surplus. But the OPEC nations could create a shortage at any time if they agreed to sell smaller amounts of oil.

▶ THE EFFECT OF RISING OIL PRICES

The increase in the price of petroleum brought great wealth to many OPEC nations. They spent large sums to develop industry and provide social services for their people. A small amount of the OPEC wealth was used to aid poor countries. A much larger share was invested in various ways in the industrialized nations. The OPEC nations hoped these investments would provide income when their oil resources were used up.

Many poorer nations in Africa and Asia have little or no oil reserves. The rising cost of petroleum caused great hardship for them. It reduced the amount they could spend to import food, fertilizer, and manufactured goods. And it took money away from projects that would have benefited their people.

Growth in the industrialized nations was long based on low-cost energy. Energy in the future will be expensive. And geologists predict that most of the world's oil will be used up within 50 years.

The actions of OPEC have done more than bring its members higher prices for their most valuable resource. The increased cost of petroleum has changed the world economy. It has made people aware of the need to conserve the oil they have and to search for new sources of energy.

E. WILLARD MILLER
Pennsylvania State University

WORLD PETROLEUM PRODUCTION*

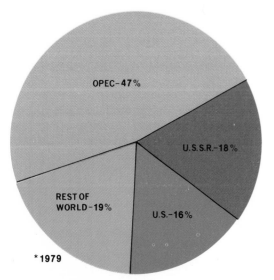

OPEC—47%

U.S.S.R.—18%

REST OF WORLD—19%

U.S.—16%

*1979

INTERNATIONAL STATISTICAL SUPPLEMENT

Independent Nations of the World

The United States

    Senate

    House of Representatives

    Cabinet

    Supreme Court

    State Governors

The 1980 United States Census

Canada and Its Provinces and Territories

INDEPENDENT NATIONS OF THE WORLD

NATION	CAPITAL	AREA (in sq mi)	POPULATION (estimate)	GOVERNMENT
Afghanistan	Kabul	250,000	15,500,000	Babrak Karmal—president
Albania	Tirana	11,100	2,700,000	Enver Hoxha—communist party secretary
Algeria	Algiers	919,593	19,000,000	Benjedid Chadli—president
Angola	Luanda	481,351	7,100,000	José Eduardo dos Santos—president
Antigua and Barbuda	St. John's	171	75,000	Vere Bird—prime minister
Argentina	Buenos Aires	1,068,297	27,900,000	Leopoldo Galtieri—president
Australia	Canberra	2,967,895	14,700,000	Malcolm Fraser—prime minister
Austria	Vienna	32,374	7,500,000	Rudolf Kirschschläger—president Bruno Kreisky—chancellor
Bahamas	Nassau	5,380	230,000	Lynden O. Pindling—prime minister
Bahrain	Manama	240	360,000	Isa ibn Sulman al-Khalifa—head of government
Bangladesh	Dacca	55,598	88,700,000	Abdus Sattar—president
Barbados	Bridgetown	168	250,000	J. M. G. Adams—prime minister
Belgium	Brussels	11,781	9,900,000	Baudouin I—king Wilfried Martens—premier
Belize	Belmopan	8,867	145,000	George Price—prime minister
Benin (Dahomey)	Porto-Novo	43,483	3,600,000	Ahmed Kerekou—president
Bhutan	Thimbu	18,147	1,300,000	Jigme Singye Wanchuk—king
Bolivia	La Paz Sucre	424,163	5,600,000	Celso Torrelio Villa—president
Botswana	Gaborone	231,804	820,000	Quett Masire—president
Brazil	Brasília	3,286,478	123,000,000	João Figueiredo—president
Bulgaria	Sofia	42,823	8,900,000	Todor Zhivkov—communist party secretary Grisha Filipov—premier
Burma	Rangoon	261,217	35,000,000	U San Yu—president U Maung Maung Kha—prime minister
Burundi	Bujumbura	10,747	4,300,000	Jean-Baptiste Bagaza—president
Cambodia (Kampuchea)	Pnompenh	69,898	5,000,000	Heng Samrin—communist party secretary
Cameroon	Yaoundé	183,569	8,500,000	Ahmadou Ahidjo—president
Canada	Ottawa	3,851,809	24,000,000	Pierre Elliott Trudeau—prime minister
Cape Verde	Praia	1,557	320,000	Aristides Pereira—president

NATION	CAPITAL	AREA (in sq mi)	POPULATION (estimate)	GOVERNMENT
Central African Republic	Bangui	240,535	2,400,000	André Kolingba—head of state
Chad	N'Djemena	495,754	4,500,000	Goukouni Oueddei—president
Chile	Santiago	292,257	11,200,000	Augusto Pinochet Ugarte—president
China	Peking	3,705,390	975,000,000	Hu Yaobang—communist party chairman Zhao Ziyang—premier
Colombia	Bogotá	439,736	27,500,000	Julio César Turbay Ayala—president
Comoros	Moroni	838	400,000	Ahmed Abdallah—president
Congo	Brazzaville	132,047	1,500,000	Denis Sassou-Nguessou—president
Costa Rica	San José	19,575	2,200,000	Rodrigo Carazo Odio—president
Cuba	Havana	44,218	9,800,000	Fidel Castro—president
Cyprus	Nicosia	3,572	630,000	Spyros Kyprianou—president
Czechoslovakia	Prague	49,370	15,300,000	Gustáv Husák—communist party secretary and president Lubomir Ŝtrougal—premier
Denmark	Copenhagen	16,629	5,100,000	Margrethe II—queen Anker Jorgensen—premier
Djibouti	Djibouti	8,494	120,000	Hassan Gouled—president
Dominica	Roseau	290	81,000	Mary Eugenia Charles—prime minister
Dominican Republic	Santo Domingo	18,816	5,400,000	Antonio Guzmán—president
Ecuador	Quito	109,483	8,400,000	Osvaldo Hurtado Larrea—president
Egypt	Cairo	386,660	42,000,000	Muhammad Hosni Mubarak—president
El Salvador	San Salvador	8,124	4,800,000	José Napoleón Duarte—president
Equatorial Guinea	Malabo	10,831	360,000	Teodoro Obiang Nguema—president
Ethiopia	Addis Ababa	471,777	31,100,000	Mengistu Haile Mariam—head of state
Fiji	Suva	7,055	630,000	Ratu Sir Kamisese Mara—prime minister
Finland	Helsinki	130,120	4,800,000	Mauno Koivisto—acting president
France	Paris	211,207	53,800,000	François Mitterrand—president Pierre Mauroy—premier
Gabon	Libreville	103,346	550,000	Albert B. Bongo—president
Gambia	Banjul	4,361	600,000	Sir Dauda K. Jawara—president
Germany (East)	East Berlin	41,768	16,800,000	Erich Honecker—communist party secretary Willi Stoph—premier
Germany (West)	Bonn	95,976	61,600,000	Karl Carstens—president Helmut Schmidt—chancellor
Ghana	Accra	92,099	11,500,000	Hilla Limann—president
Greece	Athens	50,944	9,600,000	Constantine Caramanlis—president Andreas Papandreou—premier
Grenada	St. George's	133	110,000	Maurice Bishop—prime minister

NATION	CAPITAL	AREA (in sq mi)	POPULATION (estimate)	GOVERNMENT
Guatemala	Guatemala City	42,042	7,300,000	Romeo Lucas García—president
Guinea	Conakry	94,926	5,000,000	Sékou Touré—president
Guinea-Bissau	Bissau	13,948	780,000	Joâo Bernardo Vieira—head of government
Guyana	Georgetown	83,000	880,000	Forbes Burnham—president
Haiti	Port-au-Prince	10,714	5,000,000	Jean-Claude Duvalier—president
Honduras	Tegucigalpa	43,277	3,700,000	Roberto Suazo Córdova—president-elect
Hungary	Budapest	35,919	10,700,000	János Kádár—communist party secretary György Lazar—premier
Iceland	Reykjavik	39,768	230,000	Vigdis Finnbogadottir—president Gunnar Thoroddsen—prime minister
India	New Delhi	1,269,340	684,000,000	Neelam Sanjiva Reddy—president Indira Gandhi—prime minister
Indonesia	Jakarta	735,269	147,000,000	Suharto—president
Iran	Teheran	636,294	37,400,000	Ruhollah Khomeini—religious leader Hojatolislam Ali Khamenei—president Mir Hussein Moussavi—premier
Iraq	Baghdad	167,925	13,100,000	Saddam Hussein—president
Ireland	Dublin	27,136	3,400,000	Patrick Hillery—president Garret FitzGerald—prime minister
Israel	Jerusalem	8,019	3,900,000	Yitzhak Navon—president Menahem Begin—prime minister
Italy	Rome	116,303	57,100,000	Alessandro Pertini—president Giovanni Spadolini—premier
Ivory Coast	Abidjan	124,503	8,000,000	Félix Houphouët-Boigny—president
Jamaica	Kingston	4,244	2,200,000	Edward P. G. Seaga—prime minister
Japan	Tokyo	143,737	117,000,000	Hirohito—emperor Zenko Suzuki—premier
Jordan	Amman	37,738	3,000,000	Hussein I—king Mudar Badran—premier
Kenya	Nairobi	224,959	16,400,000	Daniel Arap Moi—president
Kiribati	Tarawa	264	58,000	Ieremia Tabai—president
Korea (North)	Pyongyang	46,540	17,900,000	Kim Il Sung—president Li Jong-ok—premier
Korea (South)	Seoul	38,025	37,600,000	Chun Doo Hwan—president Nam Duck Woo—premier
Kuwait	Kuwait	6,880	1,400,000	Jaber al-Ahmed al-Sabah—head of state
Laos	Vientiane	91,429	3,700,000	Souphanouvong—president Kaysone Phomvihan—premier
Lebanon	Beirut	4,015	3,200,000	Elias Sarkis—president Shafiq al-Wazan—premier

NATION	CAPITAL	AREA (in sq mi)	POPULATION (estimate)	GOVERNMENT
Lesotho	Maseru	11,720	1,300,000	Moshoeshoe II—king Leabua Jonathan—prime minister
Liberia	Monrovia	43,000	1,900,000	Samuel K. Doe—president
Libya	Tripoli	679,360	3,000,000	Muammar el-Qaddafi—head of state
Liechtenstein	Vaduz	61	26,000	Francis Joseph II—prince
Luxembourg	Luxembourg	999	360,000	Jean—grand duke Pierre Werner—premier
Madagascar	Antananarivo	226,657	8,700,000	Didier Ratsiraka—president
Malawi	Lilongwe	45,747	6,000,000	H. Kamuzu Banda—president
Malaysia	Kuala Lumpur	127,316	13,400,000	Sultan Ahmad Shah—paramount ruler Mahathir ibn Mohammed—prime minister
Maldives	Male	115	150,000	Maumoon Abdul Gayoom—president
Mali	Bamako	478,765	6,900,000	Moussa Traoré—president
Malta	Valletta	122	370,000	Sir Anthony Mamo—president Dom Mintoff—prime minister
Mauritania	Nouakchott	397,954	1,600,000	Mohammed Khouna Ould Haidalla—president
Mauritius	Port Louis	790	960,000	Sir Seewoosagur Ramgoolam—prime minister
Mexico	Mexico City	761,602	67,400,000	José López Portillo—president
Monaco	Monaco-Ville	0.6	26,000	Rainier III—prince
Mongolia	Ulan Bator	604,248	1,600,000	Yumzhagiyn Tsedenbal—communist party secretary
Morocco	Rabat	172,413	20,200,000	Hassan II—king Maati Bouabid—premier
Mozambique	Maputo	309,494	12,100,000	Samora Machel—president
Nauru	—	8	8,000	Hammer DeRoburt—president
Nepal	Katmandu	54,362	14,000,000	Birendra Bir Bikram Shah Deva—king Kirtinidhi Bista—prime minister
Netherlands	Amsterdam	15,770	14,200,000	Beatrix—queen Andreas A. M. van Agt—premier
New Zealand	Wellington	103,736	3,200,000	Robert D. Muldoon—prime minister
Nicaragua	Managua	50,193	2,700,000	Sergio Ramírez Mercado—head of junta
Niger	Niamey	489,190	5,300,000	Seyni Kountche—head of government
Nigeria	Lagos	356,668	77,000,000	Shehu Shagari—president
Norway	Oslo	125,181	4,100,000	Olav V—king Kaare Willoch—prime minister
Oman	Muscat	82,030	890,000	Qabus ibn Said—sultan
Pakistan	Islamabad	310,403	82,000,000	Mohammed Zia ul-Haq—president

NATION	CAPITAL	AREA (in sq mi)	POPULATION (estimate)	GOVERNMENT
Panama	Panama City	29,761	1,900,000	Aristides Royo—president
Papua New Guinea	Port Moresby	178,260	3,100,000	Julius Chan—prime minister
Paraguay	Asunción	157,047	3,100,000	Alfredo Stroessner—president
Peru	Lima	496,223	17,800,000	Fernando Belaúnde Terry—president
Philippines	Manila	115,830	48,400,000	Ferdinand E. Marcos—president Cesar Virta—premier
Poland	Warsaw	120,724	35,800,000	Wojciech Jaruzelski—communist party secretary and premier
Portugal	Lisbon	35,553	9,900,000	António Ramalho Eanes—president Francisco Pinto Balsemão—premier
Qatar	Doha	4,247	220,000	Khalifa ibn Hamad al-Thani—head of government
Rumania	Bucharest	91,700	22,200,000	Nicolae Ceaușescu—communist party secretary Ilie Verdet—premier
Rwanda	Kigali	10,169	5,000,000	Juvénal Habyalimana—president
St. Lucia	Castries	238	120,000	Winston Cenac—prime minister
St. Vincent and the Grenadines	Kingstown	150	120,000	Milton Cato—prime minister
São Tomé and Príncipe	São Tomé	372	85,000	Manuel Pinto da Costa—president
Saudi Arabia	Riyadh	829,997	8,400,000	Khalid ibn Abdul-Aziz—king
Senegal	Dakar	75,750	5,700,000	Abdou Diouf—president
Seychelles	Victoria	107	65,000	France Albert René—president
Sierra Leone	Freetown	27,700	3,500,000	Siaka P. Stevens—president
Singapore	Singapore	224	2,400,000	C. V. Devan Nair—president Lee Kuan Yew—prime minister
Solomon Islands	Honiara	10,983	220,000	Peter Kenilorea—prime minister
Somalia	Mogadishu	246,200	3,600,000	Mohammed Siad Barre—head of government
South Africa	Pretoria Cape Town Bloemfontein	471,444	29,300,000	Marais Viljoen—president Pieter W. Botha—prime minister
Spain	Madrid	194,897	37,500,000	Juan Carlos I—king Leopoldo Calvo Sotelo—premier
Sri Lanka (Ceylon)	Colombo	25,332	14,700,000	Junius R. Jayewardene—president Ranasinghe Premadasa—prime minister
Sudan	Khartoum	967,497	18,700,000	Gaafar al-Numeiry—president
Surinam	Paramaribo	63,037	380,000	Henk Chin a-Sen—president
Swaziland	Mbabane	6,704	550,000	Sobhuza II—king
Sweden	Stockholm	173,731	8,300,000	Carl XVI Gustaf—king Thorbjörn Fälldin—prime minister

NATION	CAPITAL	AREA (in sq mi)	POPULATION (estimate)	GOVERNMENT
Switzerland	Bern	15,941	6,300,000	Fritz Honegger—president
Syria	Damascus	71,498	9,000,000	Hafez al-Assad—president Abdel Raouf al-Kassem—premier
Taiwan	Taipei	13,885	17,500,000	Chiang Ching-kuo—president Sun Yun-suan—premier
Tanzania	Dar es Salaam	364,898	18,000,000	Julius K. Nyerere—president
Thailand	Bangkok	198,456	46,500,000	Bhumibol Adulyadej—king Prem Tinsulanonda—premier
Togo	Lomé	21,622	2,500,000	Gnassingbe Eyadema—president
Tonga	Nuku'alofa	270	97,000	Taufa'ahau Tupou IV—king Prince Tu'ipelehake—prime minister
Trinidad & Tobago	Port of Spain	1,980	1,200,000	Sir Ellis Clarke—president George Chambers—prime minister
Tunisia	Tunis	63,170	6,400,000	Habib Bourguiba—president
Turkey	Ankara	301,381	45,200,000	Kenan Evren—head of state Bulent Ulusu—prime minister
Tuvalu	Funafuti	10	8,000	Toalipi Lauti—prime minister
Uganda	Kampala	91,134	13,200,000	Milton Obote—president
U.S.S.R.	Moscow	8,649,512	265,500,000	Leonid I. Brezhnev—communist party secretary and president Nikolai A. Tikhonov—premier
United Arab Emirates	Abu Dhabi	32,278	1,000,000	Zayd ibn Sultan—president
United Kingdom	London	94,226	55,900,000	Elizabeth II—queen Margaret Thatcher—prime minister
United States	Washington, D.C.	3,618,467	229,000,000	Ronald W. Reagan—president George H. Bush—vice-president
Upper Volta	Ouagadougou	105,869	6,900,000	Saye Zerbo—head of government
Uruguay	Montevideo	68,037	2,900,000	Gregorio Alvarez—president
Vanuatu	Vila	5,700	110,000	Walter Lini—prime minister
Venezuela	Caracas	352,143	13,900,000	Luis Herrera Campíns—president
Vietnam	Hanoi	127,202	52,700,000	Le Duan—communist party secretary Pham Van Dong—premier
Western Samoa	Apia	1,097	156,000	Malietoa Tanumafili II—head of state
Yemen (Aden)	Madinat al-Shaab	128,559	2,000,000	Ali Nasser Mohammed—president
Yemen (Sana)	Sana	75,290	5,900,000	Ali Abdullah Saleh—president
Yugoslavia	Belgrade	98,766	22,500,000	Sergej Kraigher—president Veselin Djuranovic—premier
Zaïre	Kinshasa	905,565	28,300,000	Mobutu Sese Seko—president
Zambia	Lusaka	290,585	5,700,000	Kenneth D. Kaunda—president
Zimbabwe	Salisbury	150,333	7,400,000	Canaan Banana—president Robert Mugabe—prime minister

THE CONGRESS OF THE UNITED STATES

UNITED STATES SENATE

(53 Republicans, 46 Democrats, 1 Independent)

Alabama
Howell T. Heflin (D)
Jeremiah Denton (R)

Alaska
Ted Stevens (R)
Frank H. Murkowski (R)

Arizona
Barry Goldwater (R)
Dennis DeConcini (D)

Arkansas
Dale Bumpers (D)
David H. Pryor (D)

California
Alan Cranston (D)
S. I. Hayakawa (R)

Colorado
Gary W. Hart (D)
William L. Armstrong (R)

Connecticut
Lowell P. Weicker, Jr. (R)
Christopher J. Dodd (D)

Delaware
William V. Roth, Jr. (R)
Joseph R. Biden, Jr. (D)

Florida
Lawton Chiles (D)
Paula Hawkins (R)

Georgia
Sam Nunn (D)
Mack Mattingly (R)

Hawaii
Daniel K. Inouye (D)
Spark M. Matsunaga (D)

Idaho
James A. McClure (R)
Steven D. Symms (R)

Illinois
Charles H. Percy (R)
Alan J. Dixon (D)

Indiana
Richard G. Lugar (R)
Dan Quayle (R)

Iowa
Roger W. Jepsen (R)
Charles E. Grassley (R)

Kansas
Robert J. Dole (R)
Nancy Landon Kassebaum (R)

Kentucky
Walter Huddleston (D)
Wendell H. Ford (D)

Louisiana
Russell B. Long (D)
J. Bennett Johnston (D)

Maine
William S. Cohen (R)
George J. Mitchell (D)

Maryland
Charles M. Mathias, Jr. (R)
Paul S. Sarbanes (D)

Massachusetts
Edward M. Kennedy (D)
Paul E. Tsongas (D)

Michigan
Donald W. Riegle, Jr. (D)
Carl Levin (D)

Minnesota
David F. Durenberger (R)
Rudy Boschwitz (R)

Mississippi
John C. Stennis (D)
Thad Cochran (R)

Missouri
Thomas F. Eagleton (D)
John C. Danforth (R)

Montana
John Melcher (D)
Max Baucus (D)

Nebraska
Edward Zorinsky (D)
J. James Exon (D)

Nevada
Howard W. Cannon (D)
Paul Laxalt (R)

New Hampshire
Gordon J. Humphrey (R)
Warren Rudman (R)

New Jersey
Harrison A. Williams, Jr. (D)
Bill Bradley (D)

New Mexico
Pete V. Domenici (R)
Harrison H. Schmitt (R)

New York
Daniel P. Moynihan (D)
Alfonse M. D'Amato (R)

North Carolina
Jesse Helms (R)
John P. East (R)

North Dakota
Quentin N. Burdick (D)
Mark Andrews (R)

Ohio
John H. Glenn, Jr. (D)
Howard M. Metzenbaum (D)

Oklahoma
David L. Boren (D)
Don Nickles (R)

Oregon
Mark O. Hatfield (R)
Bob Packwood (R)

Pennsylvania
H. John Heinz III (R)
Arlen Specter (R)

Rhode Island
Claiborne Pell (D)
John H. Chafee (R)

South Carolina
Strom Thurmond (R)
Ernest F. Hollings (D)

South Dakota
Larry Pressler (R)
James Abdnor (R)

Tennessee
Howard H. Baker, Jr. (R)
James R. Sasser (D)

Texas
John G. Tower (R)
Lloyd M. Bentsen (D)

Utah
E. J. (Jake) Garn (R)
Orrin G. Hatch (R)

Vermont
Robert T. Stafford (R)
Patrick J. Leahy (D)

Virginia
Harry F. Byrd, Jr. (I)
John W. Warner (R)

Washington
Henry M. Jackson (D)
Slade Gorton (R)

West Virginia
Jennings Randolph (D)
Robert C. Byrd (D)

Wisconsin
William Proxmire (D)
Robert W. Kasten, Jr. (R)

Wyoming
Malcolm Wallop (R)
Alan K. Simpson (R)

(R) Republican
(D) Democrat
(I) Independent

UNITED STATES HOUSE OF REPRESENTATIVES

(242 Democrats, 192 Republicans, 1 Vacancy)

Alabama
1. J. Edwards (R)
2. W. L. Dickinson (R)
3. W. Nichols (D)
4. T. Bevill (D)
5. R. Flippo (D)
6. A. Smith (R)
7. R. Shelby (D)

Alaska
D. Young (R)

Arizona
1. J. J. Rhodes (R)
2. M. K. Udall (D)
3. B. Stump (D)
4. E. Rudd (R)

Arkansas
1. W. V. Alexander, Jr. (D)
2. E. Bethune, Jr. (R)
3. J. P. Hammerschmidt (R)
4. B. Anthony, Jr. (D)

California
1. E. Chappie (R)
2. D. H. Clausen (R)
3. R. Matsui (D)
4. V. Fazio (D)
5. J. L. Burton (D)
6. P. Burton (D)
7. G. Miller (D)
8. R. V. Dellums (D)
9. F. H. Stark, Jr. (D)
10. D. Edwards (D)
11. T. Lantos (D)
12. P. N. McCloskey, Jr. (R)
13. N. Y. Mineta (D)
14. N. Shumway (R)
15. T. Coelho (D)
16. L. E. Panetta (D)
17. C. Pashayan (R)
18. W. Thomas (R)
19. R. J. Lagomarsino (R)
20. B. M. Goldwater, Jr. (R)
21. B. Fiedler (R)
22. C. J. Moorhead (R)
23. A. C. Beilenson (D)
24. H. A. Waxman (D)
25. E. R. Roybal (D)
26. J. H. Rousselot (R)
27. R. K. Dornan (R)
28. J. Dixon (D)
29. A. F. Hawkins (D)
30. G. E. Danielson (D)
31. M. Dymally (D)
32. G. M. Anderson (D)
33. W. Grisham (R)
34. D. Lungren (R)
35. D. Dreier (R)
36. G. E. Brown, Jr. (D)
37. J. Lewis (R)
38. J. M. Patterson (D)
39. W. Dannemeyer (R)
40. R. E. Badham (R)
41. B. Lowery (R)
42. D. Hunter (R)
43. C. W. Burgener (R)

Colorado
1. P. Schroeder (D)
2. T. E. Wirth (D)
3. R. Kogovsek (D)
4. H. Brown (R)
5. K. Kramer (R)

Connecticut
1. Vacancy
2. S. Gejdenson (D)
3. L. DeNardis (R)
4. S. B. McKinney (R)
5. W. Ratchford (D)
6. T. Moffett (D)

Delaware
T. B. Evans, Jr. (R)

Florida
1. E. Hutto (D)
2. D. Fuqua (D)
3. C. E. Bennett (D)
4. W. V. Chappell, Jr. (D)
5. B. McCollum (R)
6. C. W. Young (R)
7. S. M. Gibbons (D)
8. A. P. Ireland (D)
9. B. Nelson (D)
10. L. A. Bafalis (R)
11. D. Mica (D)
12. C. Shaw (R)
13. W. Lehman (D)
14. C. D. Pepper (D)
15. D. B. Fascell (D)

Georgia
1. R. B. Ginn (D)
2. C. Hatcher (D)
3. J. Brinkley (D)
4. E. H. Levitas (D)
5. W. F. Fowler, Jr. (D)
6. N. Gingrich (R)
7. L. P. McDonald (D)
8. B. L. Evans (D)
9. E. L. Jenkins (D)
10. D. D. Barnard, Jr. (D)

Hawaii
1. C. Heftel (D)
2. D. K. Akaka (D)

Idaho
1. L. Craig (R)
2. G. V. Hansen (R)

Illinois
1. H. Washington (D)
2. G. Savage (D)
3. M. A. Russo (D)
4. E. J. Derwinski (R)
5. J. G. Fary (D)
6. H. J. Hyde (R)
7. C. Collins (D)
8. D. Rostenkowski (D)
9. S. R. Yates (D)
10. J. Porter (R)
11. F. Annunzio (D)
12. P. M. Crane (R)
13. R. McClory (R)
14. J. N. Erlenborn (R)
15. T. J. Corcoran (R)
16. L. Martin (R)
17. G. M. O'Brien (R)
18. R. H. Michel (R)
19. T. Railsback (R)
20. P. Findley (R)
21. E. R. Madigan (R)
22. D. Crane (R)
23. C. M. Price (D)
24. P. Simon (D)

Indiana
1. A. Benjamin, Jr. (D)
2. F. J. Fithian (D)
3. J. Hiler (R)
4. D. Coats (R)
5. E. H. Hillis (R)
6. D. W. Evans (D)
7. J. T. Myers (R)
8. H. Deckard (R)
9. L. H. Hamilton (D)
10. P. R. Sharp (D)
11. A. Jacobs, Jr. (D)

Iowa
1. J. A. S. Leach (R)
2. T. Tauke (R)
3. C. Evans (R)
4. N. Smith (D)
5. T. R. Harkin (D)
6. B. W. Bedell (D)

Kansas
1. P. Roberts (R)
2. J. Jeffries (R)
3. L. Winn, Jr. (R)
4. D. Glickman (D)
5. R. Whittaker (R)

Kentucky
1. C. Hubbard, Jr. (D)
2. W. H. Natcher (D)
3. R. L. Mazzoli (D)
4. G. Snyder (R)
5. H. Rogers (R)
6. L. Hopkins (R)
7. C. D. Perkins (D)

Louisiana
1. R. L. Livingston, Jr. (R)
2. C. C. Boggs (D)
3. W. J. Tauzin (D)
4. C. Roemer (D)
5. J. Huckaby (D)
6. W. H. Moore (R)
7. J. B. Breaux (D)
8. G. W. Long (D)

Maine
1. D. F. Emery (R)
2. O. Snowe (R)

Maryland
1. R. Dyson (D)
2. C. D. Long (D)
3. B. A. Mikulski (D)
4. M. S. Holt (R)
5. S. Hoyer (D)*
6. B. Byron (D)
7. P. J. Mitchell (D)
8. M. Barnes (D)

Massachusetts
1. S. O. Conte (R)
2. E. P. Boland (D)
3. J. D. Early (D)
4. B. Frank (D)
5. J. Shannon (D)
6. N. Mavroules (D)
7. E. J. Markey (D)
8. T. P. O'Neill, Jr. (D)
9. J. J. Moakley (D)
10. M. M. Heckler (R)
11. B. Donnelly (D)
12. G. E. Studds (D)

Michigan
1. J. Conyers, Jr. (D)
2. C. D. Pursell (R)
3. H. Wolpe (D)
4. M. Siljander (R)*
5. H. S. Sawyer (R)
6. J. Dunn (R)
7. D. E. Kildee (D)
8. B. Traxler (D)
9. G. A. Vander Jagt (R)
10. D. Albosta (D)
11. R. Davis (R)
12. D. E. Bonior (D)
13. G. Crockett, Jr. (D)
14. D. Hertel (D)
15. W. D. Ford (D)
16. J. D. Dingell (D)
17. W. M. Brodhead (D)
18. J. J. Blanchard (D)
19. W. S. Broomfield (R)

Minnesota
1. A. Erdahl (R)
2. T. M. Hagedorn (R)
3. B. Frenzel (R)
4. B. F. Vento (D)
5. M. Sabo (D)
6. V. Weber (R)
7. A. Strangeland (R)
8. J. L. Oberstar (D)

Mississippi
1. J. L. Whitten (D)
2. D. R. Bowen (D)
3. G. V. Montgomery (D)
4. W. Dowdy (D)*
5. T. Lott (R)

Missouri
1. W. L. Clay (D)
2. R. A. Young (D)
3. R. A. Gephardt (D)
4. I. Skelton (D)

5. R. Bolling (D)
6. E. T. Coleman (R)
7. G. Taylor (R)
8. W. Bailey (R)
9. H. L. Volkmer (D)
10. B. Emerson (R)

Montana
1. P. Williams (D)
2. R. Marlenee (R)

Nebraska
1. D. Bereuter (R)
2. H. Daub (R)
3. V. Smith (R)

Nevada
J. D. Santini (D)

New Hampshire
1. N. E. D'Amours (D)
2. J. Gregg (R)

New Jersey
1. J. J. Florio (D)
2. W. J. Hughes (D)
3. J. J. Howard (D)
4. C. Smith (R)
5. M. Fenwick (R)
6. E. B. Forsythe (R)
7. M. Roukema (R)
8. R. A. Roe (D)
9. H. C. Hollenbeck (R)
10. P. W. Rodino, Jr. (D)
11. J. G. Minish (D)
12. M. J. Rinaldo (R)
13. J. Courter (R)
14. F. Guarini (D)
15. B. Dwyer (D)

New Mexico
1. M. Lujan, Jr. (R)
2. J. Skeen (R)

New York
1. W. Carney (R)
2. T. J. Downey (D)
3. G. Carman (R)
4. N. F. Lent (R)
5. R. McGrath (R)
6. J. LeBoutillier (R)
7. J. P. Addabbo (D)
8. B. S. Rosenthal (D)
9. G. Ferraro (D)
10. M. Biaggi (D)
11. J. H. Scheuer (D)
12. S. A. Chisholm (D)
13. S. J. Solarz (D)
14. F. W. Richmond (D)
15. L. C. Zeferetti (D)
16. C. Schumer (D)
17. G. Molinari (R)
18. S. W. Green (R)
19. C. B. Rangel (D)
20. T. Weiss (D)
21. R. Garcia (D)
22. J. B. Bingham (D)
23. P. Peyser (D)
24. R. L. Ottinger (D)
25. H. Fish, Jr. (R)
26. B. A. Gilman (R)
27. M. F. McHugh (D)
28. S. S. Stratton (D)
29. G. Solomon (R)
30. D. Martin (R)
31. D. J. Mitchell (R)
32. G. Wortley (R)
33. G. Lee (R)
34. F. Horton (R)
35. B. B. Conable, Jr. (R)
36. J. J. LaFalce (D)
37. H. J. Nowak (D)
38. J. Kemp (R)
39. S. N. Lundine (D)

North Carolina
1. W. B. Jones (D)
2. L. H. Fountain (D)
3. C. O. Whitley, Sr. (D)
4. I. F. Andrews (D)
5. S. L. Neal (D)
6. E. Johnston (R)
7. C. Rose (D)
8. W. G. Hefner (D)
9. J. G. Martin (R)
10. J. T. Broyhill (R)
11. B. Hendon (R)

North Dakota
B. Dorgan (D)

Ohio
1. W. D. Gradison, Jr. (R)
2. T. A. Luken (D)
3. T. Hall (D)
4. M. Oxley (R)*
5. D. L. Latta (R)
6. B. McEwen (R)
7. C. J. Brown (R)
8. T. N. Kindness (R)
9. E. Weber (R)
10. C. E. Miller (R)
11. J. W. Stanton (R)
12. B. Shamansky (D)
13. D. J. Pease (D)
14. J. F. Seiberling (D)
15. C. P. Wylie (R)
16. R. Regula (R)
17. J. M. Ashbrook (R)
18. D. Applegate (D)
19. L. Williams (R)
20. M. R. Oakar (D)
21. L. Stokes (D)
22. D. Eckart (D)
23. R. M. Mottl (D)

Oklahoma
1. J. R. Jones (D)
2. M. Synar (D)
3. W. W. Watkins (D)
4. D. McCurdy (D)
5. M. Edwards (R)
6. G. English (D)

Oregon
1. L. AuCoin (D)
2. D. Smith (R)
3. R. Wyden (D)
4. J. Weaver (D)

Pennsylvania
1. T. Foglietta (D)
2. W. Gray (D)
3. J. Smith (D)*
4. C. Dougherty (R)
5. R. T. Schulze (R)
6. G. Yatron (D)
7. R. W. Edgar (D)
8. J. Coyne (R)
9. B. Shuster (R)
10. J. M. McDade (R)
11. J. Nelligan (R)
12. J. P. Murtha (D)
13. L. Coughlin (R)
14. W. Coyne (D)
15. D. Ritter (R)
16. R. S. Walker (R)
17. A. E. Ertel (D)
18. D. Walgren (D)
19. W. F. Goodling (R)
20. J. M. Gaydos (D)
21. D. Bailey (D)
22. A. J. Murphy (D)
23. W. Clinger, Jr. (R)
24. M. L. Marks (R)
25. E. Atkinson (R)

Rhode Island
1. F. J. St. Germain (D)
2. C. Schneider (R)

South Carolina
1. T. Hartnett (R)
2. F. D. Spence (R)
3. B. C. Derrick, Jr. (D)
4. C. Campbell, Jr. (R)
5. K. Holland (D)
6. J. Napier (R)

South Dakota
1. T. A. Daschle (D)
2. C. Roberts (R)

Tennessee
1. J. H. Quillen (R)
2. J. J. Duncan (R)
3. M. L. Bouquard (D)
4. A. Gore, Jr. (D)
5. W. H. Boner (D)
6. R. L. Beard, Jr. (R)
7. E. Jones (D)
8. H. Ford (D)

Texas
1. S. B. Hall, Jr. (D)
2. C. Wilson (D)
3. J. M. Collins (R)
4. R. Hall (D)
5. J. A. Mattox (D)
6. P. Gramm (D)
7. B. Archer (R)
8. J. Fields (R)
9. J. Brooks (D)
10. J. J. Pickle (D)
11. J. M. Leath (D)
12. J. C. Wright, Jr. (D)
13. J. E. Hightower (D)
14. W. Patman (D)
15. E. de la Garza (D)
16. R. C. White (D)
17. C. Stenholm (D)
18. M. Leland (D)
19. K. Hance (D)
20. H. B. Gonzalez (D)
21. T. Loeffler (R)
22. R. Paul (R)
23. A. Kazen, Jr. (D)
24. M. Frost (D)

Utah
1. J. Hansen (R)
2. D. D. Marriott (R)

Vermont
J. M. Jeffords (R)

Virginia
1. P. S. Trible, Jr. (R)
2. G. W. Whitehurst (R)
3. T. Bliley, Jr. (R)
4. R. W. Daniel, Jr. (R)
5. D. Daniel (D)
6. M. C. Butler (R)
7. J. K. Robinson (R)
8. S. Parris (R)
9. W. C. Wampler (R)
10. F. Wolf (R)

Washington
1. J. M. Pritchard (R)
2. A. Swift (D)
3. D. L. Bonker (D)
4. S. Morrison (R)
5. T. S. Foley (D)
6. N. D. Dicks (D)
7. M. Lowry (D)

West Virginia
1. R. H. Mollohan (D)
2. C. Benedict (R)
3. M. Staton (R)
4. N. J. Rahall (D)

Wisconsin
1. L. Aspin (D)
2. R. W. Kastenmeier (D)
3. S. Gunderson (R)
4. C. J. Zablocki (D)
5. H. S. Reuss (D)
6. T. E. Petri (R)
7. D. R. Obey (D)
8. T. Roth (R)
9. F. J. Sensenbrenner, Jr. (R)

Wyoming
R. Cheney (R)

(R) Republican
(D) Democrat

*elected in 1981

Charles S. Robb: Elected governor of Virginia in 1981.

UNITED STATES SUPREME COURT

Chief Justice: Warren E. Burger (1969)

Associate Justices:
William J. Brennan, Jr. (1956)
Sandra Day O'Connor (1981)
Byron R. White (1962)
Thurgood Marshall (1967)
Harry A. Blackmun (1970)
Lewis F. Powell, Jr. (1971)
William H. Rehnquist (1971)
John Paul Stevens (1975)

UNITED STATES CABINET

Secretary of Agriculture: John R. Block
Attorney General: William French Smith
Secretary of Commerce: Malcolm Baldrige
Secretary of Defense: Caspar W. Weinberger
Secretary of Education: Terrel H. Bell
Secretary of Energy: James B. Edwards
Secretary of Health and Human Services:
Richard S. Schweiker
Secretary of Housing and Urban Development:
Samuel R. Pierce, Jr.
Secretary of the Interior: James G. Watt
Secretary of Labor: Raymond J. Donovan
Secretary of State: Alexander M. Haig, Jr.
Secretary of Transportation: Andrew L.
Lewis, Jr.
Secretary of the Treasury: Donald T. Regan

STATE GOVERNORS

State	Governor	State	Governor
Alabama	Forrest H. James, Jr. (D)	**Montana**	Ted Schwinden (D)
Alaska	Jay S. Hammond (R)	**Nebraska**	Charles Thone (R)
Arizona	Bruce E. Babbitt (D)	**Nevada**	Robert List (R)
Arkansas	Frank D. White (R)	**New Hampshire**	Hugh J. Gallen (D)
California	Edmund G. Brown, Jr. (D)	**New Jersey**	Thomas H. Kean (R)*
Colorado	Richard D. Lamm (D)	**New Mexico**	Bruce King (D)
Connecticut	William A. O'Neill (D)	**New York**	Hugh L. Carey (D)
Delaware	Pierre S. du Pont IV (R)	**North Carolina**	James B. Hunt, Jr. (D)
Florida	Robert Graham (D)	**North Dakota**	Allen I. Olson (R)
Georgia	George Busbee (D)	**Ohio**	James A. Rhodes (R)
Hawaii	George R. Ariyoshi (D)	**Oklahoma**	George Nigh (D)
Idaho	John V. Evans (D)	**Oregon**	Victor Atiyeh (R)
Illinois	James R. Thompson (R)	**Pennsylvania**	Richard L. Thornburgh (R)
Indiana	Robert D. Orr (R)	**Rhode Island**	J. Joseph Garrahy (D)
Iowa	Robert D. Ray (R)	**South Carolina**	Richard W. Riley (D)
Kansas	John Carlin (D)	**South Dakota**	William J. Janklow (R)
Kentucky	John Y. Brown, Jr. (D)	**Tennessee**	Lamar Alexander (R)
Louisiana	David C. Treen (R)	**Texas**	William P. Clements (R)
Maine	Joseph E. Brennan (D)	**Utah**	Scott M. Matheson (D)
Maryland	Harry Hughes (D)	**Vermont**	Richard A. Snelling (R)
Massachusetts	Edward J. King (D)	**Virginia**	Charles S. Robb (D)*
Michigan	William G. Milliken (R)	**Washington**	John Spellman (R)
Minnesota	Albert Quie (R)	**West Virginia**	John D. Rockefeller IV (D)
Mississippi	William F. Winter (D)	**Wisconsin**	Lee S. Dreyfus (R)
Missouri	Christopher S. Bond (R)	**Wyoming**	Ed Herschler (D)

*elected in 1981

THE 1980 UNITED STATES CENSUS
FINAL FIGURES

The Constitution of the United States requires that a census be taken every ten years, so that membership in the House of Representatives may be fairly apportioned (divided up) among the states.

The table below provides the final 1980 census figures for the resident population of the United States, and it indicates the representation of each state in the House of Representatives. The population figures include people living in the District of Columbia and the 50 states; they exclude citizens living outside the United States. The change in representation in the House of Representatives takes effect in January, 1983, following the elections of 1982.

STATE	RESIDENT POPULATION				REPRESENTATIVES		
	1980	1970	Change	%	1980	1970	Change
Alabama	3,890,061	3,444,354	+445,707	+12.9	7	7	0
Alaska	400,481	302,583	+97,898	+32.4	1	1	0
Arizona	2,717,866	1,775,399	+942,467	+53.1	5	4	+1
Arkansas	2,285,513	1,923,322	+362,191	+18.8	4	4	0
California	23,668,562	19,971,069	+3,697,493	+18.5	45	43	+2
Colorado	2,888,834	2,209,596	+679,238	+30.7	6	5	+1
Connecticut	3,107,576	3,032,217	+75,359	+2.5	6	6	0
Delaware	595,225	548,104	+47,121	+8.6	1	1	0
Dist. of Columbia	637,651	756,668	−119,017	−15.7	*		
Florida	9,739,992	6,791,418	+2,948,574	+43.4	19	15	+4
Georgia	5,464,265	4,587,930	+876,335	+19.1	10	10	0
Hawaii	965,000	769,913	+195,087	+25.3	2	2	0
Idaho	943,935	713,015	+230,920	+32.4	2	2	0
Illinois	11,418,461	11,110,285	+308,176	+2.8	22	24	−2
Indiana	5,490,179	5,195,392	+294,787	+5.7	10	11	−1
Iowa	2,913,387	2,825,368	+88,019	+3.1	6	6	0
Kansas	2,363,208	2,249,071	+114,137	+5.1	5	5	0
Kentucky	3,661,433	3,220,711	+440,722	+13.7	7	7	0
Louisiana	4,203,972	3,644,637	+559,335	+15.3	8	8	0
Maine	1,124,660	993,722	+130,938	+13.2	2	2	0
Maryland	4,216,446	3,923,897	+292,549	+7.5	8	8	0
Massachusetts	5,737,037	5,689,170	+47,867	+0.8	11	12	−1
Michigan	9,258,344	8,881,826	+376,518	+4.2	18	19	−1
Minnesota	4,077,148	3,806,103	+271,045	+7.1	8	8	0
Mississippi	2,520,638	2,216,994	+303,644	+13.7	5	5	0
Missouri	4,917,444	4,677,623	+239,821	+5.1	9	10	−1
Montana	786,690	694,409	+92,281	+13.3	2	2	0
Nebraska	1,570,006	1,485,333	+84,673	+5.7	3	3	0
Nevada	799,184	488,738	+310,446	+63.5	2	1	+1
New Hampshire	920,610	737,681	+182,929	+24.8	2	2	0
New Jersey	7,364,158	7,171,112	+193,046	+2.7	14	15	−1
New Mexico	1,299,968	1,017,055	+282,913	+27.8	3	2	+1
New York	17,557,288	18,241,391	−684,103	−3.8	34	39	−5
North Carolina	5,874,429	5,084,411	+790,018	+15.5	11	11	0
North Dakota	652,695	617,792	+34,903	+5.6	1	1	0
Ohio	10,797,419	10,657,423	+139,996	+1.3	21	23	−2
Oklahoma	3,025,266	2,559,463	+465,803	+18.2	6	6	0
Oregon	2,632,663	2,091,533	+541,130	+25.9	5	4	+1
Pennsylvania	11,866,728	11,800,766	+65,962	+0.6	23	25	−2
Rhode Island	947,154	949,723	−2,569	−0.3	2	2	0
South Carolina	3,119,208	2,590,713	+528,495	+20.4	6	6	0
South Dakota	690,178	666,257	+23,921	+3.6	1	2	−1
Tennessee	4,590,750	3,926,018	+664,732	+16.9	9	8	+1
Texas	14,228,383	11,198,655	+3,029,728	+27.1	27	24	+3
Utah	1,461,037	1,059,273	+401,764	+37.9	3	2	+1
Vermont	511,456	444,732	+66,724	+15.0	1	1	0
Virginia	5,346,279	4,651,448	+694,831	+14.9	10	10	0
Washington	4,130,163	3,413,244	+716,919	+21.0	8	7	+1
West Virginia	1,949,644	1,744,237	+205,407	+11.8	4	4	0
Wisconsin	4,705,335	4,417,821	+287,514	+6.5	9	9	0
Wyoming	470,816	332,416	+138,400	+41.6	1	1	0
TOTAL U.S.	**226,504,825**	**203,302,031**	**23,202,794**	**+11.4**	**435**	**435**	**0**

* The District of Columbia sends one non-voting representative to the House of Representatives but is excluded from the apportionment process.

PLACES WITH POPULATIONS OF 20,000 OR MORE

In the following tables, final figures are shown for incorporated places with populations of 20,000 or more, except in the New England states and Hawaii, for which all places of 20,000 or more are listed.

Abbreviations used in these tables are: B (borough); C (city); T (town or township); and V (village).

ALABAMA
Anniston C	29,523
Auburn C	28,471
Bessemer C	31,729
Birmingham C	284,413
Decatur C	42,002
Dothan C	48,750
Florence C	37,029
Gadsden C	47,565
Homewood C	21,271
Huntsville C	142,513
Mobile C	200,452
Montgomery C	178,157
Opelika C	21,896
Phenix City C	26,928
Prichard C	39,541
Selma C	26,684
Tuscaloosa C	75,143

ALASKA
Anchorage C	173,017
Fairbanks C	22,645

ARIZONA
Chandler C	29,673
Flagstaff C	34,641
Glendale C	96,988
Mesa C	152,453
Phoenix C	764,911
Prescott C	20,055
Scottsdale C	88,364
Sierra Vista C	25,968
Tempe C	106,743
Tucson C	330,537
Yuma C	42,433

ARKANSAS
Blytheville C	24,314
Conway C	20,375
El Dorado C	26,685
Fayetteville C	36,604
Fort Smith C	71,384
Hot Springs C	35,166
Jacksonville C	27,589
Jonesboro C	31,530
Little Rock C	158,461
North Little Rock C	64,419
Pine Bluff C	56,576
Springdale C	23,458
Texarkana C	21,459
West Memphis C	28,138

CALIFORNIA
Alameda C	63,852
Alhambra C	64,615
Anaheim C	221,847
Antioch C	43,559
Arcadia C	45,994
Azusa C	29,380
Bakersfield C	105,611
Baldwin Park C	50,554
Bell C	25,450
Bellflower C	53,441
Bell Gardens C	34,117
Belmont C	24,505
Berkeley C	103,328
Beverly Hills C	32,367
Brea C	27,913
Buena Park C	64,165
Burbank C	84,625
Burlingame C	26,173
Camarillo C	37,732
Campbell C	27,067
Carlsbad C	35,490
Carson C	81,221
Cerritos C	52,756
Chico C	26,601
Chino C	40,165
Chula Vista C	83,927
Claremont C	30,950
Clovis C	33,021
Colton C	27,419
Compton C	81,286
Concord C	103,251
Corona C	37,791
Costa Mesa C	82,291
Covina C	33,751
Culver City C	38,139
Cupertino C	25,770
Cypress C	40,391
Daly City C	78,519
Davis C	36,640
Downey C	82,602
El Cajon C	73,892
El Centro C	23,996
El Cerrito C	22,731
El Monte C	79,494
Escondido C	62,480
Eureka C	24,153
Fairfield C	58,099
Fontana C	37,109
Foster City C	23,287
Fountain Valley C	55,080
Fremont C	131,945
Fresno C	218,202
Fullerton C	102,034
Gardena C	45,165
Garden Grove C	123,351
Gilroy C	21,641
Glendale C	139,060
Glendora C	38,654
Hanford C	20,958
Hawthorne C	56,447
Hayward C	94,167
Hemet C	23,211
Huntington Beach C	170,505
Huntington Park C	46,223
Imperial Beach C	22,689
Indio C	21,611
Inglewood C	94,245
Irvine C	62,134
La Canada Flintridge C	20,153
Lafayette C	20,879
La Habra C	45,232
Lakewood C	74,654
La Mesa C	50,342
La Mirada C	40,986
Lancaster C	48,027
La Puente C	30,882
La Verne C	23,508
Lawndale C	23,460
Lemon Grove C	20,780
Livermore C	48,349
Lodi C	35,221
Lompoc C	26,267
Long Beach C	361,334
Los Altos C	25,769
Los Angeles C	2,966,763
Los Gatos T	26,593
Lynwood C	48,548
Madera C	21,732
Manhattan Beach C	31,542
Manteca C	24,925
Marina C	20,647
Martinez C	22,582
Maywood C	21,810
Menlo Park C	25,673
Merced C	36,499
Millbrae C	20,058
Milpitas C	37,820
Modesto C	106,105
Monrovia C	30,531
Montclair C	22,628
Montebello C	52,929
Monterey C	27,558
Monterey Park C	54,338
Mountain View C	58,655
Napa C	50,879
National City C	48,772
Newark C	32,126
Newport Beach C	63,475
Norco C	21,126
Norwalk C	85,232
Novato C	43,916
Oakland C	339,288
Oceanside C	76,698
Ontario C	88,820
Orange C	91,788
Oxnard C	108,195
Pacifica C	36,866

Palm Springs C	32,271
Palo Alto C	55,225
Paradise C	22,571
Paramount C	36,407
Pasadena C	119,374
Petaluma C	33,834
Pico Rivera C	53,459
Pittsburg C	33,034
Placentia C	35,041
Pleasant Hill C	25,124
Pleasanton C	35,160
Pomona C	92,742
Rancho Cucamonga C	55,250
Rancho Palos Verdes C	35,227
Redding C	41,995
Redlands C	43,619
Redondo Beach C	57,102
Redwood City C	54,965
Rialto C	35,615
Richmond C	74,676
Riverside C	170,876
Rohnert Park C	22,965
Rosemead C	42,604
Roseville C	24,347
Sacramento C	275,741
Salinas C	80,479
San Bernardino C	118,057
San Bruno C	35,417
San Buenaventura (Ventura) C	74,474
San Carlos C	24,710
San Clemente C	27,325
San Diego C	875,504
San Dimas C	24,014
San Francisco C	678,974
San Gabriel C	30,072
San Jose C	636,550
San Leandro C	63,952
San Luis Obispo C	34,252
San Mateo C	77,561
San Rafael C	44,700
Santa Ana C	203,713
Santa Barbara C	74,542
Santa Clara C	87,746
Santa Cruz C	41,483
Santa Maria C	39,685
Santa Monica C	88,314
Santa Paula C	20,552
Santa Rosa C	83,205
Saratoga C	29,261
Seal Beach C	25,975
Seaside C	36,567
Simi Valley C	77,500
South Gate C	66,784
South Lake Tahoe C	20,681
South Pasadena C	22,681
South San Francisco C	49,393
Stanton C	21,144
Stockton C	149,779
Sunnyvale C	106,618
Temple City C	28,972
Thousand Oaks C	77,797
Torrance C	131,497
Tulare C	22,475
Turlock C	26,291
Tustin C	32,073
Union City C	39,406
Upland C	47,647
Vacaville C	43,367
Vallejo C	80,188
Visalia C	49,729
Vista C	35,834
Walnut Creek C	53,643
Watsonville C	23,543
West Covina C	80,094
Westminster C	71,133
Whittier C	68,872
Woodland C	30,235
Yorba Linda C	28,254

COLORADO

Arvada C	84,576
Aurora C	158,588
Boulder C	76,685
Broomfield C	20,730
Colorado Springs C	215,150
Denver C	491,396
Englewood C	30,021
Fort Collins C	64,632
Grand Junction C	28,144
Greeley C	53,006
Lakewood C	112,848
Littleton C	28,631
Longmont C	42,942
Loveland C	30,244
Northglenn C	29,847
Pueblo C	101,686
Thornton C	40,343
Westminster C	50,211
Wheat Ridge C	30,293

CONNECTICUT

Branford T	23,363
Bridgeport C	142,546
Bristol C	57,370
Cheshire T	21,788
Danbury C	60,470
East Hartford T	52,563
East Haven T	25,028
Enfield T	42,695
Fairfield T	54,849
Glastonbury T	24,327
Greenwich T	59,578
Groton T	41,062
Hamden T	51,071
Hartford C	136,392
Manchester T	49,761
Mansfield T	20,634
Meriden C	57,118
Middletown C	39,040
Milford C	50,898
Naugatuck B	26,456
New Britain C	73,840
New Haven C	126,109
Newington T	28,841
New London C	28,842
North Haven T	22,080
Norwalk C	77,767
Norwich C	38,074
Ridgefield T	20,120
Shelton C	31,314
Simsbury T	21,161
Southington T	36,879
Stamford C	102,453
Stratford T	50,541
Torrington C	30,987
Trumbull T	32,989
Vernon T	27,974
Wallingford T	37,274
Waterbury C	103,266
West Hartford T	61,301
West Haven C	53,184
Westport T	25,290
Wethersfield T	26,013
Windham T	21,062
Windsor T	25,204

DELAWARE

Dover C	23,512
Newark C	25,247
Wilmington C	70,195

FLORIDA

Altamonte Springs C	22,028
Boca Raton C	49,505
Boynton Beach C	35,624
Bradenton C	30,170
Cape Coral C	32,103
Clearwater C	85,450
Coral Gables C	43,241
Coral Springs C	37,349
Davie T	20,877
Daytona Beach C	54,176
Deerfield Beach C	39,193
Delray Beach C	34,325
Dunedin C	30,203
Fort Lauderdale C	153,256
Fort Myers C	36,638
Fort Pierce C	33,802
Fort Walton Beach C	20,829
Gainesville C	81,371
Hallandale C	36,517
Hialeah C	145,254
Hollywood C	117,188
Homestead C	20,668
Jacksonville C	540,898
Key West C	24,292
Lakeland C	47,406
Lake Worth C	27,048
Largo C	58,977
Lauderdale Lakes C	25,426
Lauderhill C	37,271
Margate C	36,044
Melbourne C	46,536
Miami C	346,931
Miami Beach C	96,298
Miramar C	32,813
North Miami C	42,566
North Miami Beach C	36,481
Oakland Park C	21,939
Ocala C	37,170
Orlando C	128,394
Ormond Beach C	21,378
Panama City C	33,346
Pembroke Pines C	35,776
Pensacola C	57,619
Pinellas Park C	32,811
Plantation C	48,501
Pompano Beach C	52,618
Riviera Beach C	26,596
St. Petersburg C	236,893

Sanford C	23,176	Danville C	38,985	**INDIANA**	
Sarasota C	48,868	Decatur C	94,081	Anderson C	64,695
Sunrise C	39,681	De Kalb C	33,099	Bloomington C	51,646
Tallahassee C	81,548	Des Plaines C	53,568	Columbus C	30,292
Tamarac C	29,142	Dolton V	24,766	East Chicago C	39,786
Tampa C	271,523	Downers Grove V	39,274	Elkhart C	41,305
Titusville C	31,910	East Moline C	20,907	Evansville C	130,496
West Palm Beach C	62,530	East Peoria C	22,385	Fort Wayne C	172,196
Winter Haven C	21,119	East St. Louis C	55,200	Gary C	151,953
Winter Park C	22,314	Elgin C	63,798	Hammond C	93,714

GEORGIA

		Elk Grove Village V	28,907	Highland T	25,935
Albany C	73,934	Elmhurst C	44,251	Hobart C	22,987
Athens C	42,549	Elmwood Park V	24,016	Indianapolis C	700,807
Atlanta C	425,022	Evanston C	73,706	Jeffersonville C	21,220
Augusta C	47,532	Evergreen Park V	22,260	Kokomo C	47,808
College Park C	24,632	Freeport C	26,406	Lafayette C	43,011
Columbus C	169,441	Galesburg C	35,305	La Porte C	21,796
Dalton C	20,743	Glendale Heights V	23,163	Lawrence C	25,591
East Point C	37,486	Glen Ellyn V	23,649	Marion C	35,874
Griffin C	20,728	Glenview V	30,842	Merrillville T	27,677
La Grange C	24,204	Granite City C	36,815	Michigan City C	36,850
Macon C	116,860	Hanover Park V	28,850	Mishawaka C	40,224
Marietta C	30,805	Harvey C	35,810	Muncie C	77,216
Rome C	29,654	Highland Park C	30,611	Munster T	20,671
Roswell C	23,337	Hoffman Estates V	38,258	New Albany C	37,103
Savannah C	141,634	Jacksonville C	20,284	New Castle C	20,056
Smyrna C	20,312	Joliet C	77,956	Portage C	27,409
Valdosta C	37,596	Kankakee C	30,141	Richmond C	41,349
Warner Robins C	39,893	Lansing V	29,039	South Bend C	109,727
		Lombard V	37,295	Terre Haute C	61,125

HAWAII

		Maywood V	27,998	Valparaisa C	22,247
Aiea C	32,879	Melrose Park V	20,735	Vincennes C	20,857
Hilo C	35,269	Moline C	45,709	West Lafayette C	21,247
Honolulu C	365,048	Morton Grove V	23,747	
Kailua (Oahu) C	35,812	Mount Prospect V	52,634	**IOWA**
Mililani Town C	20,351	Naperville C	42,330	Ames C	45,775
Pearl City C	42,575	Niles V	30,363	Bettendorf C	27,381
Waipahu C	29,139	Normal T	35,672	Burlington C	29,529
		Northbrook V	30,735	Cedar Falls C	36,322

IDAHO

		North Chicago C	38,774	Cedar Rapids C	110,243
Boise City C	102,451	Oak Forest C	26,096	Clinton C	32,828
Coeur d'Alene C	20,054	Oak Lawn V	60,590	Council Bluffs C	56,449
Idaho Falls C	39,590	Oak Park V	54,887	Davenport C	103,264
Lewiston C	27,986	Orland Park V	23,045	Des Moines C	191,003
Nampa C	25,112	Palatine V	32,166	Dubuque C	62,321
Pocatello C	46,340	Park Forest V	26,222	Fort Dodge C	29,423
Twin Falls C	26,209	Park Ridge C	38,704	Iowa City C	50,508
		Pekin C	33,967	Marshalltown C	26,938

ILLINOIS

		Peoria C	124,160	Mason City C	30,144
Addison V	28,836	Quincy C	42,352	Muscatine C	23,467
Alton C	34,171	Rantoul V	20,161	Ottumwa C	27,381
Arlington Heights V	66,116	Rockford C	139,712	Sioux City C	82,003
Aurora C	81,293	Rock Island C	47,036	Waterloo C	75,985
Belleville C	42,150	Rolling Meadows C	20,167	West Des Moines C	21,894
Berwyn C	46,849	Schaumburg V	52,319	
Bloomington C	44,189	Skokie V	60,278	**KANSAS**
Blue Island C	21,855	South Holland V	24,977	Emporia C	25,287
Bolingbrook V	37,261	Springfield C	99,637	Hutchinson C	40,284
Buffalo Grove V	22,230	Streamwood V	23,456	Kansas City C	161,087
Burbank C	28,462	Tinley Park V	26,171	Lawrence C	52,738
Calumet City C	39,673	Urbana C	35,978	Leavenworth C	33,656
Carbondale C	27,194	Villa Park V	23,185	Manhattan C	32,644
Carpentersville V	23,272	Waukegan C	67,653	Olathe C	37,258
Champaign C	58,133	Wheaton C	43,043	Overland Park C	81,784
Chicago C	3,005,072	Wheeling V	23,266	Prairie Village C	24,657
Chicago Heights C	37,026	Wilmette V	28,229	Salina C	41,843
Cicero T	61,232	Woodridge V	22,322	Shawnee C	29,653

Topeka C 115,266
Wichita C 279,272

KENTUCKY
Ashland C 27,064
Bowling Green C 40,450
Covington C 49,013
Frankfort C 25,973
Henderson C 24,834
Hopkinsville C 27,318
Lexington-Fayette C 204,165
Louisville C 298,451
Newport C 21,587
Owensboro C 54,450
Paducah C 29,315
Richmond C 21,705

LOUISIANA
Alexandria C 51,565
Baton Rouge C 219,486
Bossier City C 49,969
Gretna C 20,615
Houma C 32,602
Kenner C 66,382
Lafayette C 81,961
Lake Charles C 75,051
Monroe C 57,597
New Iberia C 32,766
New Orleans C 557,482
Ruston C 20,585
Shreveport C 205,815
Slidell C 26,718

MAINE
Auburn C 23,128
Augusta C 21,819
Bangor C 31,643
Lewiston C 40,481
Portland C 61,572
South Portland C 22,712

MARYLAND
Annapolis C 31,740
Baltimore C 786,775
Bowie C 33,695
College Park C 23,614
Cumberland C 25,933
Frederick C 27,557
Gaithersburg C 26,424
Hagerstown C 34,132
Rockville C 43,811

MASSACHUSETTS
Agawam T 26,271
Amherst T 33,229
Andover T 26,370
Arlington T 48,219
Attleboro C 34,196
Barnstable T 30,898
Belmont T 26,100
Beverly C 37,655
Billerica T 36,727
Boston C 562,994
Braintree T 36,337
Brockton C 95,172

Brookline T 55,062
Burlington T 23,486
Cambridge C 95,322
Chelmsford T 31,174
Chelsea C 25,431
Chicopee C 55,112
Danvers T 24,100
Dartmouth T 23,966
Dedham T 25,298
Dracut T 21,249
Everett C 37,195
Fall River C 92,574
Falmouth T 23,640
Fitchburg C 39,580
Framingham T 65,113
Gloucester C 27,768
Haverhill C 46,865
Hingham T 20,339
Holyoke C 44,678
Lawrence C 63,175
Leominster C 34,508
Lexington T 29,479
Lowell C 92,418
Lynn C 78,471
Malden C 53,386
Marblehead T 20,126
Marlborough C 30,617
Marshfield T 20,916
Medford C 58,076
Melrose C 30,055
Methuen T 36,701
Milford T 23,390
Milton T 25,860
Natick T 29,461
Needham T 27,901
New Bedford C 98,478
Newton C 83,622
Northampton C 29,286
North Andover T 20,129
North Attleborough T ... 21,095
Norwood T 29,711
Peabody C 45,976
Pittsfield C 51,974
Plymouth T 35,913
Quincy C 84,743
Randolph T 28,218
Reading T 22,678
Revere C 42,423
Salem C 38,220
Saugus T 24,746
Shrewsbury T 22,674
Somerville C 77,372
Springfield C 152,319
Stoneham T 21,424
Stoughton T 26,710
Taunton C 45,001
Tewksbury T 24,635
Wakefield T 24,895
Waltham C 58,200
Watertown T 34,384
Wellesley T 27,209
Westfield C 36,465
West Springfield T 27,042
Weymouth T 55,601
Winchester T 20,701
Woburn C 36,626
Worcester C 161,799

MICHIGAN
Adrian C 21,186
Allen Park C 34,196
Ann Arbor C 107,316
Battle Creek C 35,724
Bay City C 41,593
Birmingham C 21,689
Burton C 29,976
Dearborn C 90,660
Dearborn Heights C 67,706
Detroit C 1,203,339
East Detroit C 38,280
East Lansing C 48,309
Farmington Hills C 58,056
Ferndale C 26,227
Flint C 159,611
Garden City C 35,640
Grand Rapids C 181,843
Hamtramck C 21,300
Hazel Park C 20,914
Highland Park C 27,909
Holland C 26,281
Inkster C 35,190
Jackson C 39,739
Kalamazoo C 79,722
Kentwood C 30,438
Lansing C 130,414
Lincoln Park C 45,105
Livonia C 104,814
Madison Heights C 35,375
Marquette C 23,288
Midland C 37,250
Monroe C 23,531
Mount Pleasant C 23,746
Muskegon C 40,823
Norton Shores C 22,025
Novi C 22,525
Oak Park C 31,537
Pontiac C 76,715
Portage C 38,157
Port Huron C 33,981
Romulus C 24,857
Roseville C 54,311
Royal Oak C 70,893
Saginaw C 77,508
St. Clair Shores C 76,210
Southfield C 75,568
Southgate C 32,058
Sterling Heights C 108,999
Taylor C 77,568
Trenton C 22,762
Troy C 67,102
Warren C 161,134
Wayne C 21,159
Westland C 84,603
Wyandotte C 34,006
Wyoming C 59,616
Ypsilanti C 24,031

MINNESOTA
Apple Valley C 21,818
Austin C 23,020
Blaine C 28,558
Bloomington C 81,831
Brooklyn Center C 31,230
Brooklyn Park C 43,332
Burnsville C 35,674

Columbia Heights C 20,029
Coon Rapids C 35,826
Crystal C 25,543
Duluth C 92,811
Eagan C 20,532
Edina C 46,073
Fridley C 30,228
Golden Valley C 22,775
Hibbing C 21,193
Mankato C 28,651
Maple Grove C 20,525
Maplewood C 26,990
Minneapolis C 370,951
Minnetonka C 38,683
Moorhead C 29,998
New Brighton C 23,269
New Hope C 23,087
Plymouth C 31,615
Richfield C 37,851
Rochester C 57,855
Roseville C 35,820
St. Cloud C 42,566
St. Louis Park C 42,931
Saint Paul C 270,230
South Saint Paul C 21,235
White Bear Lake C 22,538
Winona C 25,075

MISSISSIPPI

Biloxi C 49,311
Clarksdale C 21,137
Columbus C 27,383
Greenville C 40,613
Greenwood C 20,115
Gulfport C 39,676
Hattiesburg C 40,829
Jackson C 202,895
Laurel C 21,897
Meridian C 46,577
Natchez C 22,015
Pascagoula C 29,318
Pearl C 20,778
Tupelo C 23,905
Vicksburg C 25,434

MISSOURI

Blue Springs C 25,927
Cape Girardeau C 34,361
Columbia C 62,061
Ferguson C 24,740
Florissant C 55,372
Gladstone C 24,990
Grandview C 24,502
Independence C 111,806
Jefferson City C 33,619
Joplin C 38,893
Kansas City C 448,159
Kirkwood C 27,987
Lee's Summit C 28,741
Raytown C 31,759
St. Charles C 37,379
St. Joseph C 76,691
St. Louis C 453,085
Sedalia C 20,927
Springfield C 133,116
University City C 42,738
Webster Groves C 23,097

MONTANA

Billings C 66,798
Bozeman C 21,645
Butte—Silver Bow 37,205
Great Falls C 56,725
Helena C 23,938
Missoula C 33,388

NEBRASKA

Bellevue C 21,813
Fremont C 23,979
Grand Island C 33,180
Hastings C 23,045
Kearney C 21,158
Lincoln C 171,932
North Platte C 24,479
Omaha C 311,681

NEVADA

Carson City C 32,022
Henderson C 24,363
Las Vegas C 164,674
North Las Vegas C 42,739
Reno C 100,756
Sparks C 40,780

NEW HAMPSHIRE

Concord C 30,400
Dover C 22,377
Keene C 21,449
Manchester C 90,936
Nashua C 67,865
Portsmouth C 26,254
Rochester C 21,560
Salem T 24,124

NEW JERSEY

Altantic City C 40,199
Bayonne C 65,047
Belleville T 35,367
Bergenfield B 25,568
Bloomfield T 47,792
Camden C 84,910
Carteret B 20,598
Cliffside Park B 21,464
Clifton C 74,388
East Orange C 77,025
Elizabeth C 106,201
Englewood C 23,701
Fair Lawn B 32,229
Fort Lee B 32,449
Garfield C 26,803
Hackensack C 36,039
Hoboken C 42,460
Irvington T 61,493
Jersey City C 223,532
Kearny T 35,735
Linden C 37,836
Lodi B 23,956
Long Branch C 29,819
Millville C 24,815
Montclair T 38,321
Newark C 329,248
New Brunswick C 41,442
Nutley T 28,998
Orange C 31,136
Paramus B 26,474

Passaic C 52,463
Paterson C 137,970
Perth Amboy C 38,951
Plainfield C 45,555
Rahway C 26,723
Ridgewood V 25,208
Roselle B 20,641
Sayreville B 29,969
South Plainfield B 20,521
Summit C 21,071
Trenton C 92,124
Union City C 55,593
Vineland C 53,753
Westfield T 30,447
West New York T 39,194
West Orange T 39,510

NEW MEXICO

Alamogordo C 24,024
Albuquerque C 331,767
Carlsbad C 25,496
Clovis C 31,194
Farmington C 30,729
Hobbs C 28,794
Las Cruces C 45,086
Roswell C 39,676
Santa Fe C 48,899

NEW YORK

Albany C 101,727
Amsterdam C 21,872
Auburn C 32,548
Binghamton C 55,860
Buffalo C 357,870
Cortland C 20,138
Elmira C 35,327
Freeport V 38,272
Garden City V 22,927
Glen Cove C 24,618
Harrison V 23,046
Hempstead V 40,404
Ithaca C 28,732
Jamestown C 35,775
Kingston C 24,481
Lackawanna C 22,701
Lindenhurst V 26,919
Lockport C 24,844
Long Beach C 34,073
Lynbrook V 20,431
Middletown C 21,454
Mineola V 20,757
Mount Vernon C 66,713
Newburgh C 23,438
New Rochelle C 70,794
New York C 7,071,030
Niagara Falls C 71,384
North Tonawanda C 35,760
Ossining V 20,196
Plattsburgh C 21,057
Port Chester V 23,565
Poughkeepsie C 29,757
Rochester C 241,741
Rockville Centre V 25,405
Rome C 43,826
Saratoga Springs C 23,906
Schenectady C 67,972
Spring Valley V 20,537

Syracuse C	170,105
Troy C	56,638
Utica C	75,632
Valley Stream V	35,769
Watertown C	27,861
White Plains C	46,999
Yonkers C	195,351

NORTH CAROLINA

Asheville C	53,281
Burlington C	37,266
Cary T	21,612
Chapel Hill T	32,421
Charlotte C	314,447
Durham C	100,831
Fayetteville C	59,507
Gastonia C	47,333
Goldsboro C	31,871
Greensboro C	155,642
Greenville C	35,740
Hickory C	20,757
High Point C	64,107
Kinston C	25,234
Raleigh C	149,771
Rocky Mount C	41,283
Salisbury C	22,677
Wilmington C	44,000
Wilson C	34,424
Winston-Salem C	131,885

NORTH DAKOTA

Bismarck C	44,485
Fargo C	61,308
Grand Forks C	43,765
Minot C	32,843

OHIO

Akron C	237,177
Alliance C	24,315
Ashland C	20,326
Ashtabula C	23,449
Barberton C	29,751
Beavercreek V	31,589
Bowling Green C	25,728
Brook Park C	26,195
Brunswick C	27,689
Canton C	94,730
Chillicothe C	23,420
Cincinnati C	385,457
Cleveland C	573,822
Cleveland Heights C	56,438
Columbus C	564,871
Cuyahoga Falls C	43,710
Dayton C	203,588
East Cleveland C	36,957
Eastlake C	22,104
Elyria C	57,504
Euclid C	59,999
Fairborn C	29,702
Fairfield C	30,777
Findlay C	35,594
Garfield Heights C	33,380
Hamilton C	63,189
Kent C	26,164
Kettering C	61,186
Lakewood C	61,963

Lancaster C	34,953
Lima C	47,381
Lorain C	75,416
Mansfield C	53,927
Maple Heights C	29,735
Marion C	37,040
Massillon C	30,557
Mayfield Heights C	21,550
Mentor C	42,065
Middletown C	43,719
Newark C	41,200
Niles C	23,088
North Olmsted C	36,486
Norwood C	26,342
Parma C	92,548
Parma Heights C	23,112
Piqua C	20,480
Portsmouth C	25,943
Reynoldsburg C	20,661
Rocky River C	21,084
Sandusky C	31,360
Shaker Heights C	32,487
South Euclid C	25,713
Springfield C	72,563
Steubenville C	26,400
Stow C	25,303
Strongsville C	28,577
Toledo C	354,635
Upper Arlington C	35,648
Warren C	56,629
Westerville C	23,414
Whitehall C	21,299
Xenia C	24,653
Youngstown C	115,436
Zanesville C	28,655

OKLAHOMA

Altus C	23,101
Ardmore C	23,689
Bartlesville C	34,568
Bethany C	22,130
Broken Arrow C	35,761
Del City C	28,424
Duncan C	22,517
Edmond C	34,637
Enid C	50,363
Lawton C	80,054
Midwest City C	49,559
Moore C	35,063
Muskogee C	40,011
Norman C	68,020
Oklahoma City C	403,213
Ponca City C	26,238
Shawnee C	26,506
Stillwater C	38,268
Tulsa C	360,919

OREGON

Albany C	26,546
Beaverton C	30,582
Corvallis C	40,960
Eugene C	105,624
Gresham C	33,005
Hillsboro C	27,664
Lake Oswego C	22,868
Medford C	39,603
Portland C	366,383

Salem C	89,233
Springfield C	41,621

PENNSYLVANIA

Allentown C	103,758
Altoona C	57,078
Baldwin B	24,598
Bethel Park B	34,755
Bethlehem C	70,419
Chester C	45,794
Easton C	26,027
Erie C	119,123
Harrisburg C	53,264
Hazleton C	27,318
Johnstown C	35,496
Lancaster C	54,725
Lebanon C	25,711
McKeesport C	31,012
Monroeville B	30,977
New Castle C	33,621
Norristown B	34,684
Philadelphia C	1,688,210
Pittsburgh C	423,938
Plum B	25,390
Pottstown B	22,729
Reading C	78,686
Scranton C	88,117
State College B	36,130
West Mifflin B	26,279
Wilkes-Barre C	51,551
Wilkinsburg B	23,669
Williamsport C	33,401
York C	44,619

RHODE ISLAND

Bristol T	20,128
Conventry T	27,065
Cranston C	71,992
Cumberland T	27,069
East Providence C	50,980
Johnston T	24,907
Newport C	29,259
North Kingstown T	21,938
North Providence T	29,188
Pawtucket C	71,204
Providence C	156,804
South Kingstown T	20,414
Warwick C	87,123
West Warwick T	27,026
Woonsocket C	45,914

SOUTH CAROLINA

Anderson C	27,313
Charleston C	69,510
Columbia C	99,296
Florence C	30,062
Greenville C	58,242
Greenwood C	21,613
North Charleston C	65,630
Rock Hill C	35,344
Spartanburg C	43,968
Sumter C	24,890

SOUTH DAKOTA

Aberdeen C	25,956
Rapid City C	46,492
Sioux Falls C	81,343

TENNESSEE

Bristol C	23,986
Chattanooga C	169,565
Clarksville C	54,777
Cleveland C	26,415
Columbia C	25,767
Cookeville C	20,350
East Ridge C	21,236
Germantown C	20,459
Hendersonville C	26,561
Jackson C	49,131
Johnson City C	39,753
Kingsport C	32,027
Knoxville C	183,139
Memphis C	646,356
Millington C	20,236
Murfreesboro C	32,845
Nashville-Davidson	455,651
Oak Ridge C	27,662

TEXAS

Abilene C	98,315
Alice C	20,961
Amarillo C	149,230
Arlington C	160,123
Austin C	345,496
Baytown C	56,923
Beaumont C	118,102
Bedford C	20,821
Big Spring C	24,804
Brownsville C	84,997
Bryan C	44,337
Carrollton C	40,591
College Station C	37,272
Corpus Christi C	231,999
Corsicana C	21,712
Dallas C	904,078
Deer Park C	22,648
Del Rio C	30,034
Denison C	23,884
Denton C	48,063
Duncanville C	27,781
Eagle Pass C	21,407
Edinburg C	24,075
El Paso C	425,259
Euless C	24,002
Farmers Branch C	24,863
Fort Worth C	385,141
Galveston C	61,902
Garland C	138,857
Grand Prairie C	71,462
Greenville C	22,161
Haltom City C	29,014
Harlingen C	43,543
Houston C	1,594,086
Huntsville C	23,936
Hurst C	31,420
Irving C	109,943
Kileen C	46,296
Kingsville C	28,808
Laredo C	91,449
Lewisville C	24,273
Longview C	62,762
Lubbock C	173,979
Lufkin C	28,562
McAllen C	67,042
Marshall C	24,921

Mesquite C	67,053
Midland C	70,525
Misson C	22,589
Missouri City C	24,533
Nacogdoches C	27,149
New Braunfels C	22,402
North Richland Hills C	30,592
Odessa C	90,027
Orange C	23,628
Pampa C	21,396
Paris C	25,498
Pasadena C	112,560
Pharr C	21,381
Plainview C	22,187
Plano C	72,331
Port Arthur C	61,195
Richardson C	72,496
San Angelo C	73,240
San Antonio C	785,410
San Marcos C	23,420
Sherman C	30,413
Temple C	42,483
Texarkana C	31,271
Texas City C	41,403
Tyler C	70,508
University Park C	22,254
Victoria C	50,695
Waco C	101,261
Wichita Falls C	94,201

UTAH

Bountiful C	32,877
Layton C	22,862
Logan C	26,844
Murray C	25,750
Ogden C	64,407
Orem C	52,399
Provo C	73,907
Salt Lake City C	163,033
Sandy City C	51,022
West Jordan C	26,794

VERMONT

Burlington C	37,712

VIRGINIA

Alexandria C	103,217
Blacksburg T	30,638
Charlottesville C	45,010
Chesapeake C	114,226
Danville C	45,642
Hampton C	122,617
Hopewell C	23,397
Lynchburg C	66,743
Newport News C	144,903
Norfolk C	266,979
Petersburg C	41,055
Portsmouth C	104,577
Richmond C	219,214
Roanoke C	100,427
Salem C	23,958
Staunton C	21,857
Suffolk C	47,621
Virginia Beach C	262,199
Winchester C	20,217

WASHINGTON

Auburn C	26,417
Bellevue C	73,903
Bellingham C	45,794
Bremerton C	36,208
Edmonds C	27,526
Everett C	54,413
Kennewick C	34,397
Kent C	23,152
Longview C	31,052
Lynnwood C	21,937
Mercer Island C	21,522
Olympia C	27,447
Pullman C	23,579
Redmond C	23,318
Renton C	30,612
Richland C	33,578
Seattle C	493,846
Spokane C	171,300
Tacoma C	158,501
Vancouver C	42,834
Walla Walla C	25,618
Yakima C	49,826

WEST VIRGINIA

Beckley C	20,492
Charleston C	63,968
Clarksburg C	22,371
Fairmont C	23,863
Huntington C	63,684
Morgantown C	27,605
Parkersburg C	39,967
Weirton C	24,736
Wheeling C	43,070

WISCONSIN

Appleton C	59,032
Beloit C	35,207
Brookfield C	34,035
Eau Claire C	51,509
Fond du Lac C	35,863
Green Bay C	87,899
Greenfield C	31,467
Janesville C	51,071
Kenosha C	77,685
La Crosse C	48,347
Madison C	170,616
Manitowac C	32,547
Menomonee Falls V	27,845
Milwaukee C	636,212
Neenah C	23,272
New Berlin C	30,529
Oshkosh C	49,678
Racine C	85,725
Sheboygan C	48,085
South Milwaukee C	21,069
Stevens Point C	22,970
Superior C	29,571
Waukesha C	50,319
Wausau C	32,426
Wauwatosa C	51,308
West Allis C	63,982
West Bend C	21,484

WYOMING

Casper C	51,016
Cheyenne C	47,283
Laramie C	24,410

CANADA

Capital: Ottawa
Head of State: Queen Elizabeth II
Governor General: Edward Richard Schreyer
Prime Minister: Pierre Elliott Trudeau (Liberal)
Leader of the Opposition: Joe Clark (Progressive Conservative)
Population: 24,100,000
Area: 3,851,809 sq mi (9,976,185 km²)

PROVINCES AND TERRITORIES

Alberta
Capital: Edmonton
Lieutenant Governor: Frank Lynch-Staunton
Premier: Peter Lougheed (Progressive Conservative)
Leader of the Opposition: Rod Sykes (Social Credit)
Entered Confederation: Sept. 1, 1905
Population: 2,136,000
Area: 255,285 sq mi (661,188 km²)

British Columbia
Capital: Victoria
Lieutenant Governor: Henry P. Bell-Irving
Premier: William R. Bennett (Social Credit)
Leader of the Opposition: David Barrett (New Democratic Party)
Entered Confederation: July 20, 1871
Population: 2,700,000
Area: 366,255 sq mi (948,600 km²)

Manitoba
Capital: Winnipeg
Lieutenant Governor: Pearl McGonigal
Premier: Howard Pawley (New Democratic Party)
Leader of the Opposition: Sterling P. Lyon (Progressive Conservative)
Entered Confederation: July 15, 1870
Population: 1,027,000
Area: 251,000 sq mi (650,090 km²)

New Brunswick
Capital: Fredericton
Lieutenant Governor: Hédard Robichaud
Premier: Richard B. Hatfield (Progressive Conservative)
Leader of the Opposition: Joseph Z. Daigle (Liberal)
Entered Confederation: July 1, 1867
Population: 709,000
Area: 28,354 sq mi (73,436 km²)

Newfoundland
Capital: St. John's
Lieutenant Governor: Gordon A. Winter
Premier: A. Brian Peckford (Progressive Conservative)
Leader of the Opposition: Len Sterling (Liberal)
Entered Confederation: March 31, 1949
Population: 584,000
Area: 156,185 sq mi (404,517 km²)

Nova Scotia
Capital: Halifax
Lieutenant Governor: John Elvin Shaffner
Premier: John M. Buchanan (Progressive Conservative)
Leader of the Opposition: A. M. (Sandy) Cameron (Liberal)
Entered Confederation: July 1, 1867
Population: 856,000
Area: 21,425 sq mi (55,491 km²)

Ontario
Capital: Toronto
Lieutenant Governor: John Aird
Premier: William G. Davis (Progressive Conservative)
Leader of the Opposition: Stuart Smith (Liberal)
Entered Confederation: July 1, 1867
Population: 8,600,000
Area: 412,582 sq mi (1,068,582 km²)

Prince Edward Island
Capital: Charlottetown
Lieutenant Governor: J. A. Doiron
Premier: James Lee (Progressive Conservative)
Leader of the Opposition: W. Bennett Campbell (Liberal)
Entered Confederation: July 1, 1873
Population: 124,000
Area: 2,184 sq mi (5,657 km²)

Quebec
Capital: Quebec City
Lieutenant Governor: Jean-Pierre Côté
Premier: René Lévesque (Parti Québécois)
Leader of the Opposition: Claude Ryan (Liberal)
Entered Confederation: July 1, 1867
Population: 6,325,000
Area: 594,860 sq mi (1,540,700 km²)

Saskatchewan
Capital: Regina
Lieutenant Governor: Irwin McIntosh
Premier: Allan E. Blakeney (New Democratic Party)
Leader of the Opposition: Eric Berntson (Progressive Conservative)
Entered Confederation: Sept. 1, 1905
Population: 976,000
Area: 251,700 sq mi (651,900 km²)

Northwest Territories
Capital: Yellowknife
Commissioner: John H. Parker
Reconstituted as a territory: September 1, 1905
Population: 43,000
Area: 1,304,896 sq mi (3,379,684 km²)

Yukon Territory
Capital: Whitehorse
Administrator: Douglas Bell
Government Leader: Christopher Pearson
Organized as a territory: June 13, 1898
Population: 21,500
Area: 186,299 sq mi (482,515 km²)

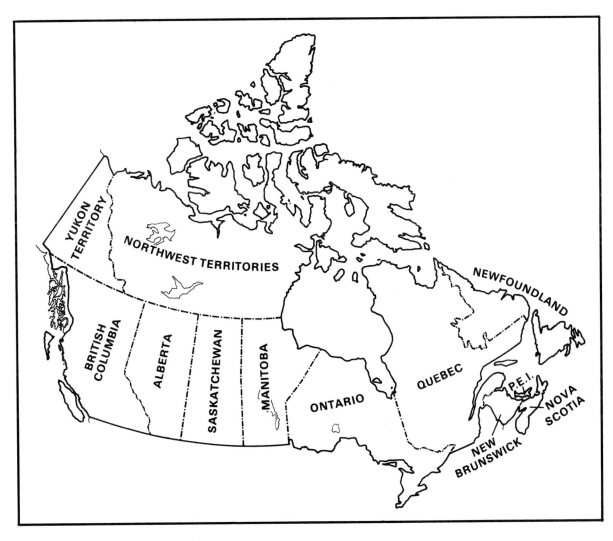

INDEX

B

C

E

Eagle, bird 79
  talons 69
  vervet's warning signal for 83
Ears
  sound location 127
Earthquakes
  Iran 24
  Los Angeles, California 195
East Germany *see* German Democratic Republic
Economic problems
  Central America 45–47
  defense buildup 57
  President Reagan's address on 16–17
  President Reagan's economic bills 29
Economics, Nobel prize in 33
Ecuador 343
  Organization of Petroleum Exporting Countries (OPEC) 340
  Roldós Aguilera, Jaime, death of 23
Edentates, order of mammals 74
Edward, British prince 39
Edward VII, British king 330
Edwards, James B., American public official 15
Edwards Air Force Base, California
  landing of space shuttle *Columbia* 95
EEC *see* European Economic Community
Eggs, birds, picture 315
Egypt 42–43, 343
  agreement with Israel 28
  Alexander the Great 255
  Mubarak, Muhammad Hosni, picture 64
  Sadat, Anwar el-, assassination of 32, 60, 62–63
  United States policy 44
Elections
  France 58–59
  Greece 58–59
  Honduras 35
  Israel 43
Electric eel, fish 73
Electric shock
  weapon of fish 73
Electron beam
  use by videodisc machines 115
Elephant, animal 78–80
  tusks 68
Elephant bird, picture 316
Elizabeth II, Queen of England
  wedding of Prince Charles 39
El Salvador 45–46, 343
Emmy Awards, television 266–67
Employee participation
  in management of jobs and working conditions 53
Emu, bird 315, 317; picture 316
Enamel work
  cloisonné 150
Endangered species
  African wildlife 78–81
Energy
  petroleum 340
England *see* Great Britain
Engle, Joe H., American astronaut 35, 96
English language
  idioms, origin of 222–23
Engraving and Printing, United States Bureau of 339
Environment
  discarded beverage containers 104
  effect on human behavior 107
  visual pollution 100–03
  water crisis 130
Epstein, Brian, British manager of Beatles 338
Equatorial Guinea 343
Erikson, John, American athlete 184

Escort, automobile 52
Eskimos or **Inuit,** people of the Arctic region 322–29
Ethiopia 343
Eugene O'Neill Memorial Theater Center, Waterford, Connecticut
  251
Europa postage stamps 145; picture 143
Europe
  castles 204–09, 211
  see also specific European countries
European Economic Community (EEC) or **Common Market** 14
  Greece 59
European Space Agency 97, 119
Exercise
  effect on heart 111
EXP, automobile 52
Eyskens, Mark, premier of Belgium 20

F

Fables, book, picture 281
Falcon, bird
  commemorative stamp 145
Falkland Islands
  postage stamps 145
Fangs, canine teeth 68
Fangs of snakes 71–72
Fanshawe Pioneer Village, London, Ontario, Canada 202
Farming
  weather 128–30
Fawn lily, wild flower, picture 117
Fennec, animal 76–77
Festivals
  garlic festival, Gilroy, California 217
  Tulip Festival, Ottawa, Canada 335
Fief, medieval feudal estate 205
Fighting methods
  judo 332
  karate 332–33
Figure skating, sport 177, 234–35
Fiji 343
  postage stamps 142
Filipov, Grisha, premier of Bulgaria 24
Films *see* Motion pictures
Fingers, Rollie, American athlete 165; picture 167
Finland 343
  Kekkonen, Urho K., resignation of 33
Fire
  rubbish dumps 103
  use by prehistoric people 34
Fish
  electric shock 73
  spines 70–71
  teeth 68–69
  unknown species discovered 37; picture 36
Fishing
  Eskimos 324–25, 327–29
FitzGerald, Garret, prime minister of Ireland 25
Flamingo, bird 79–80
Flood
  Johnstown, Pennsylvania (1889) 197
Florida
  census 352, 354–55
  launching of space shuttle *Columbia,* Cape Canaveral 94, 96
  Little League baseball team, Tampa 168
  sinkholes 131
  weather 128
Flowers
  commemorative stamps 145; picture 143
  forcing 140–41
  making bread dough flowers 153

G

hedge mazes 268—69
meeting of leaders of industrial nations, Canada 27
Northern Ireland 22
postage stamps 142, 145; picture 143
riots 26
use of garlic 216
Victoria, Queen 330
Vikings 213
young people's literature, pictures 284—85
Great Plains, region, United States 130
Great spotted kiwi, bird 317
Greece 343
elections 32, 58—59
English idiom, origin of 222
European Economic Community, membership in 14
Macedonian art 254—57
postage stamps 145
use of garlic 216
Greek mythology 256—57
animals 89, 91
maze 268
Greenland
Eskimos 322—29
Grenada 343
Gretzky, Wayne, Canadian athlete 176
Guerrero, Pedro, Dominican Republic athlete 165
Grévy's zebra, animal 78; picture 66—67
Grey Cup, football trophy 172
Griffin, mythological animal 91
Grizzly bear, animal
commemorative stamp 145
Grouse, bird
commemorative stamp 145
Guatemala 45—46, 344
Belize, dispute with 47
Guerrilla and terrorist activities
assassinations and assassination attempts 60—63
El Salvador 45
hijacking of Pakistani airplane 18
Guiles, Joelle, American marbles champion 189; picture 188
Guinea 344
Guinea-Bissau 344
Guiteau, Charles, American assassin 61
Gutenberg Castle, Liechtenstein
commemorative stamp 145
Guyana 344
Guyascutus or **Gyanousa,** mythological animal 91
Gymnastics 184—85

H

Haig, Alexander M., Jr., American public official 15
Haiti 344.
Halloween Is Grinch Night, television program 318
Halpern, David, American athlete 185
Hampton Court, England
hedge maze 268—69
Handicrafts *see* Hobbies, handicrafts, and projects
Harald Bluetooth, Danish king 214
Hare, Gerald, American photography program winner
Canadian Blue Heron, picture 229
Harrison, George, British musician 261, 338
Hart Trophy, hockey 176
Harry, Deborah, American singer 262
Haughey, Charles J., prime minister of Ireland 25
Hawaii
census 352, 355
Hays, David, American stage designer 251
Health *see* Medicine and health
Hearns, Thomas (Hit Man), American athlete 184

Heart 111
exhibit, Franklin Institute, Philadelphia, Pennsylvania 110
Heart rates 111
Hedge mazes 268—69
Heisman Trophy, football award 172
Heng Samrin, Cambodian president 37
Henrietta and the Gong from Hong Kong, book, picture 283
Hercules or **Heracles,** character in Greek mythology 91, 256
Heredity
twins 107
Heron, bird, picture 229
commemorative stamp 145; picture 143
Highgrove, Prince Charles' estate, England 40
Hijacking of Pakistani airplane 18
Hill Street Blues, television program 266
Himeji, Japan
White Heron Castle, picture 210
Hinckley, John W., Jr., American charged with Reagan assassination attempt 19, 60, 62
Hippopotamus, animal 79
Hirsch, Judd, American actor 267
Hobbies, handicrafts, and projects
body tricks 126—27
bread dough flowers 153
coin collecting 156—57
cloisonné 150
cooking 154—55
finding faces in animal and plant markings 146—47
folk painting 151
food-plant quiz and puzzle 138—39
forcing flowering plants 140—41
gift wrappings 132—36
hidden ants, word puzzle 161
making flowerpots 158—60
making treasure chests 148
maze 149
rubbings 320—21
silk flowers 152—53
sock monkeys 152
spaceship travel puzzle 137
stamp collecting 142—45
unicorn maze 149
Hockey, sport 175—76
Hoffmann, Roald, American Nobel prize winning chemist 33
Holden, William, American actor 35
Holland *see* Netherlands
Homer, Greek poet 89
Homo erectus, prehistoric people 34
Honduras 45—47, 344
election 35
Hornet, insect 77
stinger 72
Horns of animals 69—70
rhinoceros 78, 80
unicorn, mythological animal 90
Hostages, American, in Iran 14, 48—51
Laingen, Lowell Bruce, picture 65
Hotel Eden, The, art by Joseph Cornell, picture 248
Hotels
collapse of walkway, Hyatt Regency Hotel, Kansas City, Missouri 27
House of Representatives, United States
list of members 349—50
House plants
forcing of plants 140—41
making flowerpots 158—60
Houston Astros, baseball team 165—66
Houston Rockets, basketball team 169—70
Hubel, David H., American Nobel prize winning physiologist 33
Hull, John, British colonial coin maker 339
Hull, city, Quebec, Canada 334, 337
Hungary 344
Hunger strikers
Northern Ireland 22

Hunting
  Eskimos 324–25, 327–29
Hurtado Larrea, Osvaldo, president of Ecuador 23
Hutton, Timothy, American actor 252, 271
Hu Yaobang, Chinese political leader 25
Hyacinth, plant
  forcing 140–41
Hyatt Regency Hotel, Kansas City, Missouri 27
Hyena, animal 79
Hyperion, moon of Saturn 118

I

Ibex, animal 78
Ibis, bird 79
ICBM's *see* Intercontinental ballistic missiles
Ice hockey, sport *see* Hockey
Ice skating, sport 177, 234–35
Iceland 344
  Vikings 212
Idaho
  census 352, 355
Identical twins 107–09
Idioms, origin of 222–23
Igloo, Eskimo house 325–26, 328
Illinois
  census 352, 355
Imports
  automobiles 52
Impressionists, artists 319
Income *see* Wages and salaries
India 344
  British Empire 330
  communications satellite 119
  mythological animals 88–89
Indiana
  census 352, 355
Indianapolis 500, auto race 182
Indian paintbrush, wild flower, picture 117
Indians, American
  Abanaki Indian song 286
  Guatemala 46
Indonesia 344
  Organization of Petroleum Exporting Countries (OPEC) 340
Industry
  automobile manufacturing 52–53
  water requirements 130
Insects
  ant space project 98
  Children's Zoo, at Bronx Zoo, New York City 77
  faces formed from markings 146–47
  weapons 72
Intercontinental ballistic missiles (ICBM's) 55, 56
International Red Cross 196
International statistical supplement 341–61
International Year of Disabled Persons 142
Inuit *see* Eskimos
Iowa
  bottle bill 104
  census 352, 355
IRA *see* Irish Republican Army
Iran 43–44, 344
  American hostages 12, 14, 48–51
  assassinations 60
  Bahonar, Mohammed Javad, named premier 29
  Bani-Sadr dismissed as president 24
  Dwyer, Cynthia, released from jail 16
  earthquakes 24
  Khamenei, Hojatolislam Ali, elected president 32
  Organization of Petroleum Exporting Countries (OPEC) 340

  Rajai, Mohammed Ali, elected president 27
  Sobhani, Mohi, released from jail 16
Iraq 344
  Iran-Iraq war 43–44
  nuclear reactor bombed by Israel 24, 43
  Organization of Petroleum Exporting Countries (OPEC) 340
Ireland 344
  FitzGerald, Garret, became prime minister 25
Irish Republican Army (IRA) 22
Isabella II, Spanish queen 219
Islam, religion 42, 43, 44
Israel 43, 344
  bombing of Beirut, Lebanon 27
  bombing of Iraqi nuclear reactor 24
  Egyptian-Israeli peace agreements 28, 42
  Golan Heights 43, 44
Issumataq, Eskimo leader 324
Istambouly, Khaled Ahmed el-, Egyptian Muslim extremist 63
Italy 344
  castles 209
  meeting of leaders of industrial nations, Canada 27
  Spadolini, Giovanni, named premier 25
Ivory Coast 344

J

Jackal, animal 79
Jacob Have I Loved, book, picture 282
Jamaica 344
James Bay Agreement (1975) 329
Japan 344
  assassinations 61
  automobile industry 52–53
  castles 209–11
  karate 332
  meeting of leaders of industrial nations, Canada 27
  U.S. defense policy 57
Japonica, plant
  face formed from 146
Jaruzelski, Wojciech, premier of Poland 16, 32
Jaworski, Ron, American football player 171
J-car, automobile 52
John Newbery Medal 282
John Paul II, pope
  assassination attempt 23, 60, 62
Johnstown, Pennsylvania
  flood (1889) 197
Jones, Robert Tyre (Bobby), Jr., American athlete
  commemorative stamp 145
Jordan 344
Juan Carlos, king of Spain 17
Judo, fighting method 332
Jutland, Denmark 214–15

K

Kalp, Malcolm, American official, hostage in Iran 51
Kampuchea *see* Cambodia
Kansas
  census 352, 355–56
Kansas City, Missouri
  collapse of Hyatt Regency Hotel walkway 27
Kansas City Royals, baseball team 165–66
Karate, method of self-defense 332–33
Karen's New System, story 276–79

L

M

Museums
  children's art museum, Yerevan, Soviet Union 242–43
  Franklin Institute, Philadelphia, Pennsylvania, heart exhibit 110
  Ottawa, Canada 337
  Viking exhibit 213
  Viking Ship Museum, Oslo, Norway 214–15
  Viking Village, Moesgaard Museum, Denmark 214
Music 260–65
  Beatles, the 338
  commemorative coins 156
  mechanical music boxes 198–201
  symphony by Mozart, discovery of 273
Music boxes 198–201
Musk-ox, animal 323
Muskrat, animal 324
Muslims *see* Islam
Mutual assured destruction, nuclear strategy 54
MX missiles 56
Mythological animals 86–91
  Minotaur 268
  sachi, Japanese dolphins 210
Mythology *see* Greek mythology; Mythological animals

N

NAACP *see* National Association for the Advancement of Colored People
Nabavi, Behzad, Iranian public official 49
Nair, C. V. Devan, president of Singapore 22
NASA *see* National Aeronautics and Space Administration
National Aeronautics and Space Administration (NASA)
  Columbia, space shuttle, 94, 97
  Get Away Specials 98
National Arts Centre, Ottawa, Ontario, Canada 337
National Association for the Advancement of Colored People (NAACP) 30
National Basketball Association (NBA) 169–70
National Collegiate Athletic Association (NCAA) 169–70
National Gallery, Ottawa, Ontario, Canada 337
National Hockey League (NHL) 175–76
National Marbles Tournament, Wildwood-by-the-Sea, New Jersey 188–89
National Scout Jamboree, Fort A. P. Hill, Virginia 239
National Sports Festival, Syracuse, New York 184–85
National Theatre of the Deaf (NTD) 250–51
National Zoo, Washington, D.C.
  pandas, picture 84
Native Americans *see* Indians, American
NATO *see* North Atlantic Treaty Organization
Nature versus nurture controversy 107
Nauru 345
Navy, United States 57
NBA *see* National Basketball Association
NCAA *see* National Collegiate Athletic Association
Nebraska
  census 352, 357
Nebuchadnezzar, King, Biblical character 223
Nehemiah, Renaldo, American athlete, picture 181
Nepal 345
Neptune, planet 119
Netherlands 345
Neubert, Ramona, East German athlete 181
Neuschwanstein Castle, Bavaria, Germany 211
Neutron bombs 29
Nevada
  census 352, 357
Newbery Medal 282
New Braunfels, Texas
  Armadillo Alympics, picture 75

New Brunswick, province, Canada 360
  patriation issue 36
Newfoundland, province, Canada 360
New Guinea
  cassowaries 317
New Hampshire
  census 352, 357
Ne Win, U, Burmese president 34
New Jersey
  Camden high school space experiment 98
  census 352, 357
  National Marbles Tournament, Wildwood-by-the-Sea 188–89
New Mexico
  bristlecone pine trees 124
  census 352, 357
New York
  census 352, 357–58
  National Sports Festival, Syracuse 184–85
  silver, West Point 339
  weather 128
New York City
  Bronx Zoo, picture 85
  Central Park 264–65
  Children's Zoo, at Bronx Zoo 76–77
  subway graffiti 101–03
  Westminster Kennel Club dog show, picture 84
New York Islanders, hockey team 175–76
New York Yankees, baseball team 164–67
New Zealand 345
  kiwis 317
NHL *see* National Hockey League
Nicaragua 45–46, 345
Nicks, Stevie, American singer 262–63
Nicotine, chemical
  effect on heart 111
Niger 345
Nigeria 345
  Organization of Petroleum Exporting Countries (OPEC) 340
Nimitz-class aircraft carriers, ships 57
Nine-banded armadillo, animal 74
Nobel prizes 33
Noise
  effect on heart 111
Nordic skiing 177
Norris Trophy, hockey 176
Norsemen *see* Vikings
North African campaign, World War II 221
North America
  Eskimos 322–29
  Vikings 212
  see also specific North American countries
North Atlantic Treaty Organization (NATO)
  Greece 59
  U.S. defense policy 57
North Carolina
  census 352, 358
North Dakota
  census 352, 358
Northern Ireland
  Sands, Robert, death of 22
North Korea *see* Korea, Democratic People's Republic of
Northwest Territories, Canada 360
Norway 345
  Brundtland, Gro Harlem, became prime minister 16
  Conservative Party victory 30
  rosemaling, style of folk painting 151
  Vikings 213–15
  World War II 220
Notre Dame, Basilica of, Ottawa, Ontario, Canada 336
Nova Scotia, province, Canada 360
Nuclear-powered submarines 56
Nuclear reactor, Iraq
  bombing by Israeli warplanes 24, 43
Nuclear weapons 54, 55, 56, 57
Numismatics *see* Coin collecting

O

Oakland A's, baseball team 165–66
Oak Ridge Boys, music group 262; picture 239
O'Connor, Sandra Day, American Supreme Court justice, 26, 31; picture 64
Ogallala aquifer, natural underground reservoir, western United States 130
Ohio
   census 352, 358
   Soap Box Derby, Akron 184
Oil *see* Petroleum
Okinawa, island, Pacific Ocean
   karate 332
Oklahoma
   census 352, 358
Olvera Street, Los Angeles, California, picture 193
Olympias, mother of Alexander the Great 61
Oman 345
One-wattled cassowary, bird 317
Ono, Yoko, American artist and performer 260, 264
Ontario, province, Canada 360
   Canada's Wonderland, park 240–41
   London 202–03
   Ottawa 334–37
   patriation issue 36
OPEC *see* Organization of Petroleum Exporting Countries
Orange crop
   weather 128–29
Orchid, plant
   face formed from 146, picture 147
Order of Canada, civilian award
   Fox, Terry 25
Ordinary People, motion picture 252, 271
Organization of Petroleum Exporting Countries (OPEC) 340
Oregon
   bottle bill 104–05
   census 352, 358
Osbourne, Lloyd, stepson of Robert Louis Stevenson 300
Oseberg, Viking ship 215
Oslo, Norway
   Viking Ship Museum 214–15
Ostrich, bird 78–80, 314–15
   feet 69
Oswald, Lee Harvey, American charged with assassination 62
Ottawa, Ontario, Canada 334–37
   meeting of leaders of seven industrial nations 27
   meeting of President Reagan and Prime Minister Trudeau 18
Ottawa, University of, Ontario, Canada 336
Ottawa River, Canada 334, 337

P

Pacific Ocean
   fish species discovered 37
   trans-Pacific balloon voyage 34
Pahlavi, Mohammed Reza, shah of Iran 48
Pakistan 345
   hijacking of airplane 18
Paleontology
   fossils discovered in Arizona 30
Palestine Liberation Organization (PLO) 27, 43
Palestinian Arabs 43, 44
Pampas ostrich, bird *see* Rhea

Panama 45, 47, 346
   Torrijos Herrera, Omar, death of 27
Panama Canal 47
Panda, animal, picture 84
Panhellenic Socialist Movement, Greece 58
Pantry Ballet, A, art by Joseph Cornell, Picture 244–45
Papandreou, Andreas, Greek premier 32, 58–59
Papua New Guinea 346
   cassowaries 317
Parade, play, picture 251
Paraguay 346
Park
   Canada's Wonderland, Vaughan, Ontario 240–41
Parliament Buildings, Ottawa, Ontario, Canada 336–37
Parliament Hill, Ottawa, Ontario, Canada 335–36
Parton, Dolly, American singer 262
Paterson, Katherine, American author
   Jacob Have I Loved, picture 282
Patriation issue, in Canada 36
Patriots, American, 290
Paul and Virginia, art by Joseph Cornell, picture 249
Paul Revere's Ride, poem by Henry Wadsworth Longfellow 290
Pavlova, Anna, Russian dancer 273
Paz García, Policarpo, Honduran president 35
Peace, Nobel prize for 33
Peacock, bird, picture 226
Pedro, Derrick, American athlete 168
Pegasus, mythological horse 89
Pella, Macedonia 254
Pennsylvania
   census 352, 358
   Franklin Institute, Philadelphia, heart exhibit 110
   Johnstown flood (1889) 197
   Little League World Series, Williamsport 168
   mint, Philadelphia 339
   Shoe House 258
   water shortage 130
Penny, one-cent coin 157
Pérez de Cuéllar, Javier, Peruvian diplomat 37
Permafrost, frozen subsoil 323
Persian Gulf region 43–44
   Soviet military power 55
Peru 346
Petroleum (oil) 340
   Los Angeles, California 193
   U.S. Middle East policy 44
Petrouchka, story by Elizabeth Cleaver, pictures 274–75, 280
Pharmacy, art by Joseph Cornell, picture 246
Philadelphia, Pennsylvania
   Franklin Institute, heart exhibit 110
   mint 339
Philadelphia Phillies, baseball team 165–66
Philadelphia 76ers, basketball team 169–70
Philately *see* Stamp collecting
Philip, Prince, Duke of Edinburgh
   wedding of Prince Charles 39
Philip II, king of Macedonia 61, 254, 257; picture 255
Philippines 346
   Virta, Cesar, named premier 20
Photography 224–29
   ultra-high-speed photography 120–23
Physics, Nobel prize in 33
Physiology or Medicine, Nobel prize in 33
Pichiciago, animal 74
Pierce, Samuel R., Jr., American public official 15
Pine trees
   bristlecone pines 124
Pinocchio, book by C. Collodi 301–03
Pioneer spacecraft
   commemorative stamp 142; picture 143
Plansker, Jeffrey, American photography program winner
   Surreal Produce Reach, picture 227
Plants
   Arctic region 323, 328
   commemorative stamps 145; picture 143

S

V

W

ILLUSTRATION CREDITS AND ACKNOWLEDGMENTS

The following list credits or acknowledges, by page, the source of illustrations and text excerpts used in THE NEW BOOK OF KNOWLEDGE ANNUAL. Illustration credits are listed illustration by illustration—left to right, top to bottom. When two or more illustrations appear on one page, their credits are separated by semicolons. When both the photographer or artist and an agency or other source are given for an illustration, they are usually separated by a dash. Excerpts from previously published works are listed by inclusive page numbers.

10– © 1981 David Hume Kennerly—Contact
11
14 UPI
16 Joe Traver—Liaison
17 Courtesy Sinclair
18 Wide World
19 UPI
20 Source: U.S. Census Bureau; Artist, Frank Senyk
21 UPI
22 Francois Lochon-Thierry Campion—Gamma/Liaison
23 UPI
24 Catherine Leroy—Gamma/Liaison
25 CP Picture Service
26– Tony Frank—Sygma
27
28 UPI
29 Langley in *The Christian Science Monitor* © 1981 TCSPS
31 A. H. Coleman—Harvard University
32 Forbes in *The Christian Science Monitor* © 1981 TCSPS
34 Sipa Press—Black Star © 1981
35 Movie Star News
36 UPI
38 © Black Star 1981
39 Snowdon/Camera Press
40 Ron Watts—Black Star © 1981; Camera Press
41 Snowdon—Camera Press
42 Wide World
44 Owen Franken—Sygma
45 Artist, Frank Senyk
46 Marisabel Villasante de Schumacher—*The New York Times*
47 Mattison—Gamma/Liaison
48 UPI
49 © Enrico Ferorelli—Wheeler, Inc. 1981
50 John Bryson—Sygma
51 UPI
53 Andrew Sacks
54 Courtesy U.S. Air Force
55 Lee Lockwood—Black Star
56 Diego Goldberg—Sygma
58 Diego Goldberg—Sygma
59 Suzan Mulhauser—Gamma/Liaison
60 Sygma
61 The Bettmann Archive
62 Wide World
63 Elkoussy—Sygma
64 UPI; Sven Simon—Katherine Young
65 Tim Dillon—Sygma
66– © 1981 John Reader
67
68 Jane Burton—Bruce Coleman, Inc.
69 Clem Haagner—Bruce Coleman, Inc.; Robert L. Dunne; Bob & Clara Calhoun—Bruce Coleman, Inc.
70 © Keith Gunnar—Bruce Coleman, Inc.; © Stephen Collins—NAS/Photo Researchers
71 Jane Burton—Bruce Coleman, Inc., © Tom McHugh—Photo Researchers
72 © Charles E. Mohr—NAS/Photo Researchers

73 Kim Taylor—Bruce Coleman, Inc.
74 C. Haagner—Bruce Coleman, Inc.; N. Myers—Bruce Coleman, Inc.
75 Courtesy Texas Armadillo Association—Armadillo Alympics
76 Bill Meng—New York Zoological Society
77 Dennis De Mello—New York Zoological Society
78 Michael Blate—Tom Stack & Associates; © Helen Williams—Photo Researchers
79 © M. J. Griffith—NAS/Photo Researchers
80 Warren & Genny Garst—Tom Stack & Associates; © Steve Solum—Bruce Coleman, Inc.; © M. J. Griffith—Photo Researchers
81 © Daniel Cande—NAS/Photo Researchers; Dale & Marian Zimmerman—Bruce Coleman, Inc.; © Tom McHugh—Photo Researchers
82 F. S. Mitchell—Tom Stack & Associates; Dave Spier—Tom Stack & Associates; John Gerlach—Tom Stack & Associates
83 © Mark Sherman—Bruce Coleman
84 Wide World
85 Yvonne Hemsey—Gamma/Liaison; Courtesy Marine World/Africa U.S.A.
86– Artist, Michele McLean
91
92– © 1981 Jim Tuten—Black Star
93
94 Owen Flipschulke—Black Star
95 NASA
96– Brian Sullivan—*Discover* magazine © 1981
97 Time, Inc.
98 Russell T. Homan, Jr., Courtesy RCA
99 Adapted from an article appearing in the April 27, 1981, issue of *MacLean*'s magazine, by Michael Posner; Artist, Frank Senyk
100 Hal Yaeger—FPG
101 © Russ Kinne—Photo Researchers
102 © Georg Gerster—Photo Researchers; © Jim Howard—Alpha
103 © Paolo Koch—Photo Researchers
104 Barth J. Falkenberg—*The Christian Science Monitor*
105 Shostal Associates
106 Al Satterwhite—The Image Bank
107 Enrico Ferorelli
109 Thomas J. Bouchard
110 Courtesy Franklin Institute
112 Courtesy Magnavox
113 Courtesy Sony Corporation
114 Courtesy Zenith Radio Corporation
115 Courtesy RCA
116– Peter D. Capen
117
118 NASA
120 Harold E. Edgerton; Charles E. Miller
121 Zimmerman—FPG; Harold E. Edgerton
122– Harold E. Edgerton
123
124 Marv Poulson
125 Jenny Tesar; R. E. Pelham—Bruce Coleman, Inc.
126– Reprinted with the permission of the publisher,

127 The Young Naturalist Foundation, from *Owl* magazine
128 John Dickerson
129 M. Naythons—Liaison; © Curt Gunther—Camera 5
131 © 1981 Gerald David—Contact
132– Tony Thomas
133
134– Jenny Tesar
136
137 Artist, Frank Senyk. Solution: To Distant Stars
140– Artist, Michele McLean
141
146– Kjell B. Sandved
147
148 Jenny Tesar
149 Artist, Jacques Chazaud
150– Courtesy *Creative Crafts* magazine
153
154– From *Many Friends Cooking: An International*
155 *Cookbook for Boys and Girls*, by Terry Touff Cooper and Marilyn Ratner. Text © 1980 by Terry Touff Cooper and Marilyn Ratner. Illustrations © 1980 by Tony Chen. Reprinted by permission of Philomel Books.
156– Courtesy Krause Publications, Inc.
157
158– Jenny Tesar
160
161 Solution: plant; pants; anteater; giant; want; Grant; Antarctica; Santa; hydrant; lantern; slant; truant; antelope; cantaloupe; antifreeze; fantasy; pheasant; antique; pleasant; enchant
162– Barry Rabinowitz—Focus on Sports
163
164 Focus on Sports
165 Wide World; Focus on Sports
168 Vannucci Foto Services
169 Rich Clarkson—*Sports Illustrated*
170 Andy Hayt—*Sports Illustrated*
171 Wide World
172 Wide World
173 UPI

174 UPI
175 © Richard Pilling—Focus on Sports
177 UPI
178 George Tiedemann—*Sports Illustrated*
179 © United Press Canada Ltd.
180 Focus on Sports
181 UPI
182 UPI
183 Wide World
184 UPI
185 © Paul J. Sutton—Duomo; UPI
186 Jenny Tesar
188– Dan Farrell
189
190– McElroy—*Newsweek*
191
192 J. Alex Langley—DPI
193 © Chad Slattery Photography—After Image
194 James Blank—After Image
195 Ken McVey—After Image
196 Courtesy American Red Cross
197 Culver Pictures
198 Courtesy Rita Ford Music Boxes
199 Joseph B. Brignolo, Jr., from the collection of
    Gerald Planus
200 Joseph B. Brignolo, Jr., from the collection of
    Gerald Planus; Courtesy Rita Ford Music
    Boxes
201 Joseph B. Brignolo, Jr., from the collection of
    Gerald Planus
202 Victor Aziz
203 Courtesy Public Utilities Commission; Malak;
    Courtesy Public Utilities Commission;
    Courtesy Public Utilities Commission
204 © Porterfield Chickering—Photo Researchers
205– Artwork from *See Inside a Castle*
207 © Grisewood & Dempsey Ltd., London
208 Mathieu—Atlas Photo
209 © 1979 Frederick Ayer—Photo Researchers
210 Orion Press
211 Alan Clifton—Black Star
212 The Bettmann Archive
213 Lent by Schleswig Holstein Landesmuseum,
    courtesy the Minneapolis Institute of Arts;
    National Antiquities Museum, Stockholm,
    courtesy the Minneapolis Institute of Arts;
    Statens Historiska Museum, Stockholm,
    courtesy the Minneapolis Institute of Arts
214 Bruno de Hamel
215 Henry Kurtz
216 © 1979 Joyce MacDonald—*The New York
    Times*
217 Artist, Michele McLean
218 © J. P. Laffont—Sygma
219 Culver Pictures
220 The Bettmann Archive
221 © J. P. Laffont—Sygma
222– Artist, Dale Barsanian
223
224– Courtesy of Scholastic Photography Awards,
229 conducted by Scholastic Magazines, Inc. and
    sponsored by Eastman Kodak Company
230 Emily deRham; Betty Klavun
231 Betty Klavun
232 Teresa Zabala—*The New York Times;* Frank
    Lodge—*The New York Times*
233 *The New York Times;* courtesy Westinghouse
234 Diana Di Giacomo—Focus on Sports
235 Focus on Sports
236 Courtesy Boy Scouts of the U.S.A.; Courtesy
    Girl Scouts of the U.S.A.
237 *Kitchener–Waterloo Record,* courtesy Girl
    Guides of Canada; Courtesy Boy Scouts of
    Canada

238 Courtesy Girl Scouts of the U.S.A.
239· Courtesy Boy Scouts of the U.S.A.; Courtesy
    Boy Scouts of Canada
240· Courtesy Canada's Wonderland
241
242– *Soviet Life* magazine
243
244– Nelson Gallery—Atkins Museum, Kansas
245 City, Missouri, gift of the Friends of Art
246 Collection Mrs. Marcel Duchamp, Paris, photo
    by Jacques Faujour
247 Collection Mr. and Mrs. E. A. Bergman,
    Chicago
248 The National Gallery of Canada
249 © Copyright Estate of Joseph Cornell;
    Courtesy Castelli Feigen Corcoran Gallery,
    New York; Private Collection, photo by Kate
    Keller; Collection Mr. and Mrs. E. A.
    Bergman, Chicago
250– Bill Ray
251
252 Courtesy Paramount Pictures Corporation,
    © 1980
253 Courtesy Universal City Studios, Inc. © 1980;
    Copyright © 1980 United Artists Corporation,
    all rights reserved
254 The Bettmann Archive
255 George Ortiz Collection, courtesy the Art
    Institute of Chicago; Archaeological Museum
    of Thessalonike, courtesy the Art Institute of
    Chicago; Pella Museum, courtesy the Art
    Institute of Chicago
256 Archaeological Museum of Thessalonike,
    courtesy the Art Institute of Chicago;
    Archaeological Museum of Thessalonike,
    courtesy the Art Institute of Chicago
257 Pella Museum, courtesy the Art Institute of
    Chicago; Archaeological Museum of
    Thessalonike, courtesy the Art Institute of
    Chicago
258– James J. C. Andrews
259
260 Gary Gershoff © Retna Ltd.
261 Gary Gershoff © Retna Ltd; Etty Inman
    © Retna Ltd.
262 © 1981 Linda Matlow—Retna Ltd.
263 Barry Schultz © Retna Ltd.
264 O. Franken—Sygma
265 Barry Schultz—Retna Ltd.
266 NBC
267 CBS; ABC © 1981
268 The Bettmann Archive
269 © Georg Gerster—Photo Researchers
270 Bonnie Schiffman—Gamma/Liaison
271 Wide World; Greg Gorman—Sygma
272 Gamma/Liaison; UPI
273 Culver Pictures; UPI; The Bettmann Archive
274– Illustration from *Petrouchka* by Elizabeth
275 Cleaver, adapted from Igor Stravinsky and
    Alexandre Benois. Text and illustrations
    copyright © 1980 by Elizabeth Cleaver.
    Reprinted by permission of Atheneum
    Publishers
276– Text by Vivian Dubrovin from *Jack and Jill*
279 magazine © 1977 by the Saturday Evening Post
    Company, Indianapolis, Indiana. Reprinted by
    permission of the publisher; Artist, Michèle
    McLean
280 Illustration from *Petrouchka* by Elizabeth
    Cleaver, adapted from Igor Stravinsky and
    Alexandre Benois. Text and illustrations
    copyright © 1980 by Elizabeth Cleaver.
    Reprinted by permission of Atheneum
    Publishers

281 Illustrations from *Fables,* written and
    illustrated by Arnold Lobel. Copyright © 1980
    by Arnold Lobel. A Caldecott Medal winner.
    By permission of Harper & Row, Publishers,
    Inc.
282 Jacket illustration by Kinuko Craft from *Jacob
    Have I Loved* by Katherine Paterson.
    Copyright © 1980 by Katherine Paterson. A
    Newbery Medal winner. By permission of
    Thomas Y. Crowell, Publishers
283 By permission of Four Winds Press, a division
    of Scholastic Inc. from *Henrietta and the Gong
    From Hong Kong* by Winifred Rosen. Text
    copyright © 1981 by Winifred Rosen.
    Illustrations copyright © 1981 by Kay Chorao
284– Reprinted by permission of Schocken Books,
285 Inc. from *Masquerade* by Kit Williams.
    Copyright © 1979 by Kit Williams
288– Reprinted by permission from *The Christian
289 Science Monitor* © 1980; 1981. The Christian
    Science Publishing Society. All rights reserved
290– Artist, Victor Olson
299
300 The Bettmann Archive
301 The Bettmann Archive; Robert Louis
    Stevenson, *Treasure Island,* illustrated by
    N. C. Wyeth. Illustration copyright 1911, 1939
    by Charles Scribner's Sons. Reprinted with the
    permission of Charles Scribner's Sons.
    Photograph courtesy of the Brandywine River
    Museum from a private collection
302 The Bettmann Archive
303 From the book *The Adventures of Pinocchio* by
    C. Collodi, illustrations by Fritz Kredel.
    © 1946. Published by Grosset & Dunlap, Inc;
    Courtesy Walt Disney Productions. © Walt
    Disney
304– Adapted from *Scandinavian Stories,* by
312 Margaret Sperry. Illustrations by Jenny
    Williams. Illustrations © 1971 by Franklin
    Watts, Inc. Used by permission of the
    publisher
314– The Archon Press, Ltd.
317
318 Julian Wasser—© Random House
319 Los Angeles County Museum of Art: Mrs.
    Fred Hathaway Bixby Bequest
320– J. B. Brignolo, Jr.
321
322 Steve McCutcheon
324 Bob and Ira Spring; Steve McCutcheon
325 Shostal Associates
326 Steve McCutcheon
327 Shostal Associates
328 Bob and Ira Spring; Steve McCutcheon
329 The Metropolitan Museum of Art, Gift of
    James A. Hoston, 1969; Original drawing by
    Simon Tookoome, reproduced by permission
    of Sanavik Eskimo Cooperative, Baker Lake,
    N.W.T., Canada
330 Giraudon
331 Francois Lochon—Gamma/Liaison
332 Ed Ikuta
333 © Mitchell B. Reibel—Sports Photo File
334 Cliff Feulner—The Image Bank
335 George Buctel
337 Original photo supplied by the Surveys and
    Mapping Branch, Department of Energy,
    Mines and Resources, National Air Photo
    Library
338 © Henry Grossman—Transworld Feature
    Syndicate, Inc.
339 Shostal Associates
351 Jim Moore—Liaison

382

Put The World At Your Fingertips . . .

ORDER THIS EXQUISITELY DETAILED LENOX GLOBE!

The world's never looked better! Why? Because this Lenox Globe — the most popular raised-relief model made by Replogle — is as stunning to look at as the living planet it represents.

Handsomely crafted and easy-to-use, the Lenox is the latest word in the state of the mapmaker's art — an ingenious marriage of classic, antique styling with clean, modern readability.

The Lenox is a giant 12-inch globe, beautifully inscribed with eye-catching "cartouches" and colorful compass "roses" . . . solidly-mounted on an elegantly sturdy, 18-inch Fruitwood stand . . . and covered with three dimensional "mountain ranges" children love to touch!

Five pounds light, the Lenox comes complete with a 32-page **STORY OF THE GLOBE** — a richly-illustrated, full-color handbook you and your whole family will refer to over and over again.

TO ORDER, simply send us your name and address, along with a check or money order for $29.95* to:

Grolier Yearbook, Inc.
Lenox Globe
Sherman Turnpike
Danbury, Connecticut 06816

*Please note: New York and Connecticut residents must add state sales tax.

THE LENOX GLOBE . . . by Replogle. Make it yours *today.*